The Lord's Resistance Army

C000163063

The Lord's Resistance Army (LRA) is one of Africa's most notorious armed rebel groups, having operated across Uganda, South Sudan, Sudan, the Central African Republic and the Democratic Republic of the Congo. When they entered the Juba Peace Talks with the Ugandan Government in 2006, the peace deal seemed like a gift to fighters who had for years barely been surviving in Central Africa's jungles. Yet the talks failed. Why? Based on exclusive interviews with LRA fighters and their notorious leader Joseph Kony, Mareike Schomerus provides insights into how the LRA experienced the Juba Talks, revealing developing dynamics and deep distrust within a conflict system and how these became entrenched through the peace negotiations. In so doing, Schomerus offers an explanation as to why current approaches to ending armed violence not only fail but how they actively contribute to their own failure, and calls for a new approach to contemporary peacemaking.

MAREIKE SCHOMERUS, PhD, is a researcher and commentator, as well as co-editor of volumes on African secessionism and the borderlands of South Sudan. Her recent work merges behavioural science with the qualitative study of violent conflict, political contestation and governance.

The Lord's Resistance Army

Violence and Peacemaking in Africa

Mareike Schomerus

CAMBRIDGE
UNIVERSITY PRESS

Shaftesbury Road, Cambridge CB2 8EA, United Kingdom

One Liberty Plaza, 20th Floor, New York, NY 10006, USA

477 Williamstown Road, Port Melbourne, VIC 3207, Australia

314–321, 3rd Floor, Plot 3, Splendor Forum, Jasola District Centre, New Delhi – 110025, India

103 Penang Road, #05–06/07, Visioncrest Commercial, Singapore 238467

Cambridge University Press is part of Cambridge University Press & Assessment, a department of the University of Cambridge.

We share the University's mission to contribute to society through the pursuit of education, learning and research at the highest international levels of excellence.

www.cambridge.org
Information on this title: www.cambridge.org/9781108725354

DOI: 10.1017/9781108662505

First published 2021
First paperback edition 2022

A catalogue record for this publication is available from the British Library

Library of Congress Cataloging-in-Publication data
Names: Schomerus, Mareike, author.
Title: The Lord's Resistance Army : violence and peacemaking in Africa / Mareike Schomerus.
Other titles: Violence and peacemaking in Africa
Description: Cambridge ; New York, NY : Cambridge University Press, 2021. | Includes bibliographical references and index.
Identifiers: LCCN 2020037934 (print) | LCCN 2020037935 (ebook) | ISBN 9781108485920 (hardback) | ISBN 9781108725354 (paperback) | ISBN 9781108662505 (epub)
Subjects: LCSH: Lord's Resistance Army. | Insurgency–Uganda. | Juba Peace Talks–History. | Peace-building–Africa–International cooperation. | Uganda–Politics and government–1979– | Civil war–Africa.
Classification: LCC DT433.285 .S43 2021 (print) | LCC DT433.285 (ebook) | DDC 967.6104/4–dc23
LC record available at https://lccn.loc.gov/2020037934
LC ebook record available at https://lccn.loc.gov/2020037935

ISBN   978-1-108-48592-0   Hardback
ISBN   978-1-108-72535-4   Paperback

Contents

Figures

Acknowledgements

Many people have had a role in bringing this book to life. It lies in the complicated nature of writing about violent conflict that I will never be able to thank some of those people for what they have done. So rather than mentioning just a few by name, I would like you to know that if you played a part, I am grateful to you.

It is easier to publicly thank those who pushed the book over the finish line: thanks to my brother Hajo for great cover design. Thanks to two very kind and enthusiastic reviewers who might never know how much their words meant to me. And thanks to Maria Marsh and Daniel Brown at Cambridge University Press for their much-appreciated support.

Note on the Text

Most of the events described here took place before South Sudan became independent in 2011. Prior to independence, it was referred to as southern Sudan, which is reflected here.

The terms Lord's Resistance Army/Movement (LRA/M) are for ease of reading used as if they describe strictly organised entities – they do not. What they do represent is analysed in more detail in Chapter 8.

The text uses a mixture of anonymisation and attribution. This either reflects the type of permission given by the interviewee or whether a statement was given as a matter of public record or privately.

At times I use square brackets in direct quotations to clarify idiomatic expressions or figures of speech. All photos were taken by me.

Abbreviations and Acronyms

AFRICOM	United States Africa Command, unified combatant command under the United States Department of Defense, created in 2007 by presidential order
Agenda 1	Agreement on Cessation of Hostilities between LRA and GoU, first signed in August 2006 and periodically renewed
Agenda 2	Agreement on Comprehensive Solutions
Agenda 3	Agreement on Justice and Accountability
Agenda 4	Agreement on Disarmament, Demobilization and Reintegration
Agenda 5	Agreement on a Permanent Ceasefire
APG	Acholi Parliamentary Group
AU	African Union
AURTF	African Union Regional Task Force, established to fight the LRA
CAR	Central African Republic
CHMT	Cessation of Hostilities Monitoring Team
CIA	Central Intelligence Agency
CoH	Cessation of Hostilities Agreement (Agenda 1)
CPA	Comprehensive Peace Agreement between the Government of Sudan and the Sudan People's Liberation Army/Movement
DDR	Disarmament, Demobilisation and Reintegration
DPA	Department of Political Affairs (UN) now Department of Political and Peacebuilding Affairs
DPKO	Department of Peacekeeping Operations
DRC	Democratic Republic of the Congo
ESO	External Security Organisation, Uganda's intelligence agency
EU	European Union
FADRC	Forces Armées de la République Démocratique du Congo; DRC's army

FPA	Final Peace Agreement, the chapeau document to be signed by President Museveni and Joseph Kony to validate all previously signed Agenda items
GoS	Government of Sudan (Khartoum)
GoSS	Government of southern Sudan (Juba) between 2005 and 2011
GoU	Government of Uganda
HQ	Headquarters
ICC	International Criminal Court
ICG	International Crisis Group
IDP	Internally Displaced Person
IGAD	Intergovernmental Authority on Development
IOM	International Organization for Migration
JIF	Juba Initiative Fund, established by the UN to attract donors to contribute to the Juba Talks
LC	Local Council (administrative unit in Uganda)
LRA	Lord's Resistance Army
LRM	Lord's Resistance Movement
MONUC	Mission de l'Organisation des Nations Unies en République démocratique du Congo; UN Mission in the DRC until 2010
MONUSCO	United Nations Organization Stabilization Mission in the Democratic Republic of the Congo (follow-up to MONUC since 2010)
MP	Member of Parliament
NGO	Non-governmental Organisation
NCA	Norwegian Church Aid
NRA	National Resistance Army (original name for Uganda's army)
NRM	National Resistance Movement (Uganda's ruling party under President Museveni)
UNOCHA	UN Office for the Coordination of Humanitarian Affairs
OIF	Operation Iron Fist, conducted by the Ugandan army against the LRA in 2002
OLT	Operation Lightning Thunder, conducted against the LRA from December 2008 to March 2009, when it was renamed to Operation Rudia
RDC	Resident District Commissioner (Uganda)
SAF	Sudanese Armed Forces (army of the Khartoum government)

SESG	Special Envoy of the Secretary-General (UN)
SPLA	Sudan People's Liberation Army
SPLM	Sudan People's Liberation Movement
TRC	Truth and Reconciliation Commission
UN	United Nations
UNLA/F	Uganda National Liberation Army/Front
UNMIS	United Nations Mission in Sudan
UNRF II	Uganda National Rescue Front II
UNSC	United Nations Security Council
UNSG	United Nations Secretary-General
UPC	Uganda People's Congress; opposition party and party of former president Obote
UPDA	Uganda People's Democratic Army
UPDF	Uganda People's Defence Force (current name of Uganda's army)
US/USA	United States of America
VP	Vice President
WNBF	West Nile Bank Front

1 Introduction

Seeking Peace with the Lord's Resistance Army

Maybe Angelina Jolie's honeytrap could have been the end of Joseph Kony's existence as one of the world's most notorious warlords.

Jolie, a world-famous superstar of the screen, and the chief prosecutor of the International Criminal Court (ICC), Luis Moreno-Ocampo, had toyed with the idea of embedding Jolie with US troops in the Central African Republic (CAR). Her presence with the soldiers, so the plot went, would allow her to invite Joseph Kony for dinner. The leader of the Lord's Resistance Army (LRA) would then, to his surprise, soon learn that he was not in for a date with Jolie. Instead, she would help to arrest him. Even Jolie's then-husband Brad Pitt was to play a role – maybe as a soldier?[1]

The chief prosecutor of the ICC – who had issued arrest warrants for Kony and other commanders of his Ugandan LRA a few years prior – discussed these possibilities in an email exchange with Jolie obtained by the investigative website Mediapart. Ocampo later claimed that he was the victim of a cyberattack.

Yet before Jolie could fluff the table linen and clink glasses with Kony somewhere in the bush and then wrestle him to the ground to hand him over to the ICC, Ocampo and Jolie stopped communicating. It seems that Ocampo's declarations of love for Jolie were not welcome. Prior to the abrupt ending, both had seemed convinced by the approach – what more could it take but dinner with a beautiful superstar to get Kony to accept his guilt and allow peace to come?

Much, much more, it turned out. More than anyone was able to offer within the setup of how peace is commonly pursued today.

1.1 Getting Ready for Peace

Peace was going to take much more than even the representatives of the LRA and its political wing, the Lord's Resistance Movement (LRM),

---

[1] *The Sunday Times* (8 October 2017).

were envisioning when they were getting ready in the late morning of Friday, 14 July 2006. Delegates smoothed stray hairs and helped each other shave or adjust ties. The opening ceremony for what would become known as the Juba Peace Talks between the LRA/M and the Government of Uganda (GoU) was scheduled for 2 p.m. With an hour to go, the delegation of suited men and one woman was ready to depart. As a final preparation, a few briefly gathered in one of the prefabricated container hotel rooms of the RA International Hotel for a private prayer. At 4 p.m., the delegation was still waiting under the hotel's mango tree. Bored with hanging around, one of the delegates asked me to film him. He shouted into the camera: 'We want peace! The LRA wants peace!' Just after 5 p.m., cars sent by the Government of Southern Sudan (GoSS) arrived to take the delegation to the Southern Sudan Legislative Assembly building.

Juba, the capital of what was at the time called southern Sudan,[2] had at that point only been the headquarters of GoSS for a few months. The Comprehensive Peace Agreement (CPA) between the Government of Sudan in Khartoum and the former rebel Sudan People's Liberation Army and Movement (SPLA/M) had been signed in 2005, starting a six-year interim period until the referendum on independence, to be held in 2011. After years as a besieged garrison town for the Khartoum government's Sudanese Armed Forces (SAF), Juba, in July 2006, was in the early stages of reconstruction, with few stretches of paved road or permanent buildings. The Legislative Assembly was among the biggest buildings left standing after the war.

As they walked up the big staircase and across the sandy-coloured spotty carpet of the dusty lobby, nobody in the LRA/M delegation spoke. Nobody smiled. On a normal day, parliamentarians would sit in the deep brown armchairs, debating or exchanging friendly banter. On this day, the dimly lit corridors of the assembly hall were deserted. SPLA soldiers ushered the delegates into a room where representatives of the Acholi people northern Uganda's main population group, were waiting: the Ugandan Acholi Paramount Chief Rwot Achana II, accompanied by religious leaders and other delegates. The visitors hugged some delegates and patted others on the shoulder and the atmosphere instantly lightened.

Until that afternoon, I had only ever seen the parliament half-filled with newly appointed members voting on laws for newly semi-autonomous southern Sudan. Now the hall was packed with Ugandans, SPLA soldiers, South Sudanese politicians and reporters from major

---

[2] The country has been called South Sudan since its independence in 2011. I will refer to southern Sudan for the time before 2011.

Figure 1.1 Joseph Kony and his deputy Vincent Otti, June 2006

Ugandan and international news outlets. The BBC's Khartoum corres-
pondent Jonah Fisher was speaking into his recorder. Reuters had sent a
reporter from Kampala. Al Jazeera was rolling a camera. The media
presence was also a response to the shift in how the armed rebels of the
LRA had dealt with public relations in the preceding weeks. Its elusive
leader, Joseph Kony, had for the first time given a television interview –
to me – just a few weeks earlier, announcing his interest in peace.[3] He
had not been heard from or seen for years before that; appearances had
been scarce in twenty years of war. The LRA now seemed accessible,
signalling that this new attempt at peace was going to be different from
previous efforts.

The GoU delegation was already seated when the doors opened for the
LRA/M. The two groups on either side of the room seemed similar – with
two exceptions. Seated among the men of the LRA/M delegates was one
woman: Josephine Apire, an LRA affiliate based in London. Among the
representatives of the Ugandan government was one man wearing military fatigues and sunglasses: Uganda People's Defence Force (UPDF)
Colonel Charles Otema, who had for years been in charge of the military
operation against the LRA.[4] LRA/M delegate Sunday Otto, who had
been arrested by Otema a few times, kept staring at the army man even
while bowing his head for a prayer. Speaking first, southern Sudan's
President Salva Kiir Mayardit and then Gulu's Archbishop John

---

[3] Schomerus (2010a).   [4] Otema has since been demoted.

Baptist Odama both invoked a spirit of hope. The leader of the GoU delegation, Interior Minister Dr Ruhakana Rugunda, reiterated the GoU's commitment to peace. Then Martin Ojul, chairman of the LRA/M delegation, walked up to the microphone to announce that he would leave the opening words to his spokesperson Obonyo Olweny. Olweny, in the first official public appearance by the LRA/M at the Juba Talks, launched into what in my scribbled notes I described as 'a symbolic RPG [rocket-propelled grenade] attack'. First, he listed the grievances the LRA/M wanted to discuss:

> My delegation wishes to take this opportunity to inform the international community that the political agenda of the LRA/M is premised on the mission to address the basic issues of among others, political persecution and marginalisation, demeaning attitude designedly expressed by people in power to insult and demonise some ethnic groups in the country, deliberate imbalance and disparity in the development of our country, protection of the people's land against state-sponsored and state-backed land grabbers, respect for and protection of cultural diversity, abuse of democratic principles and good governance, genuine respect for international law and the territorial integrity of and peaceful co-existence with all countries, compensation and reparation for all the losses suffered as a result of civil strife and/or state-instigated schemes such as cattle rustling by NRA [National Resistance Army, a previous name for Uganda's army] soldiers that swept all the livestock in northern and eastern Uganda, equal opportunity for all, partisan army and other forces, peace and reconciliation, private sector-driven economy, professional and motivated civil service, zero tolerance for corruption, sectarianism and abuse of office, affirmative action for women, youth and the disadvantaged, IDP [internally displaced person] camps and protection of human dignity.[5]

During preparations for the opening ceremony, Olweny's speech had caused heated discussions in the LRA/M. Some delegates – and representatives of IKV Pax Christi, a Dutch organisation that played a crucial part in bringing about the Juba Talks – had advised against putting a sweeping collection of issues on the table and instead suggested sticking to pleasantries. Others wanted to use this unprecedented publicity opportunity to establish the LRA/M's political agenda. They argued that this would prove that the LRA/M had fought a legitimate war and that it would set the appropriate tone for the negotiations. Unsurprisingly, Olweny's main point, in addition to 'explain[ing] the root causes of the war to those who are genuinely concerned about the conflict in northern Uganda, its manifestations and ramifications', was that the LRA wanted to

---

[5] Olweny (2006b).

give our side of the story against extremely negative and malicious distortions, misinformation and outright lies about the role of the LRA/M in the conflict, and to a no less extent, against the people of northern Uganda ... [and] appeal to the international community to reassess its position on the LRA/M, based on prejudices and misgivings prompted by NRM's [National Resistance Movement, President Yoweri Museveni's ruling party] elaborate propaganda machinery.[6]

As he concluded his speech, Olweny's tone became firm:

Our clear and unequivocal message to the regime in Kampala is that our acceptance of these peace talks should not be interpreted that LRA can no longer fight or that we are now militarily weak. No, we are not. Should the regime in Kampala choose the path of violence and militarism in the belief that they can settle the current conflict in the battlefield by decisively defeating the LRA, then they shall be in for a rude surprise.

Colonel Otema, seated only a few rows away from me, let out an audible snort. Olweny continued:

The LRA is strong and the unfolding political events in Uganda, the ever manifesting clearer dichotomy between a small clique of an ethnic-based regime and the majority of the marginalised Ugandans can only make a now focused, more pro-people and more sophisticated and committed LRA stronger. The LRA has come of age. Never shall we remain silent about the intransigent and rapacious machinery of the NRM/UPDF.[7]

The audience was noticeably taken aback. I heard someone say loudly: 'That was a bit harsh!' Such a strong statement, delivered with military verve by someone people knew to be a member of the Acholi diaspora was unexpected for some, frustrating for others. Most journalists construed the speech as an attention-grabber to counter allegations that, as a spent force, the LRA was not a credible negotiation partner. Olweny's debut also fuelled a separate discussion. Who was the LRA, really? A safe haven for an embittered but out-of-touch diaspora? Die-hard commanders with forced recruits at their mercy? Considering that the LRA was known for recruiting through abduction, were these delegates brainwashed abductees, volunteers for a cause they believed in or, as someone behind me whispered, down-on-their-luck individuals who had joined the delegation in anticipation of a generous per diem?[8] Father Carlos Rodriguez, a longtime resident of Uganda and a significant figure in previous peace negotiations with the LRA, turned to his neighbour and asked loudly: 'When has this man last been to Uganda?'[9]

---

[6] Olweny (2006b).   [7] Olweny (2006b).   [8] Fieldnotes, Juba: 14 July 2006.
[9] Fieldnotes, Juba: 14 July 2006; also Rodríguez Soto (2009)

Within the walls of the windowless Legislative Assembly, within the space of a few minutes, I had heard or overheard a whole set of issues that somehow needed to be tackled at the Juba Talks – including how the LRA/M wanted to present itself.[10] Within the delegation, Olweny's speech had created dissonance. One delegate, a middle-aged man with an army rank who was now living in Europe, was concerned that the strong tone of the speech had closed down the possibilities for negotiations: 'The Government of Uganda will feel snubbed. They might withdraw .... The speech should have been more humble, without any inclusion of military power. Otherwise, this can be seen as a threat of war'.[11] Other LRA/M delegates left the opening ceremony in a visibly triumphant mood, convinced that their having voiced their anger and demands would allow the conflict to be resolved. Asked how he felt during the ceremony, one of the younger delegates with reportedly close connections to Joseph Kony said: 'I feel that I have done something good'.[12]

1.2   Understanding the Reality of Peace Negotiations

This delegate's feeling that something positive had been started in Juba was initially reflected in how the Juba Talks were perceived. Despite the doubtful whispers in the audience and the LRA/M's awkward opening speech, the Juba Talks are widely considered the most promising attempt at peace in the history of a violent conflict that has its beginnings in 1986 and, in 2021, is still not fully over yet. Yet the Juba Talks ended in 2008 when, despite several opportunities, LRA leader Kony did not sign the Final Peace Agreement (FPA) and the Ugandan army (UPDF) then dropped bombs on the camp of the LRA in the north-eastern corner of the Democratic Republic of the Congo (DRC). An international military offensive against the LRA continued for several years; more than ten years later the LRA still causes terror for civilians in the CAR. Joseph Kony remains a somewhat mystical figure – in many ways simply because he is still alive – while one of his main senior commanders, Dominic Ongwen, is prosecuted for crimes against humanity at the ICC in The Hague in a controversial and challenging trial.[13]

It is widely argued that the peace talks failed because Kony was not serious about peace, that the Juba Talks were an LRA ploy to regroup, that Kony's position on many negotiation points remained unclear,[14]

---

[10] Fieldnotes, Juba: 14 July 2006.   [11] Fieldnotes, Juba: 14 July 2006.
[12] Fieldnotes, Juba: 15 July 2006.   [13] Keller (2017); Branch (2017).
[14] Jackson (2009).

that the LRA was torn apart by internal strife, that the mediation set-up was not conducive to reaching an agreement, and that the international community had lacked leverage.[15] Opponents of the ICC argue that the court's arrest warrants issued for LRA senior commanders in 2005 – the young court's first-ever warrants – made a peace agreement impossible,[16] citing the Juba Talks as a watershed moment and reality check for international peacemaking. Supporters of the ICC claimed that it helped bring the LRA to the table but then laid bare the LRA's lack of commitment to accountability. All of these points made the Juba Talks difficult, but they do not conclusively explain the complex failure to reach a peace deal.

Most of these arguments foreground the content of the negotiated agreements, implying that the reason for the talks' failure was that simply no agreement could be found to satisfy. This interpretation is too easy – and yet, with the ICC seemingly having won the argument by getting an LRA commander to trial, it is also becoming ever more dominant. But the reality behind the failure cannot be reconstructed through the lens of victor's justice: The reasons are not clear cut and instead can be found in the experience of the peace process. Thus, a detailed account of what happened is warranted.

The Juba Talks were the first peace talks directly influenced by the ICC, constituting a watershed moment in peacemaking. They also left a sobering legacy, with a violent fall-out for civilians in South Sudan, DRC and the CAR, an unsatisfying peace for Ugandans and with lessons unlearned on the long-term impact of military intervention against armed rebellions in Africa.[17] How the Juba Talks are remembered and conceptualised also has long-term implications regarding how military partnerships between the United States and Uganda are understood. It is necessary to shine a light on the complex and convoluted events that were set in motion in Juba, beyond the obvious chronology of agreements signed.

The LRA/M did not sign the FPA because of how they had experienced the peace talks, not because they simply rejected the content

---

[15] See for example Spiegel and Prendergast (2008).

[16] It is widely argued that the peace talks failed because the LRA/M was not serious about finding a negotiated solution and was focused on regrouping (Day 2017), or because the arrest warrants issued for LRA senior commanders by the International Criminal Court (ICC) in 2005 – the young court's first-ever arrest warrants – made a peace agreement impossible. More recent scholarship has nuanced this blanket interpretation and instead refines what the nature of the influence of the ICC on the negotiations was (Gissel 2017; Macdonald 2017; Kersten 2016; Clark 2010a).

[17] Epstein (2017).

outright. My endeavour is thus a nuanced analysis of the experience of this confusing and multilayered process in which many actors with often conflicting objectives played a part. The Juba Talks were unique, but they also offer broader lessons about peacemaking: they teach us that peace negotiations can entrench the structures of the conflict and that how participants experience the dynamics of the process matters more than anything else for an outcome. The Juba Talks demonstrate how difficult it is to understand these processes as they happen and to use that understanding to influence them positively. As a case study and bench-mark peace process in a changed international environment, the Juba Talks can help explain why, broadly speaking, the emphasis in current peacemaking on negotiated agreements is misplaced as a measure of success – and yet, this emphasis remains. The key to making peace might instead be found in engagement with dynamics and developments that occur around the talks.

What happens on paper and what actually happens is rather discon-nected; hence I am restricting my analysis to my own observations outside the negotiation room rather than focusing on the content of the peace agreements, which are accessible for everyone to analyse.[18] Focusing on the experience of the LRA/M, I will demonstrate how fragmented narratives and dynamics within the group and in the encoun-ters between the group and outside actors failed to amount to a shared understanding of what could be achieved through negotiations.

As I spent prolonged periods of time with the LRA/M during the Juba Talks to watch and ask questions, I learned that behind seemingly accepted events, a separate set of evolving dynamics and challenges called the meaning of the negotiated agreements into question for the LRA/M.[19] In Juba, the LRA/M did not experience a deep peace process and instead encountered the same power patterns that had kept the conflict alive. Yet on another level, the Juba Talks brought peaceful change to Uganda, strengthening the argument that despite the failure to sign a final agreement, negotiating holds value in itself.

1.3   Overview

Following a chapter on the history of the conflict and attempts at peace-making, this book alternates between empirical chronologies of what

---

[18] All agreements can be found on the United Nations Peacemaker Peace Agreements Database. https://peacemaker.un.org/document-search
[19] Clark's analysis of the gacaca courts in Rwanda starts from a similar perspective (Clark 2010b).

occurred between the opening ceremony and Kony's failure to sign the FPA by the deadline of 30 November 2008 and analytical chapters. In these chronologies, I sometimes use secondary information on events that I did not witness myself, however, the narrative of events is punctuated with insights into how what happened frustrated or elated the LRA/M. The chapters also underscore the methodological and reflective challenges of researching an ongoing process.

The first analytical chapter is a narrative enquiry into how LRA members explained the inner workings and values of the LRA, including how the amorphous and contradictory LRA identity contributed to their experience of the dynamics of the talks. Further, analytical chapters reveal the LRA/M's logic beneath the confusion, outlining ideological and systematic obstacles encountered and entrenched, and distilling the particularities of the LRA/M as a negotiation partner. The final chapter concludes on broader achievements of the Juba Talks, as well as what general insights on peacemaking can be derived.

1.4   The Challenge of Peace

Peace is often assumed to be better than war; yet solving entrenched conflicts within the existing system is extraordinarily difficult. A few days before the opening ceremony of the Juba Talks, I was writing notes on what I then considered the main challenges for the talks. The challenges to me seemed pretty straightforward: simply conducting the negotiations would be difficult, I noted. The heavily armed LRA and the LRA leaders were camped out about 300 miles away in the Congolese jungle with no intention of joining the negotiations at the table in Juba, so getting their input and feeding them would be difficult, as would be protecting the population around them. Facilitation through the young GoSS might be unreliable. There was a need to figure out how to navigate the arrest warrants issued by the ICC for LRA commanders, including the leader Joseph Kony, his deputy, Vincent Otti, Okot Odhiambo, Raska Lukwiya and Ongwen, and with that to establish how to manage the tensions between localised conflicts and international justice frameworks. I presented these challenges to one of the LRA/M delegates. These were all good points, he said, but that he did not think that these were the biggest problems.

Peace, he explained to me, would require a lot of change, both inside and outside the LRA. Adjusting to new situations, thinking of the world they lived in as a peaceful environment in which tackling issues with violence was not an option, was going to be as difficult for the outside world as it was for the LRA. He explained that people mistook peace for something that was very easy and could be achieved by simply wanting to achieve it. This was not the case. It was more important that the talks be done properly. He was unsure whether the LRA would be able to get their points across; he was sceptical that the negotiations would work. Using an Acholi proverb, he put into words that how the LRA and those affected by the conflict experienced the process would be the most important part, and that getting all these things into place to reach peace was full of potential hurdles: 'Every easy thing can be very complicated', he said. 'Even something that you think is very easy and normal to do. Even eating you can bite your tongue'.[20]

How actors experience peace talks and their dynamics determines negotiation conduct and the extent to which they can change their own behaviour. The process takes centre stage, its achievements fading into the background. For the LRA/M, the process was a contradictory experience with shifting loyalties and interests. Internal dynamics within the LRA/M were profoundly influenced by their perception that they were trapped in an established hostile system, with an uneven playing field. Yet the LRA/M also struggled to transform their internal dynamics of distrust. Instead, the Juba Talks confirmed the workings of the 'system LRA/M' that continues to function on its internal trust and distrust between actors of the LRA and the LRM, as well as in collaboration with the government as all groups continuously infiltrate each other. This permanent playing-off of loyalties and betrayals in a conflict system that connects everyone to everyone is a crucial part of why the conflict has continued for so long and why civilians continue to suffer.

These complex internal functions made engaging with international actors – who functioned very differently from the LRA – even more challenging. Where the LRA/M maintains momentum and connections by establishing a pattern in which they often simultaneously reach out and pull back, international actors were aiming to establish consensus to deal with the challenges of the ICC. These two different operational modes created encounters that to the LRA/M confirmed the unevenness of the playing field. The sum of these experiences encouraged the LRA/M to maintain the status quo of the conflict, including continuing to play their own established role that had kept the conflict alive for two decades.

Individuals within the LRA/M embraced the notion of peace with ambiguity. Personal stories give an insight into how LRA/M members experience the day-to-day realities of their often-shifting identities, expressing an ambiguity vis-à-vis being an actor in war and peace.

[20] Fieldnotes, Juba: 5 July 2006.

Some of this ambiguity stems from the history of the conflict and the many frustrated attempts to end it. Crucially, the finding that peace comes with ambiguity for LRA/M members questions a range of common notions in scholarship and practice. Scholars have long recognised that peacemaking is not a linear process with clear goals. Yet, often an unquestioned assumption persists that conflict actors ultimately want to achieve peace and are willing to sacrifice their own position for this goal. With this assumption, conflict resolution theory and practice failed to capture the experience of the LRA/M in the peace talks.

As a case study, the Juba Talks allow for broader conclusions about obstacles to peace. Current approaches to peacemaking tend to under-estimate the dynamics of the process and how these entrench existing conflict-prone structures – including internal structures – and complex-ities involving outside actors receive too little attention, which often inadvertently contributes to the continuation of violent conflict. Analysis of other recent peace processes has brought out similar lessons.[21] Methods of investigation and analysis of these elements cur-rently fall short of providing the empirical information needed to develop a broader holistic perspective on how to measure success and failure to allow for a transformation of conflict resolution strategies.

1.5 The Scholarship on Peace Negotiations

For a brief moment, it all seemed easy. The Juba Talks recovered from the rocky start in the opening ceremony; over the following months, several countries pledged financial and political support. Success appeared within reach. Experienced practitioners seemed convinced that this time a peace deal was inevitable – primarily because by entering the talks, the LRA/M had sent a signal that most analysts read as a sign of weakness or as having run out of options. In October 2007, Jan Egeland said that the Juba Talks had largely progressed in patterns familiar to conflict resolution practitioners. Egeland had retired from his position as UN Under-Secretary-General for Humanitarian Affairs (the head of the United Nations Office for the Coordination of Humanitarian Affairs [OCHA]) the previous year, having been engaged in northern Ugandan issues for a long time. He had visited Juba twice during the talks, including a visit to the bush to meet with the LRA high command. Looking back in 2007, he was not concerned that both

---

[21] Vertin (2018).

negotiation partners had assured each other that they were prepared to continue fighting:

> It was classic negotiation in a sense that they both take very tough positions vis-à-vis the third party. But I was not that nervous. I felt that we had had a turning point by the end of 2006 for the simple reason that we could see that everybody enjoyed the several months of peace and quiet in northern Uganda, the first ones in 18 years.[22]

Yet since no peace deal was achieved, the assumption that the negotiations were on track and that the LRA/M had no choice but to agree to peace were proven wrong. A brief look towards existing scholarship on peace negotiations helps explain the basis of the expectations that made the Juba Talks seem a certain success and highlights the existing gaps. From the vast amount of general scholarship on peace negotiations, two areas are of particular relevance. First is the science that aims to understand negotiation behaviour primarily through modelling. What this approach crucially overlooks is the experience of those doing the negotiations. Second is the contested question whether a negotiated peace agreement does bring peace, or whether it instead sets the stage for a different phase in the conflict.

1.6   Modelling Negotiations

Social science has long established the fine-grained complexities of violent conflict. Oliver Ramsbotham et al., for example, describes the need to understand the complexity of 'hybrid struggles' that transcend 'international state and societal levels' and stresses the necessary 'shift towards seeing conflict in its context'.[23] Yet implementation of conflict resolution remains for practical reasons largely driven by a monolithic view of conflict parties – after all, there need to be clearly identifiable negotiation partners around the table – and the assumption that context can be altered through negotiations. In the Juba Talks, the tacit understanding that any kind of deal would be attractive for the LRA created the notion that the LRA/M had more to gain than to lose from getting a deal, and would thus come together around that goal. It seemed as if concluding the talks successfully was only a matter of working out the bargaining positions. Dean Pruitt's iconic 1981 representation of a simplified game theoretical view of negotiations might be considered dated by scholars in

---

[22] Telephone interview with Jan Egeland, former UN Undersecretary for Humanitarian Affairs, 15 October 2007.
[23] Ramsbotham, Woodhouse and Miall (2005: 25).

light of more nuanced understandings of conflict, but the basic message that negotiations function according to game theory models remains rather dominant when negotiation partners sit down to talk.[24]

Game theory is not simplistic, but in creating models, it fails to capture the finer dynamics of complex conflicts,[25] falling short of taking into account subtle motivations and behavioural shifts within a group and among individuals in the group. The practical application of negotiation models tends to be simplified, politicised and, as Ariel Rubinstein says, misunderstood as a tool to predict behaviour instead of as 'an abstract inquiry into the concepts used in social reasoning when dealing with situations of conflict'.[26] Bruce Hemmer et al. have argued that an emphasis on game theory has meant that more complex setups 'involving networks of many actors' remain under-studied, as they do not fit measurable patterns; crucially, game theory tends to present negotiations as an isolated event starting with a blank slate, whereas they tend to be a continuation of 'ongoing networks of relationships and social processes'.[27]

Paul Richards makes the point that a game theoretical view overlooks the social context: 'The worst wars are between groups whose basic social assumptions lead them to define quite incompatible – indeed incommensurable – needs and desires', he writes. 'Stakeholders can bargain, but first they need to agree they hold stakes in common'.[28] Bates' criticism of 'off-the-shelf models' that reduce each situation 'to one of a small number of models (prisoner's dilemma, battle of the sexes, principal agent with moral hazard, principal agent with adverse selection)' is particularly pertinent in this context. He argues that models only become informative through context, which calls into question the usefulness of the model in the first place.[29]

Naturally, models struggle to include the finer political context such as the internal dynamics of negotiators, the memories and narratives of the war and previous attempts to end it, and crucially the changing perspectives of individuals within the group of negotiators as they go through the process of negotiation. Broader issues, such as the Juba Talks' particularly challenging setup in a country emerging from war and the need to navigate tensions between national conflict resolution and an

---

[24] Pruitt (1981).

[25] See for example Watson (2002) and Dutta (1999) for a comprehensive discussion of game theory's applicability in conflict resolution.

[26] Rubinstein (1991), Game theorists counter that the gap between practice and theory is due to different methods: a practitioner sees limited appeal in randomisation. See Radner and Rosenthal (1982).

[27] Hemmer et al. (2005).   [28] Richards (2005: 19).   [29] Bates, Greif and Levi (2000).

international justice framework, are overlooked. In modelling, such intricacies would simply be marked as *b* or *o* for *other things*. Unsurprisingly, Hemmer complains that *other things* in modelling are 'usually seen as static or uncontrollable'.[30] Yet, how conflict actors in Juba perceived the negotiations shows how dynamic and tremendously important such *other things* are – to the point that they can determine whether agreements get signed or not.

1.7   What Do Peace Agreements Achieve?

The pursuit of a written peace agreement at the heart of the Juba Talks is hardly surprising. A large number of conflicts are now settled by peace agreements, rather than by an outright victory. The belief in the power of negotiation, writes Bertram Spector, remains strong as 'a meaningful and viable technique to address the conundrum of apparently irreconcilable differences, though the need for creativity is stressed'.[31] Opponents of military intervention remain focused on peace agreements as the acceptable, more humane and humanistic way to end violent conflict. Relationship building, trust, incentives and reconciliation are elements of an idealised model of conflict resolution, but Mac Ginty and Özerdem make the crucial point that pursuing peace negotiations cannot be understood as 'an attempt to reach a peace of rainbow and unicorns' but as a 'calculated attempt by the parties to a conflict to recalibrate the conflict in order to lower the conflict cost'.[32] Egeland himself, despite presenting a whole range of peace processes in his autobiography as successes that ultimately did not lead to peace, retains a seemingly unshaken belief in the approach.[33] Scholarship rarely goes beyond rather general statements in providing frameworks for negotiation. Neema Seguya, in her work on the Juba Talks, emphasises, for example, broad participation as essential. The Juba Talks, she writes, 'could have benefited from a "bottom-up" approach', which she elaborates to include 'addressing root causes of the conflict, and the inequalities in the country's economy, the changing dynamics of the conflicts', among others.[34]

Much like the five separate signed agreements that the Juba Talks produced – even though they were not endorsed with a final signature – many peace agreements do not have the desired effect. Only a few prominent peace agreements brought lasting, albeit often fragile, peace between specific conflict parties, such as the Camp David Accords between Israel and Egypt, the Good Friday Agreement, and the work

---

[30] Hemmer et al. (2005).   [31] Spector (2006).   [32] Mac Ginty and Özerdem (2019)
[33] Egeland (2008).   [34] Seguya (2010: 92).

done by the Mwalimu Nyerere Foundation.[35] With such a poor record of obvious success, there is no conclusive answer to the broader question of whether peace talks are a good way to achieve peace. Generally, argues Monica Toft, peace agreements are the least reliable way to bring peace, because systemic change needs the destruction of one conflict party, usually through military means.[36] Edward Luttwak suggests that letting a war run its course is a less costly and more reliable way to achieve peace.[37] Peace negotiations and peace agreements might simply contribute to a continuation of the conflict. Christopher Dolan has written that before the Juba Talks, peace talks between the GoU and the LRA had been a tool to entrench existing power relations and thus could be seen as 'a continuation of war by other means' which 'in essence created the space for further militarisation', an argument that will continue to ring true in this book.[38]

The greatest challenge in contemporary peacemaking might be the vast gap between theory and practice, between what scholars and analysts know is necessary to de-escalate and change conflict dynamics, and what processes are supported particularly by international organisations. In conflict resolution scholarship, the theory has long moved to a more sophisticated understanding of the holistic and structure-changing processes that are required to transform entrenched conflicts, with John Paul Lederach and Johan Galtung being the first scholars to widely introduce this language.[39] Broadly speaking, scholarship on conflicts tends to work with the notion of transformation, rather than resolution, even though Johannes Botes questions whether fine-tuning the semantics in this way has brought a chance to theory and practice, as the muddled use of terminology continues to muddle practice.[40] How the notion of conflict transformation can make the practice of peace negotiations complicated becomes clear when looking at what schools of thought exist. Heidi Burgess and Guy Burgess categorise three conceptualisations of the term conflict transformation: the first requires a recognition of national aspirations, the second encompasses deep-ranging structural institutional changes and power redistribution in order to not allow the conflict to return, and the third requires adjustment of individual beliefs and behaviour.[41]

---

[35] Ramsbotham, Woodhouse and Miall (2005). Wallensteen argues that from 1946 to 2004, durable peace agreements were achieved in more than a third of all conflicts (Wallensteen and Eriksson 2009: 13).
[36] Toft (2010).   [37] Luttwak (1999).   [38] Dolan (2005: 109).
[39] Galtung (1995); Lederach (1995).   [40] Botes (2003).
[41] Burgess and Burgess (1997: 285), cite Kriesberg, Northrup and Thorson as the most important proponents for concept 1, Harrington, Merry and Burton for number 2, and

In practice, despite this understanding, particularly peace talks with an international interest tend to fall back on a range of established procedural templates. Approaches such as negotiations (including track one and track two negotiations), mediation, diplomacy and peacebuilding are well established and preferable for peace processes under public scrutiny as they seemingly are more measurable. The Juba Talks, in particular, are an example of how such limited procedural tools ultimately stood in the way of conflict transformation – or even just preventing the conflict from moving into its next military phase.

The idea of transformation does not come from a realisation that negotiation and mediation often fall short of expectations, but that in situations of entrenched conflict those seemingly streamlined processes do not mirror the kind of conflicts they are trying to solve. These entrenched social conflicts – of which the LRA conflict was one – instead move through phases of social change, along the lines of the conceptualisations of James Coleman and Kenneth Boulding.[42] Even though scholars of conflict have since debated the exact meanings of the terms, practice in the heat of the moment tends to boil down to the much more limited procedural templates discussed above which are aimed at resolving a particular part – usually violence – of a conflict rooted in structures and individual experience. These templates do not accommodate the long-term fluidity of a transformative process. Botes argues that conflict resolution attempts are a setup for failure as they leave the system within which the conflict occurred intact. On the other hand, conflict resolution processes through the readily available toolkit are, as Bernard Mayer argues, seemingly more manageable because they seem focussed on a set of tangible issues and have a timeframe attached to them.[43] Further, the negotiated agreements tend to hold some procedural, some substantive and some institutional components to agree on schedules, ways to address grievances, agreements on root causes, and implementation monitoring.[44]

1.8   How Do Wars End?

With procedural toolkits to end war rather limited, the question does remain: how does the end of war come about? Research on how to best

---

Bush and Folger for the focus on individual change. See Burton (1996); Bush, Baruch and Folger (1994); Kriesberg, Northrup and Thorson (1989); Harrington and Engle Merry (1988).

[42] Boulding (1962); Coleman (1956).   [43] Mayer (2003).

[44] Yawanarajah and Ouellet (2003).

end war peacefully is a relatively young field that emerged in this definition only in the mid-1980s. The field is still better at asking questions
than providing answers. Daniel Chirot and Clark McCauley, for
example, question the viability of a range of approaches to end violent
conflict, such as 'pursuing leaders responsible for mass murder and
bringing them to justice? Education campaigns? Strengthening international institutions? Alleviating poverty? Building civil society?
Promoting truth and reconciliation commissions?'[45] Sidney Tarrow
wonders: 'What are the factors and the mechanisms that are likely to
produce post-war civil peace? Power sharing? Vigorous peace-making by
international institutions? Or simply stalemate and exhaustion of the
internal antagonists'?[46]

In the past, as conflicts were often studied quantitatively, the need for
data sets crowded out attention to the internal processes of conflict
parties; political context as experienced by individual conflict actors
was largely absent. More recently, even scholars who focus on quantitative approaches have complemented their work by including political
narratives.[47] The study of conflict resolution is thus rapidly evolving,
drawing on various disciplines to understand the complex nature of
conflicts that can be rooted in history, politics, geography, economics
or sociology, and more recently with an increased emphasis on culture.[48]
Jeremy Weinstein focuses on the individual motives of conflict actors by
categorising the rational choices that drive people to join rebellions.[49]
However, a crucial gap exists even in approaches that focus on individual
experiences. How dynamic processes continuously shape motivations is
rarely captured. This includes processes experienced in the resolution of
a conflict. Generally speaking, research on peace negotiations that puts
actors' experience, rather than technical issues, centre stage is almost
non-existent. Reasons for this are methodological – access is a challenge,
as outlined further below. It is also the case that some processes are so
multilayered that they become what Elizabeth Drexler calls a 'black box':
a peace process so complex that it defies analysis beyond the identification of a start and an end.[50] It is simply very difficult to stay on top of a
developing process in which insights might develop their own dynamic.

One way to deal with this in scholarship has been to focus primarily on
technical issues and scholarship on the Juba Talks is no exception.

---

[45] Chirot and McCauley (2006: 5).   [46] Tarrow (2007).
[47] Fearon and Laitin (2005), Laitin's research involves presenting so-called random
narratives to 'assess the fit of the statistical model case by case and to establish whether
the narrative of a conflict reflects the quantitative findings'. See Laitin (n.d.).
[48] Trujillo et al. (2008); Ramsbotham, Woodhouse and Miall (2005).
[49] Weinstein (2007).   [50] Drexler (2007).

However, peacemaking is as complex as the conflicts it aims to resolve. That means that peace processes are not linear, and that a detailed understanding of actors' motivations and experience is necessary.[51] In the months leading up to the Juba Talks, the LRA/M Information Bureau had published a paper that argued for a more detailed understanding of the conflict: 'The interconnectedness of the issues and parties to this conflict is far broader and more complex than is currently being perceived by both the Sudanese and Ugandan authorities'.[52]

Yet analysis of the Juba Talks tends to foreground two primarily technical aspects. The first point that has received a large amount of attention is the tension between international and national justice frameworks, and between peace and justice as it emerged during peace negotiations.[53] This is unsurprising, considering the benchmark significance of the Juba Talks as the first peace negotiations conducted with conflict actors wanted by the ICC. Although it was designed to end the worst of crimes, one of the main points of contention regarding the ICC has been the issuing of arrest warrants for actors in ongoing violent conflicts. The main argument against this instrument is that it closes off avenues for peace negotiations; the main argument for ICC activity in an ongoing conflict is that it might change conflict dynamics positively by putting actors under pressure.

The second most common analytical approach to the Juba Talks zooms in only on the modalities of conducting the talks as they relate to how the text for the agreements was reached, for example in discussions over the extent to which the process was participatory and inclusive, and addressed the root causes of the war.[54] Additionally, accounts of the Juba Talks tend to be reduced to brief chronologies – with Ronald Atkinson a notable exception[55] – yet how actors experienced the process and how this might have contributed to the failure of the talks is not generally addressed, and if so, only by using retrospectively gathered data.

It is tempting to approach an analysis of the LRA/M in the Juba Talks as a philosophical sceptic, maintaining that increased complexity, the interdependence of actors and the unreliability of those involved defy attempts at explanation and as a consequence undermine the idea that a peaceful negotiated solution is ever possible. In the Juba Talks, such

---

[51] See for example Körppen, Ropers and Gießmann (2011).

[52] LRA/M Information Bureau, 'For immediate release', 15 November 2005.

[53] A few significant examples from a huge literature are Nouwen (2013); Kersten (2012); Clark (2011); Wierda and Otim (2011); Bukuluki (2011); Afako (2010); Worden (2009); Waddel and Clarke (2008); Wijeyaratne (2008).

[54] Seguya (2010).   [55] Atkinson (2010a).

scepticism was particularly prominent, as many observers of the Ugandan conflict continue to explain the lack of peace by reference to the enigmatic inner workings of Kony's mind. This obsession with Kony as a spirit-possessed wild card has obscured other reliable and available evidence about what went wrong. Yet elements in the LRA's behaviour can be explained through a scrutiny of the LRA's own point of view. LRA members and supporters are aware of these complexities and at times willing to articulate them. The complexities were also to a certain extent observable, although observation came with methodological challenges.

1.9   A Comment on Methods

My ethnographic methods were determined by the developments that brought me to this research. On 7 November 2005, I was sitting in broad daylight at a table in an open-air nightclub in Gulu, northern Uganda, with three young Ugandan men. They were listening intently as I was speaking on the phone with the LRA's Second-in-Command, Vincent Otti. Having checked that I had enough phone credit to sustain an expensive call to a satellite phone, they had dialled a number on my mobile and handed the handset to me. The first thing I heard was a low, breathy giggle and then a voice addressing me by my nickname, Malaika, followed by an introduction: 'This is Vincent Otti'.[56]

We made conversation. I talked cautiously, not sure whether the man at the other end of the line really was the feared deputy commander of the LRA. I had learned that many people in Gulu boast about their tight connection to the LRA high command. Having close connections to the LRA was dangerous – the UPDF was keeping a very close watch on assumed rebel sympathisers – but it also came with clout. For researchers like me, people claiming to be close to the high command were endlessly fascinating. We all wanted to hear their stories and somehow get to the enigmatic Kony. When I asked Otti where the LRA was right at that moment, he laughed again. He could not say on the phone, of course, but he himself was somewhere far in the bush – maybe Sudan, maybe Uganda, maybe the DRC. The LRA was under attack, he said.

This was not my first contact with Otti. We had been exchanging pleasantries by post, hand-delivered through messengers. A note I had written had supposedly been given to Otti in the bush; at least I had paid

---

[56] My name, Mareike, sounds very similar to Malaika, which in Swahili or Arabic translates as angel. Malaikas are also spirits. See Allen (1991) or Behrend (1993, 1999a) for discussions on spirit possession in northern Uganda. Kony is said to have been possessed by different spirits. See Dolan (2005: 437).

someone US$25 as a delivery fee and for transport costs. A few weeks later, I had received a letter in return. The neat handwriting on rough, lined paper stated that the letter had been written on 28 August 2005; the red stamp at the bottom of the page read 'Lord's Resistance Army/ Movement (LRA/M)'. It was the first time I had seen an LRA letterhead. This one was signed with a simple 'Thanks' and 'Yours sincerely, Otti Vincent, c/m II'.[57]

'Madam Malaika', the letter read. 'I would like to thank the almighty God, the God of Abraham, Isaic [sic], Jacob and our ancestors for allowing our meeting through this letter though not physically'. The letter went on to express concern: Otti wanted to know who I was, but also what I – as a representative of the outside world – thought about him. He did not think that the world had the story right:

The world currently has termed us as terrorist [sic], murderers, thugs and all they can call us but we are not such. It is only that our points, agenda of the war is not being represented to the international body. So my point of argument is only if you can promise to work with us secretly without exposing things to the Ugandan government then absolutely we are also ready to work with you.[58]

I was unsure what exactly Otti expected of me, what 'working with' the LRA entailed. The young men I had met in Uganda had wanted to speak to me repeatedly over the course of several months. We had discussed why they thought that violence had been necessary to end the conditions in northern Uganda's displacement camps, their disillusionment with recent attempts at peace, and their confusion about the involvement of the ICC. They had said that Otti also wanted to understand better what the ICC was.

I asked Otti what he knew about the ICC. 'I know that they take me to the ICC and then they will hang me', he answered and laughed. It must have seemed funny to him that after two decades of barely leaving the bush between Uganda, Sudan and the DRC, he believed that he was facing execution in Europe. Equally funny must have been the thought that this institution called the 'ICC' – with offices in Europe and an Argentinean prosecutor – was trying to get to him. He added that he did not want to be executed far away from his home, the town of Atiak in northern Uganda. This would not be a fitting end to his fight against the GoU and more specifically Uganda's president, Yoweri Museveni.

In the weeks leading up to my first phone call with Otti, the young men had made clear that they also did not think much of the ICC, and that the

---

[57] Vincent Otti, personal letter to author, 25 August 2005.
[58] Vincent Otti personal letter to author 25 August 2005.

LRA wanted to have another go at a negotiated solution. In his letter, Otti wrote a description of how he thought these peace talks ought to be conducted.

Peace talks can't be under trees, on the road sides and in a gazetted area. Peace talks should be in different country where international observers can also be there. If that is followed, then we are ready to talk peace.

My conversations with Otti continued over the following months, as the LRA pursued its contacts to start a new round of peace talks. He kept reiterating to me that peace was what the LRA wanted; to prove it, they would allow me to visit them in the bush and to talk to Kony. After months of regular phone calls, Otti considered me a personal contact who had something to contribute.[59] This connection ultimately led me to the bush on the Sudan/DRC border to sit down and interview Kony. Circumstances helped, as powerful actors, namely the then-Vice-President of the GoSS, Riek Machar Teny Dhurgon, made their moves towards facilitating peace talks with the LRA.

With Machar's logistical help, I arrived as part of a larger delegation of SPLA, LRA/M representatives and peacemaking organisations in the provisional camp of the LRA on Sudan's border with the DRC in the afternoon of 11 June 2006. Along with those who were waiting to be nominated as the official LRA/M delegation for the peace talks, I was told to make myself comfortable for the night in a round clearing the LRA soldiers had created. The bush was so dense that when I strolled through, pushing aside the broad-leafed plants, I could not retrace my own steps after walking off the path for only a few seconds. Had I been lost, however, I would have easily been found. LRA soldiers were stationed at regular intervals in wide concentric circles. They were invisible to me; I could only make them out in the dense vegetation when I bumped into one. They could clearly see me much better than I could see them. At certain times, I could at least hear the decisive marching steps of the patrols circumnavigating the clearing, betrayed by the slurping sound of gumboots and the faint musky smell of clothes that had dried on some-one's body while walking through the bush.

In the evening, I was seated near Otti on a bench constructed from tied bamboo. Every now and then, a soldier entered the clearing with a military greeting and a loud request for 'Permission!' before being allowed near Otti. I saw a few young men charging their simple mobile phones (smartphones were not yet available), using solar panels with

---

[59] This gross overestimation of my capacity to influence peacemaking with the LRA shows, in my opinion, how disconnected the LRA felt.

haphazard wiring sticking out. The weaponry on display was less make-shift: most soldiers were wrapped in long ammunition belts and carried at least an AK-47, often with a mounted bayonet. One tall man shoul-dered an M-16 gun; another paraded a rocket-propelled grenade. Most LRA soldiers wore green uniforms, or at least parts of a uniform. One combined his camouflage trousers with a blue UNICEF T-shirt with a slogan campaigning for polio immunisation: 'Have you seen a paralysed child?' I spotted a woman among the armed troops, distinguished by her golden ear hoops. I asked Otti what her rank was. He pretended not to understand. 'Is that a woman?' he said, pointing at her and winking at me. 'What makes you think it's a woman?' He then told me that she was a captain, a very good captain: 'Women can also fight. She is an example'.

I had been invited to stay the night, and once the SPLA and Machar had left, the LRA noticeably relaxed. It dawned on me over the course of the evening that my visit to the LRA was as much an occasion for them as it was for me. Several commanders told me that I was the first guest to be invited by the high command.[60] One officer was relentlessly filming me with a small video camera. I later learned that his nickname was 'Record' because he was always on filming duty. The young men of the LRA mostly reacted with giggling fits when I came near them, especially when they witnessed how I tried to lug several bags at once. Immediately they came to my rescue and carried my luggage to the clearing. Three young men of LRA were helping me to put up my tent when another young woman appeared with freshly baked bread and mashed beans. She set down the metal pots without uttering a sound or making eye contact with anyone. The bread was still warm, and the men gathered around the campfire to eat. I was invited to join and to say grace for everyone. When I said that as a non-religious person, I could not do that – a slightly awkward moment – one of the men from the to-be-appointed peace delegation took off his baseball cap and quickly said a prayer. I was the first to be offered food from the shared pot and red, syrupy tea in a metal mug.[61] Shortly after, Otti sat down next to me. He ate and talked about his history with the LRA, but his mind seemed to be elsewhere as his eyes scanned the surrounding soldiers.

It was a moment of unmatched yet brief openness, lasting from mid-2005 to mid-2007, during which the LRA decided to voice their side of the story and to launch what could be called their first public relations campaign. It remains the only opportunity so far to get first-hand answers

[60] I believe they meant that I was the first white guest to interview Kony. Fieldnotes, Ri-Kwangba: 11 June 2006.
[61] Fieldnotes, Ri-Kwangba: 12 June 2006.

about thinking in the active LRA and to observe the LRA's interactions with the outside world. In the greater context of the LRA's aim to start negotiations, it is not surprising that they changed their behaviour to allow this access. I was in the lucky position to observe this opening up of the LRA. As the Juba Talks got underway, I moved to Juba and became an unofficial observer of the talks, able to attend several meetings between officials and LRA in the bush and conducting my own meetings as part of a community project to aid the Juba Talks. I was a beneficiary of the rather chaotic organisation of the early days of the peace negoti-ations, when not many questions were asked and rules were easily bent. I spent as much time as possible in the midst of it, sometimes exposing myself to intense – and justified – criticism about my unmandated presence. As the Juba Talks were taken over by the international com-munity, the talks and the LRA became less accessible. Despite a few more public appearances by the LRA high command, they were starting to close the door in September 2007, slamming it shut in November 2008.

Peace processes tend to be studied from a comparative or historical perspective, often using causal process theory to answer the broad ques-tion of why a peace agreement does or does not work. These approaches are useful when combined with the benefit of hindsight but are of lesser value in a developing process. Analysis of the motivations for and experi-ence of being a member of the LRA (or any other military group engaged in violent conflict) is often necessarily reduced by lack of access and, as has been argued, constrained by the various analytical lenses used to view the war. The most prominent of these are humanitarian or legal frame-works. What is missing in the literature is detailed data and analysis of how actors in a peace process experience their own roles and constraints in the process. Peter Wallensteen highlights the need for research to move away from 'a consolidated set of insights on which strategies work or why agreements endure' and suggests that research should instead seek 'plausible understandings that ... help to highlight policy dilemmas for further study'.[62] It is a plausible understanding of how processes are experienced by those caught up in them that I am after.

Yet, the often-explosive day-to-day interactions in peace negotiations tend to be off-limits for researchers. Only fragmented records exist of dynamics in peace negotiations as they and the political economy of the moment develop. Most in-depth analysis of peace processes happens after the fact and relies on the memory of actors – either conflict parties

---

[62] Wallensteen (2007: 5).

or mediators with a stake in the matter. Research on the LRA largely relies on material provided by ex-LRA, which naturally shapes a certain perspective.[63] Also, researching the dynamics of a complex process with guarded, manipulative or largely inaccessible actors provides its own set of methodological and analytical challenges: how I tackled those makes, I hope, also a contribution on the limitations and greater benefits of research methods in contested processes. It is in the nature of conflict actors that the information they provide is fractured, changeable and incomplete. Of course, as Thandika Mkandawire rightly stresses, asking perpetrators of crimes for their motivation usually elicits 'a retrospective account of what drove them to commit the crimes' that 'is likely to be self-serving'.[64] As such, the information provided here echoes the nature of the conflict and the difficulties of capturing precise description and broadly applicable analysis, while also providing a detailed account of what happened.

In documenting the experience of the LRA/M, I am building on extensive fieldwork conducted primarily with the LRA/M as they were going through the Juba Talks, as well as previous and subsequent work in northern Uganda.[65] I interviewed several of the major players in the Juba Talks – some of them several times – namely LRA leader Kony, his deputy Otti, South Sudan's then – Vice President Machar, who mediated the talks, and the then head of OCHA, Egeland. I visited the LRA camp in southern Sudan's Ri-Kwangba seven times, with two overnight stays in the LRA camp deeper in the bush across the border in the DRC. The longest visit had me stay in the nearby village of Nabanga for ten days, making daily visits to Ri-Kwangba 5 kilometres down a bush road. I spent time at the designated assembly area for LRA forces in Owiny-Kibul near the Ugandan border. The first time, I travelled to Owiny-Kibul on a field visit with the Cessation of Hostilities Monitoring Team comprised of LRA, UPDF and SPLA. My second stay in Owiny-Kibul lasted two weeks, during which I pitched my tent in the SPLA barracks and was kindly fed by the SPLA soldiers.

I was present at many of the milestone events of the talks, such as various opening and signing ceremonies, and Egeland's visit to the LRA in the bush. On many days in Juba, I talked, observed and debated what was going on with the LRA/M or members of the mediation team. Over the course of almost three years of travelling to southern Sudan regularly during the Juba Talks, I conducted at least 400 semi-structured interviews with participants and civilians, and held many more informal

---

[63] See for example Cakaj (2016).   [64] Mkandawire (2002: 168).
[65] Allen and Schomerus (2006).

conversations with participants in the Juba Talks.[66] In addition, I conducted research on the phone, making frequent phone calls to the bush, and met with members of the Acholi diaspora in Europe and Kenya.

This seems like astonishing access to the LRA and compared to what had been possible before and has been since, it was. Despite this, I am limited by what research was possible depending on the mood of the actors and my ability to spend time in Sudan. Numerous ethical and methodological issues appeared along the way. The Juba Talks happened in a confined and very guarded space. The situation among actors remained fluid; it was at times remarkably open, at other times all doors were closed, and I was met with hostility. With multiple actors in charge, from the LRA/M to GoSS or international agencies such as OCHA or the UN Department of Political Affairs (DPA), access was at no point guaranteed. This means that the empirical insights presented here inevitably suffer from selection bias in the sense that I was only allowed access to information when it was deemed useful or not harmful by the various actors. However, in monitoring when the LRA/M granted me access and when they pushed me away, I experienced myself how the LRA/M keeps people engaged by at times rejecting them and then inviting them back. My own experience of being trusted, being used and being betrayed sharpened my focus on this particular characteristic. Overall, this summary account underscores the subjectivity of analysis in complex processes of conflict resolution. This problem extends also to using other source material, an issue I discuss further below.

I grappled with the common researcher's dilemma that I was dealing with unreliable information, because respondents might not be telling the truth, either inadvertently or with purpose.[67] One of the international facilitators at the Juba Talks said to me that he took every statement given by LRA/M members with a grain of salt, including all the quotes I present here, as they were all tactical statements.[68] When asking an LRA/M member for information, I sometimes said that my basic

---

[66] I undertook fieldwork in Sudan and Kenya focused on the Juba Talks during the following times: 25 May to 13 June 2006, 28 June to 15 July 2006, 9–16 August 2006, 4 September to 18 December 2006, 15–26 February 2007, 28 May to 8 June 2007, 6 June to 21 July 2007, 21 September to 4 October 2007, 22 January to 16 February 2008, 13 March to 2 April 2008, 8–16 April 2008, 5–27 June 2008. Between 2008 and 2016, I travelled to Sudan and South Sudan repeatedly, often staying for several months at a time, including several months of fieldwork in LRA-affected Western Equatoria in 2013 and 2015. While not every trip had an LRA focus, I gathered information on a range of subsequent occasions. I worked again in Uganda in 2018.

[67] Gardner (2001).

[68] Personal email to author from an international advisor to the Juba Talks, 7 August 2011.

assumption was that everyone was lying and that at most half of what I was told was considered true by the teller. While that usually created a light-hearted moment of laughter, it did not solve my basic problem of how to deal with information that might have been intentionally misleading. Often, I had information that I could not even file under exaggerated truths, as the information environment was too murky to establish a relationship between facts and how they were perceived.[69]

In addition to my ethnographic fieldwork, I use primary material from the peace talks: speeches, public statements, position papers and press releases. These papers were written as part of the peace negotiations or in response to the ongoing negotiations. This is particularly true for press releases that reflect the LRA/M's anger at how events were unfolding. This material augments the information I gathered from direct interactions and interviews, and it constitutes the more public face the LRA/M wanted to project, usually written by a smaller committee within the LRA/M. Some of the public statements and position papers were drafted by no more than two people within the delegation. At all times, some of the delegates would work on statements, not all of which saw the light of day. Some of the public materials were drawn from previous material written by individuals within the delegation; other content was developed as the talks went along. In a few cases, I use material that was never published but was shared with me to show what the LRA/M was thinking. That not all public statements were signed off by the whole delegation points to internal tensions.

Further, the dynamics of the environment naturally shaped the kind of information the LRA/M produced. A separate book might be written using solely the public material the LRA/M published during the negotiations and how the changing dynamics and the responsiveness in the international environment influenced the LRA/M discourse and how it presented its public face. One particularly prominent stream of how changing dynamics were reflected in the public materials is the LRA/M's growing realisation that while the GoSS had been the initial facilitator of the Juba Peace Talks, the young government's own challenges in implementing its peace agreement far overshadowed its ability to handle an extremely complicated second peace process. The documents reflect this through a gradually changed attitude towards southern Sudan's Vice President Machar and, more generally speaking, the SPLA. When towards the end of the negotiations the SPLA re-emerged as a military

---

[69] See Watson (2006: 368) or Bourdieu's work on how the 'logic of practice' pushes respondents to give what they think are appropriate or expected answers (Bourdieu 1990 (1980)).

force that might be deployed against the LRA, rather than for its protection, the public documents became accusatory.

The documents further reflect international developments and the LRA/M's struggle to deal with those. Most prominently among the international parallel processes is the waxing and waning support for the ICC warrants. A separate analysis that focuses on just this point would produce a changing LRA/M stance on the validity of having to be accountable for their crimes. I have used this material in an interwoven way with ethnographic material to piece together a bigger picture of the LRA/M discourse during the peace talks and how these were experienced.

While it is true that my access was without precedent, I am aware that for the LRA/M so much was at stake that I largely saw a controlled external appearance. Erving Goffman calls the process in which an individual creates a front, or a biography or opinion that they would like to have, a 'front-stage presentation'.[70] I witnessed front-stage presentation as life narratives of delegates or fighters changed with each month in the public eye. From a strictly methodological point of view, gathering research data that I knew at various times to be manipulated might seem rather counterproductive. Yet by spending time with people, I tried to understand the process that went into the creation of the front-stage and how the front-stage was negotiated.[71] This seemed to me important information, as the adjusted truths of front-stage presentations were also a reflection of what Lloyd describes as 'practical dealings with [experienced] reality'.[72] When dealing with information about definitive events such as military encounters, I tried to triangulate, using LRA, SPLA, UPDF and UN sources to establish a middle ground. Nonetheless, in seeking to gain the insider's perspective of the LRA/M, as ethnographers would aim to do, I was at all times aware that embedded in this endeavour is the realisation that I could only ever deliver an outsider's report, as Melvin Pollner and Robert Emerson describe the irony at the heart of ethnography.[73]

Members of the LRA/M at various points shared insights with me; yet being actors in a situation where information came at a premium, they undoubtedly found it difficult to trust me, therefore controlling what they said to me. Further obvious constraints in delivering an analysis of the

---

[70] Goffman cited in Watson (2006: 371).   [71] Giddens (1984).

[72] Lloyd (1993: 99). See also Gardner, drawing on the philosopher Richard Rorty on the many elements of biographical knowledge, creating 'ambiguous, ambivalent, ironic, self-contradictory, multiple and contingent' narratives (Gardner 2001: 194).

[73] Pollner and Emerson (2001).

Juba Talks are that I did not attend the negotiations and that I avoided speaking in depth to GoU delegates. Conducting consciously one-sided research was necessary to not compromise my endeavour to document and analyse how the LRA/M experienced the Juba Talks. If I had been seen to talk at length with GoU delegates, members of the LRA/M would have surely avoided talking to me. As it was, how much access I was allowed was entirely dependent on the mood of the actors and how the talks were going. At times, I was accused by the LRA/M of being a spy – although it was not made clear to me for whom – or an investigator for the ICC, possibly with the power to arrest. My silver pendant in the shape of a chameleon was at various times scrutinised by Otti. I was later told that he was checking whether it was either a recording device or held poison. GoU supporters openly accused me – sometimes jokingly, sometimes angrily – of being an LRA member. While being accused was not a comfortable position to be in, neither was being seen as too close to the LRA, as evidenced in the reaction when I told a few of the LRA/M delegates that I was being harassed about belonging to them. One LRA/M delegate commented: 'What is bad about that? We can give you a membership card'.[74]

Being under scrutiny and in danger of losing my access at any moment meant that I had to simply record as much as I could, through multiple methods within my personal constraints. I do not speak Acholi and thus could not rely on classic participant observation. However, I became something of a participant observer by simply being present at many of the Juba Talks' important occasions. Additionally, as part of the programming to support the peace talks, I ran two community projects in southern Sudan's Eastern and Western Equatoria. I had observed that communities in close proximity to the designated LRA assembly sites had no access to reliable information on what was happening in Juba. I assembled a team of young South Sudanese men to act as liaisons between the local community, the LRA in Ri-Kwangba and organisations in Juba.

In Owiny-Kibul, the team was on the ground for six weeks in late 2006, travelling the area to hold community meetings to answer questions about the Juba Talks and collecting community concerns to report back to Juba. In Western Equatoria, the team spent about a month in Nabanga to liaise between the community and the LRA. In July 2007, they facilitated the first direct meeting between the administrator of the *payam* (district) and the LRA commander in charge of the Ri-Kwangba

---

[74] Fieldnotes, Juba: 10 October 2006.

camp. The *payam* administrator relayed two pressing concerns, asking the LRA to allow residents in the area to tend to their coffee plantations, which were close to the LRA assembly site. Further, he appealed to the LRA to stop harvesting honey and then destroying beehives, as honey was an important cash crop. The LRA and the *payam* administrator eventually agreed to share the honey harvest and regulate access to the coffee plantations. I was present for parts of both missions.[75]

I gathered data in the various situations in which I found myself – through observation, casual conversations, official interviews, daily reflections noted down in my research journals and feedback on my thoughts from LRA/M, GoSS or international actors. Quite often, my research consisted of spending days in the bush, exchanging a few words with LRA soldiers on duty who often did not speak much English, hoping to get some time with one of the more senior commanders. On those days, or when I waited for hours outside the negotiation room to catch a moment of conversation with members of the LRA/M, I wrote notes to capture quotes and observations, grouping observations under themes as the weeks passed by. The information is presented here as a mixture of an analytical narrative of the Juba Talks, comments by LRA/M members, and an analysis of emerging dynamics. Detail about the atmosphere and setting of the talks is vital because, as John Beattie points out, 'even the most matter-of-fact descriptions are shot through with abstractions, usually unanalysed "common sense" ones .... So description does more than merely describe; it is also in some degree explanatory'.[76]

I also draw on a range of other material that is no less problematic. I discuss in the following chapter the history of information on the LRA war and why many published sources are so unreliable. Yet, I use some of these sources to make claims. Such sources include reports from international agencies, internal government reports (thanks to whistle-blowing website WikiLeaks that published them) and media. The challenge of dealing with unreliable testimony applies just as much to these reports – in the case of media, particularly so when it comes to citing the Ugandan government-owned newspaper, *The New Vision*. I tackle this challenge by only including source material that I know for a fact not to

---

[75] Sponsored by Pact Sudan under a UN grant, the project was supposed to support the Juba Talks. Otti and Machar signed off on the presence of the community teams. The Owiny-Kibul team had to leave the area when it became unsafe. Shortly after the team facilitated the beehive and coffee agreement, Otti was killed. Neither agreement was implemented. With the deteriorating communication situation with the LRA, UN funding for community work ceased.

[76] Beattie (1959: 48).

be false because I have been able to triangulate it. However, naturally, this issue also highlights the broader methodological challenge in dealing with murky information environments. I can only assess sources if I already have some prior knowledge about their content. It is inevitable that this means that I sometimes dismiss a correct source based on previous incorrect knowledge I have, and vice versa. Concerning US internal government documents published by WikiLeaks, this control mechanism is less useful as many of the processes described happened behind closed doors. However, these documents are used to illustrate the parallel discourse that occurred within the upper echelons of the US government and how information was used and dispensed.

Throughout, I often found it difficult to keep my finger on the pulse of realities and memories that were permanently being shifted and reconstructed using multiple layers and power reassignments. In accepting this, I attempt, as Joan Acker and others write, to give 'full legitimacy to the subjectivity of the other as well as to our own'.[77] As I did my own analysis and observed others making theirs, it became obvious to me that the unreliability of the narrator was a problem with regard to both my research subjects and myself. Both sides were editing thoughts and outputs according to their own frames of reference. While some of my interviewees might have been deliberately manipulative – which made them no less valuable to me – it is important to be aware of my own shortcomings in interpretation and analysis in an extremely confusing environment. In trying to untangle rather messy information situations and present my findings in a coherent way, I am hoping to also contribute by showing the challenges and limitations of researching the complexity of these kinds of peace processes.

I have anonymised quotes from observers or advisors to the peace talks, as well as those from various LRA members and LRA/M delegates, unless these were given in public or explicitly on the record. I have retained names only where public records exist that identify a particular situation. International staff often spoke on the condition of anonymity. I refer to all LRA delegates in the masculine, since there were only two women on the delegation, and avoid specific descriptions of people. Eighteen delegates or LRA members are directly quoted throughout the book and losing background information on the speakers in exchange for anonymity is a flaw. Yet hiding people's identities is necessary. Some delegates wanted to remain anonymous. Others have returned to Uganda and no longer talk about their engagement in the Juba Talks. Some of the

---

[77] Acker, Barry and Essveld (1991: 42).

quoted LRA members cannot be reached to check whether I have represented their views correctly; some are dead. Crucially, former delegates have run into problems after the talks. In Uganda, two members of the delegation had land taken away from them; one's family has been harassed. Outside Uganda, one delegate lost his job; another was detained, accused of terrorism and threatened with extradition when he travelled to the country where his family is resident. In all cases, delegates' engagement in the Juba Talks was cited as a reason for the trouble. The events described here truly had a long-term impact.

2   The Lord's Resistance Army
A Continuum of War, Peace and Information

In June 2006, I was seated in the back of a car with the future LRA/M delegation. When we left the small town of Ibba on South Sudan's border with the DRC, ready to tackle the final two hours' drive to Nabanga to meet Kony for the first time, it started pouring. The Land Cruiser was so packed with people and equipment that I struggled to find a space for my feet between piles of bags and damp arms and legs. During the drive, two designated LRA/M delegates were talking animatedly about how the actions of the international community were responsible for continued conflict in this part of Africa. 'The UN is just a bunch of robbers. They are exploiting the wealth of Congo', one of the delegates said. The other argued that the UN showed a pro-Museveni bias by not being present in northern Uganda. I threw in that UN agencies such as the World Food Programme, UNICEF and the World Health Organization were working there, although whether supporting life in the displacement camps was a good idea was contentious.[1] The main point was, one of the delegates responded, that there were no UN soldiers to prevent UPDF attacks on the LRA: 'The soldiers are never there when you need them for protection'. UN troops, they argued, would make the situation much better for the LRA and thus stop the spiral of violence. I found this interesting. I asked if they thought that UN peacekeepers would protect the LRA – or would UN soldiers instead bring peace to Uganda, including safety for civilians from LRA attacks? At this point, another delegate interrupted the debate. He spoke to all of us when he said: 'To solve the problem, you have to understand it first'.[2]

Trying to do that in an unreleased draft paper, the LRA/M delegation in Juba had set out what they were aiming to do:

It is vital to boldly deal with the root causes of the conflict. We need to boldly deal with the past. How did Uganda come into being? How have the various groups now constituting the British thing now called Uganda been relating with one

---

[1] Branch (2011: 94).   [2] Fieldnotes Nabanga/Ri-Kwangba, 11 June 2006.

another? What are the constitutional issues that bedevilled our country? How did the war start? Why has it persisted? A simplistic approach will not work.[3]

The following day, I asked Kony what the conflict between the LRA and the GoU was about. He offered a simple explanation. 'Let me say it, Museveni he did not want Acholi to be in their land there', Kony answered. 'He want Acholi to be out, to complete, to die all. To be completed [dead], by all means. This is what Museveni is doing'.[4] It was a simple and sweeping explanation of what, in Kony's opinion, had been happening in Uganda in the previous two decades – a complicated mix of war, peace, information and personal experiences of hope, disappointment and horror. Both the simple and complicated explanations meant that many of those involved in the Juba Talks brought baggage to the process.

2.1   War

In their internal discussions during the Juba Talks, LRA/M delegates often invoked former Ugandan president Milton Obote's description of Museveni's ascent to power: 'The people of Uganda started their struggle in 1986 against a rapacious, oppressive and massacring regime led by a demented man',[5] was a typical statement. In the tumultuous year of 1986, Museveni's forces, the National Resistance Army (NRA), over-threw the government of Tito Okello, a northerner. On 17 December 1985, Museveni's NRA and Okello's military regime had signed the Nairobi Peace Agreement on power-sharing, a peaceful settlement of the civil war, and on keeping Ugandan political leadership in the hands of Okello.[6] Nonetheless, Museveni's forces marched on Kampala and over-threw Okello. People of Acholi origin, who had been working with Okello's government, were dismissed from positions of power. Violence continued after the coup, with the new government under Museveni focusing its counter-insurgency tactics on the northern part of the country, where they suspected strong support for Okello. Many of Okello's supporters, however, had fled the country. The elite group amongst them would later form the prominent and influential diaspora opposition to Museveni.

---

[3] LRA/M delegation in Juba, unpublished notes seen by author, 11 September 2006.
[4] Author interview with Joseph Kony, Sudan/DRC border: 12 June 2006. I have minimally edited Kony's quotes because his points can be unclear in written English. This way, I offer my understanding of what he said. For a full transcript of the interview see Schomerus (2010b).
[5] Obote (1990).   [6] Barnes and Okello (2002).

However, the long history of violence in Uganda before 1986 also informed the LRA conflict in many ways: riots and attacks had happened as Obote consolidated his power during his first reign and during Idi Amin's bloody regime.[7] Museveni himself had been a rebel against both Obote and Amin, and other regimes in power, since 1971. For the LRA/M, the conflict in Uganda is largely a story of betrayal, starting with what they called in a position paper Museveni's 'abrogation' of the Nairobi Peace Agreement.[8] They argue in another official statement that Museveni took power with 'a dirty record of insincerity', proving his 'treachery in negotiating and then trashing the Nairobi Peace Agreement'.[9] The impact of this treachery is all the greater for those in the LRA and elsewhere who contrast Okello's attempts at national reconciliation (despite their shortcomings) with Museveni's subsequent divisive record.[10] Museveni, wrote the LRA/M, instead abandoned national unity when he

embarked on a deliberate policy to divide the country, firstly between the Bantu and the Nilotics and Nilo-Hamites.[11] Although the Hima ethnic group from which Museveni himself comes is not of the Bantu stock, but Hematic [sic], like the Tutsis of Rwanda, he has nevertheless conveniently used this as a gimmick to win political cohesiveness and capital to galvanize his political hold on power, not only in Uganda, but also to promote his regional ambition within the Great Lakes Region and Africa as a whole.[12]

The LRA/M outlined how the election results of 2006 showed that Museveni's party, the National Resistance Movement (NRM), was

a regional, but not a national party .... Whereas the Bantu people of the southern and western Uganda overwhelmingly voted for Museveni's NRM party, the people of the northern and eastern part of the country overwhelmingly voted against the NRM party.[13]

---

[7] Berg-Schlosser and Siegler (1990).   [8] LRA/M delegation in Juba (2006).
[9] Olweny (2006a).   [10] Lomo and Hovil (2004: 10).
[11] The LRA/M's use of these contested terms suggests an essentialised view that they themselves often contest when it comes to the Acholi.
[12] LRA/M delegation in Juba (2006). This passage gives an insight into how the LRA/M instrumentalises ethnicity and history. The hamitic (here spelt hematic) creation myth of the sub-Saharan African people was extensively used by colonialists to argue the superiority of some groups of people over others. Seligman's work of the 1930s has been seminal in establishing these categories, and is today largely dismissed. Although nowadays the Hima are considered Bantu and are generally referred to as the Tutsi sub-group living in Uganda, their origins are usually located elsewhere. It is often argued that originally the Hima are Nilotic and from Sudan and were only absorbed into the Bantu languages after arriving in what is today Uganda. The fine and deeply historical distinctions presented here by the LRA/M show that they are utilising ethnic differences in a similar way to those they criticise.
[13] LRA/M delegation in Juba (2006).

The LRA/M's version of history as presented here points to the deep divisions within Uganda, including the instrumentalisation of ethnicity – a prominent feature in previous peace processes with the LRA.[14]

After Museveni took power, armed resistance grew in Acholiland, Lango and Teso. Armed rebellions in the latter two areas were largely over by the early 1990s; resistance in the north was to remain active for the next decades.[15] The Uganda People's Democratic Army (UPDA) had been formed in August 1986 and was, argues Atkinson, largely supported by a 'violated and disgruntled Acholi population'.[16] When the UPDA signed an accord with the NRA in June 1988, Alice Lakwena's Holy Spirit Mobile Forces became the most prominent and supported armed group in northern Uganda. The NRA defeated Lakwena's troops in 1987.[17] In 1988, Kony was mandated by a group of Acholi elders from his lineage to resist Museveni with force, naming his group of fighters the United Holy Salvation Army. Kony's group then in 1992 called itself the United Democratic Christian Army, before finally adopting the name the Lord's Resistance Army. The NRA seemed generally unconcerned with another emerging Acholi force, having just defeated Lakwena's forces. Yet, Kony proved a lot more resilient than expected, possibly because Kony was mandated by some Acholi elders to fight.[18] Africa's most enduring armed rebel group was then born.

Initially, the LRA's military successes against the oppressive government forces garnered support among the northern Ugandan civilian population. This was particularly so after the government's 1991 military offensive, Operation North, which was meant to end the LRA insurgency and improve security for civilians instead brought arbitrary arrests and harassment of civilians. Following Operation North and faced with the successful consolidations of the government's power over territory and people, the rebels increasingly turned against civilians, instilling fear through attacks and abductions, and recruiting most of its fighting force

---

[14] Dolan (2005: 111).

[15] The literature dealing with the history of this conflict is vast and varied. What is striking is the shift in perspective as understanding grows about the war's complexities, with Finnstroem's work marking a seminal moment in how the conflict was understood (Finnstroem 2008b). Other articles are rooted in the time they were written and linked to events that were foremost in people's minds and discussions at the time of writing. Examples are van Acker (2004) and Doom and Vlassenroot (1999). In addition to many of the academic sources quoted, Green's account of the early days of Kony's fight, including how he was supported by the Acholi elders, is comprehensive (Green 2008).

[16] Atkinson (2010b: 286)   [17] Behrend (1999a, 1999b); Allen (1991).

[18] Green (2008); O'Kadameri (2002).

by coercion.[19] However, atrocities by Kony's troops against Acholi civilians – including cutting by *pangas* – were not solely a reaction to the military offensive, but had been reported as early as 1987.[20] The LRA's reputation as a fearless rebel group, strengthened by their adherence to spiritual rules, was soon established along with the fault lines of this war. The LRA justified its violence as a protest against the oppressive GoU, although public statements by the LRA with a clear political agenda were rarely heard, except during attempts at peace, namely in 1993–94, further discussed below.[21]

While Uganda's south and west gradually became more peaceful and prosperous, other parts, particularly the north, north-east and north-west, fell behind. For a period of intense fighting in the late 1990s and early 2000s, the war garnered hardly any international attention, yet in northern Uganda, millions of people were affected by the violence committed by the rebels, the army and the government policy of forcing people into displacement camps – so-called protected villages.[22] The contested policy, officially implemented from 1996 onwards, was a government response to the war situation.[23] However, several LRA officers, including Otti stressed that the Acholi were systematically herded into camps as soon as Museveni took power. Some said that the first time Acholis were forced out of their homes was in the autumn of 1986. Others, among them Otti, argue that the policy started in 1987. One younger LRA officer, who said he was born in 1980, described how he

---

[19] The LRA also attacked civilians in DRC and the Central African Republic. In Uganda, the interaction and relationships between civilians and the LRA was complicated, see Allen and Schomerus (2006). For a more detailed history of the LRA in Sudan, see Schomerus (2007).

[20] Lamwaka (2011: 146).

[21] See Finnstroem (2008b). Kony's four-hour speech at the 1994 peace talks is generally considered to be his first major effort to give his perspective.

[22] Detailed accounts and analysis of the displacement come from Lamwaka (2011); Branch (2008b); Rodriguez (2004); Omach (2002). Displacement was at its height between 2002 and 2005, increasing as a reaction to the military offensive Operation Iron Fist (OIF). However, the causes of displacement are contested. See for example Kabonero (2006).

[23] Dolan and Hovil divide the war into six distinct phases: 1986–88, 1988–94, 1994–99, 2000–2, 2002–3 and 2003–6 (Dolan and Hovil 2006). A UNOCHA report states that in Gulu district, most 'protected villages' were established between August and October 1996 after 'a decision by the military authorities'; in Kitgum and Pader the 'villages' were established between 1995–97 (Weeks 2002). Some sources mistakenly connect the policy with OIF as late as 2002 (Mukwana and Ridderbos 2009). Others downplay the intensity of population movement in the early days of the Museveni regime (Omach 2002).

remembered people being taken into camps when he was a young child.[24] Caroline Lamwaka, the late Ugandan journalist working in Gulu at the time, seemed to confirm the LRA version at least partially. She estimated that between December 1986 and June 1988, of the 400,000 residents of Gulu district, 28,000 were displaced in Gulu town and more than 25,000 were 'residing near the various NRA detaches in the rural areas, showing signs of malnutrition and living under appalling hygiene conditions'. She described the early displacement camps:

The 'Caribbean camp' was a grotesque structure with open doors and windows without frames and fittings. A few hundred people were residing there, brought in by the army from Atiak, 42 miles northwest of Gulu, in January 1987 after a fierce battle there …. The displaced people relied mainly on meagre food from the Ministry of Rehabilitation and from relatives and friends in town. It was a humanitarian crisis of the first order.[25]

Describing what the policy of protected villages had done, the LRA wrote in 2009 that

due to the brutality of the armed conflict, the region has literally been made into a wasteland …. Tens if not hundreds of thousands of people in the region have died, and over 2 million people were displaced and encamped under genocidal conditions – mainly as a result of the government army's counter-insurgency measures.[26]

From the LRA/M's point of view, Museveni – who was steadily becoming a darling of international donors – was singularly to blame. A 1996 LRA position paper stated:

The Acholiland is threatened and it can be safe only if Museveni is toppled. The whole of Uganda will be safe only if Museveni is removed. Museveni is one man in this world that Ugandans must not trust.[27]

Kony's interpretation that the cause of the war and the reason for its continuation was primarily an anti-Acholi policy is shared by those who argue that the GoU has systematically attempted to destroy the population of northern Uganda, particularly by forcing the entire population into displacement camps.[28] To substantiate the argument that the LRA war had continued as a fight against Museveni's anti-Acholi stance, the

---

[24] Fieldnotes, Juba: 5 July 2006.   [25] Lamwaka (2011).

[26] LRA/M Peace Team (2009). The literature on the IDP situation in Uganda is vast, for example Kamara, Cyril and Renzaho (2017); Oosterom (2016); Moffett (2015); Baines and Rosenoff Gauvin (2014); Roberts et al. (2011); Stark et al. (2009); Branch (2008a); Dolan and Hovil (2006); Allen (2006); World Health Organization/Ministry of Health (2005); Hassen and Keating (2004); Mawson (1999).

[27] LRA. 1996. 'LRA policy definitions and explanations'. Unpublished LRA document.

[28] Doom and Vlassenroot (1999: 17); Jackson (2009: 324).

LRA/M referred to an alleged personal letter from Olara Otunnu to Kizza Besigye, written in early 2006. Otunnu at the time had resigned as UN Undersecretary-General and Special Representative for Children and Armed Conflict and was preparing for his political comeback in Uganda to run against Museveni in the elections of 2011. Besigye had returned from exile to run as Museveni's most threatening opponent in the 2006 elections and had faced treason and rape charges brought against him. In the letter, Otunnu criticises Museveni's remark – and by implication, the government's use of racism – that part of the reason for the continued violence was that it was 'Acholi soldiers causing the problems. It is the cultural background of the people here; they are very violent. It is genetic' and that 'the chauvinism of the Acholi has to be destroyed'.[29] Otunnu went on to write that because of such attitudes within the government and the political consequence, the Acholi had suffered the 'death of culture and values system' – in addition to twenty years in which

> two generations of children have been denied education as a matter of policy. They have been deliberately condemned to a life of darkness and ignorance, deprived of all hope and opportunity .... These children are being targeted for systematic deprivation in this way within the twisted and racist logic of genocide – to ensure that 'those people' will never rise again! ... In a society renowned for its deep-rooted and rich culture, values system and family structure – all these have been destroyed under the living conditions imposed and prevailing over the last 10 years in the camps. This loss is colossal and virtually irreparable; it signals the death of people and their civilization.[30]

Few academics would go as far as Otunnu, who, having finished his tenure at the UN, in an acceptance speech for the Sydney Peace Prize also launched a scathing public criticism of the international response to the crisis in northern Uganda:

> I must draw your attention to the worst place on earth, by far, to be a child today. That place is the northern part of Uganda. What is going on in northern Uganda is not a routine humanitarian crisis, for which an appropriate response might be the mobilization of humanitarian relief. The human rights catastrophe unfolding in northern Uganda is a methodical and comprehensive genocide. An entire society is being systematically destroyed – physically, culturally, socially, and economically – in full view of the international community.[31]

---

[29] Olara Otunnu (2006). 'Private letter to Dr Kizza Besigye (Forum for Democratic Change)'.

[30] Olara Otunnu (2006). 'Private letter to Dr Kizza Besigye (Forum for Democratic Change)'.

[31] Otunnu (2005). The language of genocide had been used before Otunnu's speech; however, his status brought new levels of attention. When Otunnu went public with

Repeating his argument in an article in *Foreign Policy* magazine, he challenged the common line that the situation in northern Uganda stemmed from a one-sided killing campaign by insane rebels.[32] While Otunnu offered the most radical interpretation regarding the intent behind northern Uganda's neglect, most scholars of the conflict in northern Uganda agree that northern Uganda's marginalisation was deliberate government policy, and that the government's commitment to finding a negotiated solution to the conflict has been questionable.[33] Otunnu's suggestion that the international community was complicit in what was happening in northern Uganda was not new – amongst scholars, Branch, Dolan and Finnström have provided empirical material to argue international complicity.[34] As early as 1990, former president Obote had concluded that a better future for Uganda was possible despite the international complicity: 'I am convinced that however long it may take and whatever protection the world affords to the oppressors, freedom shall be won and that the Pearl of Africa shall rise and shine again'.[35]

The atrocious conditions in the camps finally attracted the wider attention of the international community. In 2003, the then-UN Under-Secretary-General for Humanitarian Affairs, Egeland, made a highly publicised visit to the region, focusing in his subsequent press appearances on the plight of displaced civilians. Egeland described the situation at the time in an interview in 2007:

> It was very much a forgotten conflict, neglected conflict. I was myself shocked to my bones coming in the autumn of 2003 and I could not believe how bad it was in northern Uganda. And also checking, even in the couple of days, the international community why so little had been done really to alleviate the suffering – but also to try to bring the conflict to an end.
> Everybody had failed.
> I then went very dramatically public on BBC and later other big ... the whole BBC system and later CNN and said we have all failed, the international community, the Uganda government in northern Uganda. So why had it not

---

his criticism in 2006, the impact of his speech was not dampened by concerns about his own political interests in Uganda and his well-publicised antagonism towards President Museveni.

[32] Otunnu (2006: 45–46).

[33] Whitman presents a note from Museveni that seems to outline a plan for an Acholi genocide; the authenticity of the letter is contested as the author acknowledges (Whitmore 2010). Dolan outlines the governance system at the heart of the conflict as akin to 'social torture' (Dolan 2009). Egeland states in his book that he felt Museveni did not want a negotiated solution (Egeland 2008). Quinn points out that in the 2004–5 budget, the GoU only allocated 0.01 per cent of the national budget to conflict resolution attempts in northern Uganda (Quinn 2009: 61).

[34] Branch (2011); Dolan (2009); Finnstroem (2008b).   [35] Obote (1990).

been brought on the international agenda or on the Security Council agenda? I think because everybody wanted Uganda to remain a success story.[36]

Egeland's visit refocused attention on alleviating civilian suffering in the camps, but also on getting a peace agreement with the LRA. The renewed emphasis on peace led to another failed attempt at a negotiated agreement by the end of 2004, discussed below. With new international attention on Uganda, 2005 brought a dramatic turning point. The newly established ICC concluded a controversial two-year investigation, which in July that year led to the issuing and later the unsealing of arrest warrants for five LRA commanders, including Kony and Otti. It was just after the unsealing of the warrants that Otti sought to speak to me on the phone to ask questions about the exact procedures behind this ominous organisation 'ICC' that was coming after him – and to reiterate the LRA's commitment to peace.

2.2   Peace

Internationally, the ICC's intervention was the most high-profile attempt to address the conflict in northern Uganda before the Juba Talks. Yet the history of efforts to end the conflict is as long as the history of the violent conflict itself. When the Juba Talks opened on 14 July 2006, I saw many different expressions in the audience. Some faces showed excitement and enthusiasm; others looked sceptical with an air of weariness. This was because many of the people in the room were part of the history of peace attempts. There had been several efforts at negotiated peace between the LRA and the GoU, in addition to peace negotiations with other armed groups who had emerged from Uganda's post-1986 turmoil – most prominently the 1988 talks with the UPDA.[37]

The LRA/M delegates in Juba often described previous peace attempts as 'two-faced'. Museveni, they argued, had in the past shown the same duplicitous attitude towards peace deals that he had first displayed in 1985. They said that for as long as he had been in government, Museveni had continued 'to renege on so many agreements with so many other fighting forces, including with the LRA'; peace efforts in the past had been seen as a trap 'to either kill the LRA leaders or lure them out of the bush'.[38] Establishing trust in another peace endeavour after so many failed attempts was to prove a major challenge in Juba.[39]

---

[36] Author telephone interview with Jan Egeland, 15 November 2007.
[37] See Lamwaka (2002).   [38] Olweny (2006a).
[39] Different perspectives on peacemaking in northern Uganda can be found in Drew (2010); Lucima (2002).

The first government initiative to end LRA insurgency came in 1988. Museveni appointed Betty Bigombe to the new post of Minister of State for Pacification of Northern Uganda, Resident in Gulu – later renamed (to remove the offensive reference to 'pacification') – Minister of State in the Office of the Prime Minister, Resident in Northern Uganda. Having tried unsuccessfully for a few years to end the rebellion by encouraging family members to send messages to their fighting sons in the bush and arming villagers with arrows to defend themselves, Bigombe initiated peace talks by asking one of Kony's main civilian confidants, Yusuf Adek, to connect her with Kony. Adek had subsequently signed the Gulu Ceasefire in 1994 as a witness for the LRA. At the opening of the Juba Talks, Adek was seated as an LRA/M representative on the right side of the stage.

Thanks to Adek's initiative, the first-ever face-to-face meeting between LRA and GoU representatives occurred on 25 November 1993, in Pagik, near Gulu.[40] While the so-called Gulu Ceasefire gave Betty Bigombe the space to conduct these talks,[41] failure to reach agreement over security issues at the second meeting on 10 January 1994, almost ended the effort.[42] Crucially, the LRA were adamant that they were not defeated and were to be treated with respect by the government. They also stressed that the talks should be genuine negotiations, rather than an opportunity to set the conditions for surrender.[43] The GoU's dismissal of the LRA and the LRA's endeavour to seek recognition for their struggle created irresolvable tension.[44]

After the second meeting in January, Museveni travelled to Gulu on 6 February 1994, for a public visit. Speaking to the crowd, he announced a deadline of seven days for the LRA to surrender before talks would be abandoned in favour of a military strike.[45] Looking back, one LRA/M delegate in Juba described the situation: 'Museveni's deadline 1994 was a directive, not a deadline. It was a directive'.[46] When the deadline was not met and the LRA retreated into Sudan, the talks had failed. The war had entered a new phase. Although the LRA had been present in Sudan since the early 1990s, it was after the failed talks of 1994 that it grew into one of the most destructive forces in southern Sudan and the most effective proxy army for the Government of Sudan.[47] While the GoU generally

---

[40] O'Kadameri was a rapporteur (O'Kadameri 2002).   [41] O'Kadameri (2002).

[42] Apart from Dolan, O'Kadameri and Branch, the 1994 peace talks tend to be dealt with in the literature in a cursory and summative manner – for example Quaranto (2006); Westbrook (2000).Vinci offers an analysis of LRA motivations, but little insight into the talks (Vinci 2007).

[43] Dolan (2005: 113).   [44] Dolan (2005: 109).   [45] Rodriguez (2004).

[46] Fieldnotes, Juba: 6 July 2006.   [47] Schomerus (2007); Prunier (2004).

maintains that talks ended because of Sudan's involvement, Branch, amongst others, argues that Sudan's involvement was a consequence of the failed talks, rather than the cause.[48]

In retrospect, it became clear that the talks failed because the parties had irreconcilable objectives: the LRA wanted a political process and recognition of a political struggle, the GoU wanted the elimination of the LRA. Agreeing on security arrangements proved impossible. Government commitment to the talks was shaky: Bigombe herself has stated that there were attempts from within the government to sabotage the talks.[49] Branch also asserts that

the sabotaging of the peace talks made it clear that certain sectors within the NRA wanted the LRA to continue to exist, and would do whatever necessary to ensure that they remained in the bush. Thus, one aspect of their strategy would be to refuse, or sabotage, negotiations. The other aspect would be to repress political organization among the Acholi to ensure that they could not effectively demand an end to the war.[50]

Describing what they were experiencing in Juba, delegates regularly drew parallels between the time of the Gulu Ceasefire and the Juba Talks: their own quest for a political process and recognition, the equivocal government commitment, and the struggle to agree on security issues had in their mind remained the same. The LRA might have felt betrayed in the 1994 talks, but analysts had doubts over the LRA's sincerity and rationality then, too. Pain recounts that Kony was making decisions 'on a "spirit" basis, not rational. Therefore what is agreed today may be reversed tomorrow'.[51] The 1994 talks had shown that there were flexibility and unpredictability in Kony's decision-making process; the mainstream conclusion drawn from this was that there was a spiritual element in dealing with the LRA, which was soon mystified into a major part of how the LRA was viewed. A document by the United States Agency for International Development (USAID) later gave a less transcendental assessment of the 1994 talks and concluded that 'Kony is willing to reach out to talk when he is pressured and when he trusts the person/people he is dealing with'.[52] Yet in 1996 when the LRA killed a group of elders from Acholiland under the pretence of continuing the talks, doubts over the LRA's sincerity about wanting to end the war were reinforced.

Many who had played a role in trying to bring peace over the years gathered again at the Juba opening ceremony, bringing along their personal and institutional baggage. The memories they had of previous

[48] Branch (2005).   [49] O'Kadameri (2002: 40).   [50] Branch (2005).
[51] Pain (1997). Pain's analysis of the spirit-driven peace talks became very influential.
[52] USAID (2006).

talks, and their histories of interaction would become crucial particularly in the first year of the Juba Talks. In addition to Adek, other LRA delegates had been representatives during various peace efforts. After the failed 1994 talks, the Dutch organisations IKV Pax Christi and the Rome-based Sant'Egidio had made peace attempts. Their representatives were also seated in the audience during the opening ceremony, as was the Sudanese Acholi, Dr Leonzio Onek, who had become an important figure in the aftermath of the Gulu Ceasefire.

After the 1994 talks had failed, Onek had contacted the GoU to offer help as a negotiator between the LRA and the GoU.[53] His initiative was sanctioned at the time by Ruhakana Rugunda, then Minister for Foreign Affairs.[54] In Juba, Rugunda would lead the GoU delegation as Minister for Interior Affairs. Once the GoU had supported Onek in his quest to make contact with the LRA again, Onek sent the lawyer Alfonse Owiny-Dollo to Khartoum, where reportedly Kony could regularly be found as a guest of his supporters in the Government of Sudan. Dollo had been involved in drafting the 1988 peace agreement with the UPDA and was about to become Minister of State for Northern Uganda – he would be appointed as Deputy Chief Justice of Uganda in September 2017. To cover up the real purpose of his trip to Khartoum, Dollo even dressed as a woman, Onek said.[55] He would later give legal advice to the LRA on a visit to the bush in December 2006. In 1997, Onek succeeded in bringing representatives of the two sides face-to-face in Lancaster, UK, although not much came of that meeting. Still, some donors recognised the value of the efforts and strengthened the initiative by attaching Onek to people who were professionally involved in the field. Professor Hizkias Assefa was named to assist him in his mediating role.[56] Dr Simon Simonse of IKV Pax Christi, who in early 1998 had, as he described it, 'stumbled on the secret initiative of the Equatoria Civic Fund of Dr Leonzio Onek in which Professor Hizkias Assefa was involved', offered additional support.[57] IKV Pax Christi felt that they came close to success in 1998, having secured Dutch government support through Dutch Interchurch

---

[53] Onek was at one point accused of being the secret leader of the LRA delegation. He explained his connection, which went back to 1995, in a newspaper article: 'I had written to the government of Uganda that I wanted to offer myself, as a Southern Sudanese Acholi, to assist with negotiations between the government and LRA' (Kenyi 22 June 2006).

[54] Author interview with Sudanese advisor to peace talks. Juba: 8 December 2006.

[55] Author interview, December 2006.   [56] Kenyi (22 June 2006).

[57] Email to author from S. Simonse, IKV Pax Christi, 10 October 2007. Assefa, a prominent conflict resolution expert, was the Pax Christi-designated mediator for the Juba Talks. See for example Assefa (1992). Pax Christi's description of their involvement in Juba can be found in Simonse, Verkoren and Junne (2010: 226).

Aid 'to bring the LRA leadership to Holland to meet with GoU … the Obita/Sant'Egidio connection frustrated this attempt'.[58] Another speaker close to Pax Christi commented that this effort had been significant until 'Sant'Egidio came and hijacked the process'.[59]

What seemed like 'hijacking' to some was a team effort by Sant'Egidio and prominent member of the Acholi diaspora Dr James Obita. The Community of Sant'Egidio is a Catholic lay organisation, headquartered in Rome, which runs humanitarian and peacebuilding programmes.[60] In May 1997, representatives of the Acholi diaspora met in London for the first *Kacoke Madit*. *Kacoke Madit* ('big meeting') was a unique attempt initiated by diaspora Acholi to bring people together in search of a new avenue for solving the conflict in northern Uganda through dialogue that was not possible in Uganda. *Kacoke Madit*, although influential and adopting an ambitious approach, descended into infighting and was largely discredited by the Ugandan government, even though it is widely seen as a milestone attempt within the diaspora.[61] Attending *Kacoke Madit* for the LRA/M was Obita. Following the meeting in London, Obita sent an open letter to Museveni in late 1997, confirming the LRA/M's commitment to peace.[62] The president reacted first in an open letter condemning what he called the LRA's evasiveness and arrogance regarding peace negotiations. He then expressed the government's willingness to end the war and give an amnesty to anyone but three top commanders.[63] Sant'Egidio offered Obita an alternative LRA/GoU meeting place in Rome, but the meeting never happened and the initiative dwindled. Instead, the LRA accused Obita of being insincere and he was dismissed by the LRA leader – narrowly escaping an assassination.[64] Obita reappeared in Juba in 2007 as a member and later spokesperson of the LRA/M.

The crucial lesson from these various efforts was that rivalrous interlocutors had promising interactions with the LRA, but that the LRA withdrew after losing trust in the mediators. The two organisations had now come back to Juba where the old rivalry instantly continued. That a sympathiser of one organisation called the other's effort a 'hijacking' shines a light on the difficulty of managing diverse peacemaking interests.

---

[58] Email to author from S. Simonse, IKV Pax Christi, 10 October 2007.

[59] Fieldnotes, Juba: 6 June 2006. The speaker expressed the feeling that a similar process was now happening in Juba, as the peace talks were being held rather publicly. See also Simonse, Verkoren and Junne (2010).

[60] See for example an explanatory article about Sant'Egidio's work by one of their representatives who participated in the Juba Talks (Giro 1998).

[61] Oguru Otto (2002).   [62] Obita (1997).   [63] Museveni (1997a).

[64] Obita (2002).

Crucially, it shows how the general baggage of the peacemakers – including those of the LRA/M or the GoU who had been involved in previous efforts – remained unacknowledged. Thus, a contradictory process was set up from the start, where the pronounced intention was to clear the air by addressing root causes and political marginalisation (and admit that such marginalisation existed in the first place), yet without any explicit acknowledgement by any of the actors involved what lessons needed to be learned from past experiences.

An armistice in northern Uganda from January to December 1999 created space for the next steps.[65] The armistice was followed by the Carter Center's mediation between the LRA, the GoU, and the Sudan government. However, the final settlement of this mediation – the 1999 Nairobi Agreement – was struck between the two governments only.[66] Signed by Presidents Museveni and Omar al-Bashir of Sudan, and witnessed by former US president Jimmy Carter and Kenya's President Daniel arap Moi, the Nairobi Agreement excluded northern Ugandan community leaders and terminated talks with the LRA. Describing the Carter Center's involvement, one LRA commander said, 'Jimmy Carter's people did not speak to the right people. They did not have the right contacts. It was frustrating'.[67] The Nairobi Agreement did not include the LRA, but instead spelt out the end of each governments' support for the other's insurgencies, and paved the way for military intervention by the UPDF in pursuit of the LRA in Sudan.[68] From then on, the UPDF was officially allowed to set up bases in Sudanese territory. Crucially, however, the Agreement also put in motion an amnesty law in Uganda as an incentive for rebels to put down their weapons.

In March 1999, Uganda signed the Rome Statute of the ICC. In a parallel development that would come to characterise the tension between international and national justice procedures in Uganda, parliament then in 2000 passed Uganda's Amnesty Act. The Act allowed rebels to return to their homes without fear of criminal charges, opening the possibility to end the war without prosecutions. In the opinion of some observers in Juba, the Amnesty Act created the space for Justice Peter Onega as the head of the Amnesty Commission and IKV Pax

---

[65] Jongomoi Okidi-Olal, a Ugandan who became an investment banker and soldier in the US Army Reserve who appeared in Juba in late 2006 and seemed to be working closely with Riek Machar, in a letter to Machar takes credit for brokering the ceasefire – along with several other people. See Okidi-Olal (2006). Various sources also state that Okidi-Olal was instrumental in moving the LRA into DRC.

[66] The Governments of Sudan and Uganda (1999).

[67] Fieldnotes, Nairobi/Juba: 2 June 2006.   [68] See Schomerus (2012).

Christi to pursue the steps that would lead to the Juba Talks.[69] However, Uganda's ratification of the Rome Statute in June 2002 further complicated the interaction between the two parallel justice developments. That the US government had included the LRA on its Terrorist Exclusion List in 2001 had further muddled responsibilities.

In 2003, Museveni's half-brother, Salim Saleh, was tasked with setting up talks with the LRA, but the initiative ceased without success after the LRA refused to assemble in government-appointed ceasefire safe zones and instead asked for a ceasefire in all of northern Uganda. In response, the GoU withdrew its safe zones offer in April 2003. Saleh reappeared as a player in the Juba Talks in the spring of 2007 in the infamous Mombasa meeting, more on which later.

The 2004 talks, again initiated by Bigombe, used amnesty as the major incentive. Kony appointed his Brigadier Sam Kolo to negotiate with Bigombe. The GoU declared a ceasefire in November 2004, which was extended after its initial run of seven days. The ceasefire only applied to demarcated assembly zones.[70] These zones of about 300 square kilometres included Patiko, Atanga, Palabek and Atiak. When Acholi leaders assured the LRA that their fighters would be safe there after a peace deal had been agreed, negotiations seemed close to conclusion. However, Museveni soon reduced the ceasefire area from 300 to about 100 square kilometres and issued a new deadline for the conclusion of the negotiations. The LRA stopped trusting the negotiation process. The LRA Colonel Lubwoa Bwone emphatically argued in 2006, referring to 2004, that 'last time, it was not peace talks'. Drawing a map of the proposed 2004 assembly area along Palabek Kal road in the sand, he explained how the GoU 'made the assembly area smaller and then they sent helicopter gunships within hours of our assembly'.[71]

After the GoU bombed the LRA in the assembly area, the LRA attacked Alero in Gulu District on 1 January 2005. With this, the 2004 talks had officially collapsed; Museveni said that war had resumed. Just over a week later, on 9 January 2005, the South Sudanese rebels of the Sudan People's Liberation Army/Movement (SPLA/M) and the Government of Sudan signed the Comprehensive Peace Agreement

---

[69] Fieldnotes, 24 November 2007. The Amnesty Act was allowed to expire in 2012, in violation of the Juba agreement. However, the expiry is being challenged through a new law that has been put to parliament in 2015 to end ambiguity between the amnesty act and the International Crimes Chamber (Hazan 2017; Hovil and Lomo 2005; Afako 2002a).

[70] Afako (2002a).

[71] Author interview with Col. Lubwoa Bwone and Lt Col. Santo Alit (LRA). Ri-Kwangba: 22 September 2006.

(CPA) after many years of negotiating. During the celebrations, SPLA/M leader John Garang de Mabior announced that the LRA would be 'treated as enemies of the united Sudan'.[72] On 3 February 2005, the GoU declared a limited eighteen-day truce with the LRA in a bid to revive the flagging peace process. This effort was hampered when on 16 February 2005, LRA negotiator Kolo surrendered to the UPDF. The ceasefire ended on 22 February with no significant achievements. The next news about the LRA came on 8 March when the UPDF and LRA clashed south of Tore in southern Sudan. A captured LRA lieutenant told the UPDF that the rest of his group was already in DRC, and that he had been sent back to Sudan's Central Equatoria to escort Kony to join the others.[73]

I asked various LRA/M members how they viewed previous attempts at peace. 'Insincere', 'full of presidential directives' or 'a trap' were typical answers. Commenting on the 2004 attempt, one LRA member said that it had damaged their trust in any peace process tremendously because 'Kolo took money, and he left a lot of people behind'. Otti wrote in his letter to me: 'It is not that we are not interested in peace negotiations, but we don't trust Bigombe and her peace team. These are bias people. They are after buying our people with money'.[74] Bigombe's very public handling of the peace talks and her close engagement with the GoU had led Kampala donors to nickname the 2004 peace talks the 'friends of Betty parade'.[75] A South Sudanese politician who had spent some time in Uganda during the 2004 process explained:

people were alienated from the peace process; it was not a people-centred peace. The GoU was not interested in peace, because the more you engage northern Uganda, the more free is South and West Uganda and that is difficult for the GoU because fear of government has always been a factor in this war.[76]

Joanna Quinn echoes the sentiment that in the process, the voices of civil society had been 'largely eclipsed in the fray', although some of the leaders, notably the Acholi religious leaders, had been engaged in peace efforts for years.[77]

When the ICC announced Uganda's referral of the situation in northern Uganda to the ICC prosecutor in December 2003, critics argued that the ICC was supporting the Ugandan government by portraying the war

---

[72] IRIN (13 January 2006).   [73] UNHCR (9 March 2006).
[74] Personal letter to author from Vincent Otti, 25 August 2005.
[75] Fieldnotes, Nairobi/Juba: 2 June 2006.
[76] Author interview with Dr Julia Duany, Undersecretary Parliamentary Affairs, Government of Southern Sudan. Juba: 15 October 2006.
[77] Quinn (2009: 62).

as a one-sided LRA-problem, thus allowing the GoU to use the court as a political tool.[78] The ICC's engagement sparked a lively international debate on the court's role in conflict situations and how to balance the politics of justice and accountability with peace.[79] Local leaders in northern Uganda also voiced their concerns about the impact of potential ICC warrants on a peace process. On March 15, 2005, Acholi leaders from northern Uganda travelled to The Hague to ask the ICC to refrain from issuing arrest warrants against LRA leaders.

In June 2005, just after the Ugandan Parliament had lifted restrictions on presidential terms to allow Museveni to run again for president, the President publicly pledged to forgive Kony if he surrendered to government forces, stating that Kony would receive the same treatment and immunity from prosecution as other former LRA commanders, such as former rebel spokesman Kolo.[80] In Sudan, Garang reiterated his earlier commitment to get rid of the LRA, promising 'Kony won't be hiding there for long'.[81] The lack of credibility of any peace process was confirmed from an unexpected source. When a report by the Ugandan health ministry and its partners revealed in August 2005 that 1,000 IDPs in northern Uganda were dying every week from violence or disease, notably malaria and HIV/AIDS-related, Egeland commented: 'Given the conditions in the camps, it is not surprising that many LRA combatants remain in the bush. We have not done enough to create a "pull factor" that could draw more of the LRA to disarmament and reintegration programmes'.[82]

On 9 July 2005, the ICC issued five sealed warrants – which means they were only shared with persons authorised by the court – for LRA commanders Joseph Kony, Vincent Otti, Okot Odhiambo, Raska Lukwiya and Dominic Ongwen. The warrants were unsealed – made public – on 13 October the same year.[83] The reception was mixed. Some hailed the move as a historic step towards ending impunity for the worst of crimes.[84] Others argued that the option to discuss peace had been curtailed and replaced with a politicised, but difficult-to-execute arrest

---

[78] Clark (2011); Branch (2007); Parrott (2006).

[79] Prorok (2017); Jo and Simmons (2016); Schomerus (2015a); Gegout (2013); Nouwen (2013); Clark (2010a); Afako (2010); Baines (2009); Rodman (2009); Allen (2006); Apuuli (2005).

[80] IRIN (13 January 2006).   [81] UNOCHA–IRIN (2005).   [82] IRIN (2005).

[83] International Criminal Court (2005). Cole gives a useful brief discussion of the pros and cons of keeping ICC warrants sealed or unsealed in active conflicts (Cole 2011).

[84] UN News Service (2005).

warrant, leaving northern Uganda without any credible option to pursue peace.[85] ICC supporters later argued that it was because of the warrants that the talks came about, as Nick Grono and Adam O'Brien write: 'The threat of prosecution clearly rattled the LRA military leadership, pushing them to the negotiating table'.[86] The ICC intervention, it was hoped by its supporters, could change dynamics to spell the end for the LRA, although precisely how local negotiations would be balanced with the international warrants was never clear.

Opponents of the ICC warrants contended that they made ending violence look like an unattractive option, as Richard Dowden holds: 'Western policy, led by Britain, is to capture Kony and his fellow cult leaders and take them to the international court, while Museveni's aim is a military victory. Kony has no incentive to talk'.[87] Otti's confusion as to how exactly the ICC would deal with him – his expectation being to be hanged in The Hague – was not surprising; unbeknown to Otti, capital punishment was clearly off the cards, but that also was almost the only clear point. Yet, with all the international attention, at the time of my first contact with Otti in late 2005, it seemed as if the LRA had been cornered. The LRA, however, had quite a different view. They had observed how outside peace-building initiatives were transforming Gulu from the centre of war into an aid-industry hub; the possibility of peace with the LRA was driving business.[88] In addition to all the disincentives to engaging in peace talks, seeing the world come to Gulu was one reason why in late 2005 discussing peace became more attractive again to the LRA.

2.3   The LRA Moves towards the Juba Talks

Otti argued that 2005 was a good moment to get the LRA's points across, as the world was now paying attention. Others from the LRA stressed that they were confused by the complicated new situation and it seemed best to tackle it through negotiations. However, the LRA wanted time to understand the new situation before making any commitment, and to prove that they were not yet defeated. When I spoke to Otti in January 2006, he expected 'to carry on with war until June, July', which was about when the dry season would end. He saw continued fighting until the rainy season as the only option because there was 'money out on our heads'. He explained that Walter Ochora, the then-Gulu Resident District Coordinator (RDC), had announced this on the radio, and the

---

[85] The literature on this discussion could fill a library – see also footnote 155.
[86] Grono and O'Brien (2007: 15).   [87] Dowden (2006).   [88] See Branch (2008b).

LRA now had no choice but to be 'out to get Ochora'.[89] 'We are going to win, we are sure', Otti said, explaining that Ochora's announcement had left them with the only option to continue fighting until they were no longer threatened, since they could not have

peace talks on the phone .... Every day in the bush, we are attacked several times. We have killed several [UPDF] commanders: .... We are staying now in the bush as our home. We are scattered now. I am nowhere near the chairman.

He emphasised 'the chairman is not with me, but I will organise a phone talk. Kony is fearing a call from somebody. He will call you. He cannot be called'. Otti told me to ring him each day between 7.30 and 7.45 p.m., because the LRA would be in long prayers before that and they would keep 'praying until the end of the month'.[90]

It was during this time in late 2005 and early 2006 that Machar, with the help of IKV Pax Christi, was making contact with the LRA leadership to arrange a meeting in the bush. Machar, one of the most contentious yet skilled personalities in Sudanese and South Sudanese politics, had just been named Vice President of GoSS, after the former deputy Kiir had replaced Garang, who was killed in a helicopter crash. Machar's war history connected him to the LRA: having split from the SPLA in 1991, his subsequent South Sudan Independence Movement was one of the groups acting as connectors between the LRA and their sponsor in Khartoum.[91] Machar returned to the SPLA/M after reconciling with Garang in 2002; nonetheless, his past meant that there was substantial distrust of his motives.

On 20 December 2005, members of the SPLM said that LRA representatives had been in touch by email to respond to an SPLM offer to mediate peace talks. Machar stated that the LRA had accepted, although there had been no direct contact.[92] Parallel contacts developed through individual delegates, through Justice Onega from the Ugandan Amnesty Commission, and IKV Pax Christi.[93] Southern Sudanese local leaders

---

[89] Colonel Walter Ochora was Gulu's LC5 from 1996 to 2006. In 2006, he lost his position to Norbert Mao. In 1985, Ochora had marched with the UNLA towards Kampala to protest against President Obote's treatment of Acholi officers; one interpretation of the event is that it led to Obote's flight to Kenya, paving the way for Tito Okello's government. A great supporter of the NRM, he was best known for leading a delegation of Acholi leaders into the bush to meet with Sam Kolo before the 2004 peace talks collapsed. For the LRA, Ochora remained an important contact: he was Gulu's RDC and was seen by the LRA leadership as a nemesis as well as an important contact. He died in 2011.

[90] Fieldnotes, Juba: 7 September 2006.   [91] See Schomerus (2007); Johnson (2003).

[92] Etukuri (20 December 2005).   [93] Fieldnotes, 24 November 2007.

sought contact with the LRA by leaving messages in villages that the LRA had attacked. For months, explained the then-MP for Magwi County, Betty Acan Ogwaro, 'Riek Machar did not succeed to make contact with the LRA leadership because every group he spoke to claimed to be able to make the contact, but nobody did'.[94] In the end, she elaborated, it was a six-man team with people from Juba, the UK, Uganda and Kenya that made contact, possibly triggered by a false alarm in a newspaper.

When the newspaper claimed that one team of those searching for an LRA contact had been contacted by Kony, another team, which was led by Dr Onek, received a phone call and he was told that he would be connected to the leadership. That is how Dr Onek met the LRA representative and they rung Number Two [Otti] and spoke to him. We were looking at that connection for five to six months.[95]

On 2 February 2006, Machar succeeded in contacting Otti on the phone.[96] Shortly after, four LRA representatives met with representatives of IKV Pax Christi in Nairobi. For IKV Pax Christi, judging the credibility of the meeting was a challenge. Despite having worked on a peaceful solution for years, they had never previously encountered these men.[97] Recalling the first meeting, Onek explained that two men in particular – who were also two of my initial contacts – were 'very convincing. [One] was very articulate; he talked like an old man. He was very clever. Pax [Christi] thought we don't have any chance. This might be it'.[98]

After the meeting in Nairobi, on 14 February 2006, a small delegation of LRA/M and IKV Pax Christi took a chartered plane to Juba, paid for by IKV Pax Christi, to meet Machar face to face. Upon arrival, they were ushered towards the Vice President's office. For the delegates, it was significant that they were allowed to enter Sudan 'without having our passports stamped' – akin to the way a diplomat on a covert mission would be treated, as one of the LRA representatives said.[99] One of the original LRA/M delegates got a nickname out of this: they had entered Juba like diplomats on a mission, so the delegation from then on called him 'Ambassador'. Because Machar treated them like respected diplomats, the LRA representatives trusted his motives. In a three-hour meeting in Juba that day, Machar – sceptical that he was indeed talking to

---

[94] Author interview with Betty Achan Ogwaro, MP Magwi County Southern Sudan Legislative Assembly. Juba: 9 September 2006.
[95] Author interview with Betty Achan Ogwaro, MP Magwi County Southern Sudan Legislative Assembly. Juba: 9 September 2006.
[96] Otti (13 September 2006).   [97] See also Simonse, Verkoren and Junne (2010).
[98] Author interview with Sudanese advisor to peace talks. Juba: 8 December 2006.
[99] Fieldnotes, Juba: 12 September 2006.

LRA representatives – asked to call Otti. 'He wanted to know if we were real', one of the delegates explained.[100] Delegates and SPLA then checked each other out by comparing phone numbers and text messages sent earlier. 'Machar was friendly, he said he had been wanting to make contact for a long time', another delegate said.[101]

Machar needed to solve the LRA problem for his own country and to ensure that the CPA could be implemented in all of southern Sudan, including in the areas in the Equatorias that continued to be affected by the LRA. Additionally, Machar was unhappy about the UPDF moving freely in Sudan: 'I don't feel very comfortable under an invasion', he said in June 2006, referring to the fact that the UPDF's mandate to operate in Sudan had expired the previous January.[102] Machar was in a unique position to take the lead in a complicated situation. As Vice President of a semi-autonomous region (which was southern Sudan's status from 2005 to 2011), he was not bound to most international treaties. Sudan had not ratified the Rome Statute, thus it had no obligation to arrest and extradite those with an ICC arrest warrant against them; southern Sudan, lacking sovereignty, was under no international pressure at all.

A successful peace deal would boost both Machar's and his new government's international profile. Still, when Machar invited the delegation to stay in Juba overnight, they declined. 'We had to get straight back. We did not trust him enough to stay in Juba'.[103] However, the trust expanded far enough to allow a second meeting with Machar.[104] Yet Machar had set himself a huge task. On 24 March 2006, the UN Security Council passed a resolution that 'strongly condemned activities of militias and armed groups such as the LRA, which continue to attack civilians and commit human rights abuses in Sudan'.[105] A week later, Egeland pitched in with a comment, declaring the twenty-year conflict in northern Uganda 'the world's worst form of terrorism' during a visit to Uganda's Patongo camp for the displaced in Pader district.[106]

After the February meeting, the LRA/M had led Machar to believe that he would next, as one delegate phrased it, 'connect with Otti' in Jebel Lien, just outside Juba, in April.[107] At the last minute, Machar was given a new location for the meeting: Nabanga in Western Equatoria, on the border with the DRC – much further away. One delegate explained: 'Machar thought we were mad when we were asking for Nabanga because [Nabanga and Jebel Lien] are so far apart. But we were in

---

[100] Fieldnotes, Juba: 9 July 2006.   [101] Fieldnotes, Juba: 9 July 2006.
[102] Fieldnotes, Maridi: 13 June 2006.   [103] Fieldnotes, Juba: 9 July 2006.
[104] Fieldnotes, 24 November 2007.   [105] IRIN (2006).   [106] IRIN (2006).
[107] Fieldnotes, 24 November 2007.

control of the territory; there was nothing he could do'.[108] Exerting this control was particularly important for the LRA.[109] Onek described the first meeting in the bush on 11 April: 'It was interesting. It was scary'.[110] Heavily armed LRA fighters led Machar deep into the bush in a stern atmosphere. The outcome was an agreement between Machar and Otti to meet again – next time with Kony in attendance.

On 3 May 2006, Kony turned up at the second meeting in Nabanga. Most of those at the meeting described the moment as exhilarating. During the meeting, Machar handed Kony an envelope with US $20,000 to buy food. The interaction was filmed, presumably to provide proof to Museveni that Kony really had met with Machar. Reportedly, Salva Kiir showed the video to Museveni on 13 May 2006, as evidence that the LRA was engaged; Museveni agreed to keep amnesty for the LRA high command in place.[111] The video was leaked to Reuters in Nairobi on 24 May, causing a stir: it was the first footage of Kony in more than a decade, and his reappearance made world news. Machar's decision to hand over money was met with international criticism. However, internally in the LRA, enthusiasm for the peace effort was maintained when the SPLA held up their side of the bargain and started to deliver food provisions to Nabanga. The delegation went back to Nairobi to assemble fully, said one delegate: 'We thought this was now possible: we could start negotiations. We could start a peace process to end this thing. We could bring all our people together'.[112] They said they were unfazed, even when, on 17 May, Museveni announced that the LRA would now have a two-month ultimatum 'to peacefully end terrorism' or face a combined force of Ugandan and southern Sudanese troops. However, Museveni reiterated that if Kony 'got serious about a peaceful settlement, the government would guarantee his safety'.[113]

On 2 June – the same day Interpol sent 'wanted persons' red notices to 184 countries in connection with the ICC warrants against the LRA high command[114] – a provisional LRA peace delegation travelled to Juba, accompanied by two representatives from Sant'Egidio. A representative of IKV Pax Christi followed a few days later and was surprised to find Sant'Egidio in Juba. The two organisations did not speak to each other. Having waited a few days for a meeting with Machar, who was delayed in Khartoum, they met with the Vice President on the evening of 7 June.

---

[108] Fieldnotes, Obbo/Magwi: 4 October 2006.
[109] For LRA rules in previous talks, see Dolan (2005).
[110] Author interview with Sudanese advisor to peace talks. Juba: 8 December 2006.
[111] IRIN (30 August 2006).   [112] Fieldnotes, Juba: 28 September 2006.
[113] IRIN (30 August 2006).   [114] BBC News (2 June 2006).

Both Machar and the LRA/M reiterated their commitment to the peace effort; plans were made to travel to the bush to connect with Kony and Otti. The following day, representatives of the UN Security Council visited Juba for an extraordinary meeting on Darfur with Kiir and Machar. With the UN press corps in town, the first international news stories appeared about the rumour that an LRA delegation was in Juba.

During the meeting on Darfur, the United Kingdom Ambassador to the United Nations and head of the Security Council visiting delegation Emyr Jones Parry reiterated the international community's position on the LRA: 'LRA is a threat to the peace and stability of the region and [the Security Council] would very much like this scourge to be eliminated'. Kiir reportedly answered,

we think that arresting Joseph Kony is not the solution to the problem by itself. Arresting Joseph Kony, another leader will just surface from nowhere and so, taking Joseph Kony or the other four indictees will not be the end of the problem. Some new commanders will come up they may even be worse than Joseph Kony.

Ambassador Jones Parry then added that he would 'support the proposition of the five indictments issued by the International Criminal Court (to) be given effect'.[115]

A few days later, on 11 June 2006, again in Ri-Kwangba, near the small Western Equatorian village of Nabanga, Machar met once more with both Kony and Otti. The two LRA leaders were dressed in military fatigues and surrounded by armed young soldiers in mix-and-match uniforms. Machar arrived in civilian clothing with only minimal protection from unarmed SPLA soldiers. That the external pressures on the talks would be huge had become even clearer after the Security Council meeting on Darfur, but Machar seemed confident that mediating was going to be worthwhile.[116] He was trying to drum up international support. Waiting in the bush for Kony, he spoke on the satellite phone to representatives of President Thabo Mbeki of South Africa and President Mwai Kibaki of Kenya.[117] Later he tried to convince the White House that his undertaking was promising.[118] While he said Mbeki and Kibaki had responded positively, early support for his attempt was underwhelming to outright hostile.

After news of the latest meeting in the bush transpired, Kampala reacted with a turn-around on the earlier statement that the amnesty would stand even for the LRA leadership. The GoU now said that they

---

[115] Jada and Toure Pouch (15 June 2006).   [116] Fieldnotes, Maridi: 13 June 2006.
[117] Fieldnotes, Ri-Kwangba: 12 July 2006.   [118] Fieldnotes, Maridi: 13 June 2006.

could not meet LRA leaders who were wanted by the ICC.[119] The toing-and-froing was by many in Juba commented on as being typical of Museveni's approach. A few days later, the ICC insisted that engaging LRA rebels in peace talks would not impede the arrest and prosecution of their leaders.[120] Nonetheless, after Kony had appointed his delegates, Machar was elated and convinced that this approach to peace was going to work. One reason for the optimism was that at the time of Machar's efforts to start peace negotiations, a broad consensus seemed to exist within the Ugandan government and the international community that the LRA stood to only gain from entering peace negotiations and signing a deal. They were, at least according to their military opponents, a spent force, on the run, marginalised and deprived of their territory by the CPA.

I talked to Machar at dawn the day after his meeting with Kony and Otti; he was already working through documents while waiting for the charter plane back to Juba. He was also well aware of the wave of international criticism that was about to hit him for engaging with wanted war criminals and joked that dealing with Kony would probably be easier than dealing with all the peace-talks sceptics.[121] He predicted, correctly, that many would argue that even offering the option to pursue a peace deal was giving the LRA more than it deserved.[122] Nonetheless, on 20 June 2006, Uganda's ambassador to Juba announced that a GoU delegation was coming to Juba. On 28 June, the GoU reported that it had been formally invited by GoSS to attend talks with the LRA, and that it would send a technical team for preliminary meetings.[123]

This team arrived, led by Uganda's Minister of the Interior, Rugunda, on 3 July. After meeting with Kiir and Machar, Rugunda said at a press conference that Uganda's government was prepared to talk, that talks would take place in Juba, and that Machar would chair them – with no mention of IKV Pax Christi or Sant'Egidio. Only two days later, Museveni reiterated his offer of amnesty for all LRA, including the top commanders. He failed to address the contradictions between his various statements that the GoU would grant amnesty but would also not meet with the LRA leadership. The offer of amnesty was flat out dismissed by the LRA/M delegation. A delegate had previously explained to me that they could not take amnesty because it would imply that they had done

---

[119] IRIN (30 August 2006).   [120] IRIN (30 August 2006).
[121] Critical writing on engaging in a peace process with the LRA is plentiful, ranging from polemical rants to informed debates. See for example Quinn (2009); Feldman (2007); Onyango-Obbo (2007); Human Rights Watch (2006).
[122] Fieldnotes, Maridi: 13 June 2006.   [123] IRIN (30 August 2006).

something wrong. On 7 July, newly appointed LRA/M spokesperson, Olweny, reacted to the amnesty offer in a radio interview, stating that the LRA was not denying having committed atrocities, but they wanted to talk peace and that was why they were rejecting the idea of amnesty. On the same day, ICC Chief Prosecutor Luis Moreno-Ocampo insisted that Kony must eventually face trial.[124]

On 11 July, Machar made a final attempt to convince Otti in a meeting in Ri-Kwangba to join the LRA/M delegates in Juba. The following day, Otti declined the invitation and instead sent two additional officers as the most senior military representatives in Juba. Upon return to Juba on 14 July, Machar announced that the Juba Peace Talks would start the following day with an opening ceremony.

When the Talks commenced with the fiery opening speech by the LRA, media attention focussed particularly on the LRA/M delegation. A big question loomed large over any interaction: Who are these people? Who is the LRA/M and how do the two connect with each other? More on 'the system LRA' will follow later, yet that this question remained such a challenge points to its answer: both LRA and LRM are at the same time fixed and flexible entities, both groups at times encompass a range of actors who are loosely affiliated. This is typical: A trademark of contemporary conflicts is that they lack reliable boundaries in terms of geography, ideology and affiliation. Taking these headings, in turn, might allow to find a workable answer to the question who the LRA/M is.

2.4   Space and Ideology

Geographically speaking, the LRA/M conflict's fighting territory has shifted from northern Uganda into other countries. To help with a definition of who the LRA/M was at the time of the Juba Talks, broadening the understanding of geographic boundaries is useful. The spatial expansion has been a characteristic of conflict in other contexts, and it is worth thinking about what it means. Zachary Lomo documents how two other Ugandan rebel groups, the West Nile Bank Front (WNBF) and the Uganda National Rescue Front II (UNRF II), were in direct contact with the LRA when all three groups were operating from Sudan. Lomo's point is that all conflicts are not only inter-related, but also evoke international geopolitical issues because of the wider geographical setting: 'Although the exact nature of the relationships between the groups is unclear, the extent to which insurgents were not acting in

---

[124] IRIN (30 August 2006).

total isolation is an important dynamic that has to be taken into consideration when attempts to resolving these conflicts are being made'.[125]

In the case of the LRA, the lack of focus on territorial control has often been used to argue that the group lacks a political agenda or negotiation credibility. Instead, I propose that transcendence of geographical space, rather than being an expression of meaninglessness, emphasises that the conflict is more broadly representative of conflict dynamics in the region which are rooted in marginalisation. Daniel Pécaut states that 'the perception of space is inseparable from social experience rooted in memory'.[126] With the widening of the space of the LRA/M in the region and the diaspora, the social experience of marginalisation, 'rooted in memory' and in the experience of being ever further from home, strengthened the broader conflict landscape, which also involved other actors interested in hardening of or ending of marginalisation. The geographical reach includes the pattern of proxy wars so common to the region, in which actors reach across geographical boundaries to pursue goals at home. Additionally, the point about the memory of marginalisation links the LRA as an actor to the broader conflict landscape in time. This includes, for example, previous rebellions in Uganda, most prominently the above-mentioned groups in West Nile.[127]

The fluid geographical reach also highlights the blurred boundaries of ideology. The most obvious one is the LRA's military support of an Islamist agenda from Khartoum in exchange for material support in their fight against Museveni. Khartoum loomed large as a player during the LRA's stay in southern Sudan. During the peace negotiations in Juba, its influence was much less clear particularly because of the parallel challenges that were ongoing regarding the implementation of Sudan's CPA. During the Juba Talks, however, the relationship between the LRA and the government in Khartoum came to symbolise narratives of power relations and collusion: at no point was Khartoum's role entirely clear; the crucial question of whether or not its support to the LRA continued has been a question asked ever since. Yet as a player with major influence, Khartoum was never absent.

2.5   Affiliation

The brief history of the war provided here shows individual attachments to the LRA were often fluid between force and volunteerism, between despair about the situation in which residents of northern Uganda found

[125] Lomo and Hovil (2004: 15).   [126] Pécaut (2000: 131).   [127] See Leopold (2005).

themselves and despair at the armed response that was contributing to making the situation worse. Individuals who were assembled in Juba to represent the LRA were there for a range of reasons: because they were close to Kony or others in the high command, because they had for years supported an anti-Museveni struggle from the diaspora, or because they were so entrenched in the conflict spiral between government and LRA actors that they could turn to be on either side at any point but carried valuable insider information that made them useful while they were openly on board.

Not all delegates chose to be very public about their engagement, thus describing an individual's motivations and backstories could put them at risk. The chairperson and the spokespeople over the course of the Juba Talks can all be broadly put in the category of those who were very close to Ugandan politics: one chairperson had been known to work for government agencies and had lived in Kampala for several years, another was a member of the opposition party Ugandan People's Congress, but had been in exile. A third delegate had run for Museveni's NRM in the last elections before the talks and had failed to gain a seat. A set of delegates were drawn from the diaspora in London; often these delegates held close connections to the elders who are perceived to have been the instigators of the rebellion against Museveni.[128] Some had fled Uganda for Kenya and had never returned to their homeland. Quite a few delegates had never met Kony before, having been drawn from the often more vocal exiles. Yet who exactly the LRA and LRM were at any given point is impossible to say conclusively – again, a feature that has continued ever since.

The same applies when it comes to describing the exact nature of the relationship between LRA and LRM, and how these two are embedded in the broader conflictscape that also involves other actors – what will later be described as the 'LRA system'. While conflict resolution processes aim to single out specific actors and their roles, entrenched conflicts are in fact characterised by the inseparable interaction and overlaps between actors. For example, Ugandan politicians used the Juba Talks to express their support for the LRA's grievances, if not for its methods. Some of these politicians used their past close connection with either LRA or the GoU to achieve a prominent position within the broader Juba debate. Kristof Titeca makes this point most strongly about civil society actors, pointing out that for example, the Acholi Religious Leaders Peace Initiative has long claimed a certain kind of ownership of the LRA and

[128] Finnstroem (2003: 82ff).

thus over its narratives of grievance;[129] other actors have presented their own narratives of the LRA to suit their purposes.[130]

Finnstroem has attempted in the past to give a more accurate description of who the LRA is. He has pointed out, however, that the LRA/M tends to think of itself in terms of 'what we are not'.[131] He argues that this is a reflection of skewed outside perceptions which create the need for the LRA to justify itself in relation to what is being said about them. 'What we are not', a negative definition, thus becomes the dominant discourse within the LRA/M, with the only steady connector being 'what we are against'. However, the narratives of 'what we are', of change and ending armed resistance to enter a transformative process, are weak. The limitations caused by this overwhelming 'presence of what is missing' as Freeman calls it, become apparent in a peace process.[132] For the LRA/M to find its single voice to speak about what and who they were, became an impossible task during the talks.

The LRA/M at the Juba Talks struggled with an internal process of being a fluid entity and an external reality of having to present a united front in order to achieve any agreements. The internal narratives that nobody could ever be trusted to deliver structural change ultimately contributed to the failure of the Juba Talks. Internal betrayal and shifting affiliations are part of this. Paul Richards suggests that to transform a conflict, it is necessary to 'remake social worlds', a process that was absent from Juba.[133] At best, the remaking of social worlds occurred in the corruption, back-channel processes and lack of transparency that undermined the main process and highlighted the fluidity and opportunism of affiliation.

2.6   Information

In his letter to me, Otti had expressed concern about who I was and whether I would perpetuate the 'wrong' kind of stories, those that confirm the established government narrative.[134]

What I want to ask you are these: are you a rumour monger, an activist, a journalist or a researcher? If one of these; then whose interest are you

---

[129] Titeca (2013).   [130] Titeca and Costeur (2015).   [131] Finnstroem (2008b: 123).
[132] Freeman (2002).   [133] Richards (2005).
[134] Although Otti confirmed to me that he had indeed written this letter, and the handwriting is very similar to what I saw when he wrote in my notepad in Ri-Kwangba, I remain sceptical. Producing a letter after a supposedly elaborate adventure to get it is precisely the kind of behaviour that some LRA associates display when they want to keep the interest of an outsider, although delivering a letter from the bush is a common way of communicating within the LRA.

representing? Let me hope you are trustworthy and somebody who keeps secrets because if not then definitely you will put the life of these boys at a very high risk.[135]

The LRA notion that rumour-mongering and activism drove the availability of information was strong; these would come back later in the dynamics of the talks as control over narratives. Olweny argued: 'We give our side of the story against extremely negative and malicious distortions, misinformation and outright lies about the role of the LRM/A in the conflict, and to a no less extent, against the people of northern Uganda'.[136] Kony stated,

People are fighting with propaganda. But for me as a guerrilla, I have not yet reached. I am lacking so many things. That is why you are here. All thing from Museveni side or from some other people, because I do not have proper propaganda machineries. I do not have some other people also.[137]

As spokesperson of the LRA/M delegation, Olweny had also signed one of the early position papers, stating: 'We appeal to NRM to stop its elaborate propaganda machinery that has caused the international community to treat the LRM/A with absolute scorn, disdain and contempt, based on prejudices and misgivings'.[138] 'Time has come when the truth must be told', he exclaimed in another paper, 'and all stake-holders challenged to give their side of the story'.[139] This included establishing that it was not true

that the LRM/A has no political agenda. To say so is to underrate the problem at hand and to give the false impression that LRM/A has no cause for its armed rebellion. Failure to express its political agenda loudly in intellection [*sic*] form does not mean the lack of it. Until now we have been speaking through action. We now want to use this forum, space and time to express our agenda in words. Let the world and all the stakeholders grasp this opportunity to hear us out and be the final judges.[140]

Until the Juba Talks, information on the LRA/M message and their perspective on their own role had indeed been fuzzy. Written manifestos were scarce, and when they appeared, they were discredited by the GoU or by the LRA's atrocities.[141] The delegation argued that they had been denied media exposure, but this 'failure of the LRM/A to have access to the mass media to express its political agenda loudly in intellectual form

---

[135] Vincent Otti's personal letter to author, 25 August 2005.   [136] Olweny (2006a).
[137] Author interview with Joseph Kony, Sudan/DRC border: 12 June 2006.
[138] Olweny (2006a).   [139] Olweny (2006b).   [140] Olweny (2006a).
[141] Finnstroem argues that while past manifestos were crudely assembled, they nonetheless expressed popular sentiments (Finnstroem 2008b). The International Crisis Group (ICG) in later years argued a similar line (International Crisis Group 2008: i).

does not mean the lack of it'.[142] I asked Kony, Otti and other LRA
members why they had been so reticent to state their side of the story.
Kony emphasised that LRA manifestos were well known in Uganda; the
fact that I did not know them was my own shortcoming.[143] Otti argued
that in a 'bush war' it was difficult to distribute strong messages, especially because 'rebel supporters' faced persecution.[144] Another delegate
thought my questions were misguided: 'The cause is obvious and needs
no explanation', he said. 'We have a cause'.[145] Despite this seeming lack
of need to communicate, when appointed spokesperson, Olweny, was
elated because the 'LRA never had a proper spokesperson'.[146]

Otti several times mentioned to me that he wanted to write a book, just
as Museveni had done with *Sowing the Mustard Seed*, to explain what the
world was like in Uganda and for the LRA.[147] In November 2006, Otti
asked me about the LRA's image abroad: 'Tell me, what does the outside
world now think about LRA? Do they know about LRA? Do they
understand about LRA?'[148] The topic came up often. In July 2007,
Otti said that he had just given another television interview to Sky
News – but had not yet been able to watch the story to see if it was
'truthful'. His parting words were 'I will talk to you with your tape
recorder to set the story straight'.[149] Yet rather than being able to author
the counterpart of Museveni's Ugandan founding myth, Otti became
overwhelmed. Within the LRA, he was seen as the best person to provide
information on the LRA – and really the only person. An LRA member
explained, 'We did not have a manifesto because we did not have
anybody who could do such thing. Otti could not be waiter, cashier
and cook at the same time'.[150]

The lack of LRA/M capacity to impart its message was symptomatic of
the cause of the conflict, according to Olweny.[151] His point was that the
scale of GoU crimes, the displacement camps, and the lack of the
educational opportunities that would have given the victims the political
tools to deal with their plight had silenced Acholi people who resisted the
GoU.[152] The way the war between the GoU and the LRA had been

---

[142] Olweny (2006b).
[143] Author interview with Joseph Kony, Sudan/DRC border: 12 June 2006.
[144] Author interview with Vincent Otti, Ri-Kwangba: 14 November 2006.
[145] Fieldnotes, Juba: 23 October 2006.   [146] Fieldnotes, Juba: 6 June 2006.
[147] Museveni (1997b).
[148] Author interview with Vincent Otti, Ri-Kwangba: 14 November 2006.
[149] Author interview with Vincent Otti, Ri-Kwangba: 13 July 2007.
[150] Fieldnotes, Juba: 6 June 2006.
[151] Kriesberg argues that communities need people such as intellectuals and politicians to
shape a discourse and interpretations of the past (Kriesberg 1989: 220; 2015).
[152] For a similar point on Angola (Comerford 2003).

conducted had closed down any public sphere in which to discuss the reasons for the war; the Acholi people's livelihoods had been so severely curtailed that they were no longer able to change their situation.[153] For the LRA, the Acholi people had been turned into anonymous victims, as outlined in an LRA position paper that addressed crimes committed by the NRA:

> Our mothers, sisters and wives were raped in front of us; and in some extreme cases men were sodomised in public; and in front of their family members. This became infamously known as 'Tek Gungu' .... The NRA soldiers went to the extent of cutting men's anuses with razor blades and pouring paraffin therein to enlarge them to fit their sex organs. Evidence of all these abound, but common decency compels us to keep the victims anonymous as this phenomenon was hitherto unknown to the northern and eastern tribes of Uganda and remains anathema even to talk about it.[154]

The experience of such violence limited the extent to which information about it could be spread, according to the LRA/M's argument. The LRA/M gave as an example of limiting information through violence 'the case of the sub county chief of Patiko, Mze [Muzee] Owiny [who suffered abuse from the UPDF] ... who consequently committed suicide'.[155]

While the LRA/M continued to feel that no proper information on their plight was available, the Juba Talks reignited interest in the LRA. Increasing internationalisation of the conflict had made information on many facets of northern Uganda and the LRA more accessible. Scholarship on the LRA conflict has covered a range of issues, such as the debate about international and transitional justice,[156] the role and ineffectiveness of aid agencies in complex situations,[157] health in the displacement camps,[158] and later on the role of international advocacy[159]

---

[153] The LRA consulted the blog of a Sudanese writer published in the *Sudan Tribune* on 19 August 2006. Drawing on a wide range of supporting facts about the economic disparity between north and south, the blogger argues that the system established in Uganda resembles South Africa's apartheid regime (Akec 2006). On stealing Acholi cattle see also Jackson (2009: 324).

[154] Olweny (2006a). The notion that the crimes committed were so bad that they cannot be talked about echoes Agamben's concept of bearing witness to something so horrific it cannot be witnessed (Agamben 2002). The challenge of 'bearing witness' to violence has also been struggled with by scholars seeking to understand it, such as Kleinman, Das and Lock (1997).

[155] Olweny (2006a). This underscores Chiwengo's point that 'bearing witness to African events in literature, the media, or human rights discourse is challenging because of the power relations that undergird its representation and visualization' (Chiwengo 2008: 81).

[156] See footnote 155.   [157] For example Branch (2011).

[158] For example Accorsi et al. (2005).

[159] For example Schomerus (2015b); Taub (2012).

and the continuing efforts to deal with the LRA militarily[160] or through justice procedures and rebuilding,[161] as well as the long-term unintended consequences of programmes related to the conflict.[162] Much has been written about northern Uganda's and the Acholi people's marginalisation and deprivation, and on the role of violence in political and social developments in Uganda.[163]

Additionally, news coverage, personal writing, advocacy and popular culture (evident in Internet campaigns, feature films or graphic novels) have been abundant.[164] The war and the LRA have pop-culture allure; celebrity interest such as the brief moment of attention from Angelina Jolie helps. The elusive leadership, the brutality and duration of the conflict, the number of people affected in various ways, the geographical spread and the impact of the conflict on the developmental situation in four countries – Uganda, South Sudan, DRC and CAR – remains baffling. In its later years, the conflict drew huge interest from new and established international advocacy groups, most prominently the California-based evangelical Invisible Children; their video 'Kony2012' turned into the most successful Internet advocacy campaign to date.[165]

However, with more information being produced and researched on the LRA, two opposing developments occurred. Scholarship and some journalism gave further nuance to the complex conflict dynamics and actions of a range of actors – most prominently the LRA, the GoU and international organisations – focusing increasingly on the political economy of the conflict,[166] and along the way dismissing the simple label 'the LRA war' as inadequate.[167] Finnstroem and Dolan avoid using the term 'war' altogether, both offering more socially inclusive terminology. Finnstroem describes the state of permanent warlike activities as 'living with bad surroundings', while Dolan uses the term 'social torture' to

---

[160] For example Demmers and Gould (2018); Fisher (2014); Ahere and Maina (2013); Crook (2012); Atkinson et al. (2012).

[161] For example Macdonald and Porter (2016).

[162] For example Rigterink and Schomerus (2017).   [163] Reid (2017).

[164] International audiences became engaged, thanks to a whole series of films and documentaries on the plight of the children of northern Uganda, including an episode of Law and Order (Schomerus 2015b), the Hollywood movie *Machine Gun Preacher* or the documentaries *Lost Children* and *War Dance*.

[165] See Rauxloh (2017); von Engelhardt and Jansz (2014); LRA/M Peace Team (2012).

[166] Measuring and acknowledging the role of both perpetrating sides in the war has remained challenging. However, the GoU came increasingly under criticism for conditions in the displacement camps. The Enough Project wrote that 'the Ugandan government holds the majority of blame for herding people into camps, a move they undertook because of their inability to provide sufficient protection to them in their home villages' (Spiegel and Prendergast 2008).

[167] See Lepore on the importance of naming a war (Lepore 1998: 16).

capture how rebel and government activity destroyed the social fabric of the north.[168] During the Juba Talks, the LRA/M contested the title 'LRA war' primarily because the issues were relevant to a larger group of people than just the LRA.[169] In late 2009, the LRA/M delegation urged in its rejection of military action against the LRA 'a return to the negotiating table, to save all the peoples affected by the "Northern Uganda" conflict from further senseless, destructive and unnecessary military adventures'.[170]

In a parallel development, the more prominent pop-culture public image of the LRA became increasingly jejune. Holger Herwig has out-lined how important events 'are hardest to understand because they attract the greatest attention from mythmakers and charlatans', and the LRA war was no exception.[171] Most of the mainstream information on the LRA and the war was and remains heavy on atmospheric description, one-sided human rights reporting and simplifications about youth par-ticipation that creates and perpetuates myths about the LRA, but is light on analysis that might allow answers to the persistent basic questions.[172] A simplistic view was presented even by those close to the issues in Uganda, such as the former Ugandan government minister and peace negotiator Bigombe, who asked in an article co-written by US activist John Prendergast: 'How do you end a 19-year insurgency led by a messianic guerrilla leader with an army of abducted, tortured, and brain-washed children?'[173] The imagery of an army of brainwashed child soldiers has sustained international outrage. The LRA has been accused of everything from cannibalism to drug-running. A particularly sensa-tionalist example of storytelling is Paul Raffaele's purported 'adventures on the trail of man's darkest ritual'.[174] Robert Feldman's broad-brush assessment confidently asserts that Kony 'appears to be a delusional madman'[175] and claims that

narcotics sales also help fund LRA operations. Being involved in the drug trade has the advantage of making them available for its own use. Some of the atrocities

---

[168] Dolan (2009); Finnstroem (2008b).

[169] At other moments, however, they emphasise the 'LRA war' to stress their role as Museveni's adversary. They objected to the description of 'LRA-affected areas' with the argument that the same areas might also be called 'UPDF-affected areas'.

[170] Labeja (2009).   [171] Herwig (1987: 7).

[172] Examples of atmospheric, often disturbing memoirs that are at the same time infused with symbolism are Amony (2015); Eichstaedt (2009); Cook (2007). An accomplished, humorous approach to the question why Museveni has not been able to defeat Kony has been offered by Bussmann (2010).

[173] Bigombe and Prendergast (2006).   [174] Raffaele (2008).   [175] Feldman (2007).

that are committed are reportedly so brutal that Kony's followers rely on drugs for their courage to perform them.[176]

As all returnees and active LRA agree that they are drug-free and no evidence exists that the LRA are drug dealers, it is worth noting that Feldman's source for this information is a conference paper given in Washington, DC, by Uganda's Director of Public Prosecutions on terrorist financing.[177] More recently, with the geographical shift of the LRA, the group has been linked to both diamond and ivory trading.[178]

Dowden writes that the LRA's portrayal as a 'mindless terror gang' that was 'so evil it makes political or military analysis unnecessary' was fed by the general assumption that Africa is a place of darkness. Because of the war's virulence, Dowden argues, the assumption had long been that 'the LRA would quickly burn itself out'.[179] In Juba, the LRA/M implemented a new information policy to strongly counter the notion that they had burnt out. Their aim to influence public opinion, however, did not generate a more nuanced picture.

While many important points need to be made about the role of the GoU in the conflict, the public manifestation of the LRA/M information policy during the Juba Talks hardly moved beyond a crude whitewash, with a focus on denying atrocities and deflecting guilt for attacks on the UPDF. Privately, the LRA/M argued that the set-up of the talks had made a more nuanced public presentation impossible. I observed several moments during the talks when delegates and the high command were cornered with hostile questioning about their own atrocities. Their visible reaction seemed to be embarrassment, as if atrocities and the past should not be discussed in public. An LRA member confirmed that this impression was correct – from the LRA point of view, he said, the LRA could not talk openly about crimes they had committed, because of the threat of ICC persecution and because 'talking about it like that makes it hard to reconcile'.[180] In less public situations, members freely admitted that the LRA had committed violent crimes, although they maintained that rape was not a crime sanctioned by Kony[181] – an assertion that seems misplaced considering the witness statements for the ICC trial of Dominic Ongwen, but highlights the need to understand how complex rape and forced marriage are, as Holly Porter shows in her work.[182]

---

[176] Feldman (2007: 138).
[177] Buteera (2003). The paper is no longer available online, and the LRA has never been charged with narcotics-related crimes.
[178] Titeca (2018); Collins, Cox and Pamment (2017); White (2014).
[179] Dowden (2006).   [180] Fieldnotes, Juba/Magwi: 1 October 2006.
[181] Fieldnotes, Juba/Magwi: 1 October 2006.   [182] Porter (2016).

However, it is important to note that while for some time rape of civilians by the LRA was limited and punished, the LRA's definition of rape would likely not include intercourse in forced marriage.[183] In the early days of the talks, delegates even argued that it would be beneficial for the LRA to go to the ICC in The Hague to be tried, as it would give them an opportunity to present their evidence of GoU atrocities and provide what they referred to as 'proper information' – it is possible to think that even Ongwen and his defence team, when he was delivered to The Hague, still believed that his trial might present such an opportunity.

2.7   A Focus on Joseph Kony

Multiple theories and hypotheses exist about the behaviour of the LRA, but these tend at best to be based on accounts by those who have left the LRA and at worst are speculative, driven by ideology or even propaganda that uses evidence selectively. In thirty-five years of violence, not much was seen of Joseph Kony and not much was heard of the LRA, allowing fantastical accounts of exoticism to dominate the debate with no possibility of fact-checking. Advocacy regarding the LRA has primarily been focused on Kony as the undisputed centre of the conflict whose movements and decisions determine its continuation or end. He has been portrayed by insiders and outsiders alike as a spirit-possessed leader of charisma and brutality who has fought the war fuelled by a mixture of spiritual force, religious extremism and outside military support. Of all of these, his reported spirituality usually fascinates most.

Yet generally the assessment of Kony's role has been based on hearsay, with little consideration or evidence of Kony's own perspective or that of other active members of the LRA. Part of Kony's appeal and his ability to evoke fear lay in his invisibility, a rebel leader characterised only in the stories of those who had escaped. The invisibility of the main actor also made the LRA war seem pointless, confused and lacking a coherent agenda beyond being a thorn in the side of the government at the expense of civilians. Stories of Kony's mysterious strength and unspeakable brutality made the descriptions of this ghost-like figure even more powerful and the use of fear became a strategic 'force multiplier', as Vinci calls it, for the LRA.[184] Kony's spirituality and his presumed madness were readily picked up by international organisations and advocates to drive often hugely successful fundraising campaigns, in a fine example of what

---

[183] For a discussion on definitions of rape, see Porter (2012; 2016). For statistics on rape of civilians, see Annan et al. (2009).

[184] Vinci (2005).

Giorgio Agamben calls the commodification of evil and the messianic.[185] Professional consideration of what some claimed was a serious psychiatric condition was shambolic. Engagement with background spiritual beliefs or the notion that Kony was 'evil' was righteous and lacked insight.[186] Roland Marchal has called out this mechanism, writing that in the labelling of conflict actors, 'moralistic judgements obscure analysis'.[187]

The focus on Kony as the sole responsible actor means there is little mainstream analysis of group behaviour, or of the individual choices by LRA actors. A pop-culture focus on Kony as the root of all evil has blurred understanding of the broader context. Both the LRA and those describing the conflict have commodified these fleeting characteristics to avoid taking apart the personal and societal issues at the heart of the conflict. Presuming that Kony's military might stems from transcendental inspiration creates the perfect straw-man argument that no analysis is possible or necessary because divine forces are at work. As a broader problem, because of lack of data, most developments were analysed as if macro-level events, such as the behaviour of the GoU or the issuing of ICC warrants, could deliver direct explanations of micro-level, individual LRA behaviour.[188]

In a conflict that involves armed rebellion against a government, empirical information on the rebel perspective tends to be rare. David Cunningham and Douglas Lemke argue that a lack of systematic information is absent in civil wars, hence creating a focus on the state.[189] While the interest in the LRA war has often focussed on the LRA – with a lot less attention being paid to the GoU or the UPDF – it was the case that until 2006 the only primary data available on the thinking within the LRA was provided by those who had left the LRA. Presumably, they had also left behind some of their motivations – if they had stayed voluntarily – for being in the LRA. As much of the literature on the LRA was driven by agency-funded research reports, this has largely led to the cherry-picking of evidence to underscore previously held assumptions and programming goals. Agency research also requires certain visibility of both issue

---

[185] Agamben (1993).
[186] An example is Vinci's treatment of Kony's spirituality (Vinci 2006: 83) Vinci treats the idea that soldiers are given protection through spirituality as exotic. However, soldiers in many cultures have relied on talismans for protection (Holmes 1970: 238).
[187] Marchal (2007).
[188] Uvin makes this point about the unbalanced use of evidence (Uvin 2001: 98).
[189] Cunningham and Lemke (2013).

and findings, which is achieved more powerfully through anecdotes, giving much greater presence to powerful individual stories of victims.[190]

With a rebel leader silent on political causes and a government pushing the propaganda that the northern rebellion was nothing but a violent fight without reason – and the press largely following that line of thinking – the war was effectively depoliticised outside more nuanced scholarship, which is a phenomenon with regards to wars that was also observed in the 1990s.[191] This was echoed, for example, in remarks of the then-UN High Commissioner for Human Rights, Louise Arbour, who called the LRA a 'well-armed criminal enterprise' that did not have 'any kind of political agenda' and ought not to be 'romanticized'.[192] Maybe ironically or prophetically, it has indeed become the case that in the past few years, the link between war and organised crime is strengthening. Yet remarks such as Arbour's are characteristic for the Manichean view of the conflict – a view that had infused understanding of it at each stage of war, peace and information. The dualism was also emphasised by the ICC's engagement. Overall, it is in this prevalent interpretation that an explanation can be found for why the first months of the Juba Talks struggled with establishing a level playing field for negotiations.

2.8   Continuing Continuum

Much has been written on the LRA war, peace and information, yet rarely as if the three elements are working on a continuum. Mostly, efforts at making peace tend to be seen in isolation and as if these are moments to reset the conflict. Understanding of conflicts is gradually changing, as they are seen in the context of long trajectories. However, peace efforts that occur along the way tend to be treated as exceptional situations that take the conflict away from its usual nature, rather than simply as an extension or variation of the conflict. Such understanding was rarely applied in the more public discourse in Juba.

A look at the history of LRA war and peace shows that moments of peace were integral elements of the conflict, including the continuation of conflict dynamics around the table. Yet when the Juba Talks started in 2006, they were widely – and mistakenly – treated as a blank slate. There was hardly any debate or analysis on what roles the actors who were now gathered in Juba had played in previous efforts at peacemaking and on what kind of information they were drawing. Instead, actors such as the various international organisations, the mediator and the conflict parties largely succeeded in casting themselves in a fresh light – with the LRA in

---

[190] One of the more influential early reports is Gersony (1997).
[191] Allen and Seaton (1999).   [192] Inner City Press (2007).

the bush the notable exception. One reason for this might be found in their previous experiences with the LRA/M, which had all ended in the LRA withdrawing from the engagement. A later chapter shines a light on how the LRA/M uses this dynamic of connecting and disconnecting with outsiders to its advantage. Although this pattern was familiar to almost everyone in Juba, it was not addressed constructively. While there was initially a public focus on the root causes and the broader history of the war, the same attention was not given to lessons learned from previous peace negotiations.

Right away, this created a parallel reality between the LRA/M and everyone else. Most actors wanted to treat the Juba Talks as a clean slate to finally get the conflict resolved. For the LRA/M the Juba Talks were only another chapter in the long trajectory of the conflict and with that also a moment in which previous treatment specifically during peace processes needed to be addressed as part of paying attention to root causes. They were not surprised when the first year of the Juba Talks brought a repeat of previously experienced security concerns for LRA fighters called to assemble for peace negotiations. From the beginning, 2006 replicated hostile power dynamics that the LRA/M had wanted to tackle.

3 The Juba Peace Talks with the Lord's Resistance Army in 2006
'While Talking, There Is Troop Movement'

On 12 July 2006, two days before the scheduled opening ceremony, a group of Acholi diaspora sympathisers, participants of previous talks, and a former NRM political candidate were finding their feet to become the LRA/M delegation. Then they heard that a minister would head the GoU delegation and that Museveni had extended his deadline for LRA disarmament to 12 September. Some LRA/M delegates argued that peace talks under these circumstances would be a waste of time, instead suggesting a trip to The Hague to hand-deliver LRA evidence against Museveni and the UPDF to the ICC. They expected the ICC to look at the evidence and decide that the LRA had a point. Others felt that it was better to strengthen the process with as many representatives from northern Uganda as possible. Things grew complicated when the flipside to both approaches became obvious. Calling for justice also meant subjecting the LRA to justice; calling in more support from civil society also meant diluting the power of a delegation billed as the exclusive voice for Kony, and bringing in people who might hold grievances against both government and LRA.[1] Yet, the delegates seemed largely convinced that commitment to peace talks would bring concessions, with the ICC exonerating the LRA in the face of evidence against the government, and all northern Ugandans agreeing with the LRA.

Out of these debates emerged Olweny's fiery and divisive opening speech that made the point that past peace talks had in the end always been betrayed and had created more military pressure and thus further militarised Uganda. After this rocky start to the Juba Talks, 2006 was marked by clashing expectations, baggage from previous talks and muddled information; these were the developing dynamics that would mark the experience of the LRA/M of entering peace talks. Over everything hung the permanent threat of failure of the talks. Measures of success were very narrow indeed and the consequence of this narrow

---

[1] Wallensteen and Eriksson (2009). On the dilemma of being both victim and perpetrator, see also Mergelsberg (2010: 172); Baines (2009).

70

conceptualisation soon became obvious: the peace talks became an either/or between war and peace.

3.1   First on the Agenda: Ending Hostilities

When the LRA/M delegation arrived in Juba, GoSS – having moved to Juba in late 2005 – had just started to buy government cars, which were often the only cars on the unpaved roads of the capital, apart from a few scattered NGO or UN vehicles. The young government was struggling to find accommodation for its parliamentarians. A few aid workers and engineers lived in tented or prefabricated camps; SPLA officers or SPLM politicians occupied many of Juba's limited hotel rooms. After 6 p.m., when the BBC's *Focus on Africa* jingle had wafted from dozens of shortwave radios, it was difficult to get dinner in the markets or in the handful of restaurants. International staff, hungry for anything that did not come from a US$15 hotel buffet, made weekly pilgrimages to a corner supermarket on Hai Malakal, known to be the only one in town selling Diet Coke, Snickers bars and Heinz baked beans.

The Juba Raha Hotel was a bamboo-covered building, located under the Juba airport flight path, with a dining hall and two meeting rooms, and initially a few dozen army tents serving as rooms. Later, the Juba Raha would upgrade to 'self-contained', offering green military tents on a concrete base with a porch in the front and a shower and toilet in the back for $260 per night. The weathered dartboard next to the TV in the bar declared that this was the 'Dart Palace Juba'. Several times a day, plane noise interrupted conversations but since plane arrivals were still a rare occurrence, patrons usually entered guessing games on whether they were hearing a World Food Programme plane, the daily passenger jet from Nairobi, or the president returning from Khartoum.[2]

The Juba Talks secretariat was also a military tent, furnished with a bed, printer, computer and photocopier, doubling as the residence of the head of the secretariat. Whenever the car sirens signalling the arrival of Machar's motorcade could be heard, whoever was staffing the secretariat jumped up to greet the Vice President while the handful of journalists from Uganda and beyond came running from Juba's most reliable satellite Internet café around the corner to catch a soundbite.

Unless the journalists caught the VP in these moments of arrival or departure, it was difficult for them to communicate with peace talks officials. Mobile networks were unreliable; the best one was offering calls

---

[2] Fieldnotes, Juba: 30 September 2006.

in southern Sudan under Uganda's country code, but SIM cards were always sold out. When calling, people stood outside and away from trees, shouting into satellite phones: 'Can you hear me? Can you hear me? I cannot hear you. Change your location'. The delegation spent many hours bellowing updates down the phone, communicating the complexities of the goings-on in Juba at US$1 a minute to Otti or Kony.[3]

A first step in the talks was to agree on an agenda. The GoU did not want to cease hostilities until an overall agreement was signed; the LRA/M insisted it was a prerequisite for further talks. The parties swiftly agreed to discuss issues in the following order: (1) Cessation of Hostilities (CoH); (2) Comprehensive Political Solutions; (3) Justice and Accountability; (4) Demobilisation, Disarmament and Reintegration; and (5) Permanent Ceasefire.

As negotiations got underway, the Juba Talks were discussed at the highest levels elsewhere. A few days after the opening ceremony, UN ambassadors of the so-called Core Group – Belgium, Germany, Ireland, the Netherlands, Norway, Sweden, the United Kingdom and Canada – met at the UN in New York, joined by the heads of the Department of Peacekeeping Operations (DPKO), the Office for the Coordination of Humanitarian Affairs (OCHA) and the Department of Political Affairs (DPA). It was disclosed that UN Secretary-General Kofi Annan had suggested former president of Mozambique, Joaquim Chissano, as a special envoy to the Juba Talks. The idea garnered support, with the participants discussing various awkward scenarios regarding the ICC, including the possibility that if the UN Mission in Sudan (UNMIS) were to arrest LRA leaders under an ICC warrant, 'they would have to be turned over to the Sudanese government for further action'.[4] International support for the Juba Talks was thus hesitant, but the UN was putting structures into place to allow them to be supported.

Back in Juba, the LRA/M delegation's lack of confidence in the talks was obvious. To stabilise negotiations and build confidence, Machar and GoSS organised a large gathering of family, leaders and politicians from northern Uganda in Ri-Kwangba in late July 2006. It was a last-ditch attempt to convince Kony or Otti to directly join the negotiations. The gathering also created curious scenes, some of which were later publicly regretted. Ugandan politician Norbert Mao, for example, was photographed as he enthusiastically hugged Kony. Kony gave two significant speeches. He apologised – in Acholi, to representatives from northern Uganda and southern Sudan – for atrocities committed by the LRA. On

[3] Fieldnotes, Juba: 30 September 2006.   [4] U.N. mission of the USA (2006).

2 August, he held a befuddled four-minute press conference, with the assembled international journalists shouting questions at him.[5]

3.2   Challenges in Ceasing Hostilities

The following day, Machar continued his mission to persuade Otti to join the delegation in Juba. He further insisted that the LRA needed to disclose their deployments in southern Sudan and northern Uganda, despite Kampala's insistence that there would be no ceasefire before a final agreement was signed. Otti's response expressed the level of distrust in the facilitation and environment: 'Why is Machar making my presence in Juba a condition? There must be something hidden. After all there are no guarantees that I won't be arrested'.[6] For the LRA leadership, the pressure to come to Juba was suspicious. For the delegation, hearing from Machar that he had no trust in their ability to speak for the LRA/M was embarrassing. The situation became heated, even as Machar backed down from his demands that the LRA disclose their troops. To publicly express their distrust in Machar, Kony and Otti ordered the four men on the delegation considered representatives of the military wing to remain in the bush. Machar left, taking with him the means of transport that had brought the delegates to the bush.

The delegates remained stranded in the bush for a few days, detained and questioned by the SPLA, who made no effort to hide their disliking of the LRA/M. One of the LRA/M delegates would later complain to Machar that this had been humiliating and had left one delegate – who had travelled with only a small quantity of prescription medication – with health troubles. On 4 August, with his delegates still stuck in Ri-Kwangba without GoSS transport, Kony ordered a unilateral ceasefire to counter Machar's distrust and express the LRA's seriousness. Rugunda was not ready to respond by doing the same: 'We will wait and see what it means on the ground because the previous ceasefires have been abused'. The next day, the LRA/M delegation returned to Juba without any military representation, furious about the treatment they had received. Yet it was announced that talks would resume on 7 August. Machar had in the meantime issued invitations to Mao and community leaders from northern Uganda to strengthen the talks by coming to Juba. For the LRA/M delegates, such a unilateral move was again an expression of Machar's lack of confidence in them.

---

[5] See Green (2008).   [6] Phone call to Vincent Otti, July 2006.

On 9 August, CoH was again on the table with the GoU insisting that hostilities would not cease. The LRA/M team was angry at Machar who they said had promised that the GoU would agree to cessation if the LRA/M returned to the talks, but now the GoU had failed to reciprocate.[7] Kampala described the LRA/M walkout as unfortunate; the press widely reported that the LRA was quitting the peace talks. The following day, Ugandan military chief, Aronda Nyakairima, said that the UPDF would 'pound Kony'. The GoU demanded that the LRA release captive women and children.[8]

The GoU also demanded that within one week the LRA spell out strength, positions and particulars of its forces, inventories of arms and ammunition and other military equipment. The GoU's position paper further proposed a ceasefire monitoring team composed of ten members led by a senior official appointed by GoSS and other members from the LRA, UPDF and SPLA, as well as the AU, UN and Core Group. The GoU also suggested at which locations the LRA was to assemble: Waligo in Uganda's Kitgum District, and Nabanga under the control of the SPLA.

The LRA/M was enraged at the pressure to disclose their forces without a declared CoH. Days went by without developments, until President Kiir on 11 August invited the LRA/M to his house. In a private conversation, he talked about the SPLA struggle and how the SPLA never made a ceasefire a condition during peace talks because they knew it would create an early impasse and give them fewer means to exert pressure. The LRA/M delegates afterwards said that Kiir's talk was 'very impressive and insightful'.[9] Negotiations about a CoH were back on, but the tone had markedly changed, at least for a short while.

The need to agree to end hostilities became acute when the UPDF announced that they had killed LRA commander Raska Lukwiya – one of the five LRA commanders wanted by the ICC – in Uganda. The LRA, waiting for Lukwiya to be identified by their own sources, considered this a ploy by the GoU to make them 'feel bad. We don't' want nail for a nail, eye for an eye, tooth for a tooth. We don't want to pull out, but this is not right'.[10] When they received positive identification of Lukwiya, the LRA/M asked for three days of mourning, returning to the table with black armbands. Olweny stated that in the interest of truth, the LRA would continue talks with the GoU delegation, even if the government refused to cease hostilities and despite the fact that Ugandan soldiers

---

[7] Nyakairu and Okiror (10 August 2006).   [8] Nyakairu and Okiror (10 August 2006).
[9] Fieldnotes, Juba: 11 August 2006.   [10] Fieldnotes, Juba: 12 September 2006.

had killed Lukwiya: 'We hope that all in good time the public shall put the blame where it lays'.[11]

Feeling betrayed by GoSS, and weakened by Lukwiya's death, Otti demanded that South Africa take over the mediation. Museveni rejected the demand outright, instead suggesting that the LRA should assemble in southern Sudan only, rather than also in Uganda, as a condition for the UPDF's CoH. Museveni also said that the DRC would allow the UPDF to attack the rebels in their DRC base in Garamba Park should peace talks fail.[12] When Kiir returned from a visit to Kampala with the renewed demand that the LRA disclose their troop deployments to allow monitoring, the LRA countered that they would only assemble if the UPDF declared its weapons of mass destruction. The UPDF shrugged this off: 'We have never owned, and we do not intend to own, any weapons of mass destruction', said UPDF Captain Paddy Ankunda, the government team's spokesman.[13]

On 24 August, Museveni reportedly emailed his delegates new terms for an agreement on CoH that required LRA fighters to assemble at designated points in southern Sudan, offered safe passage, agreed to a truce for fourteen days (renewable upon review), and mandated the SPLA to provide security at the assembly points. After the LRA/M agreed to concentrate its forces in two assembly points, the GoU proposed to cease hostilities as a first step and expression of goodwill.[14] Divided by the Nile and hundreds of miles apart, the two assembly points assured the GoU that the agreement would not simply allow the LRA to regroup all of its forces in one place. The Agreement on CoH was signed on 26 August 2006, to great fanfare.[15]

The breakthrough was astonishing. I asked the LRA/M delegates how they explained the sudden success, considering all the tension. Two delegates argued that they had to sign an agreement quickly to ensure that the Talks would continue. When asked why they thought the GoU had agreed to it, they explained that the GoU did not believe that LRA would assemble, thus signing the agreement was without consequences for them. I asked whether the LRA was genuine in its commitment to assemble. Of course, the delegates answered.[16]

In retrospect, the unexpected signing established a typical pattern – divergent dynamics between the process amongst the actors and the

---

[11] Kenyi (17 August 2006).   [12] Sudan Tribune and Daily Monitor (21 August 2006).
[13] Sudan Tribune and Daily Monitor (21 August 2006).
[14] Fieldnotes, Juba: 7 September 2006.
[15] The CoH was renewed five times: on 1 November 2006, 16 December 2006, 14 April 2007, 3 November 2007 and 30 January 2008.
[16] Fieldnotes, Juba: 7 September 2006.

process on paper – but it was too soon to recognise that. The LRA/M delegates considered the agreement necessary to move things forward, yet also argued that its meaning was diminished by GoU speculation that the agreement would be easy to dismiss. With one success under its belt, international actors were more inclined to give their support. Switzerland had been the first country to back the Juba initiative, even when success seemed extremely unlikely. As talks got underway, UNICEF joined the mediation team as the first UN agency, although struggling with how to enforce child protection while supporting negotiations. Other UN agencies and the Core Group countries came on board after the signing of the CoH,[17] with the aim, writes Quinn, to give moral and financial support.[18] The UN Security Council (UNSC) called on the conflict parties to be committed, to look for long-term solutions and to do so quickly, while also affirming its commitment to bringing the LRA leaders responsible for a war crime to justice.[19]

The international support was double-edged for the LRA/M who remained unsure of what position the donor countries would take vis-à-vis the ICC. Seeing more money being pledged allowed them to voice demands. Two days after signing the CoH, the delegation wrote to Machar, apologising for delivering papers late because of

failure to establish a well-manned secretariat with sufficient logistical support. We would appreciate if you would finance the establishment of a secretariat with resource persons with the capacity to fully utilise the Internet, carry out research and supply the Delegation with information, while at the same time coordinating us with the international community and our people at home. You may also wish to be reminded that up to now, we do not have internet service at our residence.[20]

3.3   Implementation Challenges

The CoH stipulated that by 18 September, all LRA forces needed to be assembled in either Owiny-Kibul in Eastern Equatoria or Ri-Kwangba in Western Equatoria.[21] Owiny-Kibul was easily accessible from Uganda and many of the LRA troops were said to be in Eastern Equatoria anyway; the leadership was already gathered in the vicinity of the second assembly site in Western Equatoria. The UPDF agreed to let LRA soldiers pass, withdraw its troops from near the assembly areas, and cease further

[17] Personal email to author from S. Simonse, IKV Pax Christi. 10 October 2007.
[18] Quinn (2009: 62).   [19] UN Security Council (2006).
[20] UN Security Council (2006).
[21] Government of the Republic of Uganda and Lord's Resistance Army/Movement (26 August 2006).

deployment in southern Sudan. The SPLA committed itself to providing protection for LRA in both assembly areas. How many LRA fighters were expected to emerge at the assembly sites was never clear: estimates ranged from 1,000 women and children to up to 15,000 combatants, a number that was provided by the LRA/M.[22] The agreement further created a Cessation of Hostilities Monitoring Team (CHMT) with representation of the LRA, UPDF, SPLA and AU.

The day after the signing, UPDF Colonel Otema instructed troops via northern Uganda's Mega FM: 'I have received communication from the president that beginning this morning at 6 a.m., we should suspend operations against the LRA rebels to allow them to move to the designated areas for peace talks'.[23] The UPDF announced ten safe corridors in Gulu, Kitgum and Pader to 'separate the LRA from some other criminals, who might take advantage of the situation'.[24] Museveni declared: 'It is hereby directed that the UPDF should withdraw to their barracks and to the guarding of internally displaced people. They should not shoot at the LRA unless in defence of the population'.[25] Otti followed suit, announcing on Mega FM that LRA fighters were to meet the two main field commanders – Ongwen and Caesar Achellam – and proceed under their command to the assembly points.[26] On their way, LRA was neither to abduct, kill, harass nor commit any violent act against civilians nor attack the UPDF.[27] Instead, Otti pleaded with civilians:

But I also ask the civilians to allow these fighters to get some food from their gardens as they move to assemble, and this would be the last time to do this because we are sure of the positive outcome of the peace talks .... But you, as Acholi people and Ugandans, should have a close watch on those opportunists who may be interested in spoiling the peace. I know they are out there, very many and some would begin to do things that would spoil our name but tell them it is now time for peace in our land.[28]

When the CoH Agreement came into effect at 6 a.m. on 29 August 2006, crowds of people paraded through Gulu waving white flags. Flags were also planted along major roads and UPDF General Katumba Wamala handed one to a son of Kony who lived in Gulu.[29] Northern Ugandans perceived the intention to cease hostilities as a major achievement. The

---

[22] Sudan, UNICEF (2006).   [23] Ocowun (29 August 2006).
[24] Ocowun (30 August 2006).   [25] Wasike (29 August 2006).
[26] AP (28 August 2006). Ugandan forces captured Caesar Achellam in the Central African Republic on 12 May 2012.
[27] Wasike (29 August 2006).   [28] Ojwee and Lubangakene (28 August 2006).
[29] Okot (31 August 2006).

LRA now had two weeks until 12 September to assemble before the CoH was to be reviewed again. The tight deadline also put the required assembly close to the government's deadline for the successful conclusion of the Juba Talks, which the GoU had now declared for 18 September 2006.

The journeys of LRA fighters produced news of highly symbolic value. The Ugandan parliament endorsed a resolution commending the great successes so far in the Juba Talks. A few Ugandan MPs asked the ICC to revoke the warrants against the LRA's top leadership,[30] a request the ICC rebuffed, saying that they would not act on rushed 'speculation' that the talks might succeed.[31] Instead, the ICC reacted a few days later by ordering an urgent investigation into Uganda's efforts to arrest Kony and others, arguing that such efforts were vital for the prevention of further crimes. The ICC insisted that the GoU submit a written report by 6 October.[32]

Meanwhile, Ongwen, a man on the ICC's wanted list who would years later find himself on trial at the ICC, celebrated a friendly encounter at Barayomo/Lacekcot junction on 3 September 2006, with the UPDF 509th Brigade commander. Looking on as the enemies shook hands were Gulu Resident District Commissioner (RDC) Walter Ochora, Pader RDC Santa Okot Lapolo, and Bishop Onono-Onweng, who had brought 200 kilos of beans, 200 kilos of *posho* [maize porridge] and 20 litres of cooking oil to sustain Ongwen's troops on their way to Owiny-Kibul.[33] The UPDF proposed to load the LRA fighters on their trucks and drive them towards the border, but Otti came on the airwaves to reject such assistance, ordering his soldiers to reject offers of transport from the SPLA or the UPDF: 'All LRA fighters and commanders will have to walk to the assembling areas. Our legs are our vehicles'.[34]

3.4   Approaching the Assembly Deadline

The enthusiasm after the promising first steps was short-lived. Within days, the LRA/M announced that Owiny-Kibul was after all not suitable as it was heavily mined. The claim could never be substantiated,[35] but the choice of Owiny-Kibul was debated again. An assessment by UN agencies articulated some of the logistical challenges of preparing the

---

[30] Mutumba, Natabaalo and Muhumuza (8 September 2006).
[31] Muhumuza and Gyezaho (7 September 2006).
[32] The New Vision (26 September 2006).
[33] Ocowun and Mukiibi (4 September 2006); Egadu et al. (5 September 2006).
[34] Mutumba, Natabaalo and Muhumuza (8 September 2006).
[35] A local chief said to his knowledge there was no problem with mines in the area.

Figure 3.1 Vincent Otti and Dominic Ongwen, July 2007

assembly areas adequately: 'Air and road transport constraints', lack of 'qualified staffing and availability in the very short term' as well as 'staff security and psycho-social well-being' and 'landmines and other UXO [Unexploded Ordinances] that may be in surrounding areas'.[36]

While Ongwen and the UPDF engaged in handshakes, the GoU delegation returned to negotiations in Juba with two people who had been mutilated by the LRA. The display of victims outraged the LRA/M delegation. One delegate said, 'Getting the victims is bad taste. Who are the perpetrators?'[37] The LRA/M retaliated by distributing a photograph: It showed a naked woman lying on the ground with her arms restrained; a UPDF soldier is pinning her legs apart while holding a razor to her crotch.[38] The woman was identified as Candida Lakony, with the picture reportedly taken in 1999.[39] With this picture, the LRA/M wanted to counter the GoU's move of bringing victims into the negotiations, to remind everyone in Juba that the army was also a perpetrator of crimes against civilians.[40]

---

[36] UN System Southern Sudan (2006).   [37] Fieldnotes, Juba: 6 September 2006.

[38] Fieldnotes, Juba: 7 September 2006.

[39] The picture and the accompanying story had been published in the *Daily Monitor* in mid-1999. The story purported that none of the soldiers in the photograph had been charged; Candida Lakony was imprisoned on charges of theft and later giving false information to the police. I have not been able to verify whether the purported UN document from 1999 is real (Matsiko 9 September 2006) and Democratic Republic of Congo Permanent Mission United Nations. 1999. 'Torture by Ugandan soldiers – Worse than animals', June 20 (unpublished).

[40] Fieldnotes, Juba: 6 September 2006.

On 11 September, Egeland visited Juba on an official OCHA mission to discuss the humanitarian aspects of the Juba Talks during negotiations and beyond. It had become clear that dispensing funds through the UN systems was going to be a challenge, and OCHA had taken on the responsibility. In a meeting with NGOs in Juba, Egeland also asked for project ideas to support the peace talks. None of the NGOs responded.

Meanwhile, reports of LRA troops moving towards Owiny-Kibul continued to trickle through, but progress was slow. On 13 September, Otti's unhappiness with government pressure to conclude the talks was obvious:

You know I am telling you clearly listeners [of Mega FM], peace talks have no date. If he [Museveni] says the talks are expiring, I don't know what he is saying. It may be expiring on their side but not on our side because we are still continuing talking peace. You cannot say that you can talk peace and finish today while even one agenda among the five agendas has been signed just recently. The second agenda has not yet started. Now I don't understand the meaning when you say, expiry date.[41]

On 14 September, Otti came on the radio again to announce that the GoU also had to extend its 18 September deadline for the peace talks, otherwise he would order all assembled fighters to disperse so as to not be attacked unawares if the UPDF should adhere to the peace talks deadline rather than the assembly deadline, which had been extended to 21 September. Otti further declared that he and Kony would disappear from Ri-Kwangba if the deadlines were not clarified.[42]

On 17 September, delegates, facilitators and journalists went to Ri-Kwangba to see the progress of the LRA assembly. When the plane touched down in Maridi, there were no cars waiting and it seemed that UN peacekeepers had not been alerted of the arrival. Hours later, the swiftly hired cars pulled into Ri-Kwangba, in what previously had been a humble clearing in the dense forest. The clearing was now expanded to about 400 metres wide. A few huts were sprinkled across and a few logs had been arranged into a seating area. LRA commander Colonel Bwone and Lieutenant Colonel Santo Alit were in charge.

When asked whether the LRA was now getting settled here and how many there were, Bwone was cagey: 'Don't mind about numbers, don't mind about our time here. Don't mind'. He seemed uncomfortable in the new Ri-Kwangba, eyeing both the provisional CHMT and the journalists suspiciously. Alit was more at ease. 'This is now our headquarter', he said, waving his arms. Lubwoa interrupted him, clearly irked by the

---

[41] Otti (13 September 2006).   [42] Ocowun (14 September 2006).

description and the situation. 'Yes, this is what we have been given. This is now our country ... I came here to announce liberation'.[43] Before walking off he said 'We have better food if we go to the bush'.[44] An LRA/M press release later articulated his concerns: 'No medical facilities, no water, no beddings, no tents; most of the food that was delivered is rotten'.[45]

On 21 September – assembly deadline day – a group of junior LRA holding watch in Ri-Kwangba, among them Sunday Otto, complained to the press that conditions in Ri-Kwangba were still not conducive. Otto walked reporters to the only water supply: a muddy puddle.[46] Nonetheless, the SPLA head of the CHMT told reporters at a makeshift press conference that 804 LRA had assembled in Ri-Kwangba, and that he was satisfied that the LRA had fulfilled the requirements of the CoH. Both SPLA and journalists then returned to the SPLA detachment in Nabanga.

Two hours later, a Reuters journalist wanted to follow up with a few more questions and was surprised that the CHMT leader had revised his assessment: 'The LRA have not assembled; there is a violation of the ceasefire. The mediator will have to decide what to do next. Kampala will extend the deadline for assembly'. He explained that 804 fighters had assembled, but three more large groups would arrive the following day.[47] The LRA/M reacted in a radio interview to reports about this confusion: Olweny stated that conditions did not allow an assembly, stressing that the CoH allowed a two-week grace period. Museveni responded in an interview on Mega FM, calling the LRA a terrorist outfit that would be finished. Ugandan Acholi leaders protested his belligerent language.[48]

The following day, the SPLA head of the CHMT consulted with the LRA in Ri-Kwangba. Otti, angry about the reports that the LRA had not assembled, stated that the SPLA was 'sympathetic to the UPDF. You reported that we violated the ceasefire when we did not. I was here and the chairman [Kony] was also here in Ri-Kwangba', to which the head of the CHMT answered: 'It is true the UPDF are our allies. You [LRA] were our enemies. We fought you but all this has been put behind us. We want this war to end. So do not doubt our commitment'.[49] In a short press conference given by Otti with Odhiambo by his side, Otti stated

---

[43] Fieldnotes, Ri-Kwangba: 17 September 2006.
[44] Fieldnotes, Ri-Kwangba: 17 September 2006.
[45] LRA/M delegation in Juba (23 September 2006).
[46] Fieldnotes, Nabanga/Ri-Kwangba: 21 September 2006.
[47] Fieldnotes, Nabanga/Ri-Kwangba: 21 September 2006.
[48] Moro and Ocowun (26 September 2006).
[49] The Daily Monitor (23 September 2006).

that he would sign a peace deal before the ICC warrants were lifted as long as it was signed in Nabanga, but that no LRA fighter would leave the bush as long as the warrants stood. He said that the remaining women and children were all family members, so they would stay with the fighters.[50]

Museveni responded to the latest news coming out of Nabanga, saying that the ICC warrants would need to remain in place:

> The ICC ... indictments have to continue until the LRA leaders fully embrace the peace talks ... How do you ask for safety from the ICC when you haven't given safety to Ugandans? ... You have to give safety to Ugandans first. If you don't do that, you will die.[51]

He was irritated that the talks were taking too long, and also that the set-up by which he had to call Rugunda and Rugunda then had to call Kony was too complicated. Museveni's solution was to come to Juba to lead the government team himself.[52] Otti commented on this declaration in a private conversation:

> If Museveni wants to come and join the peace talks in Juba, let him fight with Martin [Ojul, the chairman of the LRA/M delegation]. Let him have it out with Martin. Why does Museveni want to come to Juba, does he not trust his own delegation? I am only sending two military men for the monitoring team. It actually means I have a lot of trust in my delegation.[53]

Upon return to Juba on 23 September, the LRA/M delegation held an impromptu press conference in the Juba Airport VIP Lounge. Krispus Ayena Odongo – as the main speaker – demanded that the GoU delegation be changed from mainly military and security personnel to a political delegation. He announced that an estimated 7,000 LRA would assemble and that all UPDF troops stationed around Owiny-Kibul had to withdraw in order for talks to continue. This was a direct order from Kony, who, Ayena said, had in the past month travelled to Owiny-Kibul to inspect the conditions and the presence of UPDF troops there. The announcement that Kony had secretly travelled across southern Sudan's Equatorial states caused great confusion.[54] Most journalists and the GoU delegation dismissed it as impossible, yet Machar – who had received reports that the LRA had been crossing the Nile without notifying the SPLA, in violation of the CoH – said he thought 'it is possible that Kony crossed, too'. He explained later that he had 'told them off for letting Kony go because if something happens to him now it

---

[50] Fieldnotes, Ri-Kwangba: 22 September 2006.   [51] Reuters (20 September 2006).
[52] Kwera (22 September 2006).   [53] Fieldnotes, Juba: 7 September 2006.
[54] Fieldnotes, Juba: 23 September 2006.

is a really bad thing to happen'.[55] The same day, the LRA/M issued a press release that contradicted the findings that the LRA had not assembled in Ri-Kwangba:

While at Ri-Kwangba, the chairman of the Cessation of Hostilities Monitoring Team, Maj. Gen. Wilson Deng, visited the designated Assembly area, where he found all the top commanders and more than 1,848 members of the LRA combatants now assembled. He was fully briefed about the inadequate preparations in the area, where there is [*sic*] no medical facilities, no water, no beddings, no tents; most of the food that was delivered is rotten; etc. This shall definitely impede the arrival of roughly 7,940 combatants unless it is urgently addressed.[56]

3.5   Talks Continue amidst Confusion

On 25 September 2006, the third round of talks started. The LRA/M issued a press statement, claiming that the increased UPDF deployment near the assembly areas posed a grave threat to the Juba Talks.[57] The UPDF countered that the army was ready to attack should the LRA fail to keep its side of the CoH bargain.[58] Otti commented a day later that the UPDF should not provoke the LRA: 'Don't play with war'.[59] The LRA/M asked for a seven-day deadline for the UPDF to withdraw, and called on the international community to provide aid to fighters in assembly areas.[60] When the US Senate passed a bill to support the Juba Peace process, for a brief moment such aid seemed possible.[61] Despite all obstacles, the Juba Talks were riding a wave of support.

It was thus jolting when news arrived about a UPDF military convoy travelling unauthorised towards Owiny-Kibul. The SPLA in Juba said that they had no knowledge of such a convoy, implying that the LRA/M's accusation of UPDF movement was unfounded. A delegate countered the SPLA line:

Since we have our information from our people, our moles in the UPDF and local people, we know it is true. The GoSS says it is not true. What can that mean? Either they are complicit with the UPDF or they are not capable of controlling their territory. Both is worrying.[62]

---

[55] Author interview with Riek Machar, Vice President of the Government of Southern Sudan, Juba: 26 September 2006.
[56] LRA/M delegation in Juba (23 September 2006).
[57] Fieldnotes, Juba: 25 September 2006.   [58] AFP (25 September 2006).
[59] Gyezaho, Harera and Matsiko (27 September 2006).   [60] LRA/M (2006).
[61] The Senate of the United States (2006).   [62] Fieldnotes, Juba: 27 September 2006.

At first, the story seemed to suggest that a group of journalists had travelled to Owiny-Kibul to see the assembled LRA, but had been turned back by the UPDF, who claimed that Ongwen and his men had left the Owiny-Kibul assembly point on 25 September.[63] The first version of the story said that UPDF soldiers had argued with the journalists that their safety could not be guaranteed now that the LRA was at large again.[64] UPDF spokesman, Felix Kulayigye, was quoted as saying: 'We were let down by the SPLA which was supposed to pick us from Ngomoromo but they didn't. We proceeded with our own UPDF protection up to Pajok with hope that we could find more SPLA protection but that wasn't the case'.[65]

In Juba, these news snippets caused confusion. Had the LRA left Owiny-Kibul? Was the UPDF moving troops towards the area? The LRA/M delegates insisted that their fighters had informed them of heavy UPDF deployment around the area; the story about the group of journalists was yet another incomprehensible element. A leading delegate was concerned: 'I do not want to have blood on my hands. I did not start the peace talks for these people to gather in the assembly points, to bring their women and children to be killed'.[66] Conjuring up the Acholi experience of being forced into camps, one LRA commander said he was worried that 'the fighters will be kept in concentration camp conditions at the assembly points'.[67] When the BBC called the unprotected bushland at Owiny-Kibul a 'reception centre' and reported that the LRA had broken the CoH agreement, without mentioning the information on alleged UPDF deployment, the LRA/M delegates in Juba were again enraged.[68] A few weeks later, the Acholi Parliamentary Group (APG) issued a report about their visit to Juba, stating that there was a feeling in Juba that 'Ugandan newspapers are the worst enemy of the peace process'.[69]

Within the delegation, the mood was volatile. Some remained convinced that the CoH would be adhered to; others argued that hiccups were to be expected. The whole delegation remained adamant that the UPDF had deployed. On 28 September, the LRA/M delegation presented a thirty-three-second video clip of a UPDF military vehicle, a

---

[63] Reuters (27 September 2006).
[64] Matsiko, Nyakairu and Gyezaho (28 September 2006); Wasike (27 September 2006).
[65] Matsiko, Nyakairu and Gyezaho (28 September 2006).
[66] Fieldnotes, Juba: 27 September 2006.   [67] Fieldnotes, Juba: 12 September 2006.
[68] Grainger (27 September 2006).
[69] Acholi MPs insisted that this statement coincided with another Reuters report on the LRA violation of the CoH that failed to mention that it would be officially established that both UPDF and SPLA had also broken the agreement (Reuters 13 October 2006).

mamba, to the mediator, claiming that the footage had been taken a few days earlier in Sudan. Machar responded with a quip: 'I did not know we had such good roads in Sudan'. Gulu District Chairman and former MP, Norbert Mao, who had been present during the showing, made fun of the huge billing the LRA/M had given to the few seconds of disputed footage.[70] He laughed about Olweny's interview on the BBC in which he had said that the LRA had 'video clips' of UPDF deployment. Another LRA delegate was listening quietly to Mao's amused depiction of the LRA/M's PR manoeuvre. Finally, he responded: 'That's the war of the words'. In the end, he also laughed when Mao concluded that the LRA/M reminded him of the Iraqi propaganda minister Al-Sahaf who, in commenting while being under US fire, 'kept claiming ... "we are pounding them, we are pounding them"'.[71]

Other LRA/M delegates were less light-hearted. They saw familiar dynamics developing. One of the delegates described how tired he was of the GoU presenting a set of conditions for the talks and their outcome to the outside world as if these were negotiations. In his argument, the talks had not yet moved beyond the government setting the rules, thus limiting political debate. 'The GoU delegation uses the same words, I wait for them every day', he said, shrugging. '"Amnesty, soft landing, deadline and expeditious"'.[72]

Although UPDF military deployment and the challenges of assembling were unresolved, the LRA/M moved to present a twenty-six-page document on comprehensive solutions, demanding that the LRA would become the north's army in the interim and that both forces be given 'equal consideration and treatment as Uganda's national armies'[73] until the force was fully integrated. The GoU outright rejected this. In Kampala, Museveni announced that Uganda would contribute US$1 million to the Juba Peace Talks.[74] The day after the LRA/M had presented its document on comprehensive solutions, the Ugandan papers reported that negotiations continued, but also that the LRA/M had threatened to abandon peace talks if the UPDF did not withdraw from southern Sudan, and that the LRA/M would review their position on this within seven days. A confidential letter from Uganda's State House to Kiir claimed that all LRA had left the assembly areas on Kony's orders, a statement which Otti denied right away: 'We have not instructed anyone to withdraw from the assembly point. But because of the impending

---

[70] Mao would go on to challenge President Museveni in the elections of 2011 as leader of the Democratic Party of Uganda and has been the Party's leader since.
[71] Fieldnotes, Juba: 30 September 2006.   [72] Fieldnotes, Juba: 30 September 2006.
[73] Mukasa and Wasike (1 October 2006).   [74] Allio (28 September 2006).

situation where we are being surrounded by the UPDF, when this situation continues I will ask them [LRA fighters] to take care of themselves'.[75] Machar stated to the delegation that increased UPDF deployment had been observed near the border, but not inside Sudan.[76]

3.6   Peace Talks Conditions

Throughout this time, the LRA/M delegates were staying in the Juba Bridge Hotel, located on a downward-sloping left turn just before the bridge across the Nile. At first, the hotel was a muddy patch with prefabricated containers behind a bamboo gate. Heavy vehicles had left huge track marks that rain turned into puddles and drinking fountains for goats. Someone somewhere in the compound was always hammering or drilling, with the owner calling this his bit to 'build the peace'. The LRA/M delegates rolled their eyes at this suggestion. They lived in prefabricated rooms with communal washing areas with erratic showers and toilet flushes.

When it was raining, an occasional mango crashing down on the corrugated iron roofs would punctuate the steady drumming of the drops. I was sitting with two delegates under the thatched roof of the bar area, waiting for the rain to stop, when we heard several close thumps in short succession. We all jumped. The two delegates regained their composure much quicker than I did. I was still clasping my heart while they laughed, pointed at the smashed mango on the ground and joked: 'We are under attack now! See, we are under attack, but the LRA is in peace! Wherever we go, we are not safe! We are under attack. Even in peace talks, we are under attack!'[77]

A few weeks later, the delegates lost their sense of humour about mangoes masquerading as artillery. The SPLA raided some of the hotel rooms, finding stacks of AK-47s and ammunition. Hundreds of them, an SPLA soldier said vaguely, maybe more. Hotel staff who had seen a suspicious truck unloading dubious cargo had tipped off the SPLA. The truck's driver was a former SAF soldier who was now part of a Joint Integrated Unit – CPA-mandated units of SPLA and SAF meant to facilitate withdrawal of SAF forces from southern Sudan. After seizing the weapons, the SPLA was vocal about who they saw as the culprit. A stack of weapons in the LRA hotel, delivered by SAF soldiers? It seemed obvious that the LRA was 'preparing for war'. The Ugandan press corps was also convinced that the LRA/M was now using the

---

[75] Matsiko, Nyakairu and Gyezaho (28 September 2006).
[76] Fieldnotes, Juba: 28 September 2006.   [77] Fieldnotes, Juba: 12 September 2006.

negotiations to launch an attack on Juba; they reported it as evidence that the LRA was 'not serious'.

Further investigation brought to light that SAF had stolen the weapons from the SPLA, with SAF securing extra arms as they were moving out of Juba. The Juba Bridge Hotel must have seemed an easy place to use for storage. The SPLA security and surveillance had slipped up and the delegation was outraged at this breach of their personal safety. 'These weapons', one delegate said, 'could have easily been used against us'. One delegate said that the suggestion that all guns in Juba's volatile environment were connected to the LRA, rather than to intra-Sudanese tension, meant a limited understanding of the challenges that arose in establishing peace, even after a peace deal had been signed. This had implications for the LRA/M too: 'Sudan is not in peace, even though they are supposed to be. So it is extremely volatile for peace negotiations, it is very easy to shake things up'.[78]

Security at the hotel where the LRA/M were staying was beefed up. Cars were stopped at the now locked bamboo gate. Bags were searched and torches shone into the eyes of drivers. It was a step up for the Juba Bridge Hotel, but a long way behind security at other camps: at Civicon, where the GoU delegation was residing, the guards wrote down car registration numbers and asked for ID from all passengers.[79] A few days after the incident, a senior GoSS representative came to see Ojul over lunch to apologise. 'I think we have mishandled the situation', he explained. Ojul accepted the apology generously, if a bit patronisingly, and turned to me as soon as the representative had left. 'GoSS knows they screwed up', he said. 'Such thing could derail the peace process but we are here for peace. But how they do this, this is not peace. We are not moving in peace now. I don't think this is what peace should look like'.[80]

3.7 The Cessation of Hostilities Monitoring Team Fact-Finding Mission

On 1 October, the hastily constituted CHMT left on its first fact-finding mission seeking to answer whether the parties to the CoH had violated the agreement. The LRA/M representatives insisted that this was not a full mission, as international representatives had not yet joined the team. Crucially for the LRA/M, the CHMT had not been given uniforms. While the convoy waited for them, the LRA/M representatives bought identical clothing in the market to show, as they said, that they were

---

[78] Fieldnotes, Juba: 30 September 2006.   [79] Fieldnotes, Juba: 30 September 2006.
[80] Fieldnotes, Juba: 30 September 2006.

'professional'. Led by international technical advisor Anton Baaré and accompanied by a few journalists – and me – the team left for Owiny-Kibul on 1 October.

Travelling through Magwi to arrive in Owiny-Kibul the following day, the CHMT waited to make contact with the scattered LRA forces, discussed what the exact boundaries of the assembly area were, and met with the SPLA and the local chief to establish what had happened here in the past few days. Both the SPLA and the chief confirmed that the LRA had been present in the area and had come to collect some of the food delivered by the SPLA in preparation for the assembly, but that they had left just a few days prior to the CHMT's visit. Both mentioned that a UPDF convoy had chased the LRA away. The LRA/M representatives argued that their people had stuck to the agreement but had been forced away by the UPDF. The UPDF pointed out that the LRA was nowhere to be found at Owiny-Kibul; hence they had broken the agreement. The latest information from LRA commander Achellam had been that the LRA were in the immediate vicinity but had to remain hidden because of the UPDF.[81] The CHMT agreed to wait until the morning to see if the LRA forces in the area would make contact.

While everyone was getting ready for the night, news from Kampala came on the radio: the UPDF announced that it was resuming operations against the LRA immediately because the CHMT had conclusively established that the rebels were not assembled. UPDF's spokesperson Kulayigye announced that the UPDF had closed all safe routes to the assembly areas:

Our team of observers in Owiny-Kibul have confirmed there is no presence of LRA at that assembling point. They have abused the Cessation of Hostilities Agreement. For that matter, we are back to war because we do not know their motive and where they are. We are back to business. It's business as usual. We are looking for the LRA. It is because of the development that we have resumed operations against the LRA.[82]

Simultaneously, it was reported that Museveni had contacted US President George W. Bush to ask for support a military 'Plan B'.[83] Tensions between LRA and UPDF representatives on the CHMT were unsurprisingly high.

The next morning, 3 October 2006, Otti called the CHMT technical advisor to tell him that the LRA fighters could no longer make contact with the CHMT at Owiny-Kibul because the UPDF had announced that

---

[81] Fieldnotes, Magwi: 2 October 2006.
[82] Ahimbisibwe (3 October 2006); Reuters (4 October 2006).
[83] Matia (5 October 2006).

they would target the LRA. While the CHMT continued to travel towards Palotaka and Pajok, Museveni met with John Edwards, the former North Carolina senator, at State House in Kampala. Museveni reportedly said that unless a comprehensive peace agreement was signed soon, Uganda was expecting US support for a military plan. He hinted that such a plan was already underway since 'the peace talks might improve Kony's life expectancy, but cannot fix an insurgency'. State House released a statement that Edwards had promised to lobby for the passing of a resolution that would allow the pursuit, disarmament and demobilisation of the LRA.[84]

In Pajok, the CHMT settled down for a meeting with local residents to shed light on the incident involving the UPDF military convoy. The SPLA Major General Deng sought to encourage the residents who found themselves in the worrying situation of having to answer to representatives of the LRA and the UPDF. 'Let there be no fear from your side. Just tell us the reality', Deng said.[85] The residents explained that on 27 September one of the elders had seen Ugandan military vehicles; shortly after UPDF soldiers came to ask for a spade to dig out a stuck bus. The elder then drove with the soldiers to the location where the bus was stuck.

There he encountered many people, men and women, black and white. Many of the people had cameras and were busy taking photos; music was blasting and even a musician was performing. The entire convoy was made up of a bus (light blue with a yellow-green top and Bugandan writing on the side), two mambas [armoured personnel carriers], two buffaloes [mine-protected clearance vehicles], two Toyota double-cabin pick-up trucks, and a lorry. Each Toyota was carrying at least four UPDF soldiers. Another vehicle had six UPDF soldiers and the mambas accommodated 'the normal crew of two UPDF soldiers standing'. It was difficult for him to determine how many men were inside the buffaloes. The locals said that the convoy came from Uganda, 'acting as the same team' and connected 'just like the fish move in the river'.

After the bus was dug out, the convoy drove to the Norwegian Church Aid (NCA) compound in Pajok. When asking where the convoy was headed, the locals were told it was going to Owiny-Kibul. The residents asked: had the delegation been cleared and authorised by the SPLA to

---

[84] Muhumuza (2006). This Resolution would later became the LRA Act in the United States.

[85] Answers were given in Acholi and translated by the assistant to the chief (in Owiny-Kibul) and by Gulu's Sheikh Khalil (in Owiny-Kibul and Pajok). Arabic answers from the local SPLA commander in Owiny-Kibul were translated by SPLA Major General Wilson Deng and SPLA Colonel Kwai.

visit the LRA in Owiny-Kibul? The answer was: 'No, we have just come to negotiate with the SPLA soldiers who are here to allow us to proceed to Owiny-Kibul and see the LRA'. The locals then asked the head of the delegation from 'which side he was exactly in Uganda'. The head of the delegation was identified as the UPDF brigade commander from Kitgum.

Informing the Ugandan delegation that they had to gain permission from the SPLA, the residents insisted that in order to see the local SPLA soldiers, the convoy would have to go to Palotaka where the forces were located. The locals further stated that they could not give 'any single authority to proceed' unless the SPLA, maybe even in Magwi [the county seat, further away], was informed, and that the delegation could only move in the presence of an SPLA officer. Letting the delegation through, explained a local elder later, was seen as potentially giving the residents of Palotaka problems. Also, he was aware that the LRA had 'just come' to the assembly point, so allowing the delegation to go there could be 'kind of dangerous'. He said, expressing his fear, the delegation 'had guns. And the uniform, they were putting ... And things were still premature'. He said the delegation could provoke the LRA because once 'two brothers fought and they have just been separated, their eyes and anger still are within them and it can really cause a lot of problems'.[86]

Spending the night of 27 September in the NCA compound (with the bill signed by the Ugandan Media Centre, the GoU's public relations branch), the Ugandan delegation attempted to contact the SPLA by radio. In the end, the governor and commissioner refused the delegation permission to proceed. The delegation returned to Uganda at around 10 a.m. on 28 September 28.

At the same time, the chief of Pajok was working on the airstrip in Owiny-Kibul, where he saw members of the LRA and shared food with them. The food was stored under the roofs of the school structure in Owiny-Kibul. The people working on the airstrip told the LRA that a bus with strangers and UPDF military vehicles were headed towards them. The Pajok chief said he was 'frightened' upon receiving the news of the convoy. The SPLA commander in Owiny-Kibul sent a junior officer to tell the UPDF forces that 'you people cannot go ahead', and that they were to wait in Pajok for confirmation from the SPLA.

The news that the convoy had returned to Uganda after being 'restrained by the SPLA' came shortly afterwards when the LRA was still in Owiny-Kibul. Nonetheless, the information that military vehicles

[86] Fieldnotes, Palotaka/Pajok: 3 October 2006.

were moving unsettled the LRA. Three days after the initial news about the convoy, locals in Owiny-Kibul found that food in one location had been poured onto the ground next to an unsigned letter that instructed the finder of the food not to take it, but to please 'cover it with canvas'. The CHMT visited the site of the poured food on 2 October, together with the chief of Owiny-Kibul and the local SPLA commander. The chief told the CHMT that the LRA forces had not informed him when they were leaving the area, but he thought they had left on 30 September.[87]

After questioning the residents, the CHMT agreed that this version of the story was correct. Later, Kampala reacted through Nankabirwa, who said, 'the [convoy] trip was sanctioned officially, it was innocent. It was genuine. It was meant to enable journalists and diplomats to verify whether the LRA had assembled or not. It was not meant to deliberately breach the agreement'.[88] The CHMT also heard from residents that there was continuing UPDF movement near the border. As the CHMT was about to leave Pajok to investigate the areas towards the Ugandan border, news came that LRA fighters were crossing the Juba-Torit road. Despite protests by the LRA contingent that they needed to continue to investigate in the border area, the CHMT returned to Magwi and then travelled onwards to Juba.[89]

The same day, Uganda's Solicitor General Lucien Tibaruha sent a letter to the ICC to confirm that 'the commitment of the Government to cooperate with, and support the Court, remains unchanged'. The letter further stated that the GoU was working with the DRC and the UN missions in Sudan and DRC to ensure effective operational planning and coordination to tackle the threat posed by the LRA, but 'for reasons of operational security, the government of Uganda is not in a position to provide the ICC with details of its operational planning or activities'.[90]

3.8   Violations

The CHMT established in its first report that all parties had violated the CoH agreement: the LRA had not fully assembled by the deadline, the SPLA had not provided the promised protection, and the UPDF had deployed military vehicles into Sudan and near the assembly area. The report was never made public: with all parties in breach, the mediation team decided to conceal details. Additionally, the CHMT was clearly not working at its fully mandated capacity: AU members had not arrived, and

---

[87] Fieldnotes, Obbo/Magwi: 4 October 2006.   [88] Wasike (15 October 2006).
[89] Fieldnotes, Obbo/Magwi: 4 October 2006.
[90] Gyezaho and Nyakairu (11 October 2006).

the team barely had the resources to travel, never mind to quickly follow up on incidents. In early October, the technical advisor to the CHMT repeatedly asked for a few relevant documents to be given to the LRA/M, such as copies of reports on small arms and the Cape Town Principles on Children Associated with Armed Groups and Armed Forces, because, explained one of the members of the CHMT, 'not enough copies were given by OCHA'.[91]

OCHA and the UN showed their commitment in other ways. On 5 October, the UN announced the Juba Initiative Fund (JIF) under the auspices of OCHA. Initially valued at $4.8 million, the fund was financed through GoSS and the GoU 'to facilitate the basic necessities of the Juba Peace Talks and support the start-up of the Cessation of Hostilities Monitoring Team'. Commenting that talks had reached a critical point, but were hindered by the LRA's failure to assemble 'out of concern about the deployment of the Ugandan Popular Defence Force in the vicinity' a press release also stated that 'the Cessation of Hostilities Monitoring Team will return to Juba today with a full report verifying the situation in Owiny-ki-Bul'. The press release quoted Egeland: 'The United Nations is firmly behind the peace process in Juba .... A conflict that has dragged on for 20 years may not be resolved according to the clock. Both sides need to show patience to ensure a successful conclusion to the peace process'.[92] Other donor governments would later support the fund, although dispensing funds remained a problem.

With military pressure being kept on the LRA near the Eastern Equatoria assembly site, Otti retracted his earlier statement regarding the ICC warrants. On 9 October 2006, he announced that the LRA would not sign a peace deal before the ICC charges were dropped. He told his fighters that if they found themselves under pressure in Eastern Equatoria, they should cross to Western Equatoria: 'They should quit [Eastern Equatoria] if possible, because they are my people. Why shouldn't they come to live with me?'[93] Intelligence reports a day later confirmed that Ongwen and about 150 LRA had crossed the Nile north of Juba, presumably because the UPDF had deployed all along the east bank in response to Otti's statement.[94] There were reports that the LRA were carrying a white flag.[95]

On 12 October, LRA reportedly clashed with Mundari militias – a group of fighters that had been supported by the Khartoum government

---

[91] Fieldnotes, Juba/Magwi: 2 October 2006.   [92] United Nations (2006).
[93] Muhumuza, Nyakairu and Kasyate (10 October 2006).   [94] Allio (13 October 2006).
[95] Fieldnotes, Juba: 17 October 2006.

during the war – at Mongalla, 15 kilometres north-east of Juba.[96] The LRA reported that the Mundari fighters had attacked them marching in single file, as if under unified military command. 'This is not militia behaviour', was the message that was delivered to the delegates from the LRA fighters who argued that the Mundari had been ordered to attack the LRA, although by whom was never made clear. The following day reports came through of more than 200 LRA attempting to cross the Nile. The UPDF spokesperson Nankabirwa commented on the developments a few days later:

We are not satisfied at all. We expect the LRA to honour their side of the agreement we signed by assembling. We have written to the mediator (Lieutenant General Riek Machar). The LRA moved away from the assembly points. They are trying to sneak back to their bosses at Garamba in DRC.[97]

To counter the accusation that the LRA was breaking the agreement, Otti ordered his forces to again assemble in Owiny-Kibul. Yet LRA troops were ambushed by the UPDF near Bilinyang, 100 kilometres south-east of Juba, during the night of 15–16 October and then again in the morning and afternoon of 16 October. Two LRA were critically injured in what the LRA/M called a 'severe provocation' and a 'very grave violation of the truce'.[98] The UPDF rebuffed those claims as 'theatrical', with spokesman Kulayigye quoted as saying:

We have not had any contact with the LRA in as many months ... Bilinyang is not an assembly point, is not a safe zone and is not a safe corridor. So it cannot affect Juba at all. They have the safe zones to use so why should they meander through Bilinyang, which by the way used to be their [LRA] base? I am urging the LRA to stop these games.[99]

He also stated that Bilinyang had been occupied for some time by UPDF troops, since it had formerly been an LRA base.[100] Until that evening, the UPDF remained adamant that there had been no incident. In the evening, the SPLA confirmed that there had been shelling.[101]

Having heard of the attack, LRA/M delegates requested – and were granted – authorisation from the SPLA to send food and medicine to LRA who had been injured and possibly remained surrounded by UPDF. Delegates went to buy food to be sent out to the bush. They described being 'followed by UPDF wherever we went in the market'.[102]

---

[96] UNMIS source. For an analysis of the Mundari militias, see Human Rights Watch (1994: 123).
[97] Wasike (15 October 2006).   [98] Grainger (16 October 2006).
[99] Nyakairu, Gyezaho and Harera (17 October 2006).
[100] Grainger (16 October 2006).   [101] Reuters (16 October 2006).
[102] Fieldnotes, Juba: 17 October 2006.

The following day, 17 October, a truck manned and authorised by the SPLA left Juba to deliver these goods to the LRA. Accompanying the truck was Achama from the LRA/M team on the CHMT. Just south of Juba, a UPDF roadblock stopped the SPLA truck. The UPDF denied the SPLA passage and detained Achama in the UPDF barracks for four hours. He described the time spent in the barracks as dangerous, and he said UPDF soldiers had repeatedly threatened to kill him because he was LRA.[103]

With Achama detained, an enraged LRA/M delegation insisted in a meeting with Machar that UPDF hostilities had to stop, and that talks could not resume until it was investigated why the UPDF had more authority in southern Sudan than the SPLA. The LRA/M expressed doubt that the SPLA could protect the LRA, either outside or inside the assembly areas, if the SPLA could be bossed around in their own country by UPDF. Then news arrived that the LRA had killed a UPDF captain near Lyria.[104] Machar was outraged at all developments. After all, neither the LRA nor the UPDF was supposed to be anywhere near where they had been operating.

On the same day, Machar briefed US Presidential Special Envoy Andrew Natsios on the talks. A confidential US diplomatic cable recounts Machar's description that 'a pronounced lack of trust between the two parties' was making progress difficult. Machar said, according to the cable, 'LRA negotiators question the GoU's motives at every turn, and force protracted debate on even trivial matters like the use of the word 'combatant'. The GoU 'stigmatizes' and 'castigates' the LRA and 'some members of the GoU negotiating team believe the LRA can only be dealt with through military means'. Asked what type of support the United States could provide, Machar noted the need for financial help and responded: 'convince Museveni that there is no military solution'. The cable states that in response to Machar's suggestions, 'Natsios made no commitments'.[105]

Starting the following day, a series of ambushes on the Juba-Torit road and an attack on the village of Gumbo outside Juba were carried out by unidentified perpetrators resembling the LRA.[106] The LRA commander, Achellam, in a phone call refused to take responsibility: 'No LRA has attacked civilians in southern Sudan ... If attacks took place, it is more

---

[103] Fieldnotes, Juba: 2 November 2006.   [104] IRIN (18 October 2006).
[105] US Embassy Khartoum (2006). It is worth noting that this conversation took place a few days after the United States allowed an easing of sanctions against southern Sudan, keeping in place sanctions against Sudan.
[106] Matia (26 October 2006).

likely UPDF who are deployed around Juba. They do this, then accuse LRA'. He stated that some LRA had scattered north of his position towards Juba, but not as far north as where the killings had taken place, he said. 'The UPDF surrounded us. We had to move for fear of being attacked .... They did not go that far'.[107] Both conflict parties suspended their participation in negotiations until the matters were clarified.

3.9   Museveni Comes to Juba

On 21 October 2006, Museveni paid a visit to the Juba Talks. What was touted in the Ugandan government newspaper as a 'major boost' to faltering peace talks soon turned into a disaster.[108] Reports about what happened in the meeting between Museveni and the LRA/M delegates, with Kiir and Machar present, were muddled. Had Museveni been hostile to the LRA/M delegation first or had the LRA/M delegation treated Museveni rudely? Everyone agreed that when Museveni moved towards the deputy LRA/M delegation chairperson Apire, she refused to shake the president's hand, demanding first an apology from him for what he had done to the people of eastern and northern Uganda. A scheduled joint news conference was cancelled; members of each delegation separately reported their perceptions of the encounter to the press.

The LRA/M spokesperson, Godfrey Ayoo, told the BBC that Museveni had been abusive, having been adamant that he was not interested in peace talks and calling the LRA/M delegates 'uninformed Ugandans who have been out of the country for 20 years'. The GoU delegate and Uganda's Deputy Foreign Minister, Henry Oryem Okello, denied that Museveni had been abusive: 'To the contrary, he used the opportunity to make it very clear that he had come all this way to support and encourage the peace process'.[109] When Museveni addressed the press, he commended Machar: 'He is a very patient and persistent person who knows how to deal with unserious people like the LRA. If it were me ...' he trailed off, before bursting into laughter without clarifying what he would do.[110]

After Museveni left, most delegates agreed that his visit had created more problems than it had solved. Between the LRA/M and GoU delegations, Museveni's appearance had created further mistrust. The LRA/M delegates were no longer sure that the GoU delegates were really conveying the President's opinion during their negotiations, since he had

---

[107] Cocks (20 October 2006).   [108] Mukasa and Osike (22 October 2006).
[109] BBC News (21 October 2006).   [110] Nyakairu (22 October 2006).

so clearly stated that he was not supporting the process. Internally, the delegates were split over Apire's reaction: some called it a necessary statement in light of the press exposure that the atrocities would receive if she refused to shake his hand. Others found it clumsy and strategically unwise to be confrontational.

3.10   Continued Violence

A few days after Museveni's visit, Machar upset the UPDF by ordering them to withdraw from Aruu, Palotaka and Magwi.[111] The LRA/M demanded a complete UPDF withdrawal from southern Sudan a few days later. The GoU countered that the LRA/M's response was 'ambiguous and diversionary .... Their demand that our troops deployed in Eastern Equatoria leave or also assemble is unacceptable because they are there under a protocol we signed with the government of Sudan'.[112]

Reports of individual car ambushes by unidentified gunmen and LRA increased.[113] Uganda's Defence Minister stated, 'We are investigating the attacks. Partial results indicate there are other groups in southern Sudan that are involved, maybe groups that do not want the peace talks to succeed .... Those could be people who are entrepreneurs of violence, who gain from the violence'.[114]

Who some of those were came to light at the end of October when the SPLA arrested seventeen suspected former government militia members near Gumbo bridge after a shooting near Civicon Oasis Camp in Juba. It transpired that a network of north Sudanese traders had staged the latest ambushes and shootings to interrupt supplies from Uganda. Increased trade across the Ugandan border after the CPA had pushed down prices in Juba markets – for example from $3 to $1 for a beer. The north Sudanese traders had wanted to make the roads to Uganda unsafe so as to maintain their lucrative trade routes from Khartoum and their quasi-monopoly on supplying Juba with goods. This was done in close collaboration with former SAF military officers who controlled the Juba market.[115]

With no let-up in the military pressure on the LRA, Otti announced that LRA fighters should not assemble at Owiny-Kibul but rather stay hidden in the bush: 'I have asked them to use their guerrilla tactics and

---

[111] Nyakairu, Harera and Matsiko (26 October 2006).   [112] IRIN (26 October 2006).

[113] Nyakairu, Harera and Matsiko (26 October 2006); Matia (26 October 2006); Ocowun and Ayugi (26 October 2006); Mukasa (27 October 2006).

[114] Musamali (27 October 2006).

[115] Mukasa (27 October 2006). This version of events was confirmed to me by UN security in Juba.

hide from them [UPDF]. But if this intensifies, do not be surprised to hear that they have clashed with the UPDF because they are looking for this themselves'.[116] Museveni reacted a few days later by saying that DRC's President Joseph Kabila and Vice President Jean-Pierre Bemba had both 'consented to Kampala's request to flush out LRA insurgents in the Congo, whether or not the Juba talks succeed',[117] adding that the GoU had only entered talks to avoid trouble with the Congolese government by going into DRC to get the LRA.[118]

Two days later, an SPLA Colonel was shot dead in Juba outside a bank. The incident caused panic as rumours spread quickly that 'Kony' had invaded Juba. Traders near the bank talked about having seen 'Kony's fighters' and said that the LRA had abandoned the peace process and was taking Juba. Such rumours persisted, even after it came to light that the murderer was a member of *Ismail* Kony's militia. Ismail Kony, a Murle from South Sudan's Jonglei State, has no connection to his namesake Joseph Kony, but in the reporting of the incident, the names had been mixed up. Ismail Kony had led his Murle militia during the war; his soldiers were to be officially integrated into the SPLA.[119] The man who killed the SPLA colonel was reportedly aggrieved at having received no pay from his new employer.[120] With the two Konys continuously mixed up, the incident deepened persistent rumours, supported by Ugandan and southern Sudanese security, that a new 'LRA Sudan' had been established:

a militia recruited by Khartoum from the large Acholi community in South Sudan .... Some of these groups organised as the Southern Sudan Defence Forces (SSDF) by Khartoum never fully integrated into the new force created after the signing of the CPA. Some of these groups like the Mundari militia commanded by Major General Clement Wani and sections of the Equatorial Defence Forces (EDF) have remained out of the reach of the Southern Sudan government.[121]

3.11   Comprehensive Political Solutions

The CoH periodically expired – and was periodically renewed. In early November, when negotiations turned towards Agenda 2 on comprehensive political solutions, the LRA/M failed to present a new position paper,

---

[116] Nyakairu, Harera and Matsiko (26 October 2006).
[117] Muhumuza (30 October 2006).   [118] Museveni (30 October 2006).
[119] Ismail Kony announced in April 2007 that he was joining the SPLA. He became Salva Kiir's peace advisor (Mayom and Kur 2007).
[120] Juba Post (6 November 2006).   [121] Izama (5 November 2006).

saying they had been too preoccupied with the safety of their troops. The LRA/M's lack of effort angered the GoU, who expressed doubt at the usefulness of the Juba Talks, as the LRA was failing to assemble or constructively move the peace talks forward.[122] The LRA/M finally presented a position paper on Agenda 2 to Machar on 6 November. Reflecting on experiences of the past few months, the paper included the demand for both parties to 'recognise the need to ensure effective protection for LRA combatants and personnel during the implementation of the agreement and to that end, the parties to adopt special security measures including a designated assembly area in northern Uganda, to be elaborated in subsequent agreements'.[123]

Further, the paper suggested the establishment of a ministry in which the LRA/M would play a role by being consulted in the appointment of a minister. The LRA/M demanded that local leaders and the donor community be responsible for the rehabilitation, reconstruction, construction and recovery of war-affected areas and other regions affected by natural or other disasters, expressing their distrust in the GoU's intentions to rebuild northern Uganda. The area concerned, the LRA/M suggested, should include Masindi as a war-affected district, which constituted a significant widening of the area under consideration. The LRA/M further requested to hold a referendum within twelve months of signing a final agreement to ask the population whether they would support Uganda's transition to federalism. The LRA/M argued that a referendum would show that 'there is genuine demand for a sizeable population of Uganda for a federal form of government as the only way for guaranteeing political stability of the country'.[124]

The GoU rejected most of the suggestions straight away, particularly taking issue with the preamble of the LRA/M's position paper, which stated: 'Having realised the futility of resolving the armed conflict ... by military means (the two parties) have heeded the hues and cries of the people of Uganda'. The GoU challenged the usage of 'futility' and 'hues and cries of the people of Uganda'. To the specific demand for protection, the GoU responded that the 'parties recognise the need to offer protection to LRA combatants and personnel during the transition from conflict to peace and to the end the parties agree to adopt security measures in subsequent agreements'. The parties managed to agree that children of LRA combatants were to be given access to education and that a special fund for northern Uganda would be established, although the GoU argued that such a fund was already in place and the demand

---

[122] Mukasa (5 November 2006).   [123] Matsiko (8 November 2006).
[124] Matsiko (8 November 2006).

thus outdated. It was further agreed that Uganda would pass an Equal Opportunities Act and involve the international community in rebuilding northern Uganda.[125]

3.12   Doubts over Continuation

A few days later, the UPDF made a newspaper statement regarding the LRA's failure to assemble at Owiny-Kibul:

the Lord's Resistance Army (LRA) have neither shown any commitment nor willingness to implement their own part of the bargain signed in the document. UPDF on the other hand has played by the rules to the letter. Whereas the majority LRA moved out of Northern Uganda to Southern Sudan, it's on record that only 45 LRA turned up at the assembly area of Owiny-Kibul for one day, picked food and moved away. As for Ri-Kwangba, LRA did not bother to make any attempts to assemble at all .... We also have strong information that LRA has effectively used the peace talks in Juba to re-organise. They have now, through their financiers and collaborators, acquired more communication gadgets, especially satellite phones. They also for the first time managed to access their underground armouries and have re-armed themselves with more guns and ammunition which had hitherto been inaccessible because of UPDF pressure .... LRA in Garamba has meanwhile moved deeper into Congo to the Ituri province and have struck alliances with Ugandan rebels there such as NALU, PRA and ADF .... The Cessation of Hostilities Monitoring Team (CHMT) is either not adequately empowered, weak to effectively monitor LRA violations or has deliberately chosen to treat LRA with kid gloves.[126]

The GoU delegation left Juba on 8 November: they argued that the stalemate over the assembly and the LRA's unwillingness to stop committing violence made their stay superfluous. It had been weeks by then since tangible progress on either the assembly or the negotiations. One LRA/M delegate felt that the LRA continued to be unfairly blamed for various attacks, even though other perpetrators had been identified: 'A hare does not eat meat, but if the leopard comes and kills the kid of the goat and then smears blood on the sleeping hare's mouth, people will come and accuse the hare', he said.[127]

On 12 November, UN Undersecretary for Humanitarian Affairs, Egeland, arrived in Juba. His visit had been much anticipated, as he had announced his intention to meet with the LRA leadership in the bush. The high-level UN meeting with an armed group was unprecedented, and contentious within the UN system. The LRA/M delegates saw its merit but were also sceptical. Otti was unsure whether Egeland

[125] Matsiko (8 November 2006).   [126] UPDF Spokesperson (7 November 2006).
[127] Fieldnotes, Juba: 6 November 2006.

Figure 3.2 Jan Egeland meets the LRA while journalists wait out of earshot, November 2006.

had the power to arrest him, but finally allowed a UN helicopter to land in Nabanga. Several helicopters descended on Nabanga, carrying Egeland, LRA/M delegates, the mediation team and a group of international journalists.

UNICEF had provided a large canopy tent for the meeting, much of which was held without the journalists allowed to listen. Egeland, who had made clear before his visit to Ri-Kwangba that he would not discuss the ICC, said that when he asked Kony why the assembly had become the problem on which the talks were stuck,

Kony's position was that they were trying, the LRA, to do their best, but they were harassed and persecuted by the Ugandan army all over Southern Sudan. So he said it is not going to last long because they are breaking the ceasefire. That was Kony's position.

Straight after leaving Ri-Kwangba, Egeland travelled to Kampala to report to Museveni. During that meeting, said Egeland, Museveni 'still maintained that the most probable outcome would be a military solution'. Egeland said of Museveni:

Well, he did not offer much in a way. What he did offer was to go with the Juba process ... he also actually agreed with me to redeploy some of his soldiers in southern Sudan as they were blocking access to one of the assembly points for the LRA. But he sort of played it two ways, as he often does. He both instructed his minister Rugunda to keep negotiating as well as he said, internal and publicly that he was very impatient, and he would actually be considering ending it all at any point if there was not enough progress.[128]

On 23 November, the chief of Owiny-Kibul confirmed that as far as he knew, there were no more UPDF in the area. While LRA troops claimed to be in the area ready to assemble, the CHMT failed to make physical contact with them on its first helicopter-supported mission to Palotaka and Owiny-Kibul. On 26 November, Caritas Uganda arrived in Owiny-Kibul to set up a support structure for the assembly. A day later, the SPLA reported that about 300 LRA were 'crossing outside Magwi near a bridge', seemingly headed towards Owiny-Kibul.

Two days later attention was diverted from events in Owiny-Kibul to Malakal in Upper Nile where heavy fighting had broken out. Proving to be a volatile union, the Joint Integrated Unit in Malakal broke apart in a trice when pro-SAF militias attacked the barracks. The formerly integrated unit descended into the worst fighting since the signing of the CPA. This required Machar's full attention; events in Eastern Equatoria faded into the background. Yet on 29 November 2006, three LRA fighters were killed during early morning clashes with the UPDF in the north of Eastern Equatoria, around Mogiri, Nisitu and Ngangala. Otti complained to the CHMT about constant military pressure on the LRA by the UPDF.

The next day, between 11 a.m. and 2 p.m., LRA and UPDF exchanged gunfire north-east of Lyria. The situation was confusing: Lyria in Central Equatoria was about 150 kilometres from the assembly area in Owiny-Kibul; both the LRA and the UPDF had yet to explain why their troops were in that area. The same day, the UPDF deployed helicopter gunships to bomb the LRA near Opari, a stone's throw from Owiny-Kibul.[129] The SPLA commander in Owiny-Kibul reported hearing helicopter gunship fire in the area from 9.30 a.m. onwards, lasting about forty-five minutes. UN security confirmed that on 30 November Ugandan Hind helicopter gunships and troops had moved across the Uganda–Sudan border, and also towards Nabanga.[130] For the SPLA

---

[128] Author's telephone interview with Jan Egeland, former UN-Undersecretary for Humanitarian Affairs, 15 October 2007.
[129] Fieldnotes, Owiny-Kibul, Juba: 4 December 2006; Mwaniki and Wepundi (2007).
[130] Fieldnotes, Juba: 30 November 2006.

holding guard in Owiny-Kibul, it was clear that this was a full military assault by the UPDF. The LRA stated that its forces had come under attack, with delegates protesting against this violation. They pointed out that the CHMT had officially confirmed that the UPDF had withdrawn from its bases in Tibika, yet had not actually been able to go there, calling into question the credibility of the work the CHMT was able to do.[131] The LRA/M delegation demanded protection of their troops, which the GoU dismissed, arguing that the LRA had no right to call for protection for their troops since most of the troops had been abducted in the first place.

On 30 November 2006, the mood in the Juba was at its lowest. The LRA/M delegation had announced that it was suspending 'face-to-face' negotiations until all UPDF had left southern Sudan, even though face-to-face negotiations had not happened anyway for quite some time. An LRA/M delegate explained how he – and others in the delegation – felt about Machar's mediation at that point. He said that in meetings, Machar was seen as abusive towards delegation leader Ojul. At one point, he said, Machar had said 'fuck you' to Ojul and told him to 'get out of here'. Machar was said to have yelled at an LRA delegate who was positioned near Kony for his protection to get away from Kony while the latter had been meeting Sudanese elders to shake hands. This was a clear sign to him that Machar did not respect LRA structures: 'Riek does not listen. He always thinks he knows best'. He said that Machar was also yelling at the mediation team – including Professor Assefa who was seen by the LRA/M delegation as more competent to handle the mediation – 'but all the mediation team keep quiet when he yells and when he is fairer and more respectful to government side'. In summary, he said Machar was 'extravagant' and 'not civilised'.[132]

In a briefing in Juba, UN security stated that they had confirmation that 'large groups of LRA might become targets' and that some of the UPDF deployed in Sudan were from the 105th battalion, comprised of former LRA. UN security stated that the 'framing of incidents is a possibility', and that the situation had made it difficult for the UN to enter Owiny-Kibul and get an understanding of the local situation. There was further suspicion, drawing on reports from border residents, that the 'UPDF might be on the way to West', meaning that troops might be moving towards the site in Western Equatoria. 'Some [UPDF] elements are moving along border regions ... there is an attempt of sorts to disrupt things on the Western side'. Overall, the UN concluded, albeit never

---

[131] Fieldnotes, Juba: 30 November 2006.
[132] Author interview with LRA/M delegate, Juba: 15 October 2006.

publicly and officially, that the 'UPDF is setting up a targeting mechanism for the assembly'.[133]

During that time, the LRA continued abductions. One young woman from Maridi, for example, recounted that in December 2006 she was taken by LRA fighters six miles from Maridi and into Garamba Park, from where she walked to Ri-Kwangba to pick up food. Most LRA, she said, were staying in Garamba Park at the time and only went to the assembly area in Ri-Kwangba to collect food, which was being delivered through Caritas Uganda.[134]

By the end of November, there was no longer any sign of engagement by either IKV Pax Christi or Sant'Egidio. IKV Pax Christi wrote in their account of the Juba Talks that the reasons for their withdrawal were to be found in Machar trying 'to get a firmer grip on the process' which meant a domination of the chief mediator that left the IKV Pax Christi team wondering 'whether it still added enough value'.[135] For the LRA/M delegates who had remained in Juba, ending their pursuit of peace seemed for the first time a plausible option, despite their being encouraged by Otti to stick to their proposed agenda of negotiating comprehensive solutions even if, Otti had said, that meant death for the fighters who were still out in the bush unprotected. Otti's reasoning was that the LRA expected to be betrayed anyway, so they had little to lose by sticking to their principles.

On 1 December, UN security reported that more UPDF gunships had been sighted above Owiny-Kibul; Caritas Uganda confirmed that non-UN helicopters had hovered over the designated assembly area at around 10 a.m. with at least one of the helicopters headed east towards Kapoeta.[136] Two days later, residents of Owiny-Kibul saw helicopters passing at 8 a.m. and at 12 noon.[137] Gunfire was heard again at 2 p.m.[138] The LRA/M stated that their forces were attacked between 11 a.m. and 2 p.m. by UPDF and SPLA, explaining that LRA fighters had been able to identify the two armies from their distinct fighting styles. In the days leading up to these events, the LRA/M had grown increasingly suspicious regarding the safety of their troops. They also said that they were

---

[133] Fieldnotes, Juba: 30 November 2006.
[134] Author (with translator Zande/English) interview with Sudanese abductee who spent March–December 2008 with the LRA. Yambio: 23 February 2009.
[135] Simonse, Verkoren and Junne (2010: 232).
[136] Fieldnotes, Juba: 1 December 2006.
[137] Residents in the area confirmed that they had spotted helicopter movement and had heard gunfire around Owiny-Kibul on 30 November and 3 December. Fieldnotes early December 2006.
[138] Fieldnotes, Juba: 3 December 2006.

witnessing a revival of the SPLA/UPDF relationship in which they had become a pawn. 'The SPLA is complicit', one delegate said, explaining that Machar's reaction to the news of the fighting between the UPDF and the LRA was that '[the LRA] should just go to the assembly areas now. After all, those people shooting you should not be in that area anyway'.[139]

'So if we get peace and we are killed, not even the mediator will speak for us', one member of the CHMT argued.[140] They had expected that Machar would put the gunship attack on the agenda. I asked the SPLA leader of the CHMT why there had been no official statement by the CHMT regarding the attack. The CHMT had not inspected the site of the attack. A CHMT visit was scheduled to the site in question, but was not carried out.[141] 'All sides have confirmed this incident, there is no need to monitor', was his response.[142] However, in the *New Vision* a few days later the UPDF publicly denied that they had attacked the LRA or had even used a helicopter in Sudan.[143]

On 7 December, a few days after the gunship attack, I attended a meeting with Acholi leaders from Uganda and representatives of Caritas Uganda who were supplying the support structure for the assembly area in Owiny-Kibul. The Caritas representative announced that the LRA were being bombed on their way to and near the assembly area.[144] 'So in peace, it means that we can be killed, that we can be surrounded, that they can bring helicopters to kill us', one LRA/M delegate said, visibly enraged.[145]

On 3 December, helicopters were again heard near Owiny-Kibul, first at 8 a.m. and then at midday, circling near the areas of the LRA route into the assembly area. The UPDF, with a presence along the Nile and along all roads in Magwi County, had positioned itself so that the troops

---

[139] Fieldnotes, Juba: 30 November 2006.   [140] Fieldnotes, Juba: 30 November 2006.

[141] Mukasa (2006).

[142] Fieldnotes, Juba: 30 November 2006. I later travelled to Lyria, where residents confirmed that a helicopter had been shooting in the area.

[143] 'THE UPDF has denied allegations by the Lord's Resistance Army (LRA) that it has violated the Cessation of Hostilities Agreement. In a meeting with a group of Acholi leaders last week, the LRA chief, Joseph Kony, had accused the UPDF of attacking his forces east of the Nile and hunting down some 300 fighters who were still in Uganda.

'We are on record of having captured four fighters in Northern Uganda, who failed to walk to the assembly points within the agreed period, and handing them over to the local councils for resettlement. We cannot be the same force hunting them down', 'UPDF Denies LRA Claims', 2006.

[144] Fieldnotes, Pajok/Owiny-Kibul: 7 December 2006.

[145] Fieldnotes, Juba: 30 November 2006.

could seal all entryways into Owiny-Kibul quickly.[146] On 9 December, the head of the CHMT denied in an interview with an international reporter that an incident involving a helicopter had taken place.[147] 'It is always the same', one delegate said angrily. 'How can the government say they want peace if they behave as if they are in war? They shoot, they kill, they lie. It does not matter if we are in Juba or in Gulu – it is exactly the same. This time, it is not the LRA obstructing the peace'.[148]

3.13   Strengthening Negotiations

In the midst of the military turmoil, other elements were put into place to strengthen the Juba Talks. On 4 December, Mozambique's former President Joaquim Chissano was finally appointed UN Special Envoy for LRA-affected Areas, mandated by UN Secretary-General Annan to 'facilitate the search for a comprehensive political solution to address the root causes of the conflict in northern Uganda and the implications of the LRA activities in the region'. Chissano's task was to 'help develop a cohesive and forward-looking policy approach among all external actors'. Annan wrote that

taking into account the independent nature of the judiciary process, my Special Envoy will also liaise with the International Criminal Court, United Nations missions in the Great Lakes region and regional actors concerned on matters pertaining to the indicted LRA leaders.[149]

Another sign that the peace talks infrastructure was developing coincided with Chissano's appointment. The same day, a drilling rig arrived in Nabanga to ensure water supply for the LRA. Building a liveable assembly area had been part of agreements made with the LRA; engagement with women and children by UNICEF and Save the Children Uganda who were to build a clinic for women and children and to send social workers to engage with LRA family members had also been sanctioned by the LRA.

Although plans for the assembly seemed to strengthen again, two days later Save the Children Uganda reviewed its proposal to send social workers to Ri-Kwangba and Owiny-Kibul and withdrew its commitment to help the assembly, explaining that it was withdrawing because family

---

[146] I was given this description of the situation in November/December 2006 by a security expert who was working in the area at the time. Author interview with international security expert, Nabanga: 13 April 2008.

[147] Personal email to author from an international reporter based in Kampala, 9 December 2006.

[148] Fieldnotes, Juba: 9 December 2006.   [149] Annan (2006).

Figure 3.3 A UN helicopter arrives in the village of Nabanga, November 2006.

tracing was not going to be a priority in the assembly area. However, a few months later the organisation's position changed again when they, along with UNICEF, supported the clinic. Staff from both organisations expressed in private meetings how difficult it was to find internally and externally acceptable terms on which to engage with the LRA.[150]

As the UN secured high-level support, leaders from Gulu worked on persuading the LRA/M to go back to the table. They were relaying messages from Uganda that people were very upset about the LRA's refusal to go back to the table and about the UPDF shooting LRA fighters on their way to the assembly. Generally, said Rwot Oywak from Pader, 'people in Gulu are very discouraged'.[151]

Then a delegation from Uganda, led by RDC Ochora and including Owiny Dollo – who had reportedly many years earlier dressed as a woman to find Kony in Khartoum to talk about the possibilities for peace – and Kony's mother travelled to Ri-Kwangba, followed a few days later by representatives of UNICEF, OCHA, the mediation team and LRA/M delegates. The delegation now included the newly arrived technical advisor James Obita, who was well known to all parties from previous attempts at peace in the late 1990s. On December 12, Kony, Otti and other members of the LRA's high command Control Altar held meetings with Dollo and the mediation team's legal advisor to discuss

---

[150] Fieldnotes, Juba: 7 December 2006.
[151] Author interview with leaders from Kitgum, Pader and Gulu. Juba: 6 December 2006.

legal options. In a long speech, Kony summed up why for him the preceding months had replicated previous failed peace attempts: 'While talking, there is troop movement from Eastern Equatoria to here, seven miles from here', he explained. He then complained about the unfairness of the international justice system. He stated:

It was us who initiated peace talks, so that we have a peaceful solution, a negotiated settlement. That is why we are talking openly about ICC. Suppose we had not opened up to peace talks, would there not be an opportunity for ICC to talk to us? If we had reported Museveni and ICC first, would they have pursued Museveni? No. They are only doing to Kony and commanders because they are weak. Is this the best way to handle matter? We are relying on lawyers to give good advice. We are committed to peace process but there are a lot of contradictions.

He gave his assessment of what had happened in the Juba Talks so far and the role the LRA had played:

We are fully committed to the peace process. We want you to take note of our concern about this process. I am talking to you, lawyers. I am sure you are aware that there is no law in the world, even the law of God, that says people should not fight. God has created man and other creatures in anticipation of war. The lion has sharp teeth, the tree has thorns and the snake is born with poison. So we shall not relent on protecting ourselves.[152]

Two days after this meeting in the bush, the GoU delegation returned to Juba to restart talks for a final round before Christmas to make sure that the year would end successfully. It was not to be. Talks were cut short when on 15 December 2006, SPLA soldiers, shooting into the air, stormed into Juba to take the Ministry of Defence because they had not been paid. With bullets being fired, Juba remained in lockdown all day. Instead of another signed agreement and consensus on the way forward, 2006 ended with uncertainty over whether an LRA assembly would be possible, whether Juba was a suitable place for these negotiations, and whether either party was committed to moving things forward. For the LRA/M, the end of 2006 also came with increased doubts over whether their pursuit of peace was being supported by either the mediator or the international community.

3.14   Conclusion

The LRA/M went into the Juba Peace Talks in 2006 with both bad memories and high hopes. The same can be said for other actors in the

---

[152] Fieldnotes, Ri-Kwangba: 12 December 2006.

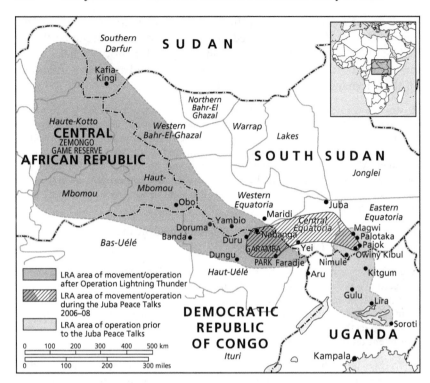

Figure 3.4 Map of areas of LRA movement. Redrawn by Cox
Cartographic Ltd from Conciliation Resources

talks, most of whom came with baggage accumulated during previous
attempts to end the conflict either peacefully or militarily. For the LRA/
M, the dynamics of the peace talks meant that 2006 quickly turned into a
replica of previous ill-fated peace processes, which they had experienced
as inadequate to open avenues that would allow discussion of substantial
issues without the threat of violence. High hopes had come, however,
from the unprecedented international profile – heightened even further
by the ICC warrants – of the Juba Talks from the very beginning. Yet it
was soon clear that chasms were emerging between how the LRA/M
experienced the talks and what others expected.

Conflict resolution scholarship puts a strong emphasis on a participatory process that involves representatives from different parts of the
community in conflict, and on confidence-building measures. Neither
were lacking in Juba. What was lacking, however, from the LRA/M
perspective was a credible sign that the talks would bring greater

attention to UPDF attacks, both in Uganda and during the Juba Talks, thus avoiding a similar military ending familiar from previous talks. With the safety and compliance of LRA troops called into question almost as soon as the CoH was signed, all achievements in 2006 were over-shadowed by the looming question of how LRA fighters could assemble safely, so as to no longer be able to attack civilians, but also so as to be able to start their own transition to a peaceful existence. It was a crucial pointer towards a continuation of the existing situation.

The events regarding the assembly and the information management about UPDF attacks proved to the LRA that structures within the peace negotiations mirrored those of the conflict; they simply became more entrenched. From the outside, the Juba Talks were mostly hailed throughout 2006 as the most promising attempt at peace ever, and the LRA was periodically blamed for not being serious. Yet the LRA/M soon perceived the Juba Talks as a set-up that maintained the existing power structures. They cited as reasons the volatile security situation, the mediator's murky information policy, clear signals that both the Ugandan military and the international justice actors maintained that they had a role to play in ending the LRA war, and growing demands from all sides.

The GoSS was juggling a volatile internal situation with having to maintain good relationships with the GoU; the GoU maintained that the talks should be over soon and was unwilling to address the issues of attacks on the LRA. Internationally, the end of 2006 brought disillusion-ment with the Juba Talks, fed by unclear information and a general distrust of the LRA/M's motives. In addition to the points made about the existing structures in Uganda, the LRA/M also increasingly focussed on the relationship between the SPLA and the GoU. With Machar as a much-disputed mediator, the LRA/M's trust in the impartiality of the SPLA towards their longstanding ally Uganda became more and more questionable. What had started with great promise in July was by December a lacklustre and complicated process.

I left Juba on the day the SPLA marched into town to demand payment, driving to the airport hearing shots. A few points seemed particularly important to me: having observed how international actors had struggled to navigate their own frameworks, including circumventing them, had emphasised that to a certain extent rules could be bent and mandates reinterpreted if needed. The lack of clarity that resulted from this process on paper did very little to move procedures forward, yet it had created a parallel space in which sideline engagements had contrib-uted constructively to the discussion. When it came to enforcing the agreements, particularly the CoH, the muddle had also created a situation in which violations were not sufficiently condemned, thus damaging trust. Crucially, 2006 had been the opportunity to discuss issues frankly with the LRA as the leadership and lower ranks were accessible and open. How they experienced the talks and what their hopes were, however, was drowned out by the broader focus on finding a way to conduct the talks in a way that would satisfy international standards.

The end of 2006 also brought into focus the disconnect between the kind of transformative process conflict actors aspire to and the procedural toolkit available – mediation, negotiation, diplomacy and peace-building, or if that fails, military intervention. Mediation and negotiation continued to confirm the LRA/M's understanding of being trapped in an unequal power relationship: the uneven set-up of the negotiation teams, with the GoU's team sporting highly qualified and powerful government representatives, rendered the tool of negotiation meaningless. Generally speaking, 2006 already showed a glimpse of why for the LRA/M committing to a signed agreement would pose a challenge, as a signature might become an endorsement of the hostile system in which the LRA/M found itself.

4 'Am I an Animal?'

Identity, Rules and Loss in the Lord's Resistance Army

Vincent Otti was sketching the LRA coat of arms on the back page of my notebook. Deeply focused, he used a thin strip of wood as a ruler to create perfect symmetry centred on Uganda's national symbol – the crane – that crowned the drawing. Having asked one of his runners to fetch coloured pens, he then added other elements: wrapped inside two palm fronds, he outlined two stone tablets with the Ten Commandments framed by a heart shape and a variation of the half-moon crescent. The 'Lord's Resistance Army' was spelt out on an elegant banner. Otti was so meticulous about the drawing that dinner was ready before he was finished. He packed away his coloured pencils and said he would continue in the morning – which he did, with the result visible on the cover of this book.

The next day, while cross-hatching the shaded parts of the emblem, he explained each element. The crane signified pride in Uganda; the palms stood for peace much like the LRA. The Ten Commandments tablets symbolised the LRA's Christian faith 'because we are resisting in the name of the Lord', the half-moon added a nod to their understanding that there was only one god, regardless of how faith was expressed. Listening to his explanation, I watched the perfectionist crafting of the LRA coat of arms and thought just how big the discrepancy was between what Otti believed the LRA stood for and how the outside world saw them.

Yet Otti's mission was to explain to that outside world what the LRA was, and crucially, what it was not. He had written to me in August 2005 about being called a terrorist that 'we are not such'.[1] Finishing the drawing, he looked up to tell me that each LRA uniform displays this emblem and that he had designed it. He pointed to the sleeve of a soldier nearby, which sported a carefully needleworked version. 'It is my work', he said, signing the drawing in my notebook with his name and rank.[2]

---

[1] Vincent Otti personal letter to author, 25 August 2005.
[2] Fieldnotes, Ri-Kwangba: 12 June 2006.

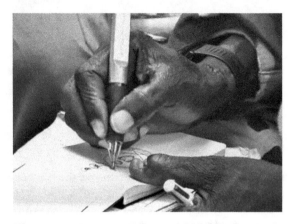

Figure 4.1 Vincent Otti draws the coat of arms of the Lord's Resistance Army.

4.1   Introduction

In conflict studies, the need to understand actors' motivations and experiences is an axiom. However, the focus tends to lie on what a group or a category of people experienced. The LRA group identity, while strong, does not adequately describe how individuals view their own complex LRA/M existence. Otti proudly stressing that he was solely responsible for the design of the LRA coat of arms was a reminder that even in an entrenched group conflict, individuals are important and that their personal experience adds up to the overall dynamics. They have all experienced what Ricoeur calls an act of 'attestation' – a moment of commitment.[3]

While spending time with the LRA/M, I collected snippets of conversations, observations and remarks. This chapter brings these together in a narrative enquiry into individuality within the amorphous and often contradictory conflict landscape.[4] A snapshot of individual sentiments during the Juba Talks, this chapter gives an insight into the extent to which the LRA experienced this time either as a deep peace process that would change their own and everyone else's thinking or as one focusing on reaching an agreement.

Experiencing the broken and fragmented individual views of LRA members also poses an analytical challenge, as seeking to find coherence through interpretation risks giving only my own rather limited perspective. It is only through narratives that a story can be told without

[3] Ricoeur (1992).   [4] See Clandinin and Connelly (2000); Bogdan and Biklen (1982).

explaining what the story is about and why things in the story proceed the way they do. The range of themes that emerged from, at times, very brief exchanges serves less as an exposition of the LRA and more as an illustration of individual experiences in the LRA. These include the need to have personal identities acknowledged and the hierarchies that emerge from that, the tension between having rules and breaking them, trust and distrust, and aspirations held in the past and the present.

4.2   Identities and Personal Choices

In a conversation in the bush, Otti was talking again about how the LRA's goals had been misunderstood. Matter-of-factly, he mentioned the injustice of being labelled 'terrorists', 'killers' and 'animals' – three words regularly used to describe the LRA. The labels had different effects on him: 'terrorist' was the greatest insult. He seemed unperturbed by 'killer'. In previous conversations, he had alluded that the LRA was proud of being an efficient military force. Being called a good killer by your enemies was a badge of honour, not an insult. In other conversations with LRA members, I had encountered that boasting about violent group successes, particularly against the UPDF and the SPLA, was common – as was being a lot less open about one's own individual role. 'Animal' seemed to amuse him tremendously. Laughing, he waved his hands to loosely point at the LRA fighters around him to indicate that nobody there was an animal. He then got up and left.

I strolled over to Colonel Bwone, who was sitting with Alfred 'Record' Otim. They were seated too far away to have overheard my conversation with Otti. When I asked if I could join them, they demanded that I take their picture, joking that I was photographing 'jungle animals'. Another LRA soldier, to whom I had not been introduced by name, walked past. He stood for a moment, then lifted up his shirt and turned his backside to me. 'Do you see my tail?' he asked, wagging his bottom at me. 'Am I an animal? Am I an animal? Can you see an animal?'

When I had asked Kony about the people who were still with him in the bush, he had argued that the LRA was also a protective force. 'We capture nobody', he answered. 'They come to us for protection. Museveni has done very bad things, they want protection. We don't capture, we don't kill, we don't rape. That's not our work. They say we are animals. Can an animal take up a gun?'[5]

---

[5] Fieldnotes, Ri-Kwangba: 12 June 2006.

During the Juba Talks, the LRA spent considerable time contesting their dehumanisation – sometimes in jest, sometimes seriously – seeking to establish that the LRA's public image was ridiculous and far-fetched. It seemed to me that there were a few motivations behind this. Since mainstream interpretation tends to discount the LRA's rationality, ridiculing the mainstream was a good way to reclaim such rationality. Emphasising the LRA's humanity redefined their violence from being animalistic to being militarily astute; shifting the LRA image from senseless to strategic was to increase political credibility in the talks. The LRA/M were well aware that their war had been depoliticised and that they had been dehumanised – and in both processes, they themselves had played a substantial part. Reclaiming both politics and humanity was an important strategy, as was stressing the legitimacy of being a rebel against a hostile government.

Colonel Bwone explained to me how he came to be an LRA rebel, presenting his devotion to armed struggle as a strategic decision. He remembered the exact moment: 'I walked over to the LRA on September 28, 1986, at 4 p.m. from Lacor. I said goodbye – to my family, to my mother – to join the rebels'.[6] He had just finished Senior 4 – junior high school. The year 1986 was a bad year in Uganda and his family expected him to struggle for the community. He saw no other choice but to fulfil his family's hope that he could do his share to make things better. When he said goodbye to his mother, he 'could not imagine' that it would be twenty years until he would see her again. The rebellion was not supposed to be his lifelong occupation; he wanted to finish 'this business' quickly and help reestablish northern-led control over the government. Despite having been in the bush all this time, he felt that he was still the same person as in the autumn of 1986: 'But I was now also a rebel'. For him, the Juba Talks had already been worthwhile because they had made it possible for his mother to visit and see him again.[7]

At first, when Bwone had heard that Machar was bringing LRA family members to Ri-Kwangba in late July 2006, he had not wanted his mother to join the visitors' delegation. He knew that at that point in the Juba Talks he would not be able to leave the bush and would have to say goodbye to her again. Even though once she had arrived, he was very happy to see his mother, watching her leave felt like 1986 all over again:

---

[6] The rebel force at the time would not have been called LRA – but Bwone chose to describe the rebels with today's name.

[7] Lubwoa Bwone's mother, Mary Atenyo, was part of the delegation and brought to Ri-Kwangba in July 2006.

again he did not know when or if he would see her again, unsure if the peace talks would make it possible for him to return to northern Uganda. He did not want to be enticed, to be given false hope through his mother's visit. After all, he had always thought that the war would make it possible for him to return to a better home, once the NRM was defeated and the situation improved. Now, sitting in Ri-Kwangba and waiting for the developments in the Juba Talks, he was no longer sure that either war or peace would bring about that improvement.

He said that he still wanted to finish the 'business of this war', but only if the terms were right. Being a rebel for life had not been Bwone's plan, but nonetheless in the summer of 2006 rebelling remained part of the plan because he still saw reason to do so. He explained that the situation that had pushed him to choose to become a rebel remained unchanged. Another senior LRA commander who was sitting with us agreed that the armed fight of the LRA was still not over because the situation was still bad and could only be changed through war or peace talks. Later, I asked him how he felt about what the LRA had achieved so far in the war and what he himself had achieved. 'I feel wasted', he said about his life. 'But only wasted for myself. I am not wasted for the fight'.[8]

Bwone and Alit often badgered me – jokingly – that I should join their fight. One day they discussed what rank I deserved. First, they thought I should start as a private like everyone else, but then offered to make me an honourable captain because I was tough enough to keep visiting them in the bush. Assigning a military rank to me was the highest reward they had to offer – even though they had giggling fits discussing it. Being tough was good, they said, and the only way to show one's strength was through military rank.

Before each visit to the bush, I spoke to Otti on the phone to arrange a meeting with him. Each time he said that it would be his duty to meet me because I, a woman, had taken on the hardship of coming to visit him in the bush. It would be impolite to not see me.

After Otti granted me an audience on the day when I was told I could be an LRA captain, Bwone and Alit started asked if I had anything to offer – beyond being able to spend time in the bush – that would allow me to work up to a higher rank. Not much, I conceded. I did jokingly mention my green belt in judo, even though I had not donned a judogi since I was 16 – and regretted this remark immediately when it dawned on me that introducing my meagre martial art skills into the discussion was probably not a good idea. I did not want to find myself in a situation

---

[8] Fieldnotes, Juba: 30 June 2006.

where LRA commanders would ask me to demonstrate judo throws, chokes and holds. Yet the thought of judo clearly intrigued Bwone; he said usually the LRA fighters practised karate kicks or kung fu jumps. They knew these from watching Bruce Lee movies. Bwone now wanted to know more about judo. I explained that while it was a martial art, it was a lot gentler than karate and used your opponent's strength to your advantage. 'Maybe it is a softer way for when the LRA is in peace', he said.

Bwone had devoted his life and existence to the LRA cause. This choice had constrained his opportunities, but he maintained other goals in life in case the armed rebellion worked out. He harboured the idea that he could still make up for the lost time and start something new. Maybe, he said, he could even go back to finish school – Senior 5 and 6 – just 'like [former LRA spokesperson] Sam Kolo did after he left the LRA'.[9] He lifted up my heavy bag to show me that he was capable of a job as my bag carrier and thus could travel the world with me. Most of his other ambitions were drawn from listening to the radio almost every day: 'I want to see glaciers and the Danube River', he said. 'I want to learn more about globalisation and global warming … and judo', he said, winking at me.

Lieutenant Colonel Alit pitched in. He was keener on returning to his old life, rather than expanding his horizons after leaving the bush. He wanted his job back: clarinet player in a military brass band. He asked me if I could bring a clarinet for him.[10] On various occasions, Alit stressed to me that he was the only one in the LRA who knew how to play an instrument. A third commander chimed in when we were talking about ambitions. He said: 'Me, I had a good upbringing. My English is better than that of the others. I keep it up'.[11] He explained that when he was a child, he had only one goal: 'I wanted to be like a walking dictionary, back in school, learn all the words from A to Z. But then the war came, and I stopped'.[12] He asked for a dictionary. I brought a dictionary on my next visit, asking a young soldier to pass it on. I never saw the commander again, so I am not sure if he ever got it.

Bwone belongs to the senior generation of commanders; he has seen waves of war and peace efforts come and go. He talked about his choice to become a rebel in a similar fashion to Otti or Alit. They all alluded to

---

[9] Former LRA spokesperson Sam Kolo went back to school after he defected from the LRA. He graduated from Gulu University with a business degree in January 2012.

[10] Author interview with Col. Lubwoa Bwone and Lt. Col. Santo Alit (LRA). Ri-Kwangba: 22 September 2006.

[11] Fieldnotes, Juba: 6 June 2006.   [12] Fieldnotes, Juba/Magwi: 2 October 2006.

having been put under pressure because NRA forces had threatened their families. Kony's explanation of why he was a rebel was different: he stressed that 'the Acholi elders' had sent him to fight Museveni – without specifying that it was a small group of Acholi elders, rather than all of them – and that he was fulfilling a task that had been assigned to him. Most senior commanders with whom I spoke seemed comfortable with their conscious choice to carry out the mandated fight for the Acholi. Several commanders hinted that Museveni had determined their lives because he had created a situation in which resistance at all cost was crucial. They had sacrificed what their lives might have been to resist him, not knowing that it would turn out to be a lifelong abandonment of once-imagined futures. They were also slightly bemused by my obvious interest in their motivations, at times saying, with a laugh, that I was posing a lot of questions that asked *why* they were doing something. It was just how things were, and often they seemed resigned to that fact.

Speaking to the younger soldiers, I came across this explanation often: things are the way they are because they just are. I talked to a group of younger LRA fighters about the kind of life they had. Captain Conggwok showed me his black arm bracelet. I asked him what it meant. 'If I take this off, I die', he said in broken English. 'Joseph put this on me eight years ago. This is our life. This is our culture in the bush'. I grabbed his hand and pointed at his red nail polish, asking him why he was wearing it. He laughed. 'This is life', he said.[13] I was not sure whether this was his answer because he spoke limited English or because some things do not need explanations.

Not all of the younger soldiers spoke English, but those who did spoke it surprisingly well. I tried to engage with a boy with a sweet face and a beaming smile: Norbert. His deep-blue Hawaiian shirt added to the general impression of cheerfulness he radiated. While carrying a few cooking pots, he laughed at my attempts to speak Acholi. When I asked him how he liked doing this work, his eyes darted. He smiled, but did not answer.

Another young man was more talkative. He was fifteen years old and guessed that he had been in the bush for ten years. He did not know what his being in the bush was supposed to achieve. Maybe it had made sense once because when I asked him what his job was he answered: 'I forgot. It is too big a question. I am only 15'. He showed me a notebook he was carrying in his pocket and compared it with my notebook. He explained that he kept a notebook with him at all times because he was still hoping

---

[13] Fieldnotes, Ri-Kwangba: 11 June 2006.

to one day go to school and he wanted to do as much as possible to be prepared. Unlike many of the others I spoke to, the status of being in the LRA was less definite for him.

I encountered a difference in understandings of their situation between the older generation, the middle and the young soldiers. The older generation – such as Bwone – seemed convinced that what they were doing was good and necessary for the community. Judging from their plans to go back to their old lives or start something new, they seemed to expect that maybe they would come out of it unhurt. The younger generation, like Norbert, could not articulate the purpose of their existence. Some expressed hope that they would leave their current life behind. Yet most were too shy, too scared or too busy asking me to take their photo to share their thoughts in detail.

The middle generation mostly described the LRA fight as a more personal issue. They talked about being proud of being an LRA member, but also about their hopes that a better future in Uganda might still be possible for them. The two worlds – being in the LRA and an imagined better life in Uganda – were distinct, but tightly connected: the latter could not be reached without passing through the former. This generation wanted to avoid two things: being in the LRA forever and living under the current conditions in Uganda.[14]

'I fight for the Acholi', one man whom I considered to be from the middle generation explained, 'but I also fight for a better life. I fight because of how I have been treated and my personal loss'. His father, he said, had been killed by Idi Amin, but he was not sure when exactly this had happened or whether it was even true. All he knew for sure was that his father had disappeared during the time of Amin's regime. His brother – of this he was certain – was shot by the NRA in 1989 for having been a member of the Uganda National Liberation Army (UNLA) on the side of Milton Obote and Tito Okello.[15] The young man remembered

---

[14] See Leonardi for a similar tension experienced by youth in southern Sudan (Leonardi 2007a). The interpretation of individual LRA being caught in the space between LRA and life in Uganda that I offer here departs from distinctions made by Allen and Mergelsberg. While transition was considered difficult, the way the two worlds were described to me emphasised that they were connected, rather than separate. Mergelsberg suggests that transitions from life at home (*kit kwo ma gang*) and life in the bush (*kit kwo ma ilum*) are 'the most painful times' (Mergelsberg 2010: 167). Allen makes a similar distinction between an inside and an outside world, with separate rules applying for each. Allen discusses the two terms *gang* and *olum* as the distinction between different spheres with different rules, with '"the bush" (*olum*) as a place of unpredictable and amoral phenomena' (Allen 2006: 44). Girling describes the meanings of the word *gang* (the home or the village, p. 7) and *olum* (which he translates as 'grass') (Girling 1960: 23).

[15] The various member groups of the UNLA initially included Obote's, Okello's and Museveni's followers, who defeated the UNLA in 1986. See also van Acker (2004).

how people were later chased from their villages by government soldiers, shot and burnt. He made a gesture to illustrate how the soldiers took razor blades to cut the anuses of those who resisted.[16] 'I feel that my revenge is both for those who suffered, but it is also for me because I was not allowed to have a good life'. 'I did this [being in the LRA] for my people. But for myself, it is very difficult', said another middle-rank commander. 'Sometimes, when I look back, I hate my life, how things have gone. I was always listening to command. Maybe it is too late for me now to have choices. I had a plan when I was in Senior 4. I wanted to study divinity. I was reading my favourite book. *Things Fall Apart.* But everything is washed away from my brain'.[17]

One of the delegates was reflecting on his own role in the peace process after returning from a visit to Ri-Kwangba, where he had met with Kony. He explained that he had a good experience meeting Kony: 'I am proud of what I have done, for my people. I have fulfilled my mission. Even the chairman, he is proud. He looked at me and then looked away and he was proud'. I asked him what was more important to him – to be proud of himself or that the chairman was proud of him? He answered: 'Myself, of course'.[18]

This exchange echoed what I had encountered before: while LRA members stressed that they had been fighting as a group and group identity was clearly crucial, individuals also said that the war was about themselves as individuals and what they had lost. At times, the importance of standing up for yourself was explained through the figure of Kony, who was also seen as an individual who by standing up for himself had stood up for the group. One day in Juba, while waiting for a meeting with Machar, one delegate turned his phone towards me and asked me to

---

[16] A number of reports list abuses by Ugandan government soldiers in rural areas, including disappearing people, rapes, beatings and extrajudicial executions (Human Rights Focus 2002; Amnesty International 1999). The practice of *tek gungu* (bent over) is well documented as a systematic way of raping both men and women. In a 2012 report on the UPDF in Uganda's north-eastern region Karamojong, Amnesty International writes about abuses: 'UPDF soldiers have allegedly used torture and other ill-treatment especially while undertaking searches. There have been reports of UPDF soldiers removing suspects' teeth, burning suspects using hot metals and hitting the muscles and veins of men around the anus and the testis' (Amnesty International 2010). In 2003 it was reported that a man had been awarded damages after being tortured by the UPDF in 1998. Although the exact methods of torture were not spelt out, doctors confirmed that he was no longer able to control his rectal function as a result of torture (Kulubya 2003). The LRA/M in their first position paper of the Juba Talks reiterated that 'NRM soldiers went to the extent of cutting men's anuses with razor blades and pouring paraffin therein to enlarge them to fit their sex organs' (Olweny 2006a).

[17] Fieldnotes, Juba: 28 September 2006. Things Fall Apart is Chinua Achebe's 1958 novel.

[18] Fieldnotes, Juba: 27 September 2006.

read a text message. He said that the chairman had sent this to him and the rest of the delegation to support their efforts in organising the peace talks. The text message read: 'HEAVEN watches over its TREASURES and you'r one of its FINEST and most PRECIOUS. Live your life knowing GOD will never take His eyes off you! Am prayin 4 u all!'[19] When I asked the delegate what this meant, he explained that 'the chairman is telling us who we are'.[20] While it seemed rather unlikely that the message was indeed from Kony, presenting it to me in this way nonetheless showed how I was supposed to perceive the connection between Kony and the LRA fighters. It seemed to be a double defence of the LRA identity against their reduction to 'animals'. An implication of this for the Juba Talks was that any change in circumstances would also lead to the loss of the one possession that LRA members had retained: their identity.

In late 2009, I asked a former delegate what he would say the purpose of the peace talks had been. He explained that in order for peace talks to be effective, they had to simplify and make goals very easy and achievable. This was difficult, he said, because with every issue tackled, it had become clear in Juba that 'things break apart'. I asked him what he meant. He explained how change was almost impossible as it came with so many contradictions: he wanted the LRA as a militant organisation to cease to exist, but for it to continue as an opposition movement ready to take up arms against Museveni if need be. He himself never wanted to take up arms again, but he felt that he might have to if the LRA came out of the peace talks too weak.[21] 'Sometimes I want other things for myself than I want for the LRA', he explained.

Contained within a strong communal identity are shifting and multifaceted personal identities. Over the course of a few years, I observed how biographies were reinvented, and how within the system LRA, individuals changed their affiliations or even their names. In Uganda, it has been quite common for LRA fighters to present themselves as LRA abductees, or for those who have never been with the LRA claimed to have been abducted, depending on which category is beneficial.[22] I heard five different autobiographies of one of the LRA members: he had either been born in the bush; or been abducted when he was young because his

---

[19] Fieldnotes, Juba: 6 June 2006, sender's caps – I have my doubts whether this message was truly sent from Kony's phone, but it is what I was told.

[20] Fieldnotes, Juba: 6 June 2006.   [21] Fieldnotes, Nairobi: 11 November 2009.

[22] Allen and Schomerus (2006). An obvious manifestation of conflicting identities is the fine line between perpetrator and victim, as discussed by Dolan (2009) or by Baines (2009) for the case of Dominic Ongwen.

uncle was in the LRA; or been abducted as an adult; or never fought in the LRA at all, but was a contact person; or had always been an infiltrator paid by the government. I am unsure whether the photograph he gave me of himself as a young boy in the bush, holding a gun, credibly rules out any of these.

The middle generation – medium-rank commanders who had been with the LRA most of their young adulthood – talked about their life in the LRA as the somewhat inevitable card they had been dealt: 'You understand that that is what you have to do, what you believe is right', one young commander explained. 'Maybe a soldier is not blamed for the wrong decision of the command, like in Iraq, but as a soldier, you do believe it is right and then you do it'.[23] Another middle-rank commander saw fighting for the Acholi cause as a rite of passage, like a transition into manhood: 'It is hard to be a man. You have many things to concentrate on. You have to look after your wife and children. You have to have a son and one thing to do also is to fight for your right'.[24] Another expressed that shaking off the LRA identity was complicated: 'I don't know what I can do in the future. If I can go back to Uganda, I don't want to be in the UPDF. I don't want to be known only as former LRA. I don't know what I can be'.[25]

One commander explained to me that Kony, of course, knew that his fighters were using violence to fight for the community. However, he said, the use of violence did not make Kony happy; instead, he was full of regrets that this was the path individual lives had had to take. I failed to grasp what the young man was trying to say. He elaborated that when he was abducted, Kony found out that he was the brother of a woman who was married to a person very close to Kony. A few months after his abduction, Kony personally came to him and apologised for the abduction. I wanted to know if he offered to let him go. No, the man replied, on the contrary. Kony said that it was good that he had come as he could now prove his worth; that was just how it was.[26] Another expressed both pride and weariness at being with the LRA. This was something, he said to me, that I would not be able to understand because I could always get on a plane back to Europe. 'I am destined to do this', he said when I asked why he was fighting. 'The difference between your life and my life is that you have the ability to choose. I don't't'.[27]

[23] Fieldnotes, Juba: 30 September 2006.   [24] Fieldnotes, Juba: 7 December 2006.
[25] Fieldnotes, Ri-Kwangba: 19 September 2006.
[26] Fieldnotes, Juba: 18 December 2006.   [27] Fieldnotes, Juba/ Magwi: 2 October 2006.

4.3   Prize Identity

While he was in a prominent position in the delegation, one delegate often stressed how long he had been an LRA supporter and how close he was to the leadership, particularly to Otti.[28] Some of his colleagues never found this particularly convincing. Over the course of the next two years, several delegates explained to me that this particular man was a con artist, that he was a government agent, that his contact with the leadership was very weak. The man in question, however, was obviously proud of being part of the Juba Talks – as were many other delegates. This was not surprising.

Within the confined space of Juba, delegates had become celebrities, along with the LRA leadership. In Juba market, photo CDs were on sale, displayed prominently next to the David Beckham posters and pirate copies of the Nollywood hits *The Abuja Connection* and *Rising Moon*. The CD sleeves showed crude photocopied pictures: Ojul shaking Kony's hand, Machar shaking Otti's hand, Kony shaking Machar's hand. Twenty photographs of great LRA encounters, to be viewed at home.[29] While, for example, Ojul's standing as a spokesperson was not entirely solid within his own group or with members of the international community, to the outside world he – along with the LRA leadership – was a celebrity.

'You should be called a hero', Bwone said to me. 'Nobody has managed to do what you did. If you write a book, there will be lots of fame for you'. It was an awkward exchange for me. Bwone was clearly teasing me, following on from a previous conversation in which he had pointed out that I was doing quite well establishing myself as an expert on the LRA. The conversation turned to a topic that I was uncomfortable discussing with the LRA: how I had managed to conduct the only interview with Kony, only to have it published in a distorted manner without receiving credit for it.[30] In 2006, after a year of preparation, I had managed to organise a sit-down television interview with Kony in the bush. I had brought along a freelancer for the BBC to give the story the greatest possible play. After the interview, the BBC distorted the story and the freelancer published my interview under his own name in *The Times* of London and *Harper's*.[31] Having been rather bruised by the experience, I cringed at Bwone's suggestion that I was a hero and shook my head. 'You are a hero', he reiterated. 'We know the interview with the chairman was a big prize. You got the prize'. Alit explained to me the story of Jacob and Esau, and said that he felt that the price of the interview had been taken from me by someone who wanted to take credit for what I had achieved, just as Jacob in the biblical story took the blessings meant for Esau.[32]

Others wanted the prize as well, and the LRA/M knew that. 'It is the longest-running war in Africa, everyone wants the fame', a delegate explained to me, commenting on how Sant'Egidio had portrayed the signing of the CoH on their website. Just like IKV Pax Christi, Sant'Egidio had played a much smaller role in the peace talks than they had hoped, thanks to Machar's role as the mediator. 'Sant'Egidio went back to Rome. They did a press conference to say that through their effort, the cessation paper was signed', the delegate said.[33] As a result, he said, Machar did not want Sant'Egidio back, because they did not acknowledge the effort put in by everyone else. Machar was, as the delegate phrased it, 'pissed off, sincerely'.[34]

Meetings with the LRA leadership had the air of celebrity encounters. On his first trip to Ri-Kwangba, Ugandan MP and later presidential hopeful Norbert Mao hugged Kony. Mao later somewhat sheepishly commented that this did not mean that he supported Kony. A reporter for Kenya's *Weekly Observer* described the scene of the arrival of a group of Ugandan MPs in Ri-Kwangba:

Otti then announces that there would be a handshake with the general [Kony]. The visitors scramble to greet the man whose 20-year rebellion has caused mayhem in northern Uganda. 'General, I am making history now. General, I am the first West-Niler to shake your hand General. General, I am now a hero', goes an excited Arua Municipality MP, Akbar Hussein Godi. Another praise singer: 'General, I am also a hero. General, they say a lot of bad things about you but I have seen you with my hands General. General, what they say about you is not true ...', that is Kumi LC-V chairman, Ismael Orot who, by the way, is an NRM member. An embarrassed Santa Okot, former Pader Woman MP, is forced to plead with Kony that the women should have their turn because they can't match men in fighting for his handshake.[35]

I experienced similar scenes. During an impromptu press conference with Otti in the bush, a handful of reporters showered him with questions. 'Do you abduct children? Do you have children in the bush? Why do you attack civilians?' the reporters shouted. Otti's answers were taciturn. At the end of the press briefing, the reporters put away their

---

[32] Author interview with Col. Lubwoa Bwone and Lt. Col. Santo Alit (LRA). Ri-Kwangba: 22 September 2006.

[33] Pax Christi Netherlands 2006 (29 August). The report of a Rome press conference by Sant'Egidio is no longer available online.

[34] Fieldnotes, Juba: 12 September 2006.   [35] Nganda and Oluka (2006).

notebooks and tape recorders, and asked to have their photo taken with Otti. All gathered for a group shot around the second-in-command. The reporter from Uganda's government newspaper, who had asked why Otti attacked civilians, wanted an individual photograph of himself and Otti. The photos were taken as the journalists were shaking hands with Otti and patting his shoulder, smiling into the camera.[36]

Otti, while seeming a bit confused about this hostility combined with reverence, clearly did not mind the celebrity status. He talked to me several times about how the world was now understanding the LRA, judging somewhat prematurely that the delegation had negotiated a more favourable attitude towards the LRA – an impression that often fuelled their more rigid negotiating positions. They felt encouraged by what was perceived to be outside support. It was similar to how, as it was phrased in a position paper, continued support through the West 'has emboldened Museveni to continue committing the genocide'. This was despite 'selfish pursuit of political, economic and military interest by nation states enthusiastically embraced to the detriment of ensuring addressing issues that ensure the realisation of Human Rights, democracy and rule of law in parts of the world where they are in danger'.[37]

When I asked Otti what he was hoping to gain from the peace talks, he said that in wanting to receive recognition for their work, the 'LRA is no different than the NGOs, the UN, and yourself'. All of you, he said – talking about the long list of international representatives, organisations and media hanging around the talks – have pursued the LRA story for professional recognition. The UN Undersecretary of Humanitarian Affairs Egeland had visited the LRA the day before. In Otti's judgment, he had visited for the same reason that the LRA wanted peace talks: to get professional recognition. Even Egeland, Otti said, wants to be recognised and wants to be able to tell the story of meeting the LRA high command.[38]

In his autobiography, Egeland describes his encounter with Otti:

'Welcome!' says Vincent Otti, Kony's deputy, striding toward us. A tall, elderly man in camouflage uniform with elaborate Soviet-made red epaulettes, he has taken the title of lieutenant general. He is waiting to greet us at the assembly point in Ri-Kwamba together with a dozen silent LRA officials .... It is an

---

[36] Fieldnotes, Ri-Kwangba: 19 September 2006.

[37] Olweny (2006a). Cockett describes a similar mechanism of perverse incentives in the Darfur conflict, where the Sudan Liberation Army and the Justice and Equality Movement received exposure to US support that allowed them to feel strengthened in their far-reaching demands for a settlement and their expectation of outside help in pushing those demands through (Cockett 2010).

[38] Author interview with Vincent Otti, Ri-Kwangba: 14 November 2006.

unprecedented meeting. No ranking UN official has ever met the LRA leadership in the twenty years they have been in hiding.[39]

I asked Otti what he thought of the meeting with Egeland, of the large press corps following him and the frantic activity as reporters called in their quotes to their newsroom, shouting into satellite phones: 'We are all here for two reasons: for money or because we want to be a hero. I would like to have money, too', he answered.[40] Violence, the main ingredient of how this status had been achieved, had faded into the background.

4.4   Rules

Within the scholarship on the LRA, the emphasis on rules is very strong, to the extent that rules are at times presented as the defining factor of identity.[41] Yet rules within the LRA were also negotiable and adjustable: it seemed more the case that the LRA's identity dictated the notion of having strict rules, rather than rules shaping LRA's identity. Most rules explained to me were grounded in the LRA's existence as bush fighters. They also served to narrow the category of unacceptable human behaviour to the smallest possible denominator. Thus, establishing strict rules also granted a certain freedom and allowed actions that were very similar to what the rules forbade, but not exactly the same. That was why, they explained, even when violent, the LRA stuck to certain rules.[42] Emphasising that these rules of conduct existed seemed important to LRA commanders. However, when nobody else was listening, they also spoke about knowing the rules and breaking them – which the LRA clearly had done many times in the way it had committed violence.

Sudanese civilians in Owiny-Kibul and Obbo in Eastern Equatoria told me that whenever the LRA came to the market, they only ever drank soft drinks, even though they sometimes asked for alcohol to take back. The LRA were adamant that they did not consume any alcohol or drugs,

---

[39] Egeland (2008).

[40] Author interview with Vincent Otti, Ri-Kwangba: 14 November 2006.

[41] The LRA as a normative communitas, in Turner's phrase, is well documented: the group follows a tight set of rules, even though these are changeable depending on circumstance. Annan et al. have written about the strict set of rules governing LRA behaviour, regarding, for example, the prohibition of sexual violence against civilians, which served 'an instrumental purpose, augmenting the LRA's command and control of diffuse mobile units, and helping to curb the spread of HIV/AIDS' (Annan et al. 2009: 21). Doom and Vlassenroot stated that the LRA raped both men and women in public (Doom and Vlassenroot 1999).

[42] This data was gathered between 2006 and 2008. Some of these rules seem to have changed since – and were probably always adjusted according to what situation the LRA found itself in.

so buying alcohol was either a bending of the rules or part of some trade that went on in the bush. One delegate explained to me that alcohol and womanising were forbidden because both distract the fighters from their mission. Smoking was prohibited because the smell of a cigarette could betray the location of a hideout.[43] Despite the supposedly strict rules on cigarettes and alcohol, I saw LRA members smoking when not in the bush. One carried a camouflaged bottle of alcohol, taking regular swigs. I saw him being taken aside by his colleagues to be reprimanded. Afterwards, I enquired about this scene. 'Did [the LRA member] tell you that he drinks?' I asked another LRA. 'We are not supposed to drink', was the response. 'They [the high command] do not need to know. When we get [to visit the high command], I have to tell him stop this'.[44]

Spiritual observance and worship were stressed as an important element of group interaction. Yet once the LRA moved out of the exact territory and structure for which these rules had been made, they seemed to become less important. Passing a mosque, I asked an LRA member whether he prayed. He looked at me with surprise, as if the answer was obvious. 'It is a must for us. When we are [outside the bush] we pray three times a day. Sometimes we pray whole days in the bush. We are LRA'.[45] In reality, praying seemed to be an afterthought on many occasions. Twice when I sat down in Ri-Kwangba to eat the honey with mandazis I had been offered, Lieutenant Colonel Alit apologised after the meal that he had forgotten to say grace.

Out of earshot of superiors, individual commanders saw no reason to pretend that the LRA was a nonviolent force but reiterated that there were certain limits to LRA violence. Raping women, he claimed, was for example not allowed because it exposed the LRA to disease. 'Abductions have happened', said one man in the Ri-Kwangba assembly area. 'I accept that. Killings have happened. I accept that. But not rape. If you rape in the LRA, you bring a big problem on yourself. The LRA does not rape. Ask the chairman. He will laugh'.[46] This is a questionable claim and one that was possibly rooted in a definition of rape that made allowances to sexual violence by simply shifting the rules.[47]

While the ban on the rape of civilians seemed to discourage LRA soldiers, nobody denied that women were forcibly taken and given to

---

[43] Fieldnotes, Juba: 9 July 2006.   [44] Fieldnotes, Juba: 6 June 2006.
[45] Fieldnotes, Nairobi: 28 May 2006.
[46] Fieldnotes, Juba: 18 December 2006. In the violence that followed the Juba Talks, the LRA were implicated for mass rape. See HRW (2009).
[47] See Porter (2012; 2016).

LRA husbands, yet the handing over of women to be wives against their will was never linked to the notion of rape. p'Bitek writes that in Acholi culture, desire is expressed very directly and often before the man and woman get to know each other in any other way.[48] Crucially, the woman has to decline the advance, which tends to be treated as meaningless. Porter argues that social relations in Acholi culture determine how crimes are perceived. In the case of rape, if victim and perpetrator have a close social relationship, victims tend to demand lesser punishment to maintain social harmony. It is possible that a similar mechanism also works the other way round: because LRA individuals feel they are doing something good for the community, forced sexual encounters are not perceived as rape.[49]

I confronted the young man with this obvious contradiction: that there had been abductions, but the LRA maintained that everyone was with them voluntarily. That there had been forced 'marriages', and yet the LRA maintained that there was no sexual violence. He explained that of course there were abductions; he himself had been abducted. However, the abductions worked differently than how they were generally portrayed. Yes, the LRA targeted able young women, but not, as he saw it, to abuse them: 'We ask them [the soldiers in the field] to bring girls, not old women. So they bring girls, but people do take care of them'.[50] To him, abduction and forced marriage were a fact of life rather than an atrocity. His argument was that the United States had been built by abducted and enslaved Africans, so it was normal to strengthen your own power by using other people against their will. Moreover, he said the LRA had a lot to offer to anyone who joined them, including to women, because there was good friendship in the LRA camp.

One day, I was being served food in the LRA camp. A young woman with short hair, wearing a blue T-shirt and ankle-length skirt placed a metal plate in front of me. Otim was standing by, as always filming my visit to the camp. He shouted out in English to me to look at the camera. The woman barely looked up, not making eye contact with either Otim or me. I asked Otim if both of us, the woman and I, should look at the camera and if we should ask the soldiers standing guard to get into the picture. I addressed the woman with an Acholi greeting and smiled. Otim was not pleased. 'Don't mind, don't mind', he said. The woman reacted with a quick, ambiguous smile and retreated backwards, half-curtseying. Otim waved her away and said that I was the guest of honour. He mumbled that the others, the woman serving food and the foot

---

[48] p'Bitek (1964 (1997)).   [49] See Porter (2012; 2016).
[50] Fieldnotes, Juba: 18 December 2006.

soldiers were ... I did not catch the word and asked him to repeat it. They were, he said, 'normal'. But they do all the work, I said, laughing, trying to make light of the awkward situation. They cook and clean and they watch over you. When I then turned to ask one of the young soldiers standing by to ask him for his name, Otim interrupted: 'I am also working', he said, waving his camera. His, he said, was an important job. Commenting on my effort to ask a soldier for his name, he just said again 'don't mind, don't mind'.[51] Rules of respect applied to some, but not others – an age-old way to justify discrimination.

Kony was adamant that everyone who was with him in the bush had come there for protection, voluntarily. Leaving aside whether this was credible, it was clear that most abductees ended up as nameless, 'normal' elements in a hierarchical society. Without being held in high esteem, they supported the LRA community through their everyday work and were vital to its functioning. Having many 'normal' ones also elevated the identities of those above them. How the normal ones were perceived internally points to the LRA/M's contradictory understanding of itself. After the failed signing, one delegate explained to me that the biggest shortcoming of the FPA was that it did not clarify what would happen to the foot soldiers, including those that were not Ugandan. It was important to take care of them and give them protection, he said, because 'most of these people are not there voluntarily'.

Otti did not tire of pointing out my achievement in travelling to the bush as a woman. He said usually women are not strong enough for such a hard journey – and that I was more like a man.[52] I said I had seen LRA women carrying great loads over long distances in the burning sun. Surely they were tougher than me. Otti shook his head in disapproval. Having spotted a female captain among the group of soldiers, I asked another commander what it was like to have women as soldiers. 'Women are the worst fighters', he answered, and because of the conversation I had just had with Otti, I misunderstood. Having had my own achievements as a tough woman touted solely by virtue of having been driven along a bumpy road, I thought he was telling me that women were not good at fighting. 'Why are they the worst fighters?' I asked. 'You should be telling me, by the way', he responded, his pointed finger implying that

---

[51] Fieldnotes, Owiny-Kibul and Palotaka: 26 November 2006.

[52] This rather light-hearted remark might hide another explanation why the LRA was open to engagement with me. Along the Sudan–Uganda border, women are often seen as bearers of outside knowledge. This particular quality means that they become like men as they get older (Allen 1994: 132). My initial contact with the LRA may have largely come about because I was seen as the bearer of outside knowledge about the workings of the ICC.

I was the expert on my own gender. I shrugged to encourage him to keep speaking. When he continued it became clear that he meant the opposite of what I had thought. 'Because they make up their mind to do something. They want to do it and then they are fierce in pursuing. Women are commanders. We have many women as high as major'.[53] What happens if a woman is a major, does she get married in the bush? 'No', he answered. 'Women with rank do not have children. Because women do not let having children be a coincidence. But if a woman commander wants a child ... they can make that decision'.[54] Again, this exchange taught me about the reality of women's lives in the LRA, and about perceptions and rules.

One LRA fighter explained that after a battle the women would be unfazed, while he would cry with anger about his experiences: 'I get very angry, and then I fight. Last time I got into a fight, I walked away, that was four months ago. Before that I got into a big fight eight months ago'. I asked him what these fights were about. He did not want to say; all he said was, 'then I go and cry and I get better'. When I said that crying was usually for women, he laughed, shook his head and explained that he could also get very angry and uncontrollably violent: 'Me, I am very bad also, but I restrain myself'.[55]

Senior commanders could express preferences when new women were abducted. The more senior the rank, the more likely it was that the commander would get to choose the woman of his liking. Younger soldiers had to hand over their shirts and the new women were required to wash them. The young man would then find his wife based on who had washed his shirt. Once the woman was handed over to the 'husband', there were certain expectations of how he would treat her. These expectations did, in the eyes of the LRA, protect the woman from rape, since rape – in their definition – did not feature in the forced marriage. A commander told me that a husband could not beat his wife – if he did, he would be punished with death. The reasoning behind this rule,

---

[53] In an article about women in the LRA that draws largely on existing stereotypes of the LRA while simultaneously aiming to refute them, Graham emphasises that Kony's spirit Silli Silindi is female and leads the female part of the LRA, the 'Mary Company'. She argues that women are seen only as less valuable fighters than men, but does not present any original evidence to prove the finding (Graham 2008).

[54] That the power of decision-making is not denied to women is unsurprising in the context of northern Uganda. After all, Alice Lakwena had been the most powerful rebel leader prior to Kony himself (Allen 1991; Behrend 1993, 1999a).

[55] Fieldnotes. Juba: 6 June 2006. Finnstroem recounts the story of two young Acholi men who said that men are more resilient than women and that women's weakness shows, for example, in their public display of grief at funerals. Restraint was considered a virtue that marked manhood (Finnstroem 2009: 64).

I was told, was that for the LRA to survive, it was very important to 'take care of each other'.

Otti and Kony insisted that the LRA was not abducting and that everyone who was with them had come for protection. In June 2006 Mary Sungu, then commissioner of Ibba County in Western Equatoria, confronted Otti in a meeting with Machar and demanded that he release women and girls abducted from her county in early 2006. Otti denied that the girls were with the LRA. Later on, in a side conversation with one of his delegates, he made the point that 'the girls are there' and had been with the LRA ever since their abduction. Machar suggested that the LRA should stop abducting because then the girls might want to voluntarily marry LRA soldiers. Everybody laughed – except the commissioner, who was the only woman in the meeting.

For me, observing from the sidelines, the episode confirmed the parallel realities of the LRA, in which conflicting facts could live side by side. The realisation that abduction was wrong sat comfortably with the notion that abduction was necessary; being a tough fighter could be reconciled with crying to get better; taking possession of women against their will, including sexual possession, was not at odds with rejecting accusations of being rapists.

4.5   Achievements

During the Juba Talks, the LRA/M initially focused on publicly reshaping the narrative of the war, away from a focus on violence and spirituality towards a politicised view of the conflict. When asked whether spirits had told him to fight this war, Kony answered:

No, no, no, no. It is not like that. God did not tell me to fight this war, no .... Many people say like that. But God did not tell me to fight the people of Uganda or to fight the government of Museveni. Only the government of Uganda want to fight us because they said that we are ... using spirits. Or spirit is with us, so he want to kill all of us. But God did not told me to fight Uganda people. He told me to teach the Uganda people how to be a democratic system, how to be in a good leader. How to work together. How to be in God's law. But not to kill the people of Uganda.[56]

Dismissing any spiritual element was part of this recasting of the narrative, and it remains difficult to assess what role spirituality played at

---

[56] Author interview with Joseph Kony, Sudan/DRC border: 12 June 2006. Agbonifo argues that religion is generally used to sanction violent acts, rather than causing them (Agbonifo 2004).

which moment and for whom.[57] In mid-2006, Kony and his delegates played down the importance of spirituality to focus on their military and political strength. Whether this translated into how junior LRA fighters related to spiritual powers is another question. A young Sudanese woman abducted from Pajok in January 2007, for example, told me that the young LRA soldiers who had taken her had asked her a range of questions straight after her abduction. These give an insight into what junior LRA soldiers still in the field at the time thought important: 'Is your mother rich? Is your father rich? Do they have poison to kill people? Are they witchcrafters?' She had answered that no, they were not rich and had no poison.[58]

In comparing the LRA to Alice Lakwena's Holy Spirit Mobile Forces, one LRA member said: 'What Alice was doing was considered witchcraft. Lakwena did not fight a strategic war, you see, because she would leave UPDF weapons behind after a battle. Kony was never about witchcraft. This was always a strategic war'.[59] One commander explained to me that thanks to the LRA, the Acholi had regained some of the power that Museveni had wanted to take from them. The LRA was a way to show the world that they were 'smart people', rather than just soldiers. 'I became a major because of my brain. I am a good fighter also. But with a good brain you can be an academic officer or a field officer',[60] he said.

The various bits of reading material I spotted in the LRA camp all seemed to emphasise military strategy – whether these books were on display to make a point or because they were really being read is difficult to say. On my first visit there, I saw three young LRA soldiers with books. One was carrying a copy of Von Clausewitz' iconic celebration of European warfare, *On War*, another an edition from the *Idiot's Guide* series – *The Complete Idiot's Guide to US Special Operations Forces* – and the third was pouring over a Tom Clancy volume titled *Special Forces* with one of the delegates, who seemed to have brought the book to the bush as a present.[61]

The move away from the image of stealthy spiritual forces towards a recasting of the LRA as military celebrities had an unexpected side effect

---

[57] See Cakaj (2016) or Titeca (2010).

[58] Author (with translator Zande/English) interview with Sudanese abductee who spent March–December 2008 with the LRA. Yambio: 23 February 2009. For a detailed historical discussion on the sigificance of poisoning in Sudan's Equtoria regions, see Leonardi (2007b).

[59] Fieldnotes, Juba: 6 September 2006.   [60] Fieldnotes, Juba: 28 September 2006.

[61] Cerasini (2002); Clancy (2001); von Clausewitz (1973) (originally published 1873). It is possible that the display of these books was a planned publicity stunt to shift the narrative on the LRA.

for them. In late 2008, I was having dinner with a former delegate when his phone rang, flashing up the number of Kony's satellite phone. He pushed the phone aside. He explained to me that since his dismissal from the delegation, he no longer took Kony's calls. I was surprised. Two years before, the same man had sounded devoted to Kony – and fearful of Kony's mind-reading powers. In May 2006 he had threatened me and told me that the chairman was reading my mind and knew my motives: 'Kony will know if you come with bad things in your heart', he had told me, waving a finger in my face. The chairman had for now decided that I did not come with bad intentions, he said, so I would be allowed to travel to the bush. Yet if I changed my intentions, I would be punished.[62] It was not clear who would punish me – a spiritual force, Kony himself, or the people sitting across from me at that moment. Over the next few months, I was repeatedly accused of having bad intentions, ranging from charges that I would arrest Kony for the ICC to the claim that my chameleon-shaped silver pendant was a hidden recording device. I was told that the chairman was particularly afraid of my necklace.

In June 2005, one of the future LRA delegates told me at length that Kony controlled thunder and lighting and had access to his mind. 'Number one always knows where I am and what I am planning', he explained. 'His power over me means I will never be able to betray him'. We were sitting in a private home in Gulu. Outside, rain poured down, lightning came and went, and thunder crashed. After one particularly loud thunderclap, the young man pointed to the sky and said that Kony knew he was speaking about him.

I was reminded of this conversation when three years later, the same man defected from the LRA to openly work for the GoU, something he had reportedly been doing covertly all along. During Operation Lightning Thunder (OLT), his face was put on leaflets dropped over Garamba Park, telling LRA defectors they should seek shelter in the churches or with the Congolese army and that they would get amnesty in Uganda and be safe. He then proceeded to deliver falsified intelligence reports to donors and tried to trick the government out of large sums of money; he spent some time in jail.[63] For his time with the LRA, the young man received amnesty twice. The suggestion that Kony could always read his mind and that it was what scared him the most was thus not particularly convincing.

---

[62] Fieldnotes, Nairobi: 25 May 2006.

[63] He posed as Bwone when delivering intelligence to US sources in Kampala about Kony's lack of interest in singing the peace agreement. For a summary, see US Embassy Kampala (2008b).

Middle- and senior-rank commanders spoke of Kony's spiritual power when they wanted to make a strong statement. The same LRA whom I had seen in a television interview talking about Kony's invincibility laughed when he told me a few weeks later that of course, he did not really believe that the chairman could not be wounded by a bullet. Another LRA member said that in his view Kony might not be invincible, but the fact that he had survived for so long was proof that the cause was right: 'I believe in the cause and I think there is a real reason why the chairman has been unharmed for so many years'.[64] For him, this was proof of the leader's legitimacy, rather than of his supernatural powers. When Otti spoke about power in the LRA, he was always very clear about his own importance. I never heard him speak with anything less than the utmost respect for Kony, but he never seemed scared or devout.[65] He never mentioned Kony's spiritual powers to me.

In stark contrast, international observers, journalists and young abductees in the LRA spoke about Kony's special powers as if they were the driving force behind events. Finnstroem has written about this 'colonial imagination' that feeds outsider's notions of the LRA.[66] 'Vincent Otti thinks Kony is the messiah', said an international observer to me, for example. The US sources reported, seemingly without questioning, that 'Colonel Bwone', acting as an informer in March 2008, had told them 'that Kony had moved at near lightning speed, travelling 270 kilometers from near Duru, DRC, to his current location in a 48-hour period'.[67] There was no comment that the steady pace of 5.6 kilometres per hour through dense bush, without a moment of rest or sleep and travelling at times in darkness, was somewhat incredible. In reality, the story had been peddled by a former LRA/M delegate who had been posing as Bwone on the phone and who had often impressed international observers with his description of Kony's superpowers.

At the dinner in late 2008, the former delegate turned off his phone after not taking Kony's call. I asked him whether he was not afraid of Kony's wrath at being treated disrespectfully. Were others in the LRA/M circle also no longer afraid? He said acting as he did – expressing his unwillingness to remain Kony's interlocutor – and being afraid of the chairman were two different things. 'People have to be afraid of the chairman, naturally', he said. However, for him, that supposed ingrained natural fear no longer translated into obeying Kony's orders.[68]

---

[64] Fieldnotes, Nabanga: 20 September 2006.
[65] In the end it seems that his authority led to his assassination, as it challenged Kony.
[66] Finnstroem (2008a).   [67] US Embassy Kampala (2008b).
[68] Interview with former LRA/M delegate. Nairobi: 10 November 2008.

A few months before, I had met with another former delegate in Nairobi to talk about why Kony had not emerged from the bush to sign the FPA. He said there had been a very simple reason for this: Kony did not show up at the signing because he was more powerful when he could not be seen. When nobody knew the LRA and what Kony was like, people were more afraid. Being seen to sign a document surrounded by former enemies would make Kony look weak. He speculated that for Kony it was important to re-establish power by becoming mysterious and hence invincible again. Being otherworldly, he said, makes for someone who is very scary: 'Kony was stronger when he was not exposed to the world'.[69] As a result of being so accessible during the Juba Talks, the 'LRA is much weaker now than it was in 2006'.[70]

4.6   Conclusion

Among observers or facilitators, establishing how the LRA ticked was a prime pursuit. Establishing patterns in their behaviour that could help explain how they would react to future events was seen as one way of making sure the Juba Talks would become a success. Yet each actor searching for patterns in LRA behaviour also brought their own prejudices and expectations to this guessing game. Thus, any mention of Kony's spirituality and the power he held over his fighters and delegates was lapped up with a mixture of disbelief and fascination. Yet another insight that could have come out of the Juba Talks was that individuals within the LRA moved through their lives with contradictions, calculations and strategies that were adjusted to their changing surroundings as is often the case in any other human existence – yet in this case, these might have been enhanced by the fact that violence was at the heart of it all.

The ways individuals portrayed themselves made it clear that inconsistency was essential to how ever-changing situations were navigated, including fluidity when dealing with supposedly firm rules. A similar pattern occurred in early 2007: after the LRA/M had made the very firm statement to not return to Juba to negotiate, the first few months were spent on interpreting that claim in a way that allowed for a continuation of the talks.

This points to the broader question of where to locate the change that peace negotiations are trying to bring. A peace deal is by definition designed to change the inconsistency that has been part of the LRA's

---

[69] Fieldnotes, Cologne: 24 September 2008.
[70] Fieldnotes, Cologne: 24 September 2008.

existence. This change also requires the possibility to have personal narratives, identity and values adjusted; maybe it is with this process that the notion of a 'holistic' process is best explained. Adjusting identities in a holistic process means that the first experience of peace is loss: loss of control, power, being. While communal benefits of peace might be clear, for individuals recasting themselves in a peace process that continues to work along entrenched power dynamics means loss of status and power.

5 The Juba Peace Talks with the Lord's Resistance Army in 2007
'We Don't Know If We Can Trust'

Towards the end of 2006, Juba had changed. Cars had started to clog the streets; a few hitherto unseen motorbike taxis were ready for passengers. Cafe de Paris, Juba's first pizza parlour, had opened in August 2006, tucked away in a corner of a half-finished building. The waiters navigated pizza or avocado vinaigrette past steel rods sticking out from unfinished concrete walls, amazed by the flocks of international customers who came to eat European food. A restaurant tucked away in a side street started karaoke nights. Sometimes the karaoke machine ran on mains electricity, which from October 2006 came on sporadically. As the first potholes were filled with mud and sand, the Juba branch of Kenya Commercial Bank opened. Tented and prefabricated camps with evocative names such as Nile Beach Hotel or Oasis Camp conquered the river's west bank, gradually limiting Juba residents' access to what was their shower room, laundromat, food supply, fridge and playground.

The year 2007 brought a different character to the Juba Talks. The frayed relationship between the LRA/M and the mediator towards the end of 2006, particularly the lack of activity to deal decisively with UPDF attacks on LRA, meant that the day-to-day negotiations had all but subsided before Christmas, along with the intense media interest. To show his continuing goodwill, Machar had sent a bull to the LRA in the bush near Ri-Kwangba for Christmas. One delegate had spent the holidays with the LRA in the bush; the others had departed to assess options to continue the talks elsewhere.

I returned to Juba in February 2007 and found that the delegates had left luggage stashed away in wardrobes or under the beds in their rooms, which were being held by the hotel. While this seemed to hint at an expected return, some of those in the SPLA who had been working on the Juba Talks said they did not think that the negotiations could be resurrected. Upon hearing that I was back in Juba, people from international agencies who had left town asked me to act as their 'eyes and ears' to find out if the Talks would resume. Neither SPLA nor international agencies had had credible contact with the LRA/M over the

Christmas period. The year 2007 started off with uncertainty about the approach on offer, but without a credible alternative.

5.1   What Will Happen to the Juba Talks?

On 9 January 2007, the second anniversary of the signing of the CPA, Bashir and Kiir announced in separate speeches that the LRA was no longer welcome in their country.[1] This statement reinforced some delegates' impression that they would not be safe in Juba and that GoSS could not be trusted. Others were less concerned about safety but were enraged by what they considered a disrespectful comment, considering the LRA was still engaged in peace talks. Ojul, announced to reporters in Nairobi: 'In view of the statements by the two leaders and security considerations, the LRA delegation for the peace talks are not going back to Juba'.[2]

A few days after Ojul had addressed reporters in Nairobi, news came that Alice Auma Lakwena, the former leader of the Holy Spirit Mobile Forces, had died in Kenya. Her family demanded a state burial for her, which the government rejected. Museveni gave responsibility for arranging her burial in Uganda to the Ministries of Defence and Foreign Affairs.[3] Delegates commented that Lakwena seemed to get more GoU honours in her death than Kony did in negotiating peace; a newspaper columnist wrote, 'Some northerners may look at the government's action of taking care of the dead, having neglected the living, as an act of hypocrisy'.[4] When asked what he thought about Lakwena's death, Otti laughed and then expressed a similar sentiment: 'Museveni likes Alice better when she is dead .... She will get a big funeral'.[5] Mao (as Gulu's District Chairman) and Ochora (as the RDC) flew to Nairobi to assure the safe return of her body, using the opportunity to meet with LRA/M delegates who were working in Nairobi on finding another venue. Lakwena's burial near Gulu was attended by scores of wailing people.

On 5 February 2007, the LRA/M delegation released a statement expressing distrust in the agenda and in Machar – arguing that Machar had been imposed on them by GoSS – and voiced their concerns for the security of fighters and delegates.

On 6 February, the US government announced the creation of a new unified combatant command 'to promote US national security objectives in Africa and its surrounding waters'.[6] The new command was to go by

---

[1] 'South Sudan's Kiir warns Ugandan LRA of military action' (2007).
[2] BBC News (2007).   [3] Egadu and Akena (2007).   [4] Nnyago (2007).
[5] Fieldnotes (phone conversations), 1 February 2007.   [6] Ploch (2011).

the name AFRICOM, and was initially to be headquartered in Germany. The LRA/M delegates commented that it was disconcerting to have a permanent US command in Africa – a view that was widely shared[7] – arguing that the United States would now play a bigger and unwelcome role in Uganda, and the Juba Talks specifically. They discussed increased US presence in Gulu and US oil interests in Uganda,[8] remarking on the long-standing partnership between the US military and the UPDF. As part of AFRICOM's relationship with the UPDF, the Combined Joint Task Force – Horn of Africa now provided counter-terrorism training to the UPDF, including training in 'how to properly search a building occupied by terrorists', as a classified US embassy cable put it.[9]

In the LRA bush camp in Garamba, the focus was reportedly still on peace. A southern Sudanese abductee who had been taken in December 2006 and given to Alfred 'Record' Otim as a wife recounted that during her first few months with the LRA, Otim was always saying 'we are coming out, we are coming out', and that generally the LRA were excited about the peace agreement they were expecting.[10] A Sudanese man who had been abducted said that during those early months of 2007, the LRA always listened to the news with everyone gathered around the radio and 'whenever there is anything about the LRA on the radio, they start laughing'. When asked to clarify whether they were laughing because what they heard was good or bad, he said he did not know.[11]

In his first months with the LRA in early 2007, the new abductees had very little to eat: 'Food in Garamba was not enough. We had to go and dig in the garden with child soldiers and in the evening, we still got very little food'. During that time, he was not aware that new guns were delivered to the LRA camp.[12] It is worth noting that much of the

---

[7] Menkhaus provides a summary of the criticism of AFRICOM (Menkhaus 2009). Marchal argues that AFRICOM is a militarisation of foreign policy which will likely lead to push back (Marchal 2007). Demmers examines AFRICOM's role in the military operations against the LRA (Demmers and Gould 2018). Tella examines the role of AFRICOM as a US foreign policy instrument (Tella 2016).

[8] Jendayi Frazer – at the time of AFRICOM's establishment, Assistant Secretary of State for African Affairs – spelt out US interests in Africa in a 2009 article. Frazer wrote: 'U.S. policy in Africa is not about love. It's about advancing America's core interests: promoting economic growth and development, combating terrorism, and fostering well-governed, stable countries' (Frazer 2009).

[9] US Embassy Kampala (2007b).

[10] Author (with translator) interview with Zande LRA-abductee, 'wife' of Alfred 'Record' Otim. Yambio: 23 February 2009.

[11] Author (with translator Zande/English) interview with Sudanese abductee who spent from March 2008 to December 2008 with the LRA. Yambio: 23 February 2009.

[12] Author (with translator Zande/English) interview with Sudanese abductee who spent from March 2008 to December 2008 with the LRA. Yambio: 23 February 2009.

information of LRA activities during and after that time came from abductee's testimony – both in my own fieldwork and in many of the reports written on the situation. Abductee's testimony comes with its own challenges, as memories might be unclear, adjusted or testimony might be changed, depending on who is asking questions and for what reason.

Meanwhile, the challenge of assembling the LRA in Owiny-Kibul and UPDF deployment remained unresolved. Officially, LRA fighters left in Eastern Equatoria were not allowed to cross the Nile. From their point of view, remaining east of the Nile was impossible because the UPDF had comprehensively deployed around the proposed assembly area and beyond. As the LRA and UPDF moved around in Eastern Equatoria, violence against civilians and clashes between LRA and UPDF continued. These were monitored by a still understaffed and under-resourced CHMT. The CHMT established that different actors were carrying out attacks, specifying that perpetrators were the LRA, the UPDF (often under the guise of the 105th battalion), and individual criminals and armed groups. Of other armed groups, remnants of the Equatorian Defence Forces (EDF) were mentioned. The EDF had been a sizeable Khartoum-aligned militia during the war. UN security staff considered Eastern Equatoria as one of the most dangerous states in southern Sudan at that time, describing it as a 'network of insecurity'.[13]

How complex this network of insecurity was transpired over the coming months. Quite disconnected from the LRA and the UPDF, economic changes in the Juba Market were creating a different kind of insecurity for Eastern Equatoria's citizens. Those who had previously held power in Juba were seeking to stabilise their control over the market in a rapidly changing environment. While the CHMT was busy trying to pinpoint the perpetrators of specific attacks, dead bodies of Somali men were appearing in Juba, usually in strategic places like the road to the SAF barracks. It turned out that a senior politician – who had been aligned with SAF during the war and afterwards received a powerful post in the government – had been involved in hiring twelve Somali men to act as a link between northern traders in Juba and remnants of the EDF in Eastern Equatoria. They paid the EDF to act as mercenaries, ambushing vehicles on the road and again interrupting supplies from Uganda. When other Juba traders realised that the road ambushes were financed

---

[13] Personal email to author from international aid worker in Juba: 4 April 2007.

by Khartoum, the dead bodies of the Somali men involved started to turn up.[14]

Despite the continued engagement of the Acholi community, the early months of 2007 were marked by the delegation's reluctance to return to Juba. Otti continuously reiterated the LRA's commitment to peace; confusion about the assembly and ongoing attacks continued. In the background, Acholi leaders and Chissano were working on finding a way to resume talks. On 2 March, Chissano met Kony in DRC, with the UN rather than GoSS providing logistics. Chissano was on a tour of the capitals of the region to drum up continued enthusiasm for the next round of talks. US documents state that Kampala was still reluctant to resume, although Machar had said to US representatives that talks would start again on 12 March.[15] Both Chissano and Machar were pushing for further international engagement, including AU observers for the CHMT and observers from Tanzania, Mozambique, South Africa and Kenya. Machar, emphasised in talks with US representatives that four-teen countries were now contributing to the UN-administered JIF, with three European countries and the GoU putting money towards humani-tarian assistance to the assembly areas.[16] Yet nothing happened.

From 1 to 4 March 2007, a group of Acholi representatives gathered in Juba for a GoSS-facilitated peace conference. No LRA representative was present. In a final document, those attending recommended that talks resume in Juba, with participants' security assured. The list of recommendations reads like a commentary on the flaws of the Juba Talks. The Acholi representatives recommended that the CoH be upheld. They elaborated that more countries, the UN, the AU, the Intergovernmental Authority on Development (IGAD) and the East African Community should join the mediation team, and that 'women and other interest groups' ought to be included and 'the Chief Mediator should define the roles and responsibilities of NGOs, groups and indi-viduals invited to facilitate, observe or participate in the Peace Talks'. The resolution further stated that those 'involved in the peace process should be enhanced through training and technical assistance', and that 'the Secretariat be strengthened and staffed with competent, professional and accountable personnel to provide effective and equitable services and equal treatment to the parties'.[17]

---

[14] Author interview with international security staff. Juba: 1 February 2008. I have since heard this story told again in a similar way by a former SPLA soldier.

[15] US Embassy Khartoum (2007).   [16] US Embassy Khartoum (2007).

[17] Acholi Peace Conference, 'Resolution from the Acholi Peace Conference', Juba: 4 March 2007.

5.2   Managing the Impasse

From the outside, it seemed as if things had largely stalled – until a press release from IKV Pax Christi on 11 April. Towards the end of 2006, IKV Pax Christi had withdrawn from its role in the mediation team. It had been instrumental in bringing about the talks, having understood its 'collaboration with the GoSS' as one in which 'Pax Christi – in the persons of Dr Onek, Professor Assefa and Dr Simonse – was to be responsible for the mediation of the peace talks while GoSS would be the host', says an article written by various IKV Pax Christi representatives.[18] However, as the Juba Talks unfolded in 2006, the role of the mediator was occupied by Machar; Professor Assefa had been sidelined.

When the peace process stalled, IKV Pax Christi came back, albeit covertly, for what they called a 'back-channel process'.[19] Having met with Museveni, who agreed that such a process would be helpful and who mandated his brother Salim Saleh to represent the GoU, Pax Christi organised a meeting from 31 March to 6 April between representatives of the LRA/M and the GoU in Mombasa, Kenya.[20] The LRA/M was represented by a selection of their delegates: Krispus Ayena, Martin Ojul, Denis Okirot, Peter Ongom and Ray Achama. Saleh, Minister of State for Microfinance, came as the main negotiator for the GoU. Sam Kagoda, Permanent Secretary for Internal Affairs and a member of the GoU delegation in Juba, accompanied Saleh. Also present for the GoU were Ambassador Joseph Ocwet (who had been instrumental in helping Betty Bigombe during her first attempt at peace), and Captain Ruhinda Maguru, his assistant.

IKV Pax Christi's motivation for the meeting was to revive the stalled peace talks by providing an alternative communication channel without interference from the big international players. With Juba having proven an unstable and pressured place, taking actors to a different location was seen as a good way to break the impasse. IKV Pax Christi describes this initiative, not as a move to

replace the Juba process, but to help it along by inserting the outcomes of the back-channel process. The Mombasa–Nairobi talks provided a safe space away from political pressures and public scrutiny. This mattered because the atmosphere in the Juba process had become highly charged and adversarial owing to intense media attention and the larger number of parties involved, each with its own interest.[21]

---

[18] Simonse, Verkoren and Junne (2010: 232).
[19] Simonse, Verkoren and Junne (2010: 233).   [20] IKV Pax Christi (2007).
[21] Simonse, Verkoren and Junne (2010: 233).

The inclusion of Saleh, who had been involved both in previous military offensives against the LRA as well as peace negotiations, seemed to guarantee buy-in from Museveni while allowing the LRA/M to engage with an actor they knew. To my mind, it was yet another manifestation of how all conflict actors brought baggage with them, but that did not necessarily mean that it could not be used to connect. With Saleh becoming a significant player at this point, it became clear how intricate the broader conflict system was in which the actors from the LRA, LRM and GoU were tightly linked.

As if to prove the point, Otti had sanctioned the meeting with Saleh and reportedly decreed who should attend for the LRA/M – although some delegates said that those attending had chosen that it would only be them and kept the meeting secret from everyone else. It is also not clear whether all parties agreed that the meeting ought to be kept private.

Publishing a press release right after the meeting – although whether all attending parties sanctioned the publicity remains contested – IKV Pax Christi announced

significant agreements between the delegates were reached on extending the Cessation of Hostilities Agreement as well as on addressing blockages in its implementation; on resolving the outstanding issues of contention in agenda item no. 2 (called 'Comprehensive Solutions'); and on specific provisions and mechanisms for agenda item no. 3, reconciliation and accountability in the war torn communities of northern and eastern Uganda. The Parties agreed that the only major issues left for the negotiations would be agenda item no. 4, Demobilization, Disarmament and Reintegration and agenda item no. 5, Formal Cease Fire.

Crucially, the press release stated that the meeting had resolved 'the East Bank Assembly Point [Owiny-Kibul] for the LRA combatants', a

major obstacle in the implementation of the Cessation of Hostilities Agreement ... and a real danger to the peace process .... The location, according to LRA was unsafe because of the presence of UPDF in the vicinity and because of land mines. LRA combatants on the East Bank have repeatedly been accused of attacks on civilians that had in fact been carried out by members of Sudanese armed groups still active on the East Bank. The agreement negotiated by General Saleh takes away a stumbling block for progress in the negotiations by allowing LRA fighters that were supposed to assemble in Owiny-ki-Bul to move to the camp in Ri-Kwangba and join the rest of the LRA forces that are supposed to assemble there. This agreement meets the express request of the LRA leadership.[22]

---

[22] IKV Pax Christi (2007).

IKV Pax Christi further outlined that significant process had been made on Agenda 2, the comprehensive political solutions to the war, by agreeing on

> measures to reinforce constitutional provisions ensuring equal opportunity and affirmative action for northern and eastern Ugandans; mechanisms, complementary to the Peace Recovery and Development Programme that counteract siphoning of availed funds to governmental and non-governmental coordination structures and empower the war-affected citizens to play an active role in their own rehabilitation and development.[23]

On Agenda 3,

> the two parties agreed that traditional institutions such as Mato Oput, Culo Kwor, Kayo Cuk, etc. should play a prominent role in the reconciliation of war-affected individuals and communities. In addition to these traditional mechanisms and underscoring the unacceptability of impunity for crimes against humanity, alternative justice systems will be put in place that will address accountability and enable victims to seek justice for grievances. To address grievances and historical conflicts at the national level the parties committed themselves to establish special forums. The Government of Uganda has agreed to ask Parliament to enact legislation that recognises traditional and alternative justice mechanisms as key elements in dealing with accountability for the offences committed during the war. Once the justice systems are effectively in place the Government of Uganda will approach the International Criminal Court regarding the indictments against the four leaders of the LRA.[24]

From 13 to 14 April 2007, a few days after the meeting in Mombasa, the delegation, Special Envoy Chissano and the LRA high command met in Nabanga to make the most of the new momentum. With both parties signing the 'Ri-Kwangba Communique', the LRA leadership agreed to restart the talks on 26 April and the GoU agreed to extend the CoH until the end of June.[25] With an addendum signed in Ri-Kwangba, the renewed CoH abandoned the idea of two assembly points and instead allowed for an assembly in Ri-Kwangba only, giving all LRA forces six weeks to arrive there.[26]

A different delegation returned to Juba to restart the talks: some delegates were disgruntled, having been excluded from the Mombasa meeting, or unhappy that their protest against the conditions in Juba had been ineffective. Others were keen to continue the talks. Some did not return at all, having been dismissed from the delegation, or withdrawn from a process they did not see as credible.

---

[23] IKV Pax Christi (2007).   [24] IKV Pax Christi (2007).
[25] Government of Uganda and Lord's Resistance Army/Movement (14 April 2007).
[26] Government of Uganda and Lord's Resistance Army/Movement (2007).

To IKV Pax Christi's astonishment, however, the continuing Juba Talks did not build on what had been agreed on in Mombasa.[27] This was not necessarily surprising, considering that so far in the Juba Talks, agreements on paper had remained disconnected from how the actors behaved in the process and what they aimed to achieve. Much like previously signed agreements, the Mombasa agreement had regulated the process, rather than decisively moved the discussions forward.

Instead of building on a solid signed agreement, the process became considerably more tense, including between IKV Pax Christi and UN representatives, who were angry about the separate initiative. Established LRA/M delegates felt excluded and eyed new arrivals with suspicion. Obita had joined the talks in Juba properly for the first time, Okot – formerly an MP for the northern Ugandan district Pader and described by the *Daily Monitor* as 'a former NRM die-hard in the Acholi sub region'[28] –was now an LRA/M delegate, and David Nyekorach Matsanga emerged as an LRA/M representative.

With the stalemate on the assembly tackled, LRA fighters were now crossing the Nile with official permission, using jerry cans to which they tied poles to pull themselves across the water. Southern Sudanese abductees, such as a young woman from Pajok who had been abducted in January 2007 on her way back from Maridi and whom I interviewed in Yambio in early 2009, were told that the LRA was now leaving Owiny-Kibul to go directly to Garamba Park.[29]

5.3   The Talks Continue

In Juba, the work continued. Agenda 2 on Comprehensive Political Solutions was signed on 2 May 2007, soon after the meeting in Nabanga.[30] However, it took until 1 June 2007, for the Juba Talks to officially restart amidst remaining confusion over trust, location, mediation and assembly. June 2007 brought significant progress on Agenda 3, with parties agreeing that both formal national justice, as well as informal local justice, would be used to handle crimes committed during the war. A parallel development, however, caused a stir in the delegation: on 10 June 2007, representatives of GoSS, the GoU and the DRC government met in Juba to work on the military 'Plan B' – a military

---

[27] Simonse, Verkoren and Junne (2010: 236).   [28] Mpagi (2007).

[29] Author (with translator) interview with Sudanese LRA abductee from Parajok. Yambio: 23 February 2009.

[30] Government of the Republic of Uganda and the Lord's Resistance Army/Movement (2007).

collaboration between the three countries against the LRA.[31] Agenda 3 was signed on 29 June.[32] Part of the agreement was that both delegations would consult with people in Uganda on their expectations of a process of justice and accountability and the agreed comprehensive political solutions. These consultations were also to include meetings with legal experts in Kampala to set up new justice mechanisms – namely a new Special Division of the Ugandan High Court – that would comply with Juba agreements while being acceptable to Uganda and the ICC. However, since no agreement could be reached on conducting the consultations jointly, the two delegations departed separately. For some of the LRA/M delegates, the consultations provided their first opportunity to return to Uganda in years – in some cases, in decades.

Back in Nabanga, Otti shared his thoughts about the process so far. Agreeing to a reconciliation process with the local community near Ri-Kwangba to sort out access to its gardens and beehives, he said:

> I think I will be here for another year. We need to be peaceful, also peaceful with my neighbours. They need to understand about LRA, and I need to understand about them so we can all have a good life. Sometimes it is hard for us because we don't know if we can trust. But to get to peace also means to learn to trust. To get to peace also means to understand when we need to stop war.[33]

A few days later, the LRA agreed with local residents on modalities to share the honey harvest from the Nabanga beehives.[34] Back in Juba, other issues that required new management strategies were settled. After initial mismanagement problems emerged in the handling of the JIF – which was now also supported by the governments of Ireland, the Netherlands, Canada and the UK – accounting firm KPMG was hired in mid-2007 to administer the funds.[35] It had become clear that the financial management of the Juba Talks had left large accountability gaps.

Up until mid-2007, the US government had stayed in the background, although the Juba Talks had received much attention from US advocacy groups – namely Invisible Children, Resolve and Enough Project – lobbying for a stronger US role. Despite acknowledging the United State's crucial behind-the-scenes role in the Juba Talks, the GoU had advised the United States against sending a Special Envoy to the talks. The GoU argued it 'would disrupt the peace process and invite unwanted propaganda and accusations from the Khartoum government'

---

[31] Fieldnotes, Juba: 10 June 2007.
[32] Government of the Republic of Uganda and Lord's Resistance Army/Movement (29 June 2007).
[33] Author interview with Vincent Otti, Ri-Kwangba: 13 July 2007.
[34] Fieldnotes, Ri-Kwangba: 15 July 2007.   [35] US Embassy Kampala (2007e).

and prompt 'Khartoum to step up its assistance to the LRA, which could scuttle progress made to date', according to a confidential US embassy cable. By contrast, Gulu RDC Ochora reportedly told the United States that since neither Machar nor Chissano had sufficient control over the LRA, 'a U.S. envoy to Juba would boost the confidence of the northern Uganda population and provide an authoritative voice to keep both parties committed to the talks'.[36]

Senator Russ Feingold of Wisconsin had written to President Bush on 14 June, expressing his desire for a US Special Envoy to northern Uganda. Senator Feingold had been working closely with both Resolve and Invisible Children who had through him lobbied for a US presence at the negotiation table in Juba. On 26 July 2007, the State Department responded to Feingold's request:

> Though President Chissano and other Ugandan leaders and northern Ugandans in regional government and civil society have quietly discouraged the United States from playing a more visible role as the current mediation proceeds, we believe the U.S. must continue to be active in seeking solutions to the situation in Uganda. Therefore, the Department is appointing a Senior Advisor on Conflict in Africa, who will, as an immediate priority, primarily focus on the conflict in northern Uganda. We plan to place Timothy Shortley, currently with the NSC's [National Security Council] Africa Office, into that position.[37]

Thus, in July 2007, Tim Shortley, now Special Conflict Advisor on the Great Lakes Region to the US Undersecretary of State on African Affairs, arrived in Juba. One of his first actions was to ask the head of the CHMT, General Deng, to arrange a meeting with DRC President Kabila. The delegates largely presumed that this was to seek further support for military action after 'Plan B' discussions at the June meeting. Under the close watch of delegates, Shortley then travelled to Uganda to instruct a number of chiefs to come to Ri-Kwangba. A confidential US embassy cable reported that during Shortley's visit to Uganda he

> encountered a consistent request for US support in keeping both the Lord's Resistance Army (LRA) and the Government of Uganda (GOU) to the agenda and moving forward, as well as a close eye on Khartoum. There is fear that the longer the Juba talks go on the greater the risk of support of the LRA by Khartoum. Further, there was wide concern that the northern Ugandan diaspora representing the LRA at the Juba talks is not representative of the Acholi people (nor other northern ethnic groups), and that they are pursuing their own political agenda potentially jeopardizing the peace process.[38]

---

[36] US Embassy Kampala (2007e).
[37] Bergner (Assistant Secretary, Legislative Affairs) (2007).
[38] US Embassy Kampala (2007d).

Delegates were suspicious of Shortley's motives. When they heard that he had arranged with Ugandan leaders to travel to Ri-Kwangba, they intervened to insist that such a trip by leaders from northern Uganda would need to be 'run by Vincent first'. When Otti was told that the United States was arranging a visit of traditional leaders, he reportedly laughed and, as one delegate explained, 'finally said let them come'. Delegates assumed that Otti had asked Kony to join the meeting, but 'Kony was confused', said delegates, because the meeting had no clear agenda and the scheduling before the consultation left him 'confused what the meeting was all about'.[39]

On his way to the meeting with the traditional leaders, Kony is said to have realised that LRA troops 'had been moved without his agreement', explained one former delegate, 'and during the meeting there were skirmishes outside, of people with guns who wanted to come in', presumably Otti's allies. Kony reportedly distrusted the situation because Otti had brought a large number of people to the meeting.[40] One of the leaders from Uganda who attended was the Paramount Chief of the Madi, Ronald Iya, who describes staying in Garamba for eight days, with Kony arriving on day four. Kony stressed that war would continue if talks failed. Iya wrote: 'It was hard to take some of the things he said seriously. What I saw from my time with the LRA commanders was that the late Vincent Otti was the force behind the peace talks'.[41] The LRA/M delegates said that after the meeting Kony is said to have gone back to his base 'with distrust because he was not sure where and why the meeting was held'.[42]

5.4 Leadership Struggle

The GoU started its community consultations in Uganda on account-ability and reconciliation with a three-day meeting in Gulu from 20 to 22 August. Attending the meeting were community leaders, IDP dele-gates, spokespeople for youth and women, and representatives of LRA victims. Broadly speaking, the consulted community seemed to be in favour of a combined legal system that would allow so-called traditional systems and formal legal procedures to augment each other. In addition, to support for justice, including against the LRA leadership, that would consider victim's views, a US observer reported that there was 'a strong desire for a truth telling process that includes UPDF'.[43] Both the

---

[39] Fieldnotes, Nairobi: 11 September 2009.
[40] Fieldnotes, Nairobi: 11 September 2009.   [41] Iya (2010: 179).
[42] Fieldnotes, Nairobi: 11 November 2009.   [43] US Embassy Kampala (2007c).

northern Ugandan leaders and the delegates stressed how much northern Uganda had changed thanks to the Juba Talks. The UN's High Commisioner for Refugees (UNHCR) was broadcasting radio messages about education, health and security in an effort to encourage IDPs to leave the camps and return to their homes.

With security stable and peace seemingly around the corner, life was notably transformed – an impression that stood in stark contrast with Museveni's messaging to the United States. On 28 August, Museveni told US senator Feingold that he had warned President Kabila that if the peace talks should fail, he ought to allow Ugandan military operations on Congolese territory, or else team up with another military partner – he suggested France – to avoid the DRC becoming 'a terrorist holiday centre'.[44]

The LRA/M's consultations were delayed until October. Not everyone viewed the separate consultations positively: with two delegations gathering input from affected populations, it was seen as likely, as one of the original facilitators of the talks said, that 'the results of both consultations may require a fresh round of negotiations to reconcile the divergent results'.[45] Yet the message that seemed to come out of both sets of consultations seemed pretty clear: the LRA should sign a deal and could then come home. In Acholiland, more so than in other districts visited, the mood generally seemed to be against the ICC, but there appeared to be broad agreement that legal procedures could and ought to happen in Uganda. A US summary of the findings of the GoU consultations states that support for 'a combination of traditional systems and the formal legal system to achieve accountability and reconciliation' was obvious as neither was considered to work on its own. This included support to amend national laws in a way that would allow the ICC to back off.[46]

Reports from other consultations and surveys conducted at around the same time show broadly similar sentiments. A joint survey by Berkeley and Tulane Universities and the International Center for Transitional Justice found that 90 per cent of respondents believed peace could be achieved 'through dialogue with the LRA', 86 per cent said peace could come through 'pardoning the LRA for their crimes'. Seventy per cent said that those who had committed crimes needed to be held account-able, with 50 per cent wanting to hold the LRA leadership to account and 48 per cent wanting to see 'all of the LRA' prosecuted. Fifty-five per cent

---

[44] US Embassy Kampala (2007a).   [45] Personal email to author: 10 October 2007.
[46] US Embassy Kampala (2007c).

wanted to see the UPDF on trial, with 70 per cent stating that the UPDF had committed human rights abuses. Twenty-nine per cent identified the ICC as the most appropriate justice mechanism; 28 per cent mentioned the Ugandan courts. Twenty per cent saw the Amnesty Commission as providing the most appropriate mechanisms.[47]

However, other reports on separate sets of consultations suggest that public opinion was more divided on what role exactly the ICC might play. Arguing that the ICC had investigated in a one-sided manner, a report on consultations held by a range of women's groups nonetheless supported the ICC because it provided 'better provisions for the rights of the accused and role of Defence Counsel than currently available under domestic law in Uganda'.[48]

Tensions between the two sets of consultations thus did not turn out to be a major issue, but other problems emerged. Although the consultations allowed some LRA/M delegates to visit family they had not seen in years, delegates eyed each other suspiciously while in Uganda. It later emerged that Ojul and Achama had accepted a personal invitation by Museveni to State House without telling the other delegates; it was unclear what they had discussed with Museveni, although they later said that they had been pressed for intelligence but had not given any away. Delegates further observed a steady presence at the various consultations of US advisor Shortley, who seemed to particularly court one of the younger delegates who supposedly drew a map for him of what exactly Ri-Kwangba looked like. One delegate later commented that these developments 'caused a great rift of trust in the delegation'.[49]

On 5 September, US assistant secretary of state Frazer introduced Shortley to President Museveni. In the confidential meeting, Museveni was generally dismissive of the peace process, calling it a 'circus', according to a confidential US memo, and stating that the LRA was being 'pampered', that Kony was a 'trickster', and that the talks were a way for the LRA to reorganise. He stated that for Kony the ICC was only problematic if 'he did not want peace' – disregarding tensions between the ICC and the peace process. He disputed that the process was strengthened by the presence of Ugandan MPs. According to the confidential US embassy memo, Museveni

downplayed the role of local politicians in the process. He described his own Government's parallel track as part of the foolery and lamented that fools have a

---

[47] Pham et al. (2007: 4–5).

[48] Greater North Women's Voices for Peace Network/Ugandan Women's Coalition for Peace/Women's Initiatives for Gender Justice (August 2007).

[49] Fieldnotes, Nairobi: 11 November 2009.

lot of audiences …. Museveni said that he himself participated in the 'foolery' and has taken Vincent Otti's telephone calls and sent the LRA cows for Christmas.

He also stressed that he had taken care of Kony's parents and, should a deal be signed, Kony 'could live anywhere in Uganda where he had not committed atrocities'. Frazer expressed her support for Museveni's efforts 'to secure Kabila's cooperation' to prepare a military response to the LRA.[50] On 8 September 2007, Presidents Kabila and Museveni met in Arusha, Tanzania. They signed an agreement of cooperation that included a clause on joint efforts to remove the LRA from eastern DRC. The agreement stipulated that the LRA had to leave Garamba by the end of December 2007 or else they would face joint military action. The LRA responded with a warning of renewed attacks.[51]

In a write-up on the peace talks by some former delegates, the authors accuse the GoU and the US government of using the consultation period

to try and compromise some members of the LRA/M peace team. Of particular concern were secret meetings that Martin Ojul, and Lieutenant Colonel Ray Achama [then still a member of the CHMT] held with President Museveni, with Internal Affairs Minister Ruhakana Rugunda (leader of the government delegation), and with Mr Timothy Shortley in Kampala between the 10th and the 16th November 2007 when the two made an unexplained break from consultation in northern Uganda.

Yet again, members of the five-man LRA/M delegation that held a secret meeting in Mombasa with General Saleh in March/April 2007, this time secretly met in Kampala with the General during the consultation exercise.[52]

On 1 October 2007, following Frazer's Kampala visit, the United States officially launched AFRICOM as a subcommand of the US European Command.[53] While Frazer had expressed continued support for the Juba Talks, she had also reiterated that the process needed to now show swift success, suggesting to the LRA/M's dismay that a timeline ought to be agreed, since otherwise the United States would publicly support regional military action to 'mop up the LRA'. In preparation, US officials were already lobbying for UN support for a military strike involving regional forces.[54]

While the local consultations on justice and accountability were going on, the LRA in Garamba was increasingly difficult to reach on the phone.

---

[50] US Embassy Kampala (2007f).
[51] 'LRA warns of fresh attacks in the North', *The New Vision*, 12 September 2007.
[52] LRA/M Peace Team (2009).   [53] Ploch (2011).
[54] Resolve Uganda (2007). It is not clear whether this was support for a Security Council resolution or peacekeeping.

Otti's silence was particularly unusual, considering he had been a vocal communicator for the LRA during the entire Juba process and had been a regular caller to northern Ugandan radio station Mega FM. The last time Otti answered a phone call from me was in late September 2007. In late October, the delegation spread the news that Otti was ill and not able to talk on the phone. With weeks passing by and no word from Otti, suspicions about his well-being grew. On 2 October, the man considered the third highest-ranking commander in the LRA, Patrick Opio Makasi, surrendered to forces of the UN's mission in the DRC (United Nations Organization Mission in the Democratic Republic of the Congo/ MONUC). He was handed over first to Congolese and then to Ugandan authorities. He reportedly informed the authorities that, as it was phrased in a private meeting by US officials, 'Kony had plans to break his troops into four task forces to abduct up to 500 Congolese girls from the Garamba area, begin new attacks in West Nile, Uganda, and to send an advance team to CAR to take up a new base of operation and to pick-up arms buried in a cache in southern Sudan'.[55] Makasi was granted amnesty on 1 November.

That same day, the LRA/M delegation arrived in Kampala to meet with Museveni two days later. The meeting went ahead without any major protocol or handshaking incidents, yet the outcome was predictable. Museveni stressed that the LRA needed to sign a deal and would be welcome to return to Uganda. The delegates asked for the GoU's support to have the ICC warrants lifted. Both parties signed an agreement to again extend the CoH, this time to the end of January 2008. In a donor briefing in Kampala on 4 December, Ojul said that the LRA would travel to Juba the following week to meet with Machar. He also reiterated the LRA/M's official message on Otti: that he was under house arrest. It was implied that there had been some wrongdoing by Otti. However, in conversations with US embassy staff in Kampala, Achama said, 'Ojul knows Otti is dead, but Ojul cannot contradict Kony, whom he fears intensely'.[56] On 17 November, Uganda's notorious tabloid newspaper *Red Pepper* pitched in with its own version of what had happened to Otti: 'Kony eats Otti's penis' was the attention-grabbing headline[57] –a headline that seemed important enough to be communicated back by US embassy staff in Kampala to their Washington, DC, superiors in a confidential cable:

---

[55] US Embassy Kinshasa (2007).   [56] US Embassy Kampala (2007g).
[57] Red Pepper, 'Kony eats Otti's penis', 17 November 2007.

In Garamba, rituals were undertaken with Otti's body parts ... with the intent of containing Otti's ghost. Kony, as executioner, has reason to fear retribution by Otti's reincarnated spirit ...

The 'Red Pepper' specializes in sensationalist stories, and often (usually) pushes the boundaries of accepted journalistic practice. However, the paper does have sources in the Ugandan security/military establishment. Kony's history of using ritual and claims of contact with spirit mediums also lends some credence to the story.[58]

The delegates remained adamant that Otti was alive but under arrest. When northern leaders requested that Otti call Mega FM as a sign of life – otherwise they would not travel to Ri-Kwangba to conclude consultations – Kony reportedly called Gulu District Chairman Mao to state again that Otti was under arrest, but not dead.[59]

In the evening of 8 December 2007, my phone rang. It was one of the former LRA/M delegates. I had last seen him in the LRA camp in Ri-Kwangba in September 2006. He was shouting: 'Vincent is dead, Vincent is dead'. Having calmed down, he explained that after Kony had killed Otti, he and others had escaped from the bush through the DRC and that they were about to bring hundreds of other fighters who had been part of Otti's group out of the bush. He told me that I needed to come and meet him in Kinshasa, bring a camera and film how a group of LRA would leave the bush, 'hundreds of them'. Then the connection was cut off. I called back; the phone just kept ringing.[60] I later learned that he, along with others, had reached MONUC peacekeepers on 18 November and had confirmed that Otti, along with some of his associates, had been killed.[61]

Otti's death remained an increasingly credible rumour until early January 2008, when first Kony and then Machar confirmed it, as well as the deaths of his close allies Ben Achellam and Alfred 'Record' Otim. They had been shot dead on Kony's orders in early October 2007, probably on 2 October. The story of what had happened transpired with facets and variations. Kony had started to distrust Otti and had believed that he had been planning his assassination. Kony had suspected – probably correctly – that Otti was prepared to sign a deal even if Kony refused. Otti had reportedly lost trust in Kony to follow through with the peace talks. Maybe he received enticing offers from various sources – options given to me were Museveni or Machar – along the lines that if he helped to get Kony out of the bush or to kill him, Otti's return to civilian

---

[58] US Embassy Kampala (2007).   [59] US Embassy Kampala (2007).
[60] Fieldnotes (phone conversations), Cologne: 8 December 2007.
[61] US Embassy Kampala (2007).

life would be facilitated smoothly. Hence Kony lost faith in his number two.

'Vincent was always the one communicating, so that led to distrust', one delegate explained. His version was that Otti had been working for the GoU and they had promised to pay him if he eliminated Kony.[62] A high-ranking SPLA intelligence officer gave the explanation that Machar – under internal political pressure to bring the talks to a close – had offered Otti money and a safe haven in return for eliminating Kony and securing a peace deal.[63] One delegate explained that Kony had learned that funds had been distributed among delegates for the consultations, but none of these found their way back to him or were spent on the consultations. He was said to have concluded that Otti and the delegation were working behind his back. The memory of the surprise visit by the Ugandan traditional leaders, of which he had been informed so late, as well as of the Mombasa meeting, of which he seems to have had less knowledge than was presumed, seemed to confirm that he was being undermined.[64]

The Mombasa meeting was regularly mentioned as having caused a rift in the leadership. Another delegate explained that Otti alone had sanctioned the meeting, without consulting Kony; it had been rumoured that the LRA/M delegates in attendance had received 60,000 Ugandan shillings from Saleh to hand to Otti in exchange for bringing down Kony.[65] Most people agreed that the Mombasa meeting had created great confusion and distrust. UN staff working on the Juba Talks were furious that IKV Pax Christi had taken their initiative too far without consulting the official facilitators. IKV Pax Christi's argument that the Mombasa meeting broke the impasse and produced a set of superior agreements to those eventually signed is also valid.[66] From IKV Pax Christi's perspective, the trust established between delegations thanks to the Mombasa meeting was evident, and the possibility that it had created internal distrust rather vague. However, when Machar met again with IKV Pax Christi's representative, Simonse, on an unrelated matter in June 2008, the vice president greeted Simonse – to the latter's great astonishment – as the man responsible for Otti's murder because of the Mombasa meeting.[67]

Many different stories circulated about how exactly Otti was killed. One delegate said that he knew Otti had pleaded for his life. One story, relayed much later from within the LRA to UN staff, was that Kony had

---

[62] Fieldnotes, Juba: 2 February 2008.
[63] Author interview with SPLA intelligence officer. Juba: 1 March 2009.
[64] Fieldnotes, Nairobi: 11 November 2009.   [65] Fieldnotes, Nairobi: 14 March 2008.
[66] Simonse, Verkoren and Junne (2010: 235).   [67] Fieldnotes, Juba: 5 June 2008.

harboured suspicions against Otti and had Otti's hut – his *tukul* – searched when he was out. When Otti returned sooner than anticipated, there was a quick shootout. 'There was no pleading, no begging for his life, and no grilling of genitals', said a UN security staff, referencing the headline in the *Red Pepper*. 'The Ugandan press has done everything possible to throw a spanner in the peace process'.[68] The LRA's third-in-command, Makasi, told Ugandan media after his escape that Kony had asked Otti for a meeting and had him arrested. Makasi said that he himself had been tipped off that he would also be arrested and had managed to flee with a group of people.

A woman from Maridi who was 'Record' Otim's forced wife recounted how Kony had come or sent someone to the place where she was staying with Otim and 'asked for his top commanders Otti, Otim, Achellam and one more to come for meeting'. Otim left her behind when he went for the meeting because she was pregnant. When Otti, travelling from his base in Garamba One, arrived at Kony's place (called Garamba Two), Kony was not there. Otti reportedly asked the bodyguards, 'Where is the big man?' He was then arrested and all four 'were taken to the bush and shot to death, their guards also .... Otti's guards were also killed'. Record Otim's wife only came to know that her husband-by-force had been killed because people had heard gunshots and told her about it. Kony then asked to divide the 'property of the people shot amongst others, including the wives', so she was given to a new husband.[69] When asked for the reason why her husband was killed, she said she did not know the reason exactly. She said what she knew was that Otim was always saying 'there would be peace, but Kony did not want peace, that they would get peace and Otti wanted out and Kony was not ready to come out', but her husband did not give her a reason why.[70]

Those who had been in Otti's camp had reportedly been either shot dead or had been disarmed and were in a gloomy mood. On 11 December 2007, President Kabila reiterated in a private meeting at his home with Shortley that DRC would 'stick to his agreement with President Museveni and ... keep the pressure on the LRA to leave Garamba or finalize a peace agreement'.[71]

Otti's death rattled the delegation, the mediation team, and the journalists. Speaking to various delegates, I learned that the killing had

---

[68] Author interview with UN security officer. Juba: 1 February 2008.
[69] Author (with translator) interview with Zande LRA-abductee, 'wife' of Alfred 'Record' Otim. Yambio: 23 February 2009.
[70] Author (with translator) interview with Zande LRA-abductee, 'wife' of Alfred 'Record' Otim. Yambio: 23 February 2009.
[71] US Embassy Kinshasa (2007).

not only challenged the delegation's coherence, but had also tainted communication between the delegates and Kony. One delegate told me: 'Adek is really disturbed by Vincent's death because he [Adek] is frank with Kony. He tells him the truth. He was the one who called Kony and said to him your own delegation is afraid to visit you'.[72] One delegate – speaking after he had just been dismissed from the delegation – said 'Kony did not tell us the truth about Vincent. First, he said Vincent was sick, then that he was under house arrest. He made me lie to the press in Nairobi, saying that Otti was okay. This makes it hard for me to make the case for the LRA'.[73] For another delegate the process had lost its momentum with Otti's death, with the focus solely on getting signatures under agreements and with both the delegation and the LRA leadership split: 'If we think about getting an agreement, but we don't think about the future after the agreement, I no longer know if it will ever end'.[74]

5.5   Conclusion

Where 2006 had been the year in which previously established conflict structures between the LRA/M and the GoU were emphasised in how the events unfolded, 2007 developed on a different trajectory. The challenging internal dynamics of the LRA/M and the many layers of the LRA/M's experience of negotiating peace became much clearer. This included internal distrust and sabotage, but also increased engagement with an ever-growing collection of outside actors which pulled the LRA/M in different directions. One way of maintaining coherence was to exert control at the very heart of the LRA. Additionally, the events in 2007 magnified the parallel processes the LRA/M was experiencing in the dynamics of the process and the signed agreements that emerged. The leadership struggle at a time when progress on paper was more successful than ever before is a manifestation both of reclaiming control and the many layers of experience in the process.

With Chissano in place as the UN Special Envoy and Shortley for the United States, the international architecture of the talks had been strengthened. But the two appointments highlighted different possibilities:

---

[72] Fieldnotes, Juba: 2 February 2008. Adek was also quoted in a confidential US embassy memo. According to the memo 'Adek confirmed that Kony was set on making money to "run his organization and run/relocate if necessary". Adek said that Kony was not interested in meeting or talking with anyone anymore and wanted to find a safe place to go. Adek said that LRA members in Garamba were terrorized and demoralized' (US Embassy Kampala 2008a).

[73] US Embassy Kampala (2008a).   [74] US Embassy Kampala (2008a).

one was that despite the ICC warrants, the broader international community was committed to somehow finding a solution in Juba. The other was that the solution could also be a military strike. For the LRA/M, increased international attention meant that the opportunity to forge outside connections also grew. This brought risks (and arguably led to the killing of Otti), but also fuelled one of the LRA/M's most powerful tools of keeping outsiders engaged by giving them access and then withdrawing it again.

6 'Reach Out a Hand and Pull It Back'
The Lord's Resistance Army's 'Connect/Disconnect' Meets International Galvanic Surges

A month before the Juba Talks started in July, on the evening of 7 June 2006, the LRA/M delegation went to the southern Sudan vice president's office. The delegates had waited for a week for their first encounter with Machar; it was necessary so that they could travel to the bush for the meeting in which Kony was to mandate them as his representatives. Machar had been delayed in Khartoum, first by political business and then by a sandstorm. Shaking Machar's hand, delegates bowed their heads and clicked their heels in acknowledgement of his authority. Once seated around a large table, host and visitors exchanged pleasantries. Machar said interest in the talks was heating up: he had received an interview request from Radio France Internationale just that morning. He was jovial, confident and very much in control. The delegates seemed deferential.

Yet the modalities of organising and paying for the peace talks weighed heavily on their minds. Designated spokesperson Olweny said, 'the financial requirement of peace is substantial. We need to leave the door open for sponsors, but the issue requires extensive discussion. We want the process to succeed. This appears to be the best chance for peace in the region'. Ojul, the designated delegation leader, concluded more bluntly: 'We want donors to come into the peace process'.[1]

Machar agreed that the LRA could not itself facilitate the talks: 'If you try to raise funds yourself you will fail', he said. 'We will also have trouble trying to raise funds, but we can facilitate. The donors need to form their own forum to manage funds. You shouldn't do this yourself'.[2] He reassured the delegation that he was in a position to gather financial and ideological support, pointing out that members of Sant'Egidio had

---

[1] Fieldnotes, Juba: 7 June 2006.
[2] Fieldnotes, Juba: 7 June 2006. With the Juba Initiative Fund (JIF), donors later did form their own forum from which to disperse funds under the auspices of the UN and GoSS, later administered and audited by KPMG.

been waiting with the delegation in Juba to travel to Ri-Kwangba: 'The Italians are members of the EU. The Swiss and the Americans have been asked to support this peace process. I have asked them to strike the LRA off the terrorists list'.[3] Everyone appeared pleased, grateful, and in awe of Machar. Moreover, everyone seemed in agreement that a priority was to establish solid international contacts to cast the net of the Juba Talks more widely. 'You have to reach out', Machar told the LRA/M repeatedly. 'We are here for peace', Olweny responded.

During the drive back, the delegation was mainly quiet, except for one short conversation. Three delegates were discussing how much international support Machar might be able to solicit. One delegate argued that reaching out was 'all well and good', but there was one thing that would cause a problem and that the mediator had yet to understand: 'We are very opinionated people also'.[4]

6.1   Introduction

'Keep the international community on your side but do not let it overpower the peacemaking momentum', suggests Wallensteen as one ground rule for peace negotiations.[5] The advice sums up what the LRA/M was trying to do: engage external or international actors but remain in control. It is often assumed that international participation benefits a peace process, particularly if one of the actors is the state. But the integrity of this process played out differently through the involvement of international actors. It is not a challenge *per se* if international actors get involved, but rather that the international community as a set of actors works in different ways from the conflict actors involved.

To describe how the LRA/M and the international external actors functioned, I will refer to the language used by members of the LRA/M: they talked frequently about their efforts to 'connect' and about 'surges' towards breakthroughs. The LRA/M progressed by alternating its levels of engagement, and simultaneously kept control by maintaining a fluid, often vague process. Progress and change came, as they described it, through reaching out in certain moments; control was maintained by pulling back in others. I call this mechanism 'connect/disconnect' and visualise it as an alternating current.

Alternating current flows in two different directions but remains powerful because the directional shift allows it to function without

---

[3] Fieldnotes, Juba: 7 June 2006.   [4] Fieldnotes, Juba: 11 October 2006.
[5] Wallensteen and Eriksson (2009: 38).

overloading the circuit. The image of an alternating current helps us to understand why LRA/M members stressed that they were always engaged with the process, even when external actors felt that the LRA/M had withdrawn. This notion also influences how the LRA/M connects to outsiders. My own experience with the LRA/M has been that periods of intense contact were followed by accusations of betrayal, yet these were always made while hinting at the possibility of absolving me. Contact was then reinstated with an emphasis that this was a gesture of forgiveness. The effect on me was that even in periods in which I was branded a traitor, I never stopped pursuing the connection.

In contrast to these waves of engagement, the external international actors – who, for the sake of brevity, are drawn here with an extremely broad brush – needed continuously developing momentum and consensus to remain committed to the peace talks. Drawing on the LRA/M description, I call this mechanism a 'galvanic surge'. The image of direct current best captures what a galvanic surge is: concentrated energy flows in one direction but has less power to sustain long distances or subtle adjustments.

Running in parallel, the two approaches created a syncopated rhythm. Profound misinterpretation occurred in moments when external momentum hit a period of lesser LRA/M engagement; at other times, strong LRA/M engagement did not coincide with external momentum. The two operational modes mismatched and thus outside support and reassurances for the process were withdrawn just when the LRA/M had entered a time of adjustment. When the LRA/M pulled back from the process – often in order to consolidate its own position – the external galvanic surge created consensus about the LRA/M's lack of commitment to a peaceful solution.

Connect/disconnect and galvanic surges highlighted the constraints on both parties' ability to pursue peace flexibly, with an open mind, a willingness to concede, and in a manner that sent a continued message of commitment. Both actors missed out because of their different ways of functioning: in retaining too much control, the LRA/M failed to use the opportunity to broaden its political support base and capitalise on the Juba agreements, such as the concessions made by the GoU regarding root causes of the conflict. External international actors displayed a lack of vision by insisting on a particular approach to peacemaking in a constrained environment, thus failing to bring about lasting change or learn lessons for future conflict resolution. Because the LRA/M and international actors conducted themselves in entrenched, yet mismatched ways, both sides struggled to utilise the Juba Talks to move towards resolution.

6.2   The Lord's Resistance Army/Movement's Connect/Disconnect

A few days before my first trip to the bush, two LRA/M delegates pulled me aside. One said: 'When you get to the bush, you will be very free'. The other added:

Don't be scared when you get to the bush. We have been in the community for a while. I might be different when I get to the bush. I will not talk openly to you like now. But don't be scared by people in the bush. It is a bit different there, but they will not be scared by you. They have seen many whites.[6]

Having 'seen many whites' is the most obvious manifestation of making an external connection, however, it was only a snapshot in a permanent process of connect/disconnect. A common perception of the LRA is that of the world's most elusive and inaccessible rebel group, emerging only for attacks or scattered peace negotiations. The LRA/Ms viewed themselves differently: their view was that they had never *not* been engaged in peace negotiations since the start of the conflict in 1986; this permanent engagement only ended with the 2008 military strike that ended the Juba Talks.[7] What from the outside seemed like inaccessibility was on the inside a continuous process of different kinds of engagement.

Roughly speaking, the LRA oscillates between two kinds of action. The first – disconnect – means exerting military strength, regrouping and recouping, evaluating the situation, fighting for survival, and closing ranks to outsiders. The second – connect – is the time when preparations for transformation are made; and relationships are forged, maintained or exploited across divides within the LRA and with the outside world. Significant shifts often happen during this time. The two stages are not clearly divided: disconnect for the LRA/M is as much a stage of engagement as connect. Support comes through connecting and control through disconnecting, yet both stages are versions of engagement. The LRA/M's relationship with civilians in Uganda and Sudan operated with this alternating current of bringing benefits and exerting brutal pressure and used both to remain a powerful and permanent presence.

The alternating current also ensured that ties were never cut. The LRA/M's narrative of how the Juba Talks happened highlights this.[8] Various LRM delegates offered stories about their continuous

---

[6] Fieldnotes, Juba: 6 June 2006.
[7] LRA/M Peace Team (2009). The fallout of the Juba Talks is the most connection-free period, a manifestation of the greatness of the failure of the talks.
[8] Opponents of the ICC warrants argued that they made ending violence look like an unattractive option, as Dowden holds (Dowden 2006). ICC supporters argue that it

contribution and long-standing (as well as often frustrating) connection to the LRA as the main motivation, for example in past efforts such as *Kacoke Madit*. Delegates explained to me that the Juba Talks had been three years in the making, with connections first made while another process, from which they were slowly disconnecting, was ongoing. 'We were appointed in 2003 because there was no trust in Kolo', explained one of the original delegates to me. Because at the time, 'everything with Kolo [his close interaction with government negotiator Betty Bigombe and his defection at the end of the previous peace process] happened exactly as predicted by Kony'.[9] Preparing the next peace talks 'was just an order from the chairman'.[10] Thus some of the future LRA delegates met up in Nairobi from November 2004 to January 2005 to strengthen support within the LRA/M diaspora. In the autumn of 2005, Otti announced on the radio that the LRA wanted peace negotiations, precisely at the time when opponents of the ICC warrants argued that the option to negotiate had been closed off. In December 2005, LRA/M representatives met with IKV Pax Christi in Nairobi for the first time; the broader contact with Machar was thus on its way.

My own experience of connecting with the LRA/M mirrors this pattern and also how connect/disconnect keeps levels of engagement. At first, I was warmly welcomed and invited to enter the world of the LRA. A brief while later, I was threatened and accused of being an infiltrator, leaving me to prove that I came with no bad intentions. After I had been allowed into the inner sanctum of the LRA by talking to Kony and staying in the camp, I was rejected again. This was based on the very plausible accusation that I had supported misleading stories in major media that had come out of the television interview with Kony. This accusation of betrayal was in one case underscored by grabbing my throat and choking me. Eager to remain engaged, I spent considerable time to prove that the accusation was unfounded. I was forgiven and allowed back for meetings, only to be cut off again a few months later. This time, the reason for the cut off was not clear. It took a few weeks for me to establish that this recent episode of disconnect was based on a case of mistaken identity and the fact that I share a similar first name with a scholar who at the time worked for the International Center for

---

was because of the warrants that the talks came about, changing dynamics in a way that would spell the beginning of the end for the LRA. Within the LRA/M, most shrug off the idea that the warrants triggered anything; they are seen as dictating the *content* of the Juba Talks rather than *causing* them. The question of cause and effect is impossible to answer, but also becomes less relevant when looking at the LRA's patterns of connect/disconnect.

[9] Fieldnotes, 24 November 2007.   [10] Fieldnotes, Juba: 28 September 2006.

Transitional Justice, Marieke Wierda. The LRA/M had thought I had failed to disclose my professional affiliation and cut me off.

While the analysis that the ICC warrants made talks more complicated is correct, it overlooks the inner logic of the LRA/M's alternating current. A prime motivator for the LRA/M to enter talks was to battle the absence of their side of the story and to use engagement in peace talks as a political tool to have their voices heard. Connecting to those who were necessary to change the public narrative – including, in the early ambitious days, the ICC itself – was a strong incentive, as was being able to talk publicly.

My own experience with the LRA's attempts to garner publicity for their perspective is interesting in this respect. One of the major motivators for the LRA to allow me to visit Kony was that I said that I would record him and it would go out internationally on radio and TV. Danny Hoffman, in writing about Sierra Leone, has argued that the choice of medium is significant: 'The narrative bloc of the violent event is shaped by the technologies and media through which it is transmitted'. What this means is that making oneself heard through official media channels brings legitimacy. He describes how in Sierra Leone, 'having one's story (re)told on the broadcast [BBC's *Focus on Africa*] constituted a form of legitimacy and verification'.[11] Due to the distorted presentation of the Kony interview – as anticipated by the LRA/M, and also by others involved in the conflict – the LRA failed to experience a verification of their side of the story. Instead, the way the interview was published for them underscored the point that within the existing structures, their side of the story was never listened to.

Colonel Bwone took a similar view on the importance of words when I asked him what the LRA expected to get out of the talks: 'We will capture power with words, not with the gun', was his response.[12] Connecting to a broader network of people to make their version of the conflict known was a crucial incentive; the risks associated with it did not change with the ICC warrants. In the end, it was precisely this broadening network and the series of connections that made the Juba Talks possible. From the LRA/M's perspective, the Nairobi meeting with IKV Pax Christi was akin to bringing in an international umpire to officiate a fair process and to establish vital outside connections.

Residents of southern Sudan's Western Equatoria experienced first-hand how this moment of connecting to the outside world changed the

---

[11] Hoffman (2005: 346).

[12] Author interview with Col. Lubwoa Bwone and Lt. Col. Santo Alit (LRA). Ri-Kwangba: 22 September 2006.

LRA's behaviour. Stationed near Ri-Kwangba from early 2006 onwards, the LRA cautiously guarded themselves against outside intruders, including the resident Azande population. The locals were told by LRA soldiers passing through the village that they were not allowed to tend to their gardens near the LRA camp. The LRA thus kept the residents under control by dictating the terms of engagement: while the LRA were to be listened to, they were not reachable. At the same time but in an entirely different location – Nairobi – the LRA connected to initiate the Juba Talks. This changed the situation in Western Equatoria, too. The experience of Reverend Moses from Ibba illustrates this. The LRA had been in his region since late 2005. The local residents had recognised them 'because of long hair. They are not shaved like our soldier. They speak a funny language'.[13] The long-haired armed men had been looting and abducting; some children were abducted in November 2005. And although they had not returned at the time I spoke to Reverend Moses in June 2006, he explained that the LRA's behaviour had changed: 'They now come to the market and buy potato plants; they get friendly with the locals'.[14] He could pinpoint when things changed: February 2006 – when, unbeknown to the Reverend – LRA/M representatives were meeting Machar in Juba. The LRA's engagement with the population changed from one of violent power assertion (disconnect) to a mutually beneficial trade relation (connect).

The first meeting in the bush between Machar, IKV Pax Christi and the LRA happened shortly after – the meeting Onek had described as being scary because the visitors were accompanied deep into the bush by heavily armed, serious-looking LRA. When I asked several senior commanders why what was supposed to be a friendly meeting had to be staged in such a frightening manner, they laughed. Lieutenant Colonel Alit, in particular, found the question funny: how else could the LRA possibly present itself to outsiders? Had they been too friendly, too ready to connect, the SPLA would just have killed them, he argued. Instead, in their encounter with outsiders, they had to simultaneously 'reach out a hand and pull it back. In a war, you cannot just shake it'.[15]

6.3   Making Broader Connections for Peace

If control was such a prominent issue for the LRA/M, what was their motivation to connect in the first place? Engaging in the peace talks came at great cost to the LRA. In April 2008, former spokesperson Olweny

---

[13] Fieldnotes, Ibba: 10 June 2006.   [14] Fieldnotes, Ibba: 10 June 2006.
[15] Fieldnotes, Ri-Kwangba: 15 July 2007.

said that making Kony a public figure and allowing him to be interviewed was a mistake: 'He was stronger when he was not exposed to the world'.[16] The LRA/M was feeding off the image of the unknown spirit-driven superhuman commander – as was the outside world, signalling back to the LRA/M that this image remained one of its strongest assets. Abandoning the unknown by connecting to the non-LRA world stripped the LRA of its power to incite fear, at least for a while. Because of this cost, it is intriguing that the Juba Talks, with wide international participation, became possible.

Using international outsiders to facilitate and make the rules, the LRA argued, would score them a political point.[17] The GoU utilised international rules in similar ways: Phil Clark argues that the GoU used the tool of state referral to the ICC for its own 'political and legal gain', citing a Ugandan politician who said 'the ICC has become Museveni's political tool'.[18] Both parties turned to outsiders for additional tools to use against their enemies – and both parties at opportune moments then argued that outsiders were interfering with a local process. Museveni made such statements when he emphasised the importance of his own Amnesty Act over the ICC's jurisdiction. Whenever the Juba Talks hit crisis points, the LRA/M would withdraw by, as Ojul put it in one of those moments, 'going back to the field to consult', which then also meant – as another delegate added – that 'no outsiders were allowed'.[19] Such moments of disconnect, needed by the LRA/M to regain internal strength, expressed the tension of peace talk participation.

Yet once the need for the connection had been identified, the opening brought in as many international actors as possible which then evolved into the Juba Talks. Despite seeing the international community as broadly complicit with Museveni, the LRA/M assumed that external actors would to a certain extent offer goodwill towards the LRA/M as the initiators of peace talks. The LRA/M surmised that international engagement with the nitty-gritty complexities of the conflict would adjust the international pro-government bias and help to create leverage on the GoU. From the LRA/M's point of view, one purpose of connecting was to widen the network, to strengthen what Mauro Sarrica calls 'social

---

[16] Fieldnotes, Cologne: 24 September 2008.

[17] I define external international actors as everyone whom the LRA/M viewed as holding a possible 'umpire' position. This vague definition makes for a somewhat mythologised version of what the 'international community' is and can do, but it draws on a notion that I have frequently encountered.

[18] Clark (2011: 1182 and 201).   [19] Fieldnotes, Juba: 12 September 2006.

representation'.[20] In the early days of the Juba Talks, strengthening those outside connections and securing resources was one of the major motivations for participation: 'Maybe we need to make contact to European politicians', a delegate explained to me: 'We need support, we need much stronger support'.[21] Through stronger social representation, the LRA/M reasoned, new energy would allow movement towards finding a way to change the situation of the LRA and Uganda. One delegate said that initially, he had found the Juba process credible 'because it was so internationally staffed' as this might allow shifting Ugandan dynamics while also tackling the problems that had arisen through the Rome Statute. After all, he said, 'the ICC remains as a biased court', a bias that the LRA/M thought they could address by engaging with international actors.[22]

6.4   An Example of Reaching Out and Pulling Back

The practice of connecting to external actors in order to gather support came with a permanent weighing of power relations for the LRA/M. A look behind the scenes at what was interpreted as the first proof that the LRA/M was not serious in its peace effort will help in understanding the many layers of action and interpretation that converged at all times. During Machar's meeting with the LRA leadership before the opening ceremony in Juba, everyone on the trip to Ri-Kwangba behaved as if the connection had been made successfully and the Juba Talks were guaranteed. Although the GoU's participation was still shaky and had not been officially announced, LRA/M delegate Ayena was on the phone inviting people from all over the world to join the delegation as observers. Otto gave interviews to journalists in which he announced that he dreamt of being Uganda's vice president. Machar, followed around by an Al Jazeera camera crew, visited Nabanga's shell of a school to assure local residents that he knew they were in a volatile situation, being physically wedged between the LRA and the outside world, but that this situation would improve as the Juba Talks progressed.

Machar's mission on this final meeting was clear: he wanted to persuade Otti to join the LRA/M delegation in Juba. Otti was at first

---

[20] Sarrica and Contarello explain how in an unfamiliar situation, group communication gives rise to representations as newly exchanged thoughts develop a new nature, a process that he calls 'social representation' (Sarrica and Contarello 2004: 550). Sarrica's outline of the stages of social representation was clearly visible in the Juba Talks.
[21] Fieldnotes, Juba: 5 June 2006.   [22] LRA/M Peace Team (2009).

nowhere to be found. The LRA had been stopped by two rivers that had merged in the rainy season. Despite, as they said, 'walking from six to six', they needed three more days beyond the scheduled meeting time to get to Ri-Kwangba.[23] One delegate, while waiting in Nabanga's school during a downpour, explained that it was a challenge for Otti to even emerge for this meeting, since the meetings had become so big and the connections expanded so quickly: 'Everyone is nervous if they don't know who they are talking to'. Various delegates said that taking Otti to Juba was too much of a security risk for him.

The following day, Machar and his entourage waited in the forest for the LRA leaders. No LRA or LRM member was to be seen, and no sound could be heard coming from the bush to announce the advance party that would signal the arrival of a high-ranking commander. Over four long hours of waiting, the discussion about the delegation was lively. All the members of the SPLM who were present were engaging in conspiracy theories about why they were being made to wait for so long. Ideas thrown around included that Kony was holding the delegation hostage. Or maybe he had confiscated their phones? At one point, a soldier spotted and killed a black poisonous snake that had crawled under one of the makeshift chairs near Machar, prompting a member of one peacemaking organisations to ask: 'Is that a message from our friends?'[24]

Onek was outraged that the LRA let the vice president of southern Sudan wait in a clearing in the bush: 'They lack respect, they should apologise to the VP'. Machar seemed unfazed. This would be his fourth encounter with the LRA command; he was used to waiting. He was engrossed in his copy of Stephen Hawking's *A Brief History of Time* and only joined in the speculations with one remark: 'Maybe they did not deliver my letter'. He had written a letter to Kony assuring him of his safety were he to come to Juba or send one of his senior commanders.[25]

Finally, the first LRA fighters emerged, followed by a rather haggard-looking delegation, and, eventually, Otti. Machar politely but firmly pointed out that he had been waiting for him for three days. Otti did not flinch: 'Last time we waited for you for 11 days', he retorted, adding that Kony was not coming to this meeting. In addition, because of the delay in his arrival, 'the delegation needs more time to talk about funda-mental issues'. Machar insisted – to no avail – that he had to meet Kony to be able to deliver a credible peace process. He wanted action, rather than deliberation: 'I need an answer in a letter', he insisted,

---

[23] Fieldnotes, Nabanga/Ri-Kwangba: 11 July 2006.
[24] Fieldnotes, Ri-Kwangba: 13 July 2006.   [25] Fieldnotes, Ri-Kwangba: 13 July 2006.

in good handwriting. The Ugandan government delegation is high-ranking; you should upgrade your delegation by sending one of the five leaders [under arrest warrant from the ICC]. Because first Uganda said, we are not talking to the top five commanders. Now they say we want one of the five, although it is not a condition. It shows that they are serious.[26]

Yet despite this pressure, Otti asserted that he would not travel to Juba. 'What are you afraid of?' Machar asked, pressing the point that the LRA needed as much media exposure as possible to broaden the connection between the LRA and the rest of the world: 'The press has to be here. More coverage of this is good and it will be better than last time'.[27] He wanted to firm up the commitment the LRA was making to connect to the outside world, to internationalise his peace talks endeavour.[28] Otti dodged the question what he was afraid of: 'We want Ochora here and the Acholi elders', he answered instead.[29] If Machar was disappointed, he did not let it show. He appeared quietly in control, ready to push his agenda step by step.

On the way back to Maridi, the convoy stopped in Ibba to buy water and snacks, and I asked one delegate how things had gone in the bush and why Kony had not appeared. 'Things don't go how we want it to go', he said. He offered an explanation of why Kony had not appeared at the meeting, even though that had been the agreement. How many outside connections Kony made was an image question: 'The rebel leader cannot always be at every meeting, otherwise he looks too junior. It is very difficult to talk to a real rebel leader'. But why, I asked, was it not possible for them to stick to the arrangements? Or indeed why did it seem impossible to send a higher rank to the negotiation table, even Otti himself, under the personal protection that Machar had promised him? The suggestion seemed ridiculous to the delegate. He was worried, he said, about handing anything over to the SPLA, because the LRA would thereby relinquish control of the process and because 'the SPLA is so unorganised'. He had heard that Onek had requested an apology from the LRA/M delegation and been outraged that they had let the VP wait so long. 'He talks to us like children', the delegate said. 'Like he is telling a girl: go to school. We have shown that we are serious. Vincent came out of the bush. We are here'.[30] For him, Otti's appearance in person to relay the news that he would not come to Juba was the strongest possible connection, and proof that the LRA was committed to the talks.

---

[26] Fieldnotes, Nabanga/Ri-Kwangba: 11 July 2006.
[27] For what had happened 'last time', see Schomerus (2010a).
[28] Fieldnotes, Nabanga/Ri-Kwangba: 11 July 2006.
[29] Fieldnotes, Ri-Kwangba: 13 July 2006.   [30] Fieldnotes, Ri-Kwangba: 13 July 2006.

Others interpreted the events differently. On the drive, the delegation listened to the BBC's *Focus on Africa* programme. The newsreader relayed the information that Kony had let Machar wait in Nabanga for five days and that in the end, Kony had still refused to send one of the commanders wanted by the ICC to negotiate in Juba. To the great dismay of some of the delegates, the BBC interpreted this as proof that the LRA had no interest in engaging. The short news headline was: 'LRA talks run into first obstacles'.[31]

6.5   Internationalisation and Africanisation

Connect/disconnect helps explain obvious contradictions in the LRA/ M's negotiation position. On the one hand, the LRA/M argued for a liberal peace – a firmly international concept – with free and fair elections, accountability, and a functioning justice system. On the other, they, at times, proposed to negotiate a power-sharing arrangement with Museveni and avoid prosecution for war crimes. Some even wanted Museveni, now an elected president, deposed by the peace agreement. A seeming contradiction emerged. The LRA/M connected to the international actors, who brought their own set of rules, but they wanted to simultaneously disconnect, countering the process put in place by the Rome Statute with their own context-specific interpretation.

At the heart of this lies a broader tension in local or regional conflicts with an international reach. The LRA/M members said that part of what they needed to do in light of the ICC warrants was to either convince the ICC that its warrants were biased or to get other international actors to agree that this was an 'African conflict between Museveni and Kony'.[32] When it was useful, the LRA cited the ICC as the instrument that had upset the fragile balance of the 'Africanness' of the conflict, arguing that this conflict was to be dealt in an African way. This argument is an extension of the broader debate about the tension between traditional local justice and international justice. In the localised and 'Africanised' justice debate, this idea usually surfaced in the focus on nonstate justice mechanisms seemingly rooted in the customs of the affected communities.[33] Reaching out to an international community that was undecided on how to deal with the LRA was part of the connection that could then be severed by rejecting the new international order to regain control. This was put particularly pointedly in early November 2006, when Egeland was expected in Juba. The LRA/M's spokesperson welcomed

---

[31] Fieldnotes, Ri-Kwangba: 13 July 2006.
[32] Fieldnotes, Nabanga: 20 September 2006.   [33] See Allen (2007).

the chance to connect with Egeland to discuss the ICC warrants with him: 'Because they are a blockade to the talks, the primary agenda is to request Egeland to use his offices to talk to the UN Security Council and the ICC to drop the warrants in the interests of peace in the region'.[34]

Hidden behind the description of 'the interests of peace in the region' was the plan to bring the GoU to the table (connect) and then expose it internationally to force acknowledgement of its part in the conflict (disconnect). This strategy was particularly obvious in the LRA/M's emphasis on international media attention, rather than on national Ugandan or Sudanese media. Even though they thought little of international actors or the international press, they calculated that the attention pay-off would be bigger.[35] Such coverage was guaranteed by selling the story as an impenetrable African war, and the LRA/M skilfully embellished and instrumentalised the supposedly unique African features of the conflict.

This Africanisation had practical implications for the LRA/M. They said, for example, that the shared 'Africanness' made overcoming hurdles possible on the personal level, as Olweny explained. At the first face-to-face meeting in Machar's office after the much fought-over signing of the CoH, the two delegations reconnected, Olweny explained, by 'shaking hands emphatically! Emphatically in that African way!'[36] Africanisation of the conflict also meant that the LRA/M wanted to specifically reach out towards African partners. On 2 September 2006, the delegation wrote a personal letter to Mangosuthu Buthelezi, head of South Africa's Inkatha Party.[37] Under the subject line 'The Just Struggle of the LRA/M', the letter addressed the LRA/M's concerns about being the disadvantaged party at the negotiation table, stating that international support had contributed to this imbalance. The letter introduced the LRA/M as 'an organisation that has been so seriously demonised and vilified for so long, but about which the world has known so little', and asked Buthelezi 'to grace the Juba Peace talks with your presence'.[38] Briefly explaining the LRA's position, the letter stated:

---

[34] BBC News (6 November 2006).

[35] The behaviour echoes what Mbembé and Rendall call 'Africanity': a 'hatred of the world at large (which also marks a profound desire for recognition)' (Mbembé and Rendall 2002: 252).

[36] Fieldnotes, Juba: 24 September 2006.

[37] The contact was established through a representative of The Earth Organisation who had come to Juba to plead with the LRA to stop killing the white rhino for food in Garamba Park. The letter makes reference to a phone conversation between Ojul and Buthelezi.

[38] Ojul, Martin. 2006. 'Letter from the LRA/M to Chief Buthelezi, Leader of Inkatha Party'. Juba.

suffice it to say that the LRA/M was formed as a response to NRM's deliberate policies of persecution and marginilisation [*sic*] of the people of northern and eastern Uganda, bordering genocide. In due course we should be able to send you our position papers in the Juba talks in order to facilitate your clear understanding of the situation. For nearly two decades the NRM Government has thrived on concealment of one of the worst human catastrophe [sic] by a well orchestrated and sophisticated propaganda machinery procured through a UK Public Relations Organisation. By the use of this machinery Museveni has slammed a ghostly smoke screen on the LRA and presented it to the international community as a murderous organisation without any political agenda. In good time, Your Highness, we should be able to explain to you that the LRA/M is not only an organisation with a truly Pan African outlook with a focused national agenda, but it is also the only serious counterbalance to Museveni's militaristic approach to politics in Uganda.[39]

The delegation further asked for Buthelezi's support in reaching the international community, for Buthelezi's presence at the Juba Talks, and for an invitation to South Africa for the LRA/M delegation to be introduced to more people who might be sympathetic.

6.6   Connect/Disconnect Tensions

The LRA/M paid for connecting by submitting themselves to forces outside its control. In war, the LRA controls people's lives, fears and experiences. In peace, the LRA/M aimed to control the narrative about the conflict with the expectation that opening up would sway opponents and sceptics. They expected that once they reached out, the biased media would be educated about what the LRA/M perceived or wanted to be the real story. At various times, delegates and LRA members talked about how the chief prosecutor of the ICC, once presented with their side of the story, would be convinced that he was wrong in seeking to prosecute only the LRA.[40] They voiced the expectation that if OCHA was satisfied that the peace talks were useful, support from the entire UN system and the international community, including the ICC, would follow. In the LRA/M's ideal scenario, making the connection would shift the power of the LRA from the mystical-disconnected to the visible-connected, and would make Kony a 'big man' on par with

---

[39] Ojul, Martin. 2006. 'Letter from the LRA/M to Chief Buthelezi, Leader of Inkatha Party'. Juba.

[40] The LRA/M's notion of the ICC as being somewhat of a fair umpire is rather reminisicient of Ho Chi Minh's telegramme to US President Harry S Truman. In 1945, the then-Prime Minister of Vietnam had written to Washington to ask for US support in Vietnam's freedom fight against the French. The letter was never answered (Minh 18 February 1946).

Machar, Museveni and Egeland. Visible power and its insignia were incentives to give up the strength that came from being elusive.[41]

The realisation that the way to power was more complicated than they had imagined came soon enough. One delegate said that in order for the LRA to become a widely supported player, they knew the LRA needed to apologise for their atrocities – and indeed Kony had done so in the July 2006 meeting with Acholi community leaders. However, the delegate argued, apologising had taken away power from the LRA that needed to be re-established. 'The problem is that now every radio station demands an apology', he said, 'but it is for the chairman to decide when to apologise. He cannot be told what to do'.[42] The theme of 'not being told what to do' emerged several times, particularly in a heated discussion I had with one delegation member when I questioned their ability to reliably contact the chairman: 'It is not easy to deal with a rebel, with someone who has been in the bush for 20 years'. I said it was obvious how difficult it was for Machar or the UN to deal with a rebel, but was it equally difficult for a rebel to deal with a rebel? Was it also not easy for him to deal with his boss? 'No', he answered. 'It is not easy, but we should not be pushed to do anything'.[43]

Despite Kony's method of maintaining power by being elusive, the LRA/M had not expected the vision of Kony as one of the world's leaders to be scuppered so quickly. With 'connect' not bringing the amount of control the LRA/M had hoped for, incentives to disconnect to regain control grew. The arrival of Ugandan MPs in Juba in September 2006 illustrated this tension well. Wanting to broaden its support base, the LRA/M initially welcomed the arrival of the MPs. Quickly, a mechanism of proxy negotiations ensued, as the MPs tried to reconcile the GoU's and the LRA/M's position papers. At first, the LRA/M delegation viewed the new players as an interruption that created an incentive to strengthen their direct connection. 'Procedures have broken down with the MPs shuttling back and forth', explained a delegate. Increasingly, as control was taken away from them – or it could be said, as the connection they had made was ignored – LRA/M delegates became furious at this intervention by a force they did not consider part of the mediation team.[44] One delegate said: 'We want face-to-face talks with Rugunda, but everyone is learning on the job'.[45]

---

[41] Dowden writes about the importance of power and the Big Man in Africa (Dowden 2008: loc959).
[42] Fieldnotes, Owiny-Kibul and Palotaka: 26 November 2006.
[43] Fieldnotes, Juba: 12 September 2006.   [44] Fieldnotes, Juba: 5 October 2006.
[45] Fieldnotes, Palotaka/Parajok: 3 October 2006.

The crisis in the talks played out in Juba Raha Hotel, with journalists and anxious observers watching to catch any movement coming out of the negotiation room. After dinner on the evening of 5 October 2006, the negotiators asked MPs and observers to leave the negotiation room so that the crisis could be contained among the negotiating parties. During a break, the MPs asked Ojul to call Kony, who refused to talk and gave the strict order that nothing was to be signed if the MPs had dealt with it.[46] Another delegate explained that the MPs simply were not sufficiently connected to the LRA experience: 'Some of these people need to be send to the bush for one month to understand suffering there, then they can come back'.[47] In the end, the measurable outcome of the MPs' engagement was negligible. One member of the delegation called the arrival of the MPs 'a big storm in a teacup. They all came, argued and went away again'.[48] For him, it was obvious that the only ones who had come with staying power were the LRA/M – even though to most outsiders it did not look that way.

The tension between the LRA/M and the MPs was at first surprising. Since many of the MPs were open about their anti-Museveni stance and their willingness to work closely with the LRA/M delegation, they seemed like obvious allies. Yet from the LRA perspective, the presence of the MPs diffused the LRA's power as a main player in the conflict and created a tension with the agenda the LRA/M had set for itself to be a political pan-Africanist negotiation partner with a truth to tell. Since the MPs represented politics in Uganda – no matter what their party affiliation – the LRA hardliners considered cooperation with the MPs to be the same as cooperation with and entrenching the existing system in Uganda.[49] 'The broader participation of MPs destabilises the process inside', one delegate explained to me. 'Some MPs are using this to stabilise their constituencies'.[50]

The LRA felt patronised. 'The MPs are not advising, but lecturing the LRA', said an observer who had joined the talks as an independent, but was clearly sympathising with LRA grievances.[51] Vis-à-vis the LRA, the MPs took the stance that negotiating comprehensive political solutions was not to be part of a peace deal. One LRA/M representative said that the MPs had given the LRA the advice 'to simply deal with combatant issues and leave all political issues to the MPs'.[52] Reacting to the

---

[46] Fieldnotes, Juba: 5 October 2006.   [47] Fieldnotes, Palotaka/Parajok: 3 October 2006.
[48] Fieldnotes, Juba: 11 October 2006.   [49] Fieldnotes, Juba: 11 October 2006.
[50] Fieldnotes, Palotaka/Parajok: 3 October 2006.
[51] Fieldnotes, Juba: 12 October 2006.   [52] Fieldnotes, Juba: 11 October 2006.

suggestion that the LRA should focus on combatant issues, one member said, 'How? It is like telling us to stop this river from flowing and then we stop it and you say, now, you cannot cross it'.[53]

The analogy of the river stopped but not being allowed to cross shows that in the LRA/M's view, transformation is denied by the very same externalities that facilitated the move towards transformation in the first place. Another stated that this meant that the MPs were in a sense boycotting the peace talks by disconnecting the LRA/M from its political demands, implying that many of the LRA/M demands were already being discussed on the political level. This was disempowering, explained one delegate: 'If you say I need two pens and the only answer you get is: 'the pens are already in place', what do you do?'[54]

Kony's order to disregard the MPs' contribution caused a new round of rumours that during the most recent visit to Nabanga, the LRA high command had already abandoned the peace process. This was compounded by the observation that a senior diaspora advisor had left that day. Additionally, Machar had reportedly become angry with the LRA/M's demand to take another break for continued consultations in Nabanga and, at the request of the member of the team affiliated with the Uganda People's Congress (UPC), to take a day off to commemorate the anniversary of Obote's death. In the morning, one delegate had said to me that 'the VP is overworked', reportedly because he had told the LRA the day before that 'nobody wanted to touch the LRA, you are seen as terrorists'.[55] 'We are still struggling with this perception problem', said the delegate, who explained that the MPs' pitching in not only put too much political pressure on the LRA, but also robbed the LRA of their political viability.[56] An incident in which the MP from Pader was overheard telling Kony on the phone that it was a possibility that the Ugandan constitution might be changed during the Juba Talks caused distrust among MPs and between the MPs and the LRA/M.[57]

Despite the LRA/M's clumsiness in garnering broader political support, signs of significant transformation were not absent in Juba, particularly when both actors stepped back from their usual way of operating to create a space to discuss Uganda's politics and conflicts. One day, walking into the Juba Raha Hotel, I caught sight of then-Gulu District Chairman Mao sitting in the shade talking to Ugandan MPs. The MPs

---

[53] Fieldnotes, Juba: 11 October 2006.   [54] Fieldnotes, Juba: 6 November 2006.
[55] On the impact of proscription – listing a group as terrorists – on peace talks, see Haspeslagh (2014).
[56] Fieldnotes, Juba: 5 October 2006.   [57] Fieldnotes, Juba: 10 October 2006.

were livid. They had read in the Ugandan papers that the talks had collapsed because of LRA allegations that the UPDF was ambushing LRA fighters in the proposed assembly areas. That much was true, and it was also true that in return, the GoU had claimed that the LRA had not assembled and had thus violated the CoH. The rest was a journalistic interpretation: in a press release the LRA/M had actually stated that they would reconsider their participation in the talks should the UPDF remain in their vicinity. The papers reported this as an LRA threat to abandon the talks in seven days.

'This is too aggressive', said one MP. 'The LRA is not politically astute. Instead of calling Museveni's bluff by not threatening to walk out of talks, they fall into the trap of putting blame for possible failure of talks on themselves'. This confirmed my observation. The LRA was so concerned about being the inferior negotiation partner and with maintaining control that they easily lost sight of when the bigger political picture might be advantageous for them. I asked what he meant by 'calling his bluff'. 'Museveni wants to make the LRA quit the talks', he explained. Mao pitched in: 'That is why every statement of the LRA is exaggerated by the government. It is to make these people sound unreasonable'. Mao suggested that the LRA should announce that they would run patrols and ask for a car with a machine gun from the SPLA to do so: 'They can call Museveni's bluff if there are now skirmishes between the LRA and the UPDF near the assembly area because it proves that both LRA and UPDF are there'.

'Now that LRA is no longer in Uganda, it would be a good time for Museveni to have the talks collapse', another MP said. 'If talks collapse, UPDF will make sure that the LRA does not get back into Uganda. There are really no pockets left for them'. He added that Museveni had even admitted that new troops had been deployed to southern Sudan. They recognised a familiar pattern: 'When UPDF was accused of doing stuff in Rwanda, Museveni deployed troops to patrol borders to prove that UPDF was not there. Imagine!' Generally, another MP said, an opportunity had been missed. It had been two weeks since the signing of the CoH, 'these should have been used to get concessions from Museveni on comprehensive solutions. The LRA should have used that time while they are still in Uganda. Also, the UN says Agenda 2 was an impressive document. But nothing is being said about that in the press'.

It was interesting to see a Ugandan politician express the thought that the LRA might act as a political player but was at the same time depoliticising itself through a misplaced focus. This seemed to be a shift in perception, both of the LRA/M, and also of their potential usefulness to push the individual political agendas of MPs.[58] It was a glimpse of a transformative process in which it would become more firmly established that both conflict parties were playing a role in the continuation and entrenchment of the conflict. The change was even perceptible during a UK parliamentary discussion in early 2007: 'Museveni is a more or less democratically elected leader', argued a UK parliamentarian. 'But it would also be helpful if the Ugandan government could make clear that resolution is at the heart of what they want'.[59] To counter allegations that they were biased in their analysis, advocacy groups, such as the International Crisis Group (ICG), started to qualify each record of supposed LRA atrocities. They now mentioned the possibility that others had committed the crimes, for example: 'Since April, armed actions attributed (not always accurately) to the LRA resumed in Sudan's Western Equatoria state and the Bas-Uélé district of the Congo (DRC)'.[60] For the LRA/M, these admissions translated into a changing overall image of the LRA – a premature conclusion.

6.7   Misinterpretation of Disconnect

The waves of engagement in the Juba Talks were externally interpreted in a black-and-white manner. Moments of seemingly wavering commitment to the talks by the LRA/M were taken as signs of insincerity and as using the Juba Talks for military regrouping. It is worth looking at a few examples that illustrate how the Juba Talks were perceived by the LRA/M and why they reacted in a way that jeopardised the talks.

After they had connected for the Juba Talks, delegates wondered whether they would be treated as equal partners around the table. Frustration visibly grew within the delegation, particularly when they felt their efforts to connect were not being repaid in kind. Ayena at one point animatedly explained to me that 'Kony is very committed. Otti not so much, he is a bit more volatile and the government response so far is less than nothing'.[61] A few months into the peace talks, one delegate said that the mediation team was doing a bad job of preserving the 'dignity of the LRA', confirming to me that the last few months from the LRA's point of view had been mainly spent proving their own worthiness. At various points, the delegation was in a state of disarray at what they perceived to be disrespectful treatment. When the CHMT was formed, the LRA and

---

[58] Fieldnotes, Juba: 28 September 2006.
[59] Author notes from Westminster Adjournment Debate on the Juba Peace Talks, UK Parliament: 23 January 2007.
[60] International Crisis Group (2008: i).   [61] Fieldnotes, Juba: 11 October 2006.

UPDF contingents on the team observed each other's moves closely. In the early days, in particular, the LRA members were vocal about being treated unfairly by the UPDF members. When I asked what they thought of their UPDF colleagues, I was told that the UPDF colonel especially was 'a bit bossmatic' and was not prepared to connect with his LRA colleagues on the same level.[62]

When the LRA/M delegation was moved to the outskirts of town to the Juba Bridge Hotel, delegates were sure that this was a move to get them further away from the proceedings. They took it as a reason to spend numerous days waiting around the Juba Bridge Hotel, not knowing what was supposed to happen, but resigned to the fact that they had no way to find out. 'We are disconnected', was how delegates commonly explained their experience in the peace talks, both around the table and in terms of infrastructure. It took a few months for UNICEF to sponsor a computer and a satellite Internet connection for the LRA/M's use at their hotel.[63]

The lack of communication could be seen as an oversight by the mediation team, but it also highlighted the LRA/M's behavioural patterns. Rather than seek out the (at the time admittedly few) opportunities to communicate by different means, they used the situation as an incentive to disconnect, emphasising their marginalisation and the insincerity of the peace talks. This experience of the peace talks would later turn out to make new rounds of talks more complicated. This concept has been widely reflected in scholarship: William Zartman argues that as conflict continues, grievances become more rather than less complex, posing ever greater challenges to resolution.[64] The same can also be said for peace processes: making the connections to the Juba Talks also meant that the dynamics of the process itself added new layers to the conflict through the way the LRA/M felt treated. These new layers of conflict in turn needed to be peeled away before old grievances could even be addressed.

The perceived – and real – power imbalance between all negotiation partners and the mediation team caused major disconnects. In late September 2006, Otti said that he would completely withdraw from communication with the GoU delegation or the mediator, because they treated his delegates unfairly. 'Vincent does not talk to anyone anymore, not to Rugunda or Machar', one delegate explained. 'He told Machar that he was turning into a headache. Machar was shocked and Vincent just told again Machar was giving him a headache'.[65] Otti confirmed his connect/disconnect relationship with Machar to me: 'I like Riek Machar. He is neutral, but sometimes not neutral enough. But now I don't speak

---

[62] Fieldnotes, Juba/Magwi: 2 October 2006.   [63] Fieldnotes, Juba: 6 September 2006.
[64] Zartman (2006: 258).   [65] Fieldnotes, Juba: 28 September 2006.

to him'. However, for Otti this did not by any means signal an end of his engagement with the talks: his disconnecting was just supposed to usher in a new kind of engagement. He saw a solution in African internationalisation: 'Maybe we can get more help from South Africa and some more observers'.[66]

At one point in November 2006, the delegation had asked for time off for consultations with the high command in the bush. Because progress in the talks was negligible, Machar was reluctant to let them go. On the morning of 6 November, a member of the peace talks secretariat visited the LRA/M in their hotel and threatened that if they were to go to Ri-Kwangba, it would be a repeat of the incident in July 2006 when GoSS had abandoned an obstinate LRA/M delegation and left them behind in the bush. After hearing this threat, a visibly upset delegation gathered under a large mango tree. Ojul had been scheduled to fly out to Nairobi that day – to connect with the German ambassador in Nairobi, he said. Now Ojul reiterated several times that such incidents confirmed the need to move the Juba Talks elsewhere: 'They [GoSS] think we have nowhere to go. But there is German support and support from Italy'.[67]

However, delegates wondered, was the threat of abandonment by GoSS an official message from Machar? Or had just one member of the mediation team shown his temper? The connect/disconnect mechanism as it played out in the LRA/M's relationship with Machar became clear. The delegates were furious about being threatened, reacting with the desire to immediately drop their connection to Machar: it was a clear moment of disconnect. However, they countered their anger by connecting and shortly after, delegates went to Machar's office. The LRA never fully trusted Machar, yet he was also the cornerstone of the peace effort – the only person who could provide genuine help. Internally, the LRA/M is a network of trust and distrust; their outside relationship with Machar was working with the same mechanism.

After the messengers had been dispatched to Machar, a delegate explained to me that he saw one major ongoing problem with the talks: 'We never moved beyond this as a favour to the LRA', he said. 'We are always told we should be thankful more than anything else. We are beggars'.[68] The notion of a peace agreement as a generous concession to the LRA was a problem. He recalled an event from mid-September,

---

[66] Author interview with Vincent Otti. Ri-Kwangba: 22 September 2006.

[67] Fieldnotes, Juba: 6 November 2006. The hope that Germany would support the LRA/M in moving the talks elsewhere was very high, and Sant'Egidio's June 2006 suggestion that talks could be held in Rome was still resonating.

[68] Fieldnotes, Juba: 6 November 2006.

when his delegation refused to go and visit Ri-Kwangba because none of them had been paid the allowance that had been agreed as part of the Juba Talks. They did not accept assurances that their money would be processed later. The chartered plane, already on its way from Kenya's Lokichogio, flew back empty, at a cost of $20,000 to GoSS. He felt that this was a good example when everyone had treated the delegates as beggars, an image that continued to haunt the LRA/M delegation in 2006 and the early months of 2007. Months later, one member said that he felt that through the last few months, not only had some of the LRA/M's position papers been changed, but 'the government is not making any concessions at all. They are treating us like beggars. They are not connecting'.[69]

6.8   Galvanic Surges

In June 2010, I received an email from someone who had worked for UNICEF in Uganda just before the warrants for the LRA were issued. He described working in the aid community in Kampala during the time leading up to the issuing of arrest warrants for the LRA leaders as

the most surreal situation, where practically everyone I knew in Uganda agreed on one analysis (this will make peace impossible and get lots of people killed) and the external analysis (this will force the LRA to the table) were the exact opposite. It was deeply frustrating, and I find it problematic when the international community create these narratives that then get taken up as true and somehow work themselves into good practice.[70]

The galvanic surge of shared opinion and developing consensus among external international actors offered a stark contrast to the LRA/M's alternating current of moving towards change and a successful peace negotiation. A few weeks into the peace talks, I overheard Machar speaking on the telephone with the White House. The United States had so far shown no particular interest in the talks. Additionally, Machar had received a lot of dissension from international organisations and the press for meeting Kony, handing him money and facilitating the peace talks. Chatting to a White House representative, Machar gave a general overview of the situation in Juba. Defending his decision to entrust $20,000 in cash to Kony, he said that 'we saw the money trickle back into our civilian community'. When asked how he would deal with negotiating peace without the main person present, he replied that he

---

[69] Fieldnotes, Cologne: 1 January 2007.
[70] Personal email to author from former international UNICEF staff in Uganda, 20 June 2010.

was 'thinking about other talk models, not face-to-face talks'. He explained that he was looking for diplomatic support from Rwanda and that 'Norway has offered'. Signing off, he emphasised that outside assistance was needed – including from the White House: 'There is no good news unless you guys support us'.[71]

In pleading for White House backing and the greater international support that might follow from that, Machar was onto the right mechanism to ensure success. When his contact with the LRA first became known, international reactions were largely subdued. Neither the LRA nor Machar had the credibility to push this process through; the debate about how to deal with the ICC warrants in peace negotiations brought no clarity. When it has to overcome obstacles and break new ground, the wider international community, including in this case advocacy groups, the press, the ICC, the UN and various governments, functions best when broad consensus creates momentum and reinforces mutual confidence. Such a galvanic surge of support benefits those who are part of it in many ways. Funding is easier to secure if groups and initiatives can show they are close to success or represent a cause that is widely considered relevant. The policy environment is more easily convinced when multiple actors send the same message. Advocacy groups can forge operational alliances based on consensus, which then allows the pitching of a streamlined mass-compatible message. Machar, reasoned correctly that if momentum developed that supported the Juba Talks, the galvanic surge of outside opinion would allow some of the more difficult points, for example the ICC warrants, to be swept up in the general enthusiasm for a negotiated peace.

In other moments, Machar, needing the galvanic surge of opinion, acted out different versions of public support or opposition, depending on which would be more helpful to move issues along. One day, Machar and the then-MP for Magwi County, Ogwaro, were waiting in Ri-Kwangba. The peace talks were scheduled to begin the next day, and Machar elaborated to Ogwaro that he fully expected some local opposition in Juba: 'There will be demonstrations against the peace talks. People will be saying "we don't want [the LRA] here"'. Ogwaro agreed that members from her constituency who had suffered the most under the LRA presence in southern Sudan would indeed want to protest: 'The Acholi will demonstrate', she replied. Thinking of how often the Sudanese Acholi had been accused of being complicit with the LRA

---

[71] Fieldnotes, Juba: 6 September 2006.

and the disharmony it had created in southern Sudan, Machar liked that idea. 'That will exonerate you', he said. 'Let's stage it!'[72]

How the galvanic surge developed in the Juba Talks was clearly visible. In the early days, when Machar was asking the White House for support, his own and IKV Pax Christi's initiative was backed only by a Swiss government willing to take a risk and stay under the radar. The galvanic surge of criticism, on the other hand, hit the early days of the talks: human rights groups like Amnesty International and Human Rights Watch questioned the legality of engaging the LRA in talks, other donor governments were unwilling to fund the initiative, and the ICC insisted that executing the warrants had priority. As the talks moved along, the galvanic surge moved towards supporting the talks. It took a few weeks for Egeland, possibly motivated by the huge exposure the conflict had gained after his visit to northern Uganda, to involve OCHA as the lead organisation within the UN to help facilitate talks, and yet another few weeks for the prominent UN support to be no longer referred to as 'Egeland's "rogue project"',[73] as Baaré recounts. Egeland explained that his support was based on the need to fill a gap that had arisen because other parts of the UN system were not ready to commit resources in the early days:

What of course was a weakness in the process ... was that the political department of the UN and those who know peace mediation, and indeed on a professional basis, were not really involved. Because there were no resources from their side. That is why by default my own organisation OCHA was asked to and encouraged to go into ... We are not supposed to deal with peace processes. OCHA was supposed to coordinate the humanitarian responses. But since nobody was able to organise a meaningful international support to the southern Sudanese peace effort, we did it. And I think that was very important because if we hadn't, the whole thing would have been fell apart [sic] very early and we could have had a much bigger conflict again upon our hands much earlier.[74]

The scaffolding of the peace talks strengthened week by week. With Switzerland and then OCHA and UNICEF on board, the galvanic surge meant that criticism became more subdued. Instead of stressing the need to execute the warrants, the ICC foregrounded its role as the force that brought about the promising Juba Talks and made Uganda safe again. The swelling of the galvanic surge does not imply that all international

---

[72] Fieldnotes, Ri-Kwangba: 13 July 2006.   [73] Baaré (2008).
[74] Telephonic author interview with Jan Egeland, former UN-Undersecretary for Humanitarian Affairs, 15 October 2007.

actors were heading towards unanimity; however, often the extent to which a range of international actors was gradually working towards signing a peace agreement that would satisfy the ICC to not pursue its warrants is in retrospect often underplayed. A few months into the talks, the UN installed Mozambique's former president Chissano as the special envoy of the UN secretary-general. When success seemed probable, the broad consensus changed: even US advocacy group, Invisible Children, who had been critical of the talks and in support of military options (and would later return to that stance) appeared in Juba as great advocates of the peace talks. Finally, AU observers arrived to strengthen the CHMT. More countries started donating and sending observers, including from the EU, the USA and the AU (from Mozambique, DRC, Tanzania, South Africa and Kenya).

Once momentum was created, international actors were keen to move things along to show that their engagement was a game-changer. The situation had not become less complicated with more international engagement, but the galvanic surge created a space in which the external rule book could be bent. As waves of opinion washed over Juba, the galvanic surge interpreted the Rome Statute at various times as the greatest obstacle to or the greatest facilitator of a peaceful solution. Whether international opinion supported the idea that the ICC warrants could be addressed without delivering Kony and his commanders to The Hague depended less on what happened in Juba, and more on how various international actors supported each other in believing that it could be done. Through this mechanism, international opinion often became disconnected from current dynamics in the Juba process, creating skewed incentives along the way.

6.9   Skewed Incentives and Cognitive Dissonance

Those participating in the galvanic surge tried to find loopholes in their own rule book. For the international community navigating the new requirements of the Rome Statute, the Africanisation argument was useful: it allowed the glossing over of the lack of clarity on how to deal with the ICC. Depending on the power of the galvanic surge, the ICC was viewed as a powerful instrument, a much-needed last resort to end violence, or as the ultimate obstacle to achieving a negotiated solution with perpetrators wanted by the ICC. Those who saw the ICC as useful cited it as the main LRA motivation for entering talks. The ICG's bold statement that 'the threat of prosecution clearly rattled the LRA military leadership, pushing them to the negotiating table', however, was hard to verify, since nobody had had a conclusive conversation to find out whether the LRA was rattled.[75] Judging from conversations, it seemed that it was not the threat of prosecution that was occupying the LRA imagination. After all, they had a rather limited understanding of what an ICC warrant meant, as Otti indicated in my first phone call with him. It was rather the humiliation of being singled out as war criminals. This also influenced external actors' behaviour, as it conveyed the idea that even if no peace deal was reached, there was still another obvious way to tackle the problem through criminal prosecution.

With increased momentum, the mismatch of international guidelines and the practice of galvanic surges became increasingly obvious. Having moved the process onto the international stage, 'parochialising' it again fulfiled a powerful purpose: it allowed the LRA to argue that the international system was patronising, and the international system to show its cultural awareness, which effectively covered up its own contradictory frameworks. As Baaré, the technical advisor on issues of demobilisation, wrote:

As the stature of the Juba process grew, the international community, including the UN, saw in their support to the GoSS and the Juba process a way of possibly managing the tricky political situation presented by the LRA. It allowed them to describe the process as an 'African solution for African problems' while still supporting the ICC warrants. In practice, this meant that donors and supporters of the process could engage with the parties while still stating that a final peace agreement should adhere to the Rome Statute (1998), which in principle allows national prosecution instead of prosecution by the ICC, one of the key demands of both the LRA and GoU.[76]

A galvanic surge attracts bandwagoning. During moments when it seemed more likely that a deal would be signed, support for the process increased tremendously, corners could be cut and the LRA was further encouraged to connect. Support was withdrawn when the process seemed at its weakest, contributing to a downward spiral. I experienced how the galvanic surge developed momentum after the US LRA Bill had been signed. Invisible Children, as one of the main lobbying organisations in support of the Bill, told me that they had been holding back on spending their funds in Uganda in anticipation of the signing of the LRA Bill. The reasoning for keeping cash was so 'that we are able to spend a

---

[75] International Crisis Group (2008: 15). Sam Kolo, however, reportedly talked about Kony's fear of the ICC.

[76] Baaré (2008).

lot of money once the act leads to action'.[77] With money released as soon as the LRA Bill was signed, the bill – for whom the money spender had lobbied – would instantly look like a success. Yet, it was just a repetition of a self-referential pattern.

Engaging only when success was guaranteed meant that in the early days of the talks, Juba-based NGOs answered with dead silence around the table when they were asked during Egeland's visit to step forth with supportive programmes at a point when the talks were extremely uncertain. Proposals started to come in when success seemed likely and, as Dave Eaton calls it in describing peace work in Kenya, the 'business of peace' started rolling.[78] In September 2006 – when the process was not without hitches, but certainly promising – the US Senate passed a bill to support the peace process.[79] Aware that outside support would strengthen his own role and solicit more support, Machar was delighted when I told him about the Senate resolution: 'Get it to me so that I can brag!' he exclaimed. He was so excited about the support that when he saw me chatting to Ayena shortly afterwards, he interrupted to ask: 'Are you exposing my secret?'[80] He also gave a succinct description of how the galvanic surge was utilised by those joining it: 'Museveni will only come [to Juba] when there is one little thing left so that he can quickly solve it and then be the hero'.[81]

The LRA/M experienced this wave-like engagement as a double standard or even abuse of powerful office. It alienated them from opportunistic external actors.[82] In a meeting with UN officials, Kony addressed the crowd and explained where he saw those double standards:

When Egeland went to northern Uganda, he had personal interviews with people in camps. People were very clear: 'We were brought here by government'. Now people are dying by thousands in Kitgum and Pader. Now world is doing nothing

---

[77] Fieldnotes: US Department of Defense expert meeting 'Eliminating the threat to civilian and regional stability posed by the Lord's Resistance Army'. Washington, DC: 30 September 10.

[78] Eaton describes the decades of inefficient peace work along the Uganda–Kenya border that is being replicated due to NGO interests (Eaton 2008: 243). In the case of Save the Children Uganda, the position on whether or not to support the peace process see-sawed during the entire process.

[79] The Senate of the United States (2006).

[80] Author interview with Riek Machar, Vice President of the Government of Southern Sudan. Juba: 26 September 2006.

[81] Author interview with Riek Machar, Vice President of the Government of Southern Sudan. Juba: 26 September 2006.

[82] Buruma and Margalit make a similar point in their explanation of antagonism towards the United States, fed by American power or American support that comes across as an overbearing father – or for turning away when help is needed (Buruma and Margalit 2005: loc18–20).

about it. Is this fairness of the world? I want the world to understand [this double standard] if there is to be a final resolution of conflict in this world.[83]

He expressed his bewilderment with the UN system: 'What I want us to understand clearly is business of UN. What is UN? Me, you, and everybody. You go to Uganda, people working for the UN. Sudan – same. UN is the people. Should not be used out of context like dragon'.[84] What he meant by the dragon analogy became clearer a little later: it was the image used to explain that the UN chose to intervene only when it felt strong enough to succeed without a doubt – invincible like a dragon. Specifically, Kony's reasoning went, the UN made sure of this by only tackling tasks with guaranteed success; it would not intervene when its opponents still seemed strong enough to stand a chance of keeping the upper hand:

You know arms are traded across the border of Sudan and Uganda. What does that mean? In short while, war is going to break between Sudan and Uganda. What is UN doing about that? They are allowing to happen, provided you are the strong man.[85]

There were obvious reasons for the galvanic surge, and the LRA/M were well aware that they were offering strong benefits to those outsiders to whom they had connected – including me. They repeatedly referred to the business opportunities for peacemakers. Sant'Egidio, who were very prominently engaged in the early days of the talks but whose commitment waned as the peace talks faltered, stated in a paper written by a member that a prerequisite for those wanting to facilitate peace was to have 'no ulterior motives besides peacemaking. Not having a hidden agenda or personal interests is perceived by the parties in conflict as a guarantee of serious mediation marked by a spirit of justice'.[86] Yet the LRA/M recognised that gaining recognition by being a peacemaker is itself an ulterior motive. If that recognition seems within reach, more people and organisations emerge to share it. Incentives to join peace talks, particularly with a galvanic surge, become skewed as a singular notion of success – the signing of a deal – arises. Bandwaggoning pushes the galvanic surge even faster.

Examples of how the skewed incentives played out abound: trying to catch the galvanic surge, those interested in making peace had for years enacted cognitive dissonance by pursuing templates of peacemaking that had failed in the past. Continuing with the same patterns

---

[83] Fieldnotes, Ri-Kwangba: 12 December 2006.
[84] Fieldnotes, Ri-Kwangba: 12 December 2006.
[85] Fieldnotes, Ri-Kwangba: 12 December 2006.   [86] Giro (1998).

was based, against better judgement, on the belief that somehow it would work this time. Stephen Van Evera has examined organisational processes of self-evaluation, and his assessment could help explain why neither the LRA/M nor external actors were able to significantly change their behaviour to move towards a peaceful solution. He has identified the inability of state institutions to evaluate their own beliefs and propaganda,

to test ideas against logic and evidence, weeding out those that fail. As a result, national learning is slow and forgetting is quick. The external environment is perceived only dimly, through a fog of myths and misperceptions.

Any significant shift in perception would, of course, threaten the standing of the incumbent leadership, including possibly the leadership of a critical opponent. 'As a result', Van Evera concludes, 'the "free market-place of ideas" often creates a confusion-sowing competition among charlatans that generates more darkness than light'.[87]

An international aid worker gave me an example of how the cognitive dissonance between belief in solutions and their reality played out. Having worked closely with donors in Uganda, he commented on the relentless competition in the international diplomatic and aid community to emerge as the successful facilitator of an LRA peace agreement. In Kampala in 2004, donors had agreed that they would all pull the same strings to facilitate peace talks. Nobody would make separate attempts, to avoid a situation in which various peace talks facilitators were in competition with each other and could thus be manipulated by the LRA. Specifically, it was decided that nobody would pay any LRA contacts to make a connection to Kony. While individual donors such as the Netherlands did coordinate with NGOs to stop attempts at peace, donor competition remained fierce. Shortly after the agreement had been made within the donor and agency crowd, explained the aid worker,

everybody started giving money and satellite phones. The image of being the one person who walks into the bush, takes Joseph Kony by the hand and says to him, you, Joseph, and I, we will walk slowly to Gulu, step by step, and we will make peace – to be the one person that brings Kony out of the bush – that image makes people stupid.[88]

---

[87] Evera (2002).

[88] Fieldnotes, New York: 24 September 2010. The LRA knew how to sell the most powerful good they had to offer: the promise of peace. In Gulu, most aid workers become aware after a while that many people ran scams promising access to Kony. The GoU is not immune to this: a famous story involved a porter at Lacor hospital who conned Salim Saleh out of 50,000 Ugandan shillings by promising to take him to Kony.

Or, as one delegate put it to me after a day when the various interests of other players in the Juba Talks had been foregrounded in discussions of the roles of the two conflict parties: 'The question of who kills first is not only between LRA and the government. It is also the problem solving that becomes like a competition'.[89] His point was that with the jostling for success among external actors, the LRA/M delegation (which at that particular point had been struggling with its internal dynamics) was also able to play the external actors off against each other. The focus, he said, was no longer on solving the issues, but on who would be able to take the most credit – in other words, who would be able to say that they were the person leading Kony out of the bush, holding his hand. That is why after initial hesitation the LRA's connect phase was greeted with great enthusiasm.

By September 2007, the impact of the galvanic surge was impressive. In a confidential meeting with US senator Feingold in Kampala, members of the diplomatic community emphasised their engagement in the peace process. The Dutch hoped for a US role in influencing Museveni directly while being able to provide intelligence. Norway acknowledged that while the country supported the ICC, internal debate on justice and peace was a lot more nuanced, leading to the withdrawal of Norway's support for the EU's terrorist list to allow more flexibility in the Juba Talks. The UK supported the United States by keeping the LRA on their terrorist list to maintain the pressure to sign a peace deal. Several donor nations had contributed the JIF to pay for the GoSS peace secretariat and for LRA/M delegation expenses, including per diems.[90] Yet at the same time, away from Juba, other galvanic surges were at play which would become important again. US diplomatic personnel on the ground acknowledged in a confidential briefing that there was a discrepancy between the real impact of the Juba Talks and the advocacy-driven narrative prevalent in Washington.

Having witnessed IDP returns and a secure northern Uganda, US embassy staff filed a report stating: 'It is clear to post that the briefings provided by advocacy NGOs to the Hill are not giving sufficient weight to positive developments in the north at the Juba talks'.[91] The previous year, on 9 November 2006, the six Gulu Night Centres had been asked to close since so few children were using them for night commutes; children sleeping in the towns of northern Uganda for protection had been one of the most prominent images of the war and the root of the organisation Invisible Children. Probation and Social Welfare Officer

---

[89] Author interview with LRA/M delegate. Juba: 15 October 2006.
[90] US Embassy Kampala (2007e).   [91] US Embassy Kampala (2007b).

Joseph Kilama had said that all centres with fewer than a hundred children were expected to close before 15 November.[92] For international groups, whose galvanic surge of support rested on a different vision of the situation in northern Uganda, time seemed to have stood still. US confidential cables describe how on 10 August 2007, Invisible Children's CEO Ben Keesey had updated the US ambassador to Uganda on his organisation's activities, such as 'visiting U.S. college campuses ... to update audiences on the current night commuter statistics'.[93]

One of the main people on the LRA side in the early stages of the Juba Talks came to epitomise how external actors seek out the information that fits their galvanic surge at that moment. A few months after his defection from the LRA in late 2007, this former delegate was arrested after a satellite phone call was traced as having been placed by him from a hill in Kampala. The phone call had been made to intelligence agencies to deliver inside LRA information in the final stages of the Juba Talks. The caller had identified himself as 'Colonel Lubwoa Bwone', and had been chillingly open about Kony's real motivations in the peace talks. Both the United States and the GoU considered 'Bwone', the man on the phone, 'a very reliable source'. US sources documented the information coming from the supposed 'Bwone', who said he was 20 miles inside CAR and 30 miles from Kony. He confirmed on 16 March that UPDF and ICC reports of Kony's relocation to CAR were true, that he himself had travelled with Kony, and that he was now with Odhiambo, and General Bok Abudema, 'who were laying landmines to prevent an attack on Kony'.

'Bwone' was telling the United States precisely what they had suspected as the Juba Talks had failed to deliver a swift peace agreement: that Kony was working closely with Khartoum to spread a regional war and that he had sophisticated weapons. Khartoum, 'Bwone' said, was also supporting the Acholi diaspora. 'Bwone explained that this was being achieved because Kony had linked up "in CAR with Chadian rebel leader Mahamat Nouri, who allegedly had 2,000 people with him"' as the embassy cable stated. It further said that Kony would also take LRA fighters to 'Bahr-el-gazel[sic]. Rankand-file [sic] LRA call it Darfur'. Several sources, including 'Bwone', said that Khartoum was moving the LRA to Darfur to work with the *Janjaweed* militia. 'Bwone' stated that Khartoum's intention was not to allow the 'SPLA fellows to have their elections in Juba', the US transcript reads. He confirmed that Kony had heavy weapons, including 'four unused large weapons that can shoot

---

[92] Eriku (9 November 2006). [93] US Embassy Kampala (2007c).

down aircraft, weapons that had been abandoned in southern Sudan, and ammunition delivered by the Arabs'.[94] Having detailed Kony's thinking – and incidentally given the United States exactly the kind of information that confirmed their worst fears – the man on the phone who claimed to be 'Bwone' had said he wanted to defect, but needed money to do so. It was the request for money that initiated the tracing of the call and led to the discovery that the former LRA man had planted exactly the kind of information international intelligence had hoped for in his call from Kampala, which they had relayed to their headquarters.

In an earlier chapter, I have written about information and discourse on the LRA. The incident of the fake insider information given by 'Bwone' to the US embassy in Kampala shows how discourse creates galvanic surges and vice versa. The fake phone caller had identified which information would most resonate with the embassy because it supported beliefs already held and increased the chances that the United States would pay money to help the informer escape, playing on their confirmation bias. Because the information seemed to fit, all disbelief could be suspended, creating instead the next wave of opinion that was to inform the next steps.

6.10   Acting in Dissonance: Connect/Disconnect and Galvanic Surges

The galvanic surge sent confusing signals to the LRA. One example of mixed messages was the LRA/M's interaction with the media. With the LRA an accessible force and a delegation in Juba ready for interviews, the early days of the talks attracted intense press interest. For many journalists, the experience of covering the LRA meant creating a personal connection so as to be allowed to travel to the bush – and then to report as if they had come to the bush on their own intrepid account. This contradictory setup often translated into bizarre scenes, as lines between being a reporter and carrying of the trophy of making it to the LRA camp blurred, sending confusing signals to the LRA.

Otti clearly enjoyed the attention. He appeared from the bush for an impromptu press conference with impeccably ironed clothes, his previously grey hair died jet black. Yet he also often seemed puzzled during his public encounters because journalists would first attack him for keeping children captive as soldiers, as did, for example, a journalist from the

---

[94] US Embassy Kampala (2008b).

Figure 6.1 Vincent Otti presents himself for a press conference,
September 2006.

New Vision in the press conference on 19 September 2006. The same
journalist then asked Otti if he could have his picture taken shaking Otti's
hand and patting him on the shoulder.[95]

Moments like this strengthened the LRA/M's view of themselves as
strong and viable negotiation partners. They also became manifestations
of how the LRA maintained people's interest in them. By promising
different levels of access, withdrawing and reinstating it, they let outsiders believe that they were important and on the cusp of a breakthrough
towards a particular insight. During my own research, I went through
many incarnations of becoming connected and disconnected.

As enthusiasm for a peace deal gained momentum, the business of
peace talks became increasingly attractive for the LRA/M. Promises of
visits to Rome by Sant'Egidio and of air tickets to the United States by
Shortley strengthened the LRA/M in their understanding that they had
retained control of the situation and could increase their demands. Talk
of ICC warrants being suspended or overruled by Uganda's government

---

[95] Fieldnotes, Ri-Kwangba: 19 September 2006.

and meetings with ambassadors had the same effect.[96] In those moments, the LRA/M was a visible and viable force. Yet what became increasingly clear was that by connecting, the LRA/M had also initiated their own loss of control over the conflict, causing a retreat into the one mechanism that the LRA knew to regain that control: disconnecting.

The failure to sign the FPA is the most prominent example of disconnect to regain control and to reclaim LRA ownership of the process. Interpreting disconnect as withdrawal and a failure of the process, the externals stopped support for the Juba Talks. Lack of support made it more difficult for the LRA/M to reconnect, as it ended the LRA/M's belief in the external umpire position and moved the process onto the military level. The expectation that external actors would be just had created the moment of connect for the LRA/M. As the galvanic surge reached a consensus that the LRA/M was not serious and that military pressure was needed, no incentive was left to prevent the LRA from disconnecting. However, the moment of disconnect was precisely when moments of transformation occurred, however slowly – for example, when the LRA/M was facing up to its own complicated internal dynamics and how these obstructed the path to peace. Profoundly misinterpreting this as withdrawal meant that support for the process faltered when the time was needed for the conflict to be transformed.

For external actors, interpreting moments of disconnect as 'alternating current' rather than withdrawal was challenging to impossible. The misinterpretation of disconnect created a galvanic surge for ending support. Signalling the end of support in the eyes of the LRA/M meant that external actors were losing their umpire position. One international advisor to the secretariat blamed misunderstood linearity for the slow negotiations: he explained to me that one problem was that the LRA/M was negotiating in a linear way. They were moving back and forth, rather

---

[96] How this impression might have been created becomes clear when reading the description of the 'Rome Platform' by Sant'Egidio in relation to the Mozambican civil war.

The Rome Platform of January 1995, organised by the Community of Sant'Egidio, represents the first and only political attempt to end this bloody war. The aim was to get all parties to sit down and recognise each other as part of the same nation. In the Rome Platform, the FIS condemned violence and started its return to a terrain of political confrontation. The 'peace offer' called on the military to accept the presence of political alternatives, of a new pole with which to negotiate. The democratic and lay opposition forces that signed the Platform were to act as buffers between the two contenders. The formula used in Rome was to bring the FIS back into the political framework, moderating it and forcing it to take on commitments toward the public. (Giro 1998)

than approaching issues simultaneously on two levels: one the official level for the leaders, and a back-channel process to carve out deals with the GoU. His point was that the LRA/M was simply not tactical, displaying either full commitment or none at all, and this was confusing. It was a different way to describe the alternating current.

Machar gave a telling portrayal of how connect/disconnect and galvanic surge failed to align. In the early days of the talks, he said that the GoU did not offer any concessions, allowing the LRA/M to be heard much more clearly if they chose to be heard. I spoke to Machar a few days after the upsetting incident in late July 2006 when LRA/M delegates had been left behind in Ri-Kwangba and Kony in reaction had ordered the military representatives to stay in the bush. Machar was annoyed that the lack of military men at the negotiating table was sending the signal that the LRA wanted to quit the talks, but more so that they were losing their voice by sending this signal. 'They behave as if they want to quit', he said. 'Cars have been waiting for fighters in Nabanga for the last four days. Sometimes they are just delaying things. The government is arrogant. The LRA can keep the moral high ground if they continue to be engaged'.[97]

The lack of tactics to keep the moral high ground became obvious in the Museveni handshake debacle. When Museveni came to Juba to visit both delegations, the deputy delegation leader, Apire, refused to shake his hand unless he apologised first for atrocities committed against the Acholi. Rather than an opportunity to gain the publicity upper hand by extending the hand of peace – to fully connect – it had become a moment in which the LRA/M had made clear that they had yet to clarify what their aim was in the Juba Talks – that they were prepared at any point to disconnect.[98] The message this sent to the external actors about the LRA/M's commitment was devastating, as it was interpreted simply as lack of interest in peace.

The ending of Chissano's mandate as the UN Special Envoy to LRA-affected Areas in 2009 was interpreted in very similar ways by both the LRA/M and the advocacy group Resolve: both saw it as a UN signal that there was no longer any interest in pursuing a negotiated peace. In his final briefing to the UNSC, Chissano made a very different point: he called for a principled approach by the UN to support the peace process. His perspective was clearly informed by a more flexible understanding of the process, and by the realisation that in this case, the UN was choosing to stick to its own rules in some moments but not in others. For better or

---

[97] Fieldnotes, Juba: 6 September 2006.   [98] Fieldnotes, Juba: 6 November 2006.

for worse, as one aid worker for a UN agency pointed out, in moments where the success of bending the rules seems unlikely, 'in HQ, approaches tend to become very principled'.[99]

6.11   Conclusion

For the LRA/M, connecting and disconnecting are ways to keep actors engaged, but also to consolidate internal thinking. Keeping people at arm's length is a way to exert control. A similar mechanism of tightening and loosening connections works internally and holds together the system LRA. What was striking to observe was how little outside actors used these LRA characteristics strategically. Instead, each moment of disconnect was viewed as being of grave consequence and led to a faltering commitment to the talks as energy flowed backwards. An uninterrupted commitment to talks and cessation of violence is preferable, but also unrealistic as belligerents edge towards each other. The interpretation of disconnect as a final stance on a peaceful solution, however, is detached from reality. International commitment based on uninterrupted forward movement of the current assumes that the process simplifies choices, and that if it fails to do so it has failed as a process. The alternating current is certainly a reflection on the challenges of the process, but its existence cannot be used to judge the quality or sincerity of it.

In mismatching an alternating-current mode of engagement with direct-current mode, the Juba Talks produced contradictions that neither actor was able to overcome and opportunities for genuine change were missed. The LRA/M failed to strengthen their connections as they were too concerned with maintaining control, and they failed to gather support by being perceived as unreliable. They experienced the international actors as too focused on achieving a goal rather than on engaging in the long haul of addressing political solutions. In turn, external actors failed to pursue challenging issues and maintain the stamina to overcome complex set-ups in moments of crucial change. In the end, both actors retreated into the familiar patterns that have sustained the conflict – before and since the Juba Talks. Each side walked away from the Juba process with confirmation that their initial assessment of the other had been correct.

Operationally managing the LRA/M's connect/disconnect mode without prejudging it presented a great political risk. Creating subtlety within

---

[99] Fieldnotes, New York: 24 September 2010.

an international response that is reliant on broad support within all its institutions remains one of the great challenges in international processes. However, the Juba Talks highlighted an unresolved tension within the international community: rules are not clearly defined and tend to be abandoned or reinstated depending on which way the wave of support goes. This highlights the international inability to engage with complex issues in a nuanced way. Instead of adjusting their approach when they lacked clarity, external actors in Juba chose to reduce their assessment of the process to judgements of the LRA/M's motivations. This assessment strengthened support for leverage through military pressure and ultimately a military strike, causing those motivations to falter. The fallout of this chain of reasoning was a prolonged conflict, many more lives lost, and many more people displaced or subjected to horrible living conditions, much more money spent on continuing the war than was spent on trying to make peace, and a diminished possibility for a nuanced peace process in the future.

The clash of operating modes led to both the LRA/M and external actors feeling confirmed in their thinking. A transformative process needs a different mindset and a willingness to engage on all levels with the complexities of how rebel groups seek peace and how the international system best and most credibly navigates its own set of rules. External actors had made their peacemaking framework much more complicated through the introduction of the Rome Statute, and were struggling to navigate it. Thus, neither the LRA nor the external actors were able to credibly establish a working mechanism that would steady the LRA/M's modus of connect/disconnect, deliver credible concessions from both belligerents, and be implementable regardless of divided international opinion.

7   The Juba Peace Talks with the Lord's Resistance Army in 2008
'Maybe We Came Too Close to the Enemy'

When I returned to Juba in mid-January 2008, I encountered different moods in the LRA/M delegation. Some expressed frustration over the uncertainty of the peace process; others were intimidated by or defiant towards the LRA leader. Machar and some of the international observers acknowledged the LRA/M's internal struggles but seemed determined to separate these from bringing the talks to a successful conclusion. On my follow-up stays during almost all of March and the first half of April, and then most of June, these two parallel strands of the Juba Talks seemed to continue.

The year 2008 was to be a confusing year. Previously less obvious patterns of mistrust and miscommunication came to the fore, as did the parallel preparations for war and peace. Of the international actors, the United States took on a new and prominent role, working behind the scenes to assure military preparations while being an observer at the talks. Within the delegation, roles of individuals became increasingly confusing, facilitating the often-lazy assertion that the LRA/M just did not want peace. Nonetheless, I mistakenly thought throughout most of the year that despite increasing brinkmanship, the peace process would continue. This chapter chronicles the events that led to the end of the Juba Talks with a particular focus on the flows of information and various backchannels that contributed to the return to war in December 2008.

7.1   January Changes

In January 2008, delegates and UN staff from Juba met with the LRA in Ri-Kwangba for the first time since Otti's death had been confirmed. Amongst those representing the LRA was Achellam. A member of UN security asked Achellam if he was at the meeting as the new number two, replacing Otti. Achellam responded that he was only representing Kony because Kony had 'another engagement', and that he was not number two. In fact, he reportedly said, 'applications for the post are being

Figure 7.1 Joseph Kony and Okot Odhiambo, June 2006.

screened'.[1] An LRA/M delegate said that when he had asked Odhiambo, whether he would be the new number two, Odhiambo had been unwilling to comment directly on Otti's death, but instead mentioned that nobody who had ever held the post of second-in-command had survived.[2]

Delegates recalled the January meeting as extremely difficult; they felt betrayed, mourned for Otti, and no longer knew how to engage with those in the bush. Just after the delegates had left Ri-Kwangba, Kony ordered a personnel reshuffle in his delegation, dismissing Ojul, and Ayoo as chair and spokesperson, to be replaced by Matsanga and Obita, respectively. The new chairman delivered a letter to Machar in which Kony asked for the dismissal of Achama and Okirot from the CHMT. They were both ordered to return to the bush. The dismissals again fuelled rumours that the reason for Otti's death and for the dismissal of a range of prominent delegates was to be found in the Mombasa meeting, at which all of those dismissed had been present. Former delegates wrote in their disgruntled repudiation of the Juba Talks:

The dismissal of Martin Ojul, in particular and the reconstitution of the LRA/M delegation on the 22nd January 2008, and the dismissal of two LRA officers in the CHMT from the LRA in early February were partly a result of the above secret meetings [with Museveni during consultations and the Mombasa meeting],

[1] Author interview with UN security officer. Juba: 1 February 2008.
[2] Fieldnotes, Juba: 2 February 2008.

which were meant to compromise, infiltrate, lure and/or destroy the LRA peace team during the consultation exercise in Uganda.[3]

Having just been dismissed from the CHMT, one of the two young men was visibly distraught. He was twiddling his chunky satellite phone in his hands and barely looked up from the sheet of paper he was reading. 'I am not sure what to do', he said.

How is this possible after all the hardship? We walked hundreds of miles through the bush, breaking through security, getting to Kitgum, hiring a car, meeting Martin, meeting Assefa and Simon, then the first meeting with the VP on February 14, the first meeting ever! It was the first time the VP spoke to Vincent; we were getting everything off the ground.

But now, he continued, the delegation was being 'renewed' and he and his colleague were 'said to be Martin's partners, so we have to go'. He had last spoken to Kony a few days before: 'The chairman said nothing to me on Tuesday night. But the chairman is now being influenced by Matsanga; there are many stories about Matsanga. Matsanga only went to Nabanga last time, he did not even go to Ri-Kwangba'. I asked him what he was going to do – was he going back to the bush as ordered? 'I am not sure if I should go and have no future at all', he replied. 'But I cannot stay in Juba, it is too expensive'. He looked at the paper in his hand. 'I am not sure whether this is really the best for Ugandan people'.[4] His colleague, also freshly dismissed, was more matter of fact. I asked him whether he was following the order to return. He answered:

We are just on standby, next time you might not find us here. What has been decided has been decided. You cannot ask questions. This is how it has been decided; there is nothing I can do about it. There was an assassination attempt on Kony, so this was what happened. But this demoralised the delegation and myself.

In the end, all those dismissed departed for Nairobi. In the delegation, the dismissal of Ojul, Ongom, Ayoo, Okirot and Achama was widely discussed. One delegate speculated that their having found agreement on too many issues was the reason for the breakdown of trust, confirming the division between the process and the agreements it produced, and that those now leaving 'had come too close to being settled. Look at the timing: all of this comes after our tour of Uganda with all its implications. Maybe we came too close to the enemy'. I was not sure I understood what that meant. Did he mean that travelling to Uganda to meet the

---

[3] LRA/M Peace Team (2009).   [4] Fieldnotes, Juba: 2 February 2008.

president was a bad decision? I asked if that was not precisely what was needed in a process that aimed to bring two parties together. He answered: 'Maybe the delegation had gone too far in what they have negotiated? But then why is the new delegation saying that it is now very easy? I am not sure it makes sense to me. I can only speculate about motives'.

'LRA is now split into two camps', explained another former delegate when I asked him how he felt about his dismissal. He was upset about Otti's death and described to me the scene in Ri-Kwangba when he learned that Otti had been killed. 'That man is a madman, killing Vincent when pleading for his life. I was going to resign but [another delegate] held my mouth shut', said the same man who had previously boasted about his tight connection with the high command.

'It's all fixed now', said another delegate. '[One delegate] and [another delegate] are government moles so from now on it will be GoU and GoU at the table. But there is nothing more we can do. We have taken it this far; it is to our colleagues now to run the last laps. If they want to run the laps with the government, there is nothing we can do'.

In contrast, Obita, who was taking over as spokesperson, seemed in a good mood. 'I would say we look at the first week of March to sign the agreement, otherwise we will give Machar a heart attack', he joked. Then he became serious. 'Kony is ready to sign. We have to renew the CoH and then consult the consultations documents for a few days and then get back into it. We can start with Agenda 3 because it is easier to deal with implementation protocols than with Agenda 2. Two is more complicated. But I am in very good spirits'.[5]

Yet despite Obita's optimism, the delegation in Juba was struggling to maintain coherence. One delegate commented that it was unfair that Ojul, who had led the delegation for close to two years, was now being blamed for the perceived failure of the talks. 'It is not good how they said it that [Ojul] was leaving with disgrace. He needs a rest. Sometimes troubles come up and then you have to be careful and withdraw for a while. Maybe you can come back later, maybe you cannot'.[6]

In the midst of the confusion, Museveni reiterated that everything needed to be signed by 31 January 2008. 'The UPDF is all over the place now for the 31st deadline', said a UN security advisor. 'It is now all very political, with the United States pushing for military and with the [UN Department of Political Affairs] playing stupid political games. They want it fixed once and for all, so it will just all go back to the beginning',

---

[5] Fieldnotes, Juba: 30 January 2008.   [6] Fieldnotes, Juba: 2 February 2008.

elaborating that the push for military action would void the progress made.[7]

With much talk of the deadline on the radio, the LRA withdrew deeper into Garamba Park. A woman who was abducted from Ezo in March 2008 said that she often had to walk from Garamba to collect food in Ri-Kwangba. From January, it took much longer – 24 hours – to walk from the LRA camp in Garamba to reach Ri-Kwangba.[8] Despite the shaky situation, said one South Sudanese abductee, the LRA was still talking about peace: 'They were digging [they were doing agriculture which implies they expected to stay in one place for a long time], waiting for outcome of peace talks. Everyone was waiting for outcome of peace talks'.[9]

With another GoU deadline looming, Chissano travelled to Kampala from 25 to 27 January to discuss the resumption of talks with Museveni. Museveni had agreed to give the talks another month; Chissano needed him to confirm this in writing to President Kabila, as it went against the agreement Museveni and Kabila had struck. A confidential US cable states: 'Chissano said that Kabila felt under pressure from the United States to take action against the LRA at the same time Congo had agreed with Uganda to take no action until January 31. As a result, Kabila was insisting on a letter from Museveni'. Despite reports that an increased number of Congolese troops were in the area around Dungu, to protect civilians from LRA attacks and contain the LRA – action that Chissano saw as critical – it was also clear that the DRC's military attention was focused on its own offensive against General Laurent Nkunda and his troops, who had been very active and had committed atrocities against civilians.[10]

On 27 January, Chissano met for three hours with Shortley during which he asked whether the United States 'were interested in supporting action against the LRA. Senior Advisor Shortley said that we would get back to him', reads a US memo about the meeting, further stating that Chissano 'did not come across as opposing military actions, as long as it did not push the LRA, which would likely scatter into small groups, deeper into Congo. He did not have a high level of confidence in the capability of regional forces to take on the LRA'.[11]

---

[7] Fieldnotes, Juba: 2 February 2008.
[8] Author (with translator) interview with female Sudanese LRA abductee from Ezo. Yambio: 23 February 2009.
[9] Author (with translator Zande/English) interview with Sudanese abductee who spent March–December 2008 with the LRA. Yambio: 23 February 2009.
[10] US Embassy Kampala (2007h).   [11] US Embassy Kampala (2007h).

The internal LRA/M developments radically altered the dynamics between the negotiation parties. In the early days of the Juba Talks, the mediator had seen the LRA/M as holding the 'moral high ground',[12] despite the tension and often unreasonable demands. In Machar's view, the LRA/M seemed to have come to the talks willing to address issues – unlike the GoU, who in his view had simply wanted to clinch an unchallenging deal. Machar had experienced the GoU as the obstinate party. When the LRA/M delegation unravelled during the process of consultations – when Otti's death became official – the delegation split and communication with Kony became near impossible, that was when the GoU displayed reason, patience and understanding, argued Machar. An international advisor to the talks described the position of the GoU:

GoU is really very constructive and says there is no such thing as a deadline in the sense of an ultimatum. But things are not moving at all, so far .... A situation of no progress whatsoever will of course lead to deadlines indeed becoming ultimatums. If they don't get their act together soon, we might seriously getting [*sic*] at risk of military action.[13]

The GoU stated that it remained positive towards the peace process and would allow time for the LRA to sort out their internal problems until the process was to start again. For some of the delegates, the GoU's stance was not surprising. They argued that the GoU had never wanted a deal; with a deal less likely they could, of course, appear to be more generous. Behind the scenes, the GoU was indeed pursuing different avenues. In meetings with the United States, the GoU delegation said that

the GOU would contain Kony's ability to act, by denying him access to arms caches in southern Sudan and northern Uganda. The GOU also has alerted the Central African Republic of Kony's reported intentions to relocate there. The GOU would continue to encourage LRA defections, and take all measures to defend its borders from incursions. Second, while the GOU was highly sceptical of the current LRA negotiating team's authority to negotiate for Kony, the GOU would continue to participate in the Juba Peace Talks.[14]

New rumours about continued upheaval within the LRA emerged. A statement by the International Organisation for Migration (IOM) said that Odhiambo had been in touch with them, wanting to defect. A US cable recounted that IOM's Uganda country director was maintaining contact with people claiming to be Odhiambo and Ongwen, believing them to be genuine callers, 'despite indications to the contrary and

---

[12] Fieldnotes, Juba: 6 September 2006.
[13] Personal email from international advisor to author, 30 January 2008.
[14] US Embassy Kampala (2007g).

warnings from the [Ugandan] External Security Organization (ESO) that the callers are not genuine'.[15] Analysts publicly speculated about the likelihood of Odhiambo's defection.

Unsurprisingly, Odhiambo never appeared at IOM-facilitated meeting points to aid his defection. It later transpired that the phone calls had most likely been made by a former LRA soldier. This man, who was also featured in documentaries by Invisible Children, had been trying to extract money from international and GoU officials in return for the promise of defection. It was a similar scheme to that pursued a year earlier by a former delegate who had impersonated LRA commander Bwone to extract donor money and plant information. A confidential US government document showed that Invisible Children had implicated the person purported to be behind the Odhiambo rumour to the GoU, and that he was arrested on 5 March 2009.[16]

Meanwhile, the security situation in southern Sudan had again deteriorated. On 20 January 2008, an LRA group was seen moving from Morobo to Tore in Western Equatoria; another moved in Central Equatoria from Lire towards Kajo Keji. This movement caused great concern and coincided with – or was the cause of – a few violent incidents. Eastern Equatorians thought that some LRA were still among them, but that they were not causing any trouble, and might be waiting for new orders. Rumours of airdrops circulated but could never be verified. Coordination between GoSS, GoS and security forces was limited. Residents around Obbo reported that the UPDF there was selling guns and ammunition to civilians. They had reported this to the UPDF in Kajo Keji, to no avail.[17]

Many attacks in Equatoria were apparently misattributed to LRA – although some attacks were clearly traceable to be LRA – and this affected talks. A number of attacks were reported in Central Equatoria; the area around Yei was particularly unstable. In an ad hoc meeting for aid agencies in Juba, the attacks were described as following 'known LRA patterns', with systematic and extensive looting and abductions, but with releasing abductees in many cases after they had done their work as porters.[18] In Kajo Keji, three SPLA soldiers were killed in a suspected LRA attack, but one of their killers was recognised to be a former SPLA soldier.

In February 2008, Agence France-Presse (AFP) ran a story about a massacre of 136 people by 300 LRA near Kajo Keji. The UN was unable

[15] US Embassy Kampala (2009a).   [16] US Embassy Kampala (2009c).
[17] Author interview with local journalist. Juba: 31 February 2008.
[18] Fieldnotes, Juba: 13 February 2008.

to confirm that such a massacre had happened. Reporting on the Kajo Keji attack on 4 February was confusing. The Danish Refugee Council and UN security spoke of thirty-six killed – a hundred fewer than AFP had reported – while the SPLA said four.[19] With the overly large number of LRA fighters (300) reportedly involved in the attack, even the Ugandan military dismissed the reports.[20] Some of the security problems indeed turned out to be homegrown. One victim of the attacks described his experience: 'The people who attacked spoke Arabic and wore green uniform. They were those that call themselves "No Unit"'.[21] 'No Unit', it came to be known, was a group of disgruntled SPLA soldiers who had defected from the SPLA after receiving no pay.[22] They had started attacks in the Yei area, renouncing their SPLA loyalty through their name 'No Unit'.

I followed up with the AFP reporter who had written about the supposed large massacre. He said that he had received his information from three sources in southern Sudan and a western diplomat. One government source told him 'that the dead were indeed 141'. Because the official did not want to go on the record, he had been unable to publish the higher number. 'All the three/four sources have confirmed that the LRA killings will be downplaed [sic] or censured [sic] for the sake of talks'.[23] This particular massacre was never confirmed, but it was clear that suspicions were also growing within GoSS that Machar was keeping a lid on LRA activities in order to conclude the talks. Small-scale abductions by the LRA were definitely happening at this time. Also, in early 2008, the UN in Juba was informed about a substantial LRA attack in CAR, in which an unconfirmed but large number of people were killed or abducted. Such atrocities were impossible to square politically with continued perseverance in the peace talks. An international member of the mediation team commented on the news about LRA activity in CAR: 'The only solution in Juba was to swipe this under the carpet. I found that at the time quite difficult to swallow'.[24]

A young Zande man who was taken by the LRA in March 2008 from Ezo recounted what happened to him after he was abducted around that time: 'When they abduct people, they gather them and pray [with] them in Acholi. They then put crosses on forehead, chest and foot using a mixture of water and ashes. After that, there were no more prayers.

---

[19] US Embassy Kampala (2008d).   [20] US Embassy Kampala (2008d).

[21] Author interview (with translator from Arabic) with Tore resident (displaced to Yei). Yei: 31 March 2008.

[22] Author interview with local journalist. Juba: 31 January 2008.

[23] Personal email to author from reporter, 13 February 2008.

[24] Personal email to author from an international advisor to the Juba Talks, 7 August 2011.

I never saw the LRA pray after that'. He was forced to speak only Acholi from his first day with the LRA: 'We were told "forget your mother tongue or you will be beaten to death if you say you don't know Acholi. When you understand first, you are better. If you are slow to learn you will be beaten until you know it"'. He also noted that while Acholi remained the language of the LRA, some of the LRA fighters spoke other languages, 'but not fluently. Some Lingala, Zande, Kiswahili. When they come to someone's house and are confused with geography, they ask for directions in local language'. He mentioned that one LRA 'speaks Lingala like a Congolese, but he is Acholi. He also speaks Arabic'.[25]

7.2   Final Talks

In the midst of confusion and accusations of a cover-up from all sides, talks restarted on 30 January with Matsanga leading the LRA/M delegation. The reopening ceremony was held in Juba Raha Hotel – a more humble affair than previous ceremonies. Chissano listened – stone-faced – as a row of speakers, including the GoU, listed the achievements of the past few months. The LRA/M emphasized unaccomplished items and grievances. Representatives of the AU, who had been brought in to strengthen the process, were also in the audience. From the point of view of the LRA/M delegates and some of the mediation team, the AU representatives were necessary to ensure Machar's impartiality as a mediator. The Juba Talks had become a regional process, which allowed for their continuation, but also made it more difficult to navigate the different interests.

After the ceremony, a delegation of women demonstrated in the Juba Raha grounds, holding up placards thanking the mediator and demanding peace. The day after, the delegates attended a workshop held by the International Centre on Transitional Justice on attitudes to justice and accountability in preparation for negotiations on Agenda 3.

The process was strengthened by EU observers, in addition to a number of African dignitaries and military personnel who had been engaged in the process since the previous November. This last round was the first to see the presence of US representative Shortley in the mediation room, mandated by US Assistant Secretary of State Frazier 'to work with the mediator and parties on moving the peace process forward'

---

[25] Author (with translator Zande/English) interview with Sudanese abductee who spent March–December 2008 with the LRA. Yambio: 23 February 2009.

Figure 7.2 Women demonstrating at the reopening ceremony, January 2008

in a process that, a US statement read, 'cannot be open-ended'.[26] Another extension of the CoH was one of the first points to be discussed. The latest version of the CoH was to expire on 29 February 2008, and the GoU was unwilling to discuss a further extension, stressing instead their confidence in progress in Juba and their expectation that an agreement on a permanent ceasefire would be signed by that date.[27]

From what then followed, this did not seem an unreasonable expectation. From the end of January 2008 and into March, events accelerated. With Matsanga as the head of the delegation, the talks proceeded at a previously unknown speed. After only four days of negotiations on the issue, on 19 February 2008, the parties signed an annexe to Agenda 3 on accountability and reconciliation that stipulated Uganda's commitment to establishing a Special Division of the High Court to deal with crimes committed in this war.[28] Agenda 5 – a permanent ceasefire – was signed on 23 February, with the ceasefire to come into force twenty-four hours after the signing of the FPA. Former delegates watched from Nairobi as Matsanga signed the outstanding agreements despite the fact, as they wrote later,

[26] US State Department (2008).   [27] US Embassy Kampala (2008d).
[28] The history of the International Crimes Division of the High Court has not been without troubles since its inception, notably during the trial of LRA Thomas Kwoyelo. See Moffett (2016); Macdonald and Porter (2016); Human Rights Watch (2015, 2012).

that all the major points contained in the LRA 'Position Papers' which the LRA/
M wanted dealt with seriously, were thrown out without consultation with
chairman of LRA peace talks. For example, the matters on Agenda No. 2,
dealing with 'The Root Causes of the conflict' were brutally handled and put to
rest, without clear solution, to bring about lasting reconciliation! All other items
were likewise manipulated and concluded in a manner that tantamount to mere
adoptions of Uganda government 'Position Papers' and without detailed
consultations with General Joseph Kony![29]

In Juba, various facilitators of the peace talks commented with dismay on
their observations of US representative Shortley, who was, in the view of
an international security official 'going around to the donors to ask them
to stop funding the talks, while being an observer and now he is also
involved in money giving to the delegation'.[30]

In late February 2008, Machar was making plans for an official grand
signing ceremony for early April in Juba, coupled with the expectation
that all agreements would be signed by 25 March. Talking to US officials, who also asked that GoSS 'be prepared to take military action in
coordination with its neighbours against the LRA in the event that Kony
refuses a peace agreement and returns to fighting', Machar, reportedly
expressed confidence that Kony would sign, and replied: 'Let me be a
peacemaker now', before agreeing that military action 'would be the
outcome of failed talks'. In a confidential memo, the US representative
commented on the meeting:

Given reports that Kony has no intention of reaching an agreement, the
negotiations in Juba appear to proceed in a parallel reality. However, the
process keeps his fighters engaged in peace rather than war and could ensure
some defections from frustrated LRA fighters if Kony doesn't follow through with
his half-hearted participation in the peace process. The wily Riek Machar cannot
be trusted, and we hope he is passing along sound information and not just
stringing us along.[31]

On 28 February, the LRA/M delegates travelled to Ri-Kwangba to
present the texts of the final agreements to Kony. They travelled without
the Langi legal advisor who had been a delegate from the first gathering
of the delegation. Krispus Ayena Odongo – who would later defend
Dominic Ongwen at the ICC – had resigned or been dismissed, fuelling
further speculation that ethnic divisions between Acholi and Langi were
widening in the delegation.[32]

---

[29] LRA/M (2008).
[30] Author interview with international security staff. Juba: 1 February 2008.
[31] US Embassy Khartoum (2008).   [32] US Embassy Kampala (2008d).

What exactly happened at the February meeting remains unclear. The broadest consensus seems to be that Matsanga stayed behind in Nabanga when the delegates went to Ri-Kwangba. In Ri-Kwangba, delegates reportedly met with LRA commanders Alit and Thomas Kwoyelo, but it seems they spoke to Kony only on the phone. Because of pressure to conclude things in Juba, the delegates stayed in Ri-Kwangba only briefly. Initially, it was unclear what message they had been given by Kony. Nevertheless, events the following day seemed to imply that Kony had liked the agreements. As the rumour spread in February 2008 that 400 members of the LRA were moving in CAR, the information situation once again became unclear. While the rumour was widely reported, even a UPDF spokesman called it unreliable since it stemmed from a single source.[33]

On 29 February, the final two documents were signed: an agreement on Demobilisation, Disarmament and Reintegration (DDR), and the implementation protocol.[34] Some of the observers were baffled at the speed at which things were now progressing, lauding Matsanga's leadership and lambasting Ojul's much slower record. Most of the LRA/M delegates, however, were less impressed and instead felt relegated to the sidelines. At this stage, they already talked about that the agreements might turn out to be meaningless. It had become clear that successes happening on paper and how the LRA/M delegates were experiencing their peace process were two different things.

What remained unsigned was the agreement that would validate all the others, the chapeau FPA. The signing of the final agenda on implementation caused a confrontation: Matsanga claimed that the GoU had agreed that they would not push for a signing date in exchange for some language changes in the implementation protocol. He said the LRA/M needed time to travel to The Hague to argue against the ICC warrants, and had also asked for time to prepare for Easter celebrations. The GoU insisted that signing should take place no later than 28 March (which was when the latest round of the CoH was due to expire), which prompted Matsanga to walk out of the negotiation room, calling the GoU delegates 'thieves' and 'liars'.[35] The LRA/M delegates insisted that the FPA would need to be signed by Kony himself. Before that could happen, however, they wanted reassurance from the ICC that it would honour the agreement. No commitment from the ICC was forthcoming, and after days of

---

[33] US Embassy Kampala (2008d).
[34] Government of Uganda/Lord's Resistance Army/Movement (29 February 2008a; 29 February 2008b).
[35] US Embassy Khartoum (2008).

debate and changed dates, Machar finally managed to have the LRA/M agree to a signing ceremony in Ri-Kwangba. For the GoU, Rugunda would be present as the most senior GoU representative to avoid a confrontation between Kony and Museveni at this late stage. A few days later, a celebratory ceremony in Juba was to be held at which Museveni was supposed to countersign; GoSS was already handing out printed guest passes for the event.

In the LRA camp, preparations were made for both war and peace. A fifteen-year-old boy from Central Equatoria, who was abducted in January 2008, said he was kept in a group of about thirty Equatorians. His group was only used to carry things, and they were told that they would be trained militarily 'once he understood the LRA policy', but others who had been abducted earlier were trained.[36] A man from Ezo who was abducted in March 2008 said that while he was in captivity, 'the LRA used to tell them that they were preparing themselves to take over Uganda government and those who are Sudanese could then stay in the professional army'. He said that when he was abducted in March 2008, he was told that the LRA 'are not fighting and were going for peace'. He also noted that at the time of his abduction, most LRA were wearing their hair shaved.[37] When in the bush and actively fighting, the LRA had been famous for dreadlocks. A number of the commanders had cut their hair before showing themselves publicly to shed the bush fighter image.

From all accounts from within the LRA camp and from the LRA/M delegation, it remains impossible to say with certainty whether at this stage the LRA believed in war or peace. No clear evidence exists to conclude that either Kony was planning to definitively sign or that he was just stringing everyone along to play for time. Judging from how he had acted all along in the Juba Talks, it seems most likely that Kony was preparing for both options, depending on what developments might still occur.

7.3   The Missing Signature

For six days, from 9 to 15 April 2008, the basic AFEX compound in Nabanga played host to a tight concentration of rumours, narratives, politics, threats and hope. A total of 150 people waited for developments

---

[36] Author (with translator) interview with male teenager from Central Equatoria, fifteen years old, abducted by the LRA for twelve months (2008–9). Yambio: 23 February 2009.

[37] Author (with translator) interview with male teenager from Central Equatoria, fifteen years old, abducted by the LRA for twelve months (2008–9). Yambio: 23 February 2009.

Figure 7.3 Dignitaries and delegates wait for the final signing ceremony, April 2008.

to happen a few kilometres away in the bush. The people were South Sudanese, Ugandans, Kenyans, Europeans and Americans. Local village leaders waited alongside a former president of Mozambique; journalists sat with those desperate to avoid press exposure. Soldiers stood guard over pacifists, priests chatted with atheists, and activists and victims lined up behind each other for food at mealtimes. Members of Kony's family were there: a sister – who looked just like him – and his uncle. A few cooks scrambled to feed the masses with ever-dwindling supplies. They had expected to cook for 70 mouths for two days, and now had to feed 150 for a week. Local women watched with worried amazement as dozens of foreigners pumped dry one of two local boreholes. In the midst of all this sat an LRA/M delegation, unsure whether its leader would follow through and deliver a signature under the FPA.

The wait for Kony's signature had begun when, on 9 April, press and observers were flown to Nabanga in UN helicopters. Machar and senior visitors arrived on the morning of 10 April, greeted by ululating women. Everyone travelled onwards to Ri-Kwangba and found a space to sit under a canopy tent. A generator for the printer and photocopier was ready to go; hot food was waiting to be served.

Ri-Kwangba was guarded by a handful of junior LRA soldiers; nobody of rank was in sight. Some of the LRA/M delegates, including the leaders Matsanga and Obita, walked into the bush. When the two leaders of the delegation reemerged shortly thereafter, their long faces signalled that something was wrong. They had not been able to meet with Kony. Machar told everyone to relax and have lunch. Matsanga insisted that the signing would still go ahead. After lunch, the Acholi elders walked into the bush because Kony reportedly wanted to talk to them. As it turned out, he only spoke to them on the phone, and said that he was ten days' walk away.[38] Beyond this discouraging news, there was little information, so everyone returned to Nabanga for the night – including the LRA/M delegation, which on previous visits had stayed in the bush behind Ri-Kwangba with the LRA.

Simultaneously in Nairobi and London, the broader LRA/M system was at work. One of the former delegates – Olweny, who had been dismissed from the delegation more than a year before this signing ceremony – said Kony called him in Nairobi. The LRA leader reportedly told his dismissed spokesperson that he was unsure what exactly the delegation had negotiated regarding Agenda 3 on accountability and reconciliation, and whether it was safe for him to come out of the bush. Olweny said he suggested that Kony renegotiates with a new delegation that, crucially, would include him, Olweny. Kony's doubts about Agenda 3's clarity were reportedly also communicated to a London-based anti-Museveni hardliner, Alex Oloya, who headed a group calling itself Atoocoon.[39]

On 11 April, Matsanga resigned as leader of the delegation. In an improvised press conference at which journalists crowded around him, he cited a lack of clarity about Kony's wishes as a reason.[40] Apparently, Kony was unclear about parts of the agreement, despite the fact that each individual component of the agreement had already been signed by his delegation.

The UN called this one of the expected scenarios; the GoU seemed relaxed. The elders went back to Ri-Kwangba and encountered an LRA colonel who had little to say about what would happen with the signing ceremony. There was no sign of further activity in Ri-Kwangba. Upon hearing this, the GoU delegation climbed onto one of the UN-provided helicopters; most reporters, some of the diplomats and the representatives of Sant'Egidio who had come to attend the signing ceremony joined them in travelling back to Juba. Machar withdrew into a tukul and held private meetings. It transpired that he had wanted to meet the high

---

[38] Iya (2010: 180).

[39] 'Atoo' in Acholi is the 'name given to a child, many of those brothers and sisters have died' (Girling 1960: 23).

[40] Fieldnotes, Nabanga: 11 April 2008.

Figure 7.4 David Nyekorach Matsanga resigns from the LRA/M delegation, April 2008.

command before the signing but was advised by the delegation that Kony would only arrive on the day itself. The second day passed. Everyone was waiting for a phone call from Kony. At night, more than twenty people squeezed into the lunch tent to sleep on the dirty floor.

On 12 April, rumours surfaced about a leadership struggle between Kony and Odhiambo. Odhiambo had reportedly been killed three weeks prior by a group of former LRA soldiers who had defected with Otto in late 2007. The story was that the former LRA had come back with the well-equipped 105th battalion of the UPDF. Another version said that Kony himself had shot Odhiambo on their way back from the January meeting with the delegation. The whispers accused one of the delegates of lying because he claimed to have spoken to Odhiambo just a week before. Nothing could be verified. Nobody openly claimed to have had recent contact with Kony.

My phone rang. It was one of the former delegates calling from Nairobi. He wanted an update, and nobody else in Nabanga, including his former colleagues in the delegation, was taking his calls. He said he also could not get through to Kony.

Then more information transpired about a statement by the London-based group Atoocoon, headed by Oloya. The statement purported to come directly from Kony: 'The Lords Resistance Army suspends all contacts with the Uganda government and dissolves peace negotiation team with immediate effect. Agreements 2, 3, 4, 5 nullified'. The statement accused 'observers, Mr. Chissano (UN) and other parties associated with the peace talks' of having misled the LRA. The mediator was accused of not being neutral, the international community of lacking 'Understanding and Full Commitment', the ICC of being biased, Chissano of incompetence and a lack of 'expertise and experience in all fields of Conflict Resolution'. As well as judging the talks poorly managed, the statement also lamented that IDPs in Uganda had remained in camps and the 'Lack of Seriousness by the Government of Uganda in which it has rejected all demands made by the LRA. The intimidation, bullying and bribery of LRA delegates and its programs of ending the war with military force is not helpful to ending conflict'.[41]

Oloya concluded in his electronic press release that Kony would not sign, and that

> In the interest for peace the High command has appointed Mr Alex, Mr Obonyo [Olweny] and Mr Bill to forge a new negotiation delegation under a political structure to salvage the peace negotiation which has now collapsed. We have the confidence under this credible formation; peace is achievable with the correct modalities for negotiation with Uganda.[42]

News of this press release was received with confusion in Nabanga, and was noted in Juba, New York, London and Washington, DC. Delegates were reluctant to comment on the authenticity of the statement. With everyone confined to the small camp in Nabanga, more rumours circulated. Someone said that more LRA soldiers were arriving in Ri-Kwangba, and this was usually a sign that the leader was near. Another rumour contradicted this: apparently Ri-Kwangba was deserted, and Kony nowhere in the vicinity. The handful of LRA still present in the camp were meant to keep up the pretence. Someone claimed that the ICC had sent word that they had military intelligence about Kony's whereabouts. According to this source, Kony was far away. Delegates dismissed this as ICC propaganda and said that in fact Kony was close.

It was unclear who had the most reliable information: Obita was considered closest to Kony, although some delegates said not to listen to Obita. They argued that only Anywar (who could be seen standing aside from everyone, speaking into a mobile phone with a concerned expression) had contact with Kony. A third delegate said to not trust Anywar, because Kony had asked for Dr Onek to come by and explain the few pages of the FPA that were not clear to him. When Onek went

---

[41] LRA/M (attributed to Joseph Kony) (2008).
[42] LRA/M (attributed to Joseph Kony) (2008).

alone to Ri-Kwangba to meet Kony, he found nobody. It was said that Oryem could have predicted that Kony would not be waiting; after all, Oryem was closest to Kony. Maybe it was not Oryem but one of the Ugandan traditional leaders, Rwot Oywak who was closest to Kony, someone argued. Kony, it was said, had asked Rwot Oywak to be the new chairman of the delegation because he no longer trusted Obita.

People were talking about friction in the delegation and the Acholi diaspora. It was said that before leaving Juba to join the signing ceremony in Ri-Kwangba, Matsanga and Obita had been fighting. Text messages had been sent to Kony from the diaspora, saying that he would be attacked within minutes if he came out. One seasoned delegate explained that LRA infighting had become bad ever since Otti's death. 'Every time there is a visit, people defect. Phone numbers are exchanged, so Kony worries about meetings'.[43] Another mentioned that the CIA now had a Gulu base on the top floor of the Bank of Uganda, and that all those who had defected from the delegation were now working with Ugandan intelligence, the External Security Organisation (ESO). Neither development had made it easier to convince Kony to commit himself to peace.

If he was surprised or frustrated, Machar did not let it show. 'There is still a strong sentiment within the Acholi community against peace', Machar said, seated under the straw roof of a tukul in the less crowded half of the compound. 'I have no clear information'. The Ugandans were impressed that Machar had not left: 'He is sitting it out. He is gaining confidence and trust that way, he has always done that', explained one Ugandan leader. Machar seemed calm, still: 'The CoH is no longer valuable to Kony since he has broken it', he explained. 'Neither Kony nor I have trust in the delegation, so we need direct contact. Because Kony can negotiate an exit package, but he needs to negotiate it. The Acholi are very divided. Many are ashamed of the LRA, but they use them as a mascot'.[44]

News transpired that upon his return from Nabanga, Matsanga had been arrested in Juba airport with $20,000 that he had been given by Museveni to deliver to Kony but had stolen instead. Matsanga also reportedly had a letter from Museveni to Kony, offering safety guarantees and advising the LRA leader to spend the money on a function in Ri-Kwangba. Before his resignation, Matsanga had mentioned this letter from Museveni. He said Museveni had written it in 'begging language' because 'a golden handshake was always an option from the US or Kampala'.[45] Later it turned out that the stories were untrue: Matsanga

---

[43] Fieldnotes, Nabanga: 12 April 2008.   [44] Fieldnotes, Nabanga: 12 April 2008.
[45] Fieldnotes, Nabanga: 12 April 2008.

reportedly had handed the money back to the GoU. The letter Matsanga had carried, promising safety and money for the Ri-Kwangba function, was addressed to himself, not to Kony. Or maybe he never had a letter at all; it remained unclear. It also turned out that Matsanga had donated $1,000 to the process and handed a $100 bill to every Acholi leader just before he left.

It now seemed certain that both Odhiambo and Achellam had been killed.[46] UN security confirmed that three LRA groups were moving; they classified them as being 'with Kony', 'anti-Kony', and 'moving towards Kony for extra protection'. Ongwen was reported to be in CAR. The US Special Envoy Shortley was giving out information on the phone in a loud voice: 'You can write this if you want. I am not saying you have to, I just want to give you a sense of things'.[47] Later, to the great amusement of some of the journalists, Shortley walked around the camp complaining that there was no cold water to drink.

On 13 April, Chissano arrived. The news spread that the CIA had tracked LRA phone calls and they were coming from near Nabanga. The dignitaries gathered in different corners of the compound or disappeared for long meetings in Machar's tukul. Over lunch, the representative of the Canadian government handed around paperwork regarding military action against the LRA prepared for the UNSC. When asked why the Canadians had done this work despite not being members of the UNSC and whether they had discussed their suggestion with Uganda, they admitted that they had not, but that it had been debated with other countries. When challenged, the Canadian had to concede that none of these other countries were African.

Later that night, beer provisions ran out. Someone claimed that contact with Kony had been established; a phone call had been made. One of the journalists had learned that US secretary of State Condoleezza Rice had offered assistance, but that Museveni had declined. 'He does not like interference, or only if it is absolutely positively good for him', explained one of the Ugandan community leaders.

On 14 April, news came that groups had been tracked moving towards Nabanga from Yei and CAR but were still a long way away. The last remaining reporters prepared to leave; the three founders of Invisible Children loaded their video equipment and then themselves onto the helicopter. Once the press had left, everyone seemed to relax. Politics were now discussed more openly. One story was that in a phone call the previous night, Kony had asked for $500,000 to be paid to him directly in

---

[46] This was later found to be untrue but remained a persistent rumour.
[47] Fieldnotes, Nabanga: 12 April 2008.

exchange for his signature. Another story was that no money had been discussed, it had only been transmitted that the high command was meeting and that they were near Nabanga – but nobody believed it. Uganda's civil society leaders suggested sending the message that they would go into Ri-Kwangba one last time to say goodbye. By the time I got into a helicopter on 15 April, the rumour was that the LRA had asked for a payment of US$2 million to be shared by everyone, and an extra $800,000 for Kony.[48] On 18 April, Kony called and demanded a meeting with Ugandan leaders to discuss Agenda 3 on 10 May.

A few weeks after the first failed signing ceremony, the London group around Oloya issued another statement. 'We condemn without reservation in the strongest terms it deserves, the tactics being used by the Ugandan government in which it's using the name of United States Army as a gunboat system to persuade LRA in signing the bogus FPA or be attacked', it said.[49] The LRA/M saw the military option coming more sharply into focus than during the better days of the talks. A former delegate argued that the talks had entered a different stage as their lack of sincerity had been exposed, the rifts in the delegation pointing to government infiltration. 'The answer is a new, proper delegation, we start afresh and from the beginning', he said.[50]

When the Ugandan leaders returned with Machar and UN representatives for the meeting on 10 May, they did not see Kony, nor did they have any communication with him. After seven days of waiting, a member of the mediation team gave a frank assessment of the situation: 'Of course the peace process is tits up. Everybody kind of agrees that Joseph has closed the door with a big bang. No communication so no dialogue so we are back at square one!'[51]

What had happened? Some in the LRA/M argue that Kony was unsure about a few points in the FPA, particularly regarding accountability and justice. He had not been able to discuss and clarify these points with his delegation, particularly the issue of whether using so-called traditional justice procedures like *mato oput*, a reconciliation ceremony after a homicide, really were the answer to ICC warrants.[52] He had asked for the

---

[48] Fieldnotes, Nabanga: 16 April 2008.   [49] LRA/M (2008).
[50] Fieldnotes, Cologne: 24 September 2008.
[51] Personal email to author (name of writer withheld), 24 August 2008.
[52] The LRA/M later published 'the main reasons he [Kony] cited for wanting the agreement to be revisited', such as increased clarity on accountability procedures, implementation of DDR as well as welfare arrangements for LRA soldiers, and 'the absence of a clear and satisfactory provision in the Agreement as a whole for the participation of the LRA/M in government in the post-conflict dispensation' (LRA/M Peace Team 2009).
  For discussions of Mato Oput, see Allen (2007); Afako (October 2006, 2002b).

'signing ceremony' to be a meeting with the delegation, the Acholi religious leaders and Rwot Acana to clarify those points. He had not clarified his concerns in April or May. The meeting in May failed, claimed the delegation in a written statement, because the former delegation leader 'Matsanga had called Kony and informed him that Dr Obita was coming with American snipers to assassinate him, and that a large number of UPDF tanks had also crossed the border from Uganda into Sudan headed for Ri-kwangba'.[53] However, lack of communication about the FPA or security concerns and Kony's unreliability meant that even supporters of the peace process were losing patience: 'The LRA's failure to attend the scheduled meetings and to advance the peace process undermines its own interest', Machar wrote in a statement.[54]

Machar himself was coming under increased pressure. His commitment to the peace talks with the LRA had always been closely scrutinised by other members of GoSS. Various points of criticism had been mentioned: that he should focus on southern Sudanese business only, or that he was doing this only to increase his international profile, that the talks were costing GoSS too much money, that he was trying to appease the LRA to call on them in case of an armed struggle within southern Sudan similar to the SPLA split of 1991.[55] In late May 2008, during the second SPLM convention in Juba, Machar declared his candidacy as SPLM chairperson, openly challenging Kiir. The move almost cost him the vice-presidency: opposition to his desire for power was voiced loudly by others. In an emergency meeting of the SPLM Interim Political Bureau, provisions were made for three deputies to make Machar withdraw his leadership challenge. It was a foreshadowing of the deep divisions that would lead to civil war in independent South Sudan in 2013.

The LRA/M delegates suspiciously eyed several parallel developments, increasingly aware that time was running out for a peaceful solution. Former delegates who had been sidelined in the various internal struggles published a statement highlighting the GoU's collaboration with other armies, including the United States:

Many times the government has used the threat of foreign or regional troops coming into an alliance of operation to crush the LRA. This even when peace talks are in progress. The SPLA, Congolese troops, Rwandese and Ethiopian troops are often said to be preparing for a joint operation. Even the UN troops in Congo, MONUC, whose mandate is to keep peace, are thrown into the fray. When, since the Korean War of the 50s, has the United Nations ever fought a war

[53] LRA/M Peace Team (2009).   [54] Government of Southern Sudan (2008: 2).
[55] When the SPLA/M split eventually came in 2013, the LRA played no role as a fighting force on any side.

on behalf of a sovereign state, not against another sovereign state but against a rebel force? The Uganda government seems to have succeeded in roping in the United States Army and Marines in the conflict. These powerful forces are now all over Northern Uganda carrying out humanitarian, development and capacity building activities. All this certainly have not gone down well with the LRA forces in the bush who see themselves as besieged from all sides. Very recently, in the past couple of weeks, large movement of UPDF troops has taken place from the UPDF 4th Division base in Gulu towards Garamda Parks [sic].[56]

For the LRA/M, the reported troop movement was proof that peace talks again would be betrayed in favour of military action. For most observers and most advocacy groups, it showed that finally, the day of reckoning for the LRA through military action had come. News of a second meeting between military officials of GoU, GoSS and the government of DRC emerged on 2 June; it was instantly obvious that these were meetings to discuss joint military operations against the LRA.

On 5 June, the LRA attacked the SPLA detachment in Nabanga. The SPLA had acted as a buffer between the LRA in Ri-Kwangba and civilians in Nabanga since 2006. In the attack, the LRA killed fourteen civilians and seven soldiers. A South Sudanese abductee in the LRA camp said that after the attack on the SPLA, the LRA fighters brought home SPLA guns, new uniforms and new bags they had looted.[57] From the point of view of one of the SPLA commanders in charge in Nabanga at the time, the LRA attacks on the SPLA were prompted by news of the military meeting on the radio. He said: 'I also heard the news on the radio that SPLA, UPDF, DRC were going to team up against LRA, so I think that was the reason'.[58]

Members of the mediation team provided a different perspective. Considering that Kony had not been engaged with the negotiations on the final two agreements, an international advisor suggested that the attack was also partly prompted in order

to violate the holy peace-ground of Nabanga, to make the peace process more difficult without saying no. And it worked, the next meeting was cancelled because the SPLA, angry as they still were, did not allow food to go through. And the GoU reacted to that by working towards a peace agreement that as they knew had not been shown to Kony by Matsanga and would not be signed. After all, to have the peace agreement ready would make it more difficult for Kony and others to say that a new round of talks should be started.[59]

---

[56] Olweny and Otukene (2008).

[57] Author (with translator Zande/English) interview with Sudanese abductee who spent March–December 2008 with the LRA. Yambio: 23 February 2009.

[58] Amoru and Mugyema (2008); BBC News (2008).

[59] Personal email to author from international advisor to the Juba Talks, 7 August 2011.

Some of the LRA/M delegates saw the reasons for this attack differently: having struggled in the past with being protected by the SPLA – a force very friendly towards Museveni – they had repeatedly reported to the mediator that they distrusted the SPLA detach in Nabanga. They claimed that one of the soldiers, who had been introduced to them as a Sudanese Acholi, was, in fact, a UPDF soldier disguised in SPLA uniform. According to the LRA/M, he had been there since at least 2007. They interpreted his presence not only as proof that the UPDF was preparing to attack the LRA in Ri-Kwangba, but further that the peace talks were never mediated and supported by a neutral southern Sudanese government.[60]

Delegates in Juba became uncomfortable. The rumour mill grew noticeably more active. UN security personnel had monitored intelligence that showed that Kony was still in the DRC, despite the delegation's information that he had moved to CAR. Activity had been observed across the DRC border near Yei, where an unscheduled and unidentified helicopter had landed in the last week of May – it was unclear whether it had brought or taken people, delivered supplies or been piloted by UPDF or SAF. In Tore, further north, an arrest was made of a SAF soldier who said he had been waiting for a plane. The speculation there was that he was supposed to coordinate with LRA who were being transported to Chad to fight for SAF there, yet none of this could be verified.[61]

On 18 June, Kony reemerged, calling Chissano's office to schedule another meeting with him. Two days later, Matsanga popped up in Juba to announce that he had been reappointed by Kony to lead the LRA/M delegation. The only remaining member of the LRA on the CHMT left the CHMT to become a negotiating delegate. Chissano's office followed Kony's request and scheduled a confidential meeting for 30 July – the former president of Mozambique judged Kony's wish for clarity justified, because the accountability agreement was particularly complex in its implications and groundbreaking within international justice.[62] Before the meeting, Kony demanded food and water to be delivered by Caritas, because since the attack on the SPLA detachment, the SPLA had no longer been willing to deliver provisions to the LRA. Engaging Caritas swiftly proved impossible, since the contract with them to support the LRA assembly had expired. Machar, expressing goodwill, organised two trucks of food, which the LRA refused to accept since they had come from the SPLA.

---

[60] Fieldnotes, Nairobi: 26 June 2013.   [61] Fieldnotes, Juba: 10 June 2007.
[62] Personal email to author from international Advisor to the Juba Talks, 7 August 2011.

On 30 July, the scheduled meeting between Kony and Chissano did not take place; several other attempts to meet also failed. Looking back on these months, an advisor to Chissano stated that he had limited sympathy with Kony's claim that he needed more clarity, because Kony did not appear at meetings and because he had said in a phone call: 'Please tell Machar and Chissano to come. I understand now that I do not have to go immediately to Uganda when I sign, and that I am the one being seen as blocking progress. Therefore, when they come I will sign'.[63] However, another suggested signing date at the end of August came and went without progress. On 11 September 2008, Machar wrote in a statement that Kony had talked about his lack of understanding of some of the elements of the negotiated settlement, namely the clauses on justice and accountability and on how the DDR procedures would actually treat and integrate the LRA. This lack of understanding had caused his reluctance to sign: 'Whilst that failure came at great cost and inconvenience, General Joseph Kony's desire to understand the full implications of the agreement is not invalid', Machar wrote.[64]

Although the CHMT had inspected the site before the agreed meeting date of 24/25 August, skirmishes ensued between the LRA and SPLA. Machar described the situation as having been caused by 'uncoordinated troop deployments along the borders', which resulted in an interruption in food supply to the LRA.[65] Although initially another meeting had been proposed for September, it was clear that whoever was trying to get the LRA/M back together for a credible peace effort was scrambling – even Kony himself. Reportedly, he was trying to meet his delegation, but many had since turned their backs on their own time as delegates. After it had reportedly been communicated to Kony that Obita was planning to come with American snipers, it became increasingly difficult to make contact.[66]

On 28 August, the US State Department named Kony a Specially Designated Global Terrorist in Executive Order 13334, which under the US's declared War on Terror allowed increased military action against the LRA and its leader. The mechanism behind using the terrorist label is spelt out by Marchal, who writes:

---

[63] Personal email to author from international Advisor to the Juba Talks, 7 August 2011.
[64] Government of Southern Sudan (2008: 2).
[65] Government of Southern Sudan (2008: 2).
[66] Fieldnotes, Nairobi: 11 November 2009. The delegates who had heard about this threat said that the information had been relayed to Kony by Jolly Okot, Uganda's Country Director for Invisible Children, who was working as an informant for the US government. This allegation has also been made publicly.

The current 'war on terror' allows the US administration to militarize its African policy through the establishment of AFRICOM. US military officials claim that this new structure will work hand in hand with civilians to build boreholes and schools, as European colonial armies did. The problem, as with their predecessors, is that that is not all they do.[67]

On 17 September, the LRA attacked Dungu in Haut-Uele district in DRC's Orientale Province in what they said was a response to increased deployment of Congolese forces in the area. In the next few months, LRA attacks would occur in the area stretching from East Faragi to Western Duruma, a distance of about 450 kilometres. As a result, schools were closed for fear of abduction, and residents in Dungu protested at the DRC government and the international community's inability to provide protection. The OCHA and MONUC offices in Dungu town were destroyed.[68]

On 1 October 2008, AFRICOM became a standalone command.[69] Kiir countered his deputy's positive attitude towards the peace talks, stating that GoSS was no longer prepared for the process to continue indefinitely. In a meeting in Kampala, Machar and Chissano agreed on a final deadline for Kony's signature: 30 November. In parallel, preparations for a military strike continued.

The final deadline of 30 November was 'properly communicated' to Kony, explained one delegate to me.[70] However, Kony had argued that he had been under the impression that the April, May and September meetings were to be opportunities to see the negotiated agreements. Kony had then arranged a meeting with his delegation for 18 November, to clarify outstanding issues before the 30 November deadline. One South Sudanese abductee said that until November, the LRA in the camp 'were saying there would be peace'.[71] The delegates tried to get to Ri-Kwangba in time for the meeting on 18 November. At that point, however, patience with the LRA's to-and-fro had largely expired. 'We tried to get transport and food support, but we could not', explained a former delegate to me. 'So we only arrived on 28th, too late to discuss before the deadline'.[72] In the evening of 28 November, Kony came to greet his visitors, returning for an afternoon meeting the following day.

---

[67] Marchal (2007).   [68] Fieldnotes, Kampala: 1/2009.   [69] Ploch (2011).
[70] Fieldnotes, Nairobi: 11 November 2009.
[71] Author (with translator Zande/English) interview with Sudanese abductee who spent March–December 2008 with the LRA. Yambio: 23 February 2009.
[72] LRA/M Peace Team (2009).

Along with the delegates, a group of leaders from Uganda had also joined the meeting. The visitors were subjected to unusually harsh security checks. Afterwards, some of the leaders were more complimentary than others about their encounter with Kony: while some said that Kony was still willing to go for peace, even if the time seemed not right, Iya, for example, found that 'much of what [Kony] said was not coherent; at times he seemed to not remember things he had just said'. Kony made a few major points, according to Iya. He expressed his distrust of Machar, the SPLA and the Congolese forces, said that he did not fear the ICC but also would not sign an agreement if the warrants were still in place, that he did not know all the details in the signed agreements and that he wanted to speak directly to Museveni. He accused his delegation of being thieves and said that his commanders felt the agreement did not give them much.[73] An account of the meeting from a confidential US cable – with the information provided by Acholi leaders – states that Kony reportedly accused his previous delegation leader, Ojul, of stealing donor money and being on the GoU payroll, thus voiding the agreements that had been signed by Ojul.

Kony said that Matsanga, with Labeja present as his trusted person, should lead his delegation. Further elaborating, Kony stated that Chissano had failed to meet his promise to request UNSC deferment of the ICC warrants after the signing of Agenda 3 in June the previous year – an action that, as Chissano's team emphasised, had never been promised before the signing of the FPA. Asking to be paid the $10,000, which Museveni had sent for him, Kony said that Machar had blocked the payment. The money, notes a US memo about the meeting, was 'diverted by the mediation team'.[74] Kony then left Ri-Kwangba without speaking to Chissano or Machar, who were waiting not far away. In a side meeting with elders, Ongwen reportedly said to the Acholi Paramount Chief, Acana, that senior LRA commanders would not allow Kony to sign a deal unless future prospects and demobilisation packages for senior commanders were clearly defined.[75]

Young South Sudanese abductees who had been staying at the LRA camp in Garamba said that after Kony returned from the November meeting, something changed. A young woman from Eastern Equatoria, who had been with the LRA since January 2007, said that from November onwards LRA fighters were talking about the failure of the Juba Talks, and she saw that 'they started now killing, they went into

---

[73] Iya (2010).   [74] US Embassy Kampala (2008c).
[75] US Embassy Kampala (2008c).

villages differently'.[76] The young man from Ezo, who had remarked on the shaved hair of the LRA at the time of his abduction in March 2008, said that after the last meeting in November with the elders, the LRA fighters 'came back and said there is no more peace' and started turning their hair into dreadlocks: 'After they came back from Nabanga, the LRA told us to grow our hair into dreads, women should stop plaiting their hair because peace talks are no longer there'.[77]

From 5 to 8 December, LRA/M delegates and Machar travelled to Kinshasa. Not all LRA/M delegates were allowed in the meetings with the president, but Machar said that Kabila was supportive of maintaining a dialogue with Kony as the cheaper and safer option to prevent attacks on civilians. To the two LRA/M delegates accompanying the SPLM/GoU delegation to Kinshasa, Kabila said that he was against military action because 'you don't disturb a beehive'.[78] In recounting the days between the meeting in Nabanga and the launch of the military offensive against the LRA, delegates said that Kony asked for clarification on a few outstanding issues. One clarification concerned the sequencing of dealing with the ICC warrants: did Kony have to sign first, or could the warrants be withdrawn first? On 8 December, in a meeting of Museveni, Machar and Matsanga in Kampala, Museveni said that Kony had to sign the document first before he could deal with the ICC warrants.[79] He expressed his willingness to talk to Kony directly, but also insisted that the LRA ought not to receive any further assistance until they were fully assembled in Ri-Kwangba.[80] Delegates said that all misunderstandings about the challenges inherent within the agreement were clarified by 10 December 2008: 'On December 10, Kony was ready to sign'.[81]

7.4   Operation Lightning Thunder

On 13 December 2008, recounted a 27-year-old female South Sudanese abductee, residents of the LRA camp were called to Kony. 'Kony told forces you people have to scatter, there will be an attack tomorrow, on 14', she said. However, she and the people she was with did not believe Kony's prediction, so they went to the garden they were tending instead. Kony had left his camp at 12, and soon afterwards they heard what

---

[76] Author (with translator) interview with Sudanese LRA abductee from Parajok. Yambio: 23 February 2009.

[77] Author (with translator Zande/English) interview with Sudanese abductee who spent March–December 2008 with the LRA. Yambio: 23 February 2009.

[78] Fieldnotes, Nairobi: 11 September 2009.

[79] Fieldnotes, Nairobi: 11 September 2009.   [80] US Embassy Kampala (2008c).

[81] LRA/M Peace Team (2009).

sounded like aerial bombing of Kony's camp.[82] A 20-year old man from Ezo said that on 13 December, he had been chosen to leave the LRA camp to carry meat from some buffaloes and fish, 'but Kony sent a message to come back quickly because war has started'.[83] Another young South Sudanese man who was at Kony's camp said that 'when Kony told people of the attack, Kony took off during bombardment. Kony's camp split in three forces'. He said that during the bombing, he was told to run with Kony's forces, 'but the forces ran into an ambush so I could take off from the ambush. When we heard gunshot we ran away, so I don't know what happened to the others'.[84] The young woman described the attack: 'People were scattered. The helicopter went back to DRC. People went back to get some things'. Her group of more than fifty people, many of whom were not LRA, then walked for two months to reach CAR.[85]

The bombs were the beginning of what came to be known as Operation Lightning Thunder (OLT). A joint press statement from all involved forces said

The Armed Forces of Uganda (UPDF), DRC (FARDC) and Southern Sudan (SPLA) in a joint intelligence-led military operation this morning, the 14 Dec 2008 launched an attack on the LRA hideouts of terrorist Joseph Kony in Garamba, Democratic Republic of Congo. The three Armed Forces successfully attacked the main body of bandits and destroyed the main camp of Kony codenamed Camp Swahili setting it on fire. Military operations against these terrorists are continuing.[86]

The operation had been prepared with the aid of AFRICOM, which had provided aid in planning and logistics to the tune of about $7 million. Within days, it was clear that the image of lightning and thunder had been ill-chosen. Plans of dividing up the area into a neat grid and having infantry jump out of planes into each square had remained fantasies.[87] The quick-strike had been delayed, and the tardy aerial action had failed to kill the LRA leadership and instead had scattered the LRA across a wide area with no ground troops to prevent the spread, fulfilling precisely what Chissano had outlined as the worst-case scenario.

---

[82] Author (with translator) interview with female Sudanese LRA abductee from Ezo. Yambio: 23 February 2009.
[83] Author (with translator Zande/English) interview with Sudanese abductee who spent March–December 2008 with the LRA. Yambio: 23 February 2009.
[84] Author (with translator) interview with male teenager from Central Equatoria, abducted by the LRA for twelve months in 2008–9. Yambio: 23 February 2009.
[85] Author (with translator) interview with female Sudanese LRA abductee from Ezo. Yambio: 23 February 2009.
[86] FARDC, UPDF, SPLA (2008).   [87] Atkinson (2009b).

On 16 December 2008, Chissano gave a closed briefing to the UNSC to inform them that military action had been launched. He outlined how Kony had seven opportunities to sign the FPA and had not done so, but on the contrary had continued to fight civilians in the DRC, CAR and southern Sudan. The UNSC was supportive of the military operation as a way to put pressure on Kony to sign the peace deal.[88] However, both Chissano and Machar maintained that other roads to peace needed to stay open. In an interview on Al Jazeera, Machar said that he had been arm-twisted by Undersecretary of State Frazier to go for the military option. Despite the military pursuit, the GoU reiterated periodically that the option to sign the FPA remained open for Kony.

In the December 2008 issue of its report, the UNSC mentioned various ideas regarding 'what role regional stakeholders, Chissano and the Council can play in the developing and implementing a new strategy to bring the LRA back to the peace process, or if Kony does sign, to support implementation of the Final Peace Agreement'.[89] Distancing itself from UN obligations of civilian protection, the report stated that 'a consideration for the Council may be what role, if any given the current situation in eastern DRC, the UN and stakeholders in the region could have'.[90]

The Security Council stated that in September the

Secretary-General indicated that a continued facilitation role of the Envoy was critical to help the parties overcome current obstacle and create a propitious environment for implementing the future Final Peace Agreement. If the Final Peace Agreement is signed, the Secretary-General would expect the Envoy to play a key role in supervising its implementation. In the event of further delays, the Special Envoy was expected to continue to provide good offices and facilitation.[91]

The Council explicitly stated 'another option, albeit unlikely given the fragility of the peace process and instability in the region, would be to terminate the mandate'.[92] Chissano's mandate as the UN Special Envoy was, however, allowed to expire on 30 June 2009, because, as the secretary-general now stated, Chissano had

achieved the main objectives of his mandate with the conclusion of negotiations in March 2008 when agreements were signed on all substantive issues, including by the representatives of the Lord's Resistance Army (LRA). While the final peace agreement has yet to be implemented due to LRA leader Joseph Kony's

---

[88] UN Security Council (2009).   [89] UN Security Council (2008 December).
[90] UN Security Council (2008 December).
[91] UN Security Council (2008 December).
[92] UN Security Council (2008 December).

refusal to honour his commitments and sign the agreement (he maintains the position that the arrest warrant of the International Criminal Court (ICC) against him and other LRA leaders must first be lifted), the Secretary General considered that Chissano had completed his assignment.

The support office for Chissano established in Kampala was closed on the day the mandate expired. The Council responded in a letter of 29 May saying that members had 'taken note' of the Secretary-General's intention.[93]

As nonmilitary options diminished, the Enough Project published a paper that further advocated the military pursuit of the LRA, emphasising this point in briefings with diplomats in Kampala, where, according to a US embassy cable, analyst Spiegel recommended

that the military operations continue with a focus on killing the senior LRA leadership and increasing efforts to protect the Congolese civilian population. She advocated a multi-lateral discourse on planning and increased MONUC capability, along with increased U.S. Government support, including planning support, intelligence, and logistics. She explained that Congolese President Kabila's internal problems, including opposition to the operation from eastern DRC parliamentarians, had been a problem, but that the lack of human rights abuses by the UPDF coupled with continued LRA depredations resulted in a positive perception of the UPDF presence among Congolese civilians.[94]

Other assessments of OLT are less jubilant and view the option of a targeted assassination more critically. In August 2007, Museveni had told US officials 'a military operation against the LRA would be "easy" or "not hard"'.[95] His confidence might have lulled the US military into a false expectation of success. Yet it was clear that Kony had been warned of the impending airstrike through his contacts in the UPDF.

Operation Lightning Thunder scattered the remaining LRA forces across southern Sudan, the DRC and CAR at great cost to civilian lives.[96] That protection of civilians had quickly become a problem was clear when Ugandan foreign minister Sam Kutesa asked MONUC on 9 February whether it could provide logistical support for the deployment of a further 2,000 UPDF troops to strengthen protection. Unable to transport Ugandan troops under its mandate, MONUC offered to support OLT in different ways, for example by improving roads and air strips and moving its own troops closer to areas of OLT action. Additionally, MONUC was providing logistical support for Armed

---

[93] UN Security Council (2009).   [94] US Embassy Kampala (2009b).
[95] US Embassy Kampala (2007a).
[96] Atkinson et al. (2012); Schomerus (2012); Atkinson (2009a, 2009b); Schomerus and Tumutegyereize (2009).

Forces of the DRC (FARDC) troops under its DRC-focused mandate.[97] The LRA conducted a series of brutal attacks; the combined presence of soldiers of various government armies created a volatile environment in which civilians were exposed to human rights violations. A confidential but leaked report commissioned by the Social Science Research Council provided fieldwork-based evidence that in 2011 UPDF soldiers in CAR were plundering resources; in DRC the Ugandan soldiers were accused of systematic rape, violence and of profiting from prostitution.[98]

Without a credible protection force, civilians were on the run from aerial attacks just as much as the LRA. What abductees with the LRA were supposed to do during OLT was unclear. Leaflets thrown out of planes by the UPDF to persuade LRA fighters to come out stated that fighters or abductees should surrender to barracks or churches. Barracks and churches had not been told to welcome LRA fighters, and in any case LRA fighters would not have been able to reach them without passing through villages, likely causing havoc there or being killed. 'The military operation was not properly planned, that's why it is dragging on', commented an SPLA officer in early 2009. 'It is more difficult and complicated the longer it drags on'.[99]

Drag on it did. From the military perspective of one of the supposed partners, the SPLA, OLT had been ill-conceived, ill-planned, ill-executed and extremely damaging, setting up the region for years of further instability. Assessing the UPDF preparations for the strike against the LRA, a senior SPLA commander commented that they had used MIG-21 planes to bomb them, and that they had stationed tanks near the border in Koboko:

It was as if they were going to fight a conventional army, but that was not the case .... Also, SPLA, UPDF and DRC forces never sat down together. SPLA was supposed to seal the borders and they were drunk. The US helped plan this, but Western systems normally undermine how our systems work. US officers will rely on equipment. They want to do their own intelligence gathering without relying on basic local intelligence. The State Department has no experience with realities on the ground. The UPDF troops were in Koboko for days. It was like they were going to a party. There was no alliance between SPLA and UPDF. The GoU wanted to keep the operation secret from Machar. The SPLA was not very happy. The SPLA just said to some forces, just go and sit there, let the Ugandans see if they really are the best. The LRA needs a counterinsurgency force. SPLA could

---

[97] US Embassy Kampala (2009a).

[98] The report was never made public, but was discussed in the Ugandan media: 'Editorial: Uganda's image at stake in CAR' (2012).

[99] Author interview with Yambio-born former UNICEF Ops manager. Yambio: 25 February 2009.

do it, but they were not involved because the Ugandans in their mambas [military vehicles] are too arrogant.[100]

The SPLA officer explained to me that he knew OLT would be a disaster when he heard reports that the UPDF was in the DRC preparing for the strike, but that the Ugandan soldiers were eating sardines and rice every night in their camp. 'But really! It was the UPDF eating rice and sardines. It takes a long time to cook and eat rice. If you are in a hurry, you don't eat rice. But this is the UPDF arrogance. Wherever they go, they come with their own problems'.[101]

Arrogance was also brought up by an international advisor to the talks: 'The US pressure for the military option also comes from American military arrogance', he explained to me almost a year before OLT. At the time he thought it would be impossible for the UPDF to remain engaged in a military operation on Congolese ground for more than a few months at most: 'The UPDF is also under performance pressure. This needs to be a neat and successful military operation; they cannot hang out in DRC and certainly not plunder anymore'.[102]

Yet on 1 March 2009, Presidents Joseph Kabila and Museveni met to sign a Memorandum of Understanding about extending the military cooperation indefinitely, with reviews every three months. The UPDF remained in the DRC and the CAR.[103] The UPDF news about OLT success came trickling in from the beginning, often disproved as quickly as it had been disseminated. In June 2009, the United States reported that the UPDF was continuing 'to make steady progress', measured on, amongst other things the fact that 'between May 18 and 29, the UPDF killed 41 LRA fighters, including Brigadier General Cesar Achellam and Lt. Col. Okello Okuti'.[104] Achellam, however, emerged from the bush in 2012, very much alive. Civilian reports about the failures of UPDF engagement and atrocities committed by all sides continued. Yet, a confidential memo regarding US/Ugandan military cooperation outlined in December 2009 that the United States had 'received verbal assurances' from the Ugandan Defence Ministry that US intelligence was

---

[100] Author interview with SPLA intelligence officer. Juba: 1 March 2009.
[101] Author interview with SPLA intelligence officer. Juba: 1 March 2009.
[102] Fieldnotes, 24 November 2007. The International Court of Justice had found the UPDF guilty of plundering in DRC in a 2005 judgement (International Court of Justice 2005).
[103] The military operations against Kony, jointly conducted by United States and mainly Ugandan forces, was called off for good in April 2017, eight years later (Burke and Mwesigwa 2017 (May 1)).
[104] US Embassy Kampala (2009b).

being used in the pursuit of the LRA 'in compliance with Ugandan law and the law of armed conflict'. The memo elaborated that

furthermore, Uganda understands the need to consult with the U.S. in advance if the UPDF intends to use US-supplied intelligence to engage in operations not governed by the law of armed conflict. Uganda understands and acknowledges that misuse of this intelligence could cause the US to end this intelligence sharing relationship.[105]

The memo thus implies that failure to notify the United States constitutes a misuse of its intelligence, rather than giving a general condemnation of any violation of law of armed conflict. The implication of this memo is far-reaching: it allows the conclusion that the military partnership was to work along rather fluid interpretations of international obligations.

7.5   Conclusion

The year 2008 was marked by competing forces in the Juba Talks and ultimately a conservative view of how peace talks were measured and deemed successful. The final year in a process that stretched out over three years became a moment when the peace process narrowed even more towards achieving milestones, rather than acting as a catalyst for change. Challenges that had existed since the beginning came to the fore. In a conflict that had been substantially driven by rumours, 2008 showed how muddled hearsay can drive those divorced from reliable information structures to action. In Kony's case, it is impossible to conclusively say what his intentions were, but it is fair to argue that the different signals sent by different parties added to the confusion.

The military fallout that began in December 2008 shows the gravity of the decision to abandon the often-frustrating process in favour of what mistakenly continues to be sold as the quicker solution: military action. Leverage had certainly worked in exerting pressure on the LRA. For some of the LRA/M delegates, the final choice between signing a peace deal or facing military action, however, underscored the perception they had held all along: that the Juba Talks were not comprehensive peace talks or a deep peace process, but a way to ultimately pressure the LRA/M into signing an agreement. Of course, such an assessment is cursory and neglects the many concessions the government made in the agreements, and which influence northern Uganda's development until today. But in terms of how delegates perceived the Juba Talks at this point, they

---

[105] US Embassy Kampala (2009d).

argued that ultimately, the Talks reinforced the power structures they were trying to address in which at some point, the GoU would again revert to badly executed military action.

Abandoning the talks in favour of a military strike also meant that actors failed to capitalise on the advances made thus far. The juxtaposition of process and pressure, which crystallised particularly in the final frantic weeks leading up to OLT, meant that broader political gains remained unacknowledged as the whole process was unfairly branded a failure.

On the international and facilitation side, the hawks and doves fought in the background over which approach would ultimately prevail. This dichotomy also brought again to light the profound challenges in engaging with an unreliable actor such as the LRA/M. Most international actors by the end of 2008 had simply lost patience with an inept delegation and an obstinate LRA leader; ending negotiations could thus be done from the moral high ground. Within the LRA/M, relationships had broken down, and different agendas were being played out. As these internal dynamics unfolded, they were generally seen as proof that the LRA/M was dysfunctional. However, the insights into the inner working of the LRA/M which were particularly obvious in 2008 actually showed something very different: how in times of crisis the LRA/M system worked and why ultimately the LRA/M stood as much in the way of an agreement as the GoU.

8 'LRA Has Already Become a System'

Representation and Distrust in the Lord's
Resistance Army

On a normal negotiation day in the first part of the Juba Talks in 2006, the LRA/M delegates were driven from their hotel to the negotiation venue, Juba Raha Hotel; the white minibus crawling and climbing through the potholes on the road that connects Hai Cinema with Konyo Konyo Market. It was the worst road in town. On the minibus dashboard sat a sign reading 'Delegation'. On a good day, a usually bored-looking soldier was riding shotgun; however, on many days, the delegation's armed escort did not show up.

In the first few months of the talks, reporters from Uganda's *New Vision* and *Daily Monitor*, as well as various news agencies such as AFP and AP, would hang around the Juba Raha Hotel. Reuters was the only international news agency with a local stringer, a young man from Ikotos who had fought against the SPLA on Machar's side during the SPLA split. The BBC Khartoum reporter occasionally made an appearance for important events. At various points, foreign freelancers with television crews showed up. For Uganda's *Daily Monitor*, keeping a staff member in Juba for this length of time was 'the most expensive story we have ever done', said the reporter.[1] Whenever members of the delegation appeared in the doorways, the journalists jumped up to collect a quote or engage in an informal chat. On bad negotiation days, they were handed a written statement. On particularly bad days, the LRA/M delegation would read out a written statement and then disappear without further comment.

Most people at the margins of the peace talks spent their days waiting: for decisions to be made, for transport, for the LRA/M delegation. From the day of the opening of the talks, when the LRA/M was three hours late because their transport had not materialised, lateness had become their signature habit, causing considerable tension. The delegation leader had to promise the mediator and the GoU delegates to 'keep better time'.

---

[1] Fieldnotes, Juba: 30 September 2006.

The day after this promise had been made, I was sitting in the LRA/M's Juba Bridge Hotel. The GoU delegation was staying at the Civicon camp – much to the resentment of the LRA/M delegation, who liked to point out that while the GoU enjoyed self-contained prefabricated housing units, their own Juba Bridge Hotel had no functioning toilet. The GoSS had replied that it had been necessary to move the LRA/M to the more remote hotel to avoid attention. On this particular day, an important afternoon meeting about next steps was scheduled for 3 p.m. I was waiting with another delegate – a usually quiet man from the diaspora – to hitch a lift in the minibus back to the Juba Raha Hotel. Just before three, the familiar white van pulled up. Apart from my conversation partner, nobody from the delegation was anywhere to be seen. At a quarter past three, one of the leading delegates walked through the camp wrapped in a towel on his way to take a shower. The LRA/M delegate sitting next to me let out an audible sigh. 'Now I understand why the LRA never made it out of the bush', he said.[2] It was a playful expression of a weary realisation that, along with the outside pressure the LRA/M was experiencing at the Juba Talks, internally they were also stuck in their own detrimental ways.

'The LRA has its own problems and I am the first to admit it', said a former delegate in November 2009. When asked why in his opinion the talks had failed, another delegate said it was because 'Kony is being used and allowing himself to be used. But if you think there is only one human being at the heart of it, it is wrong'.[3] In the opening speech of the talks, Olweny had made a similar point: 'Even if they were to succeed, God forbid, in apprehending the five indicted leaders, LRA has already become a system. The war can only become more intensive', he had said.[4] However, analysis of the LRA continues to focus on Kony as the centre of gravity and of the conflict.

More nuanced understandings of conflict networks have called into question seemingly straight lines of command that have been emphasised in conflict resolution, military strategy, and more recently, international criminal prosecution. Gernot Grabher and David Stark advocate for shifting attention 'from the attributes and motivations of individual personalities to the properties of the localities and networks' in which war happens.[5] Stanley Wassermann and Katherine Faust suggest that examining networks, rather than individual relationships, allows better analytical insight into complex conflicts.[6] This is particularly poignant when looking at the LRA conflict also as a conflict of marginalisation

---

[2] Fieldnotes, Juba: 30 September 2006.   [3] Fieldnotes, Nairobi, 1 November 2009.
[4] Olweny (2006b).   [5] Grabher and Stark (1997).   [6] Wassermann and Faust (1994).

both in the national and broader international context. Gunnar Sørbø et al. write in their description of internal wars that 'rather than being a transitory problem ... internal war can be seen as the emergence of essentially new types of social formation adapted for survival on the margins of the global economy'.[7] Connecting a local, seemingly person-alised conflict to broader processes of political and economic marginal-isation is necessary in the case of the LRA.

The Ugandan government, the US military and various advocacy groups have pushed the notion that if Kony were put under pressure, the LRA would automatically falter.[8] I had a typical conversation with a former employee of a UN agency in Kampala. He was convinced that Kony was the 'linchpin', and that killing him would turn the LRA's military behaviour into criminal behaviour 'where individual interests supersede group interest, thus it will be easier to coax them out of the bush'.[9] Paul Jackson – without empirical evidence to support this – echoes this typical assessment: 'Kony himself holds the key to peace – a cult cannot function without its high priest. Remove the high priest and the structure falls apart'.[10] Jeffrey Kaplan describes the LRA as a 'para-digmatic exemplar' of a group that has

turned inward, becoming localistic rather than international, and manifest[s] intense ethnic, racial, or tribal mysticism. They are millenarian and chiliastic in nature, and seek to create a new society – based on the creation of new men and women – in a single generation.[11]

Kaplan's description is both one dimensional and profound. In a sense, the LRA/M did seek to create a new society by pushing for deep change and for the overhaul of Uganda's politics, using violence against their own people as means. At times it seemed as if the delegation wanted to turn back the clock by comprehensively addressing Museveni's betrayals from twenty years ago, and in doing so redesign history in the Acholi's favour. Many delegates, however, were aware that such ambitious goals would require a change not only in LRA violence, but in LRA/M dynam-ics. Unreliable behaviour in negotiations, lack of clarity on who was mandated to negotiate, and the sketchy link between the high command

---

[7] Sørbø, Macrae and Wohlgemuth (1997).
[8] Glimpses of a growing understanding of the more complex set-up of the LRA emerged during the Talk. ICG wrote, for example: 'Whether [Kony] comes out of the bush to sign a peace agreement is less relevant to avoiding an eventual new revolt in northern Uganda than whether the government makes serious efforts to keep its promises to that region' (International Crisis Group 2008). A similar argument appears in a follow-up report (International Crisis Group 2010).
[9] Fieldnotes, New York: 24 September 2010.   [10] Jackson (2009: 326).
[11] Kaplan (2007).

and its civilian negotiators had earned the group the reputation of being dysfunctional. In his letter to Machar, on/off LRA/M delegation leader Matsanga gave a similar description: 'But sir LRA issue is a complex that one shouldn't blame you for the total chaos that reins the movement of LRA'.[12]

But the chaos served a purpose. It confirmed the LRA/M's status as a marginalised group – unable to act with cohesion and bring about change because of outside pressure exerted by hostile structures. The battle against such disempowering structures also implied that all LRA/M actions were justified. By maintaining this status quo, the LRA/M was able to uphold its position that they wanted peace but were not able to get it, without having to examine their own role in the failure of the talks. Their overwhelming cognitive stance was that the LRA/M as an organisation was deeply embedded in a hostile context, meaning that if any LRA/M demands were rejected or their behaviour criticised, this was proof that broader forces were at work to silence its voice. As a result, the LRA/M was weak at assessing its own performance and making necessary concessions and compromises.

Also, individuals within the LRA/M deeply distrusted and mistrusted each other. This network of distrust meant that others interpreted individual support for concessions at the negotiation table as having been manipulated by systemic forces. At the same time, distrust acted as glue in the delegation. Having been infiltrated by government agents, LRA/M delegates chose to react by keeping the enemies close to allow for better control. Distrust amongst delegates, seeming disconnect between LRA and LRM, and also infiltration through government agents are what maintains the broader LRA system.

8.1   Who Represents the LRA?

When it became clear that the negotiation would be conducted by a team of LRA sympathisers from the diaspora – the LRM – discussions in the media and international organisations centred on whether this 'diaspora delegation' was the right negotiation partner.[13] Ugandan opposition politician Mao commented in a newspaper article on 8 November

---

[12] Nyekorach-Matsanga (2008).
[13] Contested representation is not a new issue in LRA peace talks. See Pain (1997). The LRA and LRM have a long history, however volatile. In the 1990s and leading up to the Juba Talks, the relationship was usually described as one that was invoked whenever convenient to either side. While the LRM stands accused of providing material support to the LRA ever since the war started, the LRA certainly draws much of its views on the outside world from members of the diaspora. The LRM at times used the existence of

2006: 'It is good that those who have been backing the LRA have come out in the open, but their biggest problem is that they are still stuck in the politics of 1986. They seem to think that being in exile is a badge of honour'.[14] An article in the *Monitor* described the LRA/M team as 'a group of people who have maintained contact with the LRA over the years' and who were now pushing a political agenda that had not existed before. The lack of direct access to Kony and Otti – exacerbated by the fact that complicated information had to be relayed on expensive and crackling satellite phone lines – created convoluted and often unreliable communication paths for the GoU and the mediation team, as well as for the LRA/M delegates themselves.

The *New Vision* latched onto 'the striking contrast between a mostly illiterate rebel army hiding out in the bush and their educated represen-tatives flown in from abroad'. The paper questioned whether these could be legitimate representatives of Kony: 'Of 17 LRA representatives at the peace talks, only five are rebel fighters, while 10 are Ugandans living in the UK, the United States, Kenya and Germany. The remaining two are LRA sympathisers from Kampala'.[15] Egeland described the LRA/M delegations as 'more professional mediators ... these are the people of the diaspora. They are pretty good, actually too good, because they were demanding more and more per diems and more and more projects and assistance and agreements that went far beyond what should be in such talks'.[16]

It was a standard joke among UN support staff at the peace process that the Juba Talks for some delegates were mainly a period of personal improvement: 'As the talks went on, watches were growing', observed one international staff member. 'A few months into the process I saw [one of the delegates] with a $5,000 dive watch on his wrist'.[17] One alienated former delegate put down his thoughts about his former col-leagues' claim to the ownership of the peace process in a letter to Machar and various northern Ugandan and Sudanese leaders:

[Two delegates] told me in no uncertain terms that although I had been requested by their principals to support them, I should know from the start that

---

the LRA to make a political point but seemed to have very little direct contact with their supposed military wing. However, whenever the political development moved from issuing statements towards having to be a legitimate negotiation partner, the two groups converged. Overall, viewing LRA and LRM as part of the same system is a more appropriate description.

[14] Mao (8 November 2006).   [15] 'Why do Ugandan exiles support LRA?' (2006)
[16] Author telephone interview with Jan Egeland, former UN-Undersecretary for Humanitarian Affairs: 15 October 2007.
[17] Author interview with international security expert. Nabanga: 13 April 2008.

the peace talks was their DEAL and hence I should follow what they told me to do and say not what I thought was the correct thing to do and say. I could at first not believe my ears, but as time went by, what I heard was true. And by the way the two don't follow the proceedings in the conference hall as they partially understand English, the language of communication during the talks. The two are also the ones who give out per diem to the delegates and give what they think is enough not what they are given by the GoSS and the rest they pocket. If asked why not the amount given by GoSS, they simply say that is enough for delegates, the rest they would take to Otti, which is never true as the GoSS always have special package for Otti and the rest of the LRA soldiers. They also solicit funds from other sources without Otti and other members of the delegation knowing. But they make sure they send to Otti whatever he wants and at all costs. That is why they have acquired property such as mataus [sic, minibus taxis], houses and plots in Nairobi. The peace process is really their DEAL![18]

Summarising his impression of the delegation, one international advisor said 'the problem with a group like the LRA is that they have very few friends and therefore you end up with a delegation of funny people'.[19] Each individual delegate had brought their own story with them to the negotiation table. One delegate recalled his time as an opposition soldier in the UPDA as a time of suffering. Another had endured personal losses, with family members still suffering harassment in Uganda. Delegates had left behind possessions or careers in Uganda, or the hope for careers and success that they had held in 1986. Very few of them had spent time in Uganda in the past years or decades; those who did had experienced either government scrutiny or a failure to launch a political career. They deeply distrusted each other. In his first meeting with the soon-to-be delegates, Machar was frank about his concerns and reminded the delegation that during the least peace talks, the LRA's negotiator Kolo had surrendered to the UPDF. Was the same about to happen again, he asked?

The president of Uganda committed to the peace process, but are you a solid delegation representing the LRA? If you are, you have to avail yourself to the rest of the world. The leader of the movement must have confidence in his delegation. The first thing to resolve is how many should be in the delegation. When Betty Bigombe negotiated the peace, the leader of the delegation defected.[20]

Many instances during the talks seemed to confirm that the delegates and the high command were rather detached from one another. Despite publicly endorsing his delegation, Otti also emphasised that he was

---

[18] Name of writer withheld by author, 'Letter to Riek Machar re: Acholi Peace Conference in Juba', April 2007; sender's caps.

[19] Personal email to author from international Advisor to the Juba Talks, 7 August 2011.

[20] Fieldnotes, Juba: 7 June 2006.

crucial in expressing the LRA's standpoint: 'If I don't speak for LRA, there is no LRA', he said.[21] On 27 September 2006, Otti contradicted a position taken by his delegation. Reportedly at the request of the high command, the delegates had tried to get Rugunda off the GoU team. Otti weighed in via the press to say that he wanted Rugunda to stay. The delegation's legitimacy was shaken and talk about the need for direct negotiations with Kony grew louder.[22]

In the online discussion space Acoli Forum, the relationship between the LRA leadership, the LRM delegation and the Acholi elders was the subject of heated debate after a newspaper article reported that Otti had called RDC Ochora after the opening of the peace talks to say that Olweny's harsh speech 'was not cleared with the High Command'. This had followed initial confusion over whether Kony and Otti had accepted an amnesty offer from the GoU after the delegation had declined it.[23] One participant, signing his post with the name Alfred, argued:

the RDC Walter Ochora is playing his gimmick in order to create confusion between the LRA High command and their negotiating team. I wonder why the LRA high command want a separate talk with Acoli delegation when they entrusted their representative? ... Otii [sic] Vincent must also learn to be Respectfull [sic] of his representative doing a very difficult job to defend him and his commanders in the talk. Un necessary [sic] phone call interviews with the government officials and press interviews regarding the negotiation is not the best way forward. The LRA High Command must leave press interview to their leader of the delegation.[24]

Reacting to the debate about the delegation's legitimacy, LRA/M delegate Ayena stood up in the Juba Raha Hotel's meeting hall. He was reportedly angry and argued that the delegation as it stood before the mediation team had been fully mandated by Kony. Even if Kony had appointed a dog, he said, and written a letter confirming the mandate and attached it to the dog's collar, the dog would need to be treated with respect. There was thus, he concluded, no reason to doubt the legitimacy of the delegation. When asked about their legitimacy to represent the high command, most delegates, referred to 12 June 2006, when Kony had signed off on the list of delegates.[25]

---

[21] Author interview with Vincent Otti, Ri-Kwangba: 14 November 2006.
[22] Cocks (27 September 2006).   [23] Izama and Gyezaho (2006).
[24] Alfred. 2006. 'Subject: Re: [Acoli Forum] More hurdles in Juba talks', *Acoli Forum*.
[25] On 12 June 2006, Otti met with Machar and the delegates in a clearing near Nabanga to finalise the delegation. I was meeting with Kony in a clearing further in the bush. During the interview Kony received a phone call from Otti to clarify some issues with the

The *East African* quoted GoU deputy delegation leader and Minister for International Affairs Okello Oryem as having declared 'in frustration … "If we were dealing with Kony's real demands, we would have signed an agreement by now and been out of this place"'. Oryem made the point that the demands set out by the delegates were 'mainly the personal position of the non-combatant arm of the LRA', which he saw as an attempt 'to derail the process'.[26] Kony, reported the government, had only asked for his personal safety and the removal of his name from the list of terrorists.[27]

The demands Oryem saw as expressing personal positions covered a range of issues. These included the closure of IDP camps, disbandment of the UPDF as Uganda's national army, the establishment of an army that would pledge loyalty to the people rather than the president, army reform to establish forces whose composition would reflect Uganda's national character, the admission of atrocities committed by the UPDF, and a power-sharing agreement between the LRA and GoU.

Referring to these demands as of great importance to Uganda's population as a whole, the delegation rejected suggestions that they might not have a good grasp on what the LRA wanted to negotiate. A member of the mediation team concluded after the Juba Talks that the delegation

did not have any (or at least not much) influence on the leadership. I always felt that LRA-leadership used them to be between them and the rest of the world. And that the delegation did not have much of a political opinion, and that the opinion that they did have was not necessarily of relevance for the LRA .... There was a link between them and a political problem, but they were only the consequence of the Northern Ugandan problem (and later a cause, as the conflict itself and the IDP-camps became the biggest N-Ugandan problem). That poses a difficulty, because there was something to talk about, but who was supposed to talk? Of course that was the reason the parliamentarians came on board, but that didn't necessarily help the 'LRA-problem' (in terms of getting them out of the bush and ending the violence).[28]

In an unsigned discussion paper that the LRA never used publicly, the writer develops the LRA/M's counterargument against the accusation that the delegation was not a bona fide representative of the LRA or indeed of any political agenda:

delegation. Kony okayed the delegation then, and later signed the official appointment letter.

[26] 'LRA "externals" accused of killing talks' (2006).

[27] 'LRA "externals" accused of killing talks' (2006).

[28] Personal email to author from international advisor to the Juba Talks, 7 August 2011.

Before LRA did a human face-lift to its political wing by naming about 16 persons to its peace negotiation team, the NRM Kampala regime, its backers, governments and organisations in USA and Europe claimed it was impossible to engage LRA because it neither had a political wing nor a political agenda. They went further arguing that business can only be done with LRA, if its leader Joseph Kony publicly named a spokesperson/and his representative(s).

It is therefore alarmingly socking [sic] that the proponents of the views above, with ease are changing goal-post by questioning the genuineness and credibility of the political representatives named by Joseph Kony witnessed by the authorities of southern Sudan. None else except LRA and its leadership can say who genuinely represents their course [sic] and interests ...

Annoying too is the notion that the LRA team must only be considered genuine if it has a military representation on its peace negotiation team. This notion exposes Uganda as a state pervaded by the culture of military supremacy. It also means in essence that nothing binding can be done without the involvement and endorsement of the military.[29]

The text above is a good example of how the delegates viewed their role in the broader context: despite individually admitting that the delegation lacked technical capacity, as a group they tended to define every obstacle they encountered in Juba as a manifestation of the militarised and marginalising system they were fighting. Criticism of their representatives confirmed that their marginalisation was so entrenched in the broader political context that it was impossible to represent political demands. The system as they knew it was continuing to work.

8.2   Battling a Hostile Environment

On 30 September 2006, the *New Vision* published a photo of the LRA/M delegates carrying white plastic chairs into the mediation hall of the Juba Raha Hotel. It was common to see people carrying chairs back and forth, and the delegation was amused by the newspaper coverage. One delegate said to me jokingly that this proved that a level playing field had not been established at the Juba Talks: 'I want to say to the mediator we are so disadvantaged, we even have to bring our own chairs'.[30] While said in jest, I had encountered the sentiment before: that the LRA/M's marginalisation was so entrenched that not even outside help was able to create the conditions in which their situation could change. An SPLA officer who had observed the Juba Talks commented on how ingrained the dynamics between the conflict parties were – possibly too ingrained to be changed even in peace. He had observed it in Kony's refusal to sign

---

[29] Unnamed author (LRA/M member of the Juba Delegation), unpublished and undated.
[30] Fieldnotes, Juba: 30 September 2006.

the FPA, and in Museveni's treatment of the peace process which he considered lacked the necessary concessions: 'When Museveni sees opportunity for peace, his rhetoric changes from partner in peace to victor in peace. You need to concede pride and ego that you are the victor. If you don't, I will think your peace deal is bait'.[31]

Many analysts agree on Uganda's continued politics of exclusion and marginalisation.[32] It is not surprising that the LRA/M sees itself deeply embedded in them. Delegates and fighters viewed their own actions as reactions to systemic constraints imposed on them. Systemic marginalisation and depoliticisation had a wide reach, in their view. Delegates remained adamant that they were on a political mission and had been fighting or living in exile for the opportunity to be at the negotiation table to address Uganda's problems. They argued that the hostile political system in Uganda was now deliberately depoliticising their cause. This impression was enhanced when international actors seemed to pursue a similar route of the depoliticisation of northern Uganda's most obvious problem. The Enough Project wrote that Shortley, the US special envoy at the Juba Talks, called 'for the de-linking of the Juba peace process from returns and redevelopment in the North. Other international donors should join the call to press the Ugandan government to deliver on these promises now'.[33] What sounds like a suggestion that more quickly benefits the people of northern Uganda sounded to the LRA as if their connection to northern Uganda's underdevelopment was being trivialised.

Years of subdued reaction from the international community to what the LRA/M referred to as the genocide of Acholi was seen as part of the broader hostile system. The LRA/M argued that the international community had misused 'a golden international human rights opportunity, attention and focus'. Uganda had shown its true colours in its refusal to include the situation on the UN agenda, thereby 'denying ... us, the people of Uganda to reap from, benefit and enjoy the collective universal defence and promotion of the respect for men's fundamental rights to life, security, peace and development'.[34]

The powerful LRA/M notion that they were speaking for an entire affected constituency had a direct impact on how delegates described themselves in Juba. In their view, they represented all those who had been aggrieved by Museveni's politics. If this representation had violent flaws, it was because the system had silenced the LRA/M's political

---

[31] Author interview with SPLA intelligence officer. Juba: 1 March 2009.
[32] For example Alava (2019).   [33] Spiegel and Prendergast (2008).
[34] LRA/M Peace Delegation Information and Publicity Secretariat, 'Press Release: Stop the concealment of genocide in Uganda', 13 October 2007.

capacity to have a voice without violence. I asked Otti why – at the time of the assembly in Owiny-Kibul – he had not allowed his soldiers to be transported by the SPLA but had instead encouraged civilians to provide bicycles and food to LRA soldiers passing through. He explained that he had to make a distinction between those who were 'part of LRA' and those, like the SPLA, who were not. I noted that I was unsure that all civilians in northern Uganda would agree with the characterisation that they were 'part of LRA'. Otti responded with conviction: 'LRA is northern Uganda. We are northern Uganda'.[35]

From Otti's perspective, the Juba Talks strengthened this mandate. 'I am in really good spirits about the peace talks', he said in September 2006 when I asked him how he was judging the progress. 'I am happy to have more family connection now, more contact'.[36] I asked him to elaborate: why was it so important to have contact? I had always been told that LRA fighters could not go home because they had committed violence. Otti found this rather amusing. He explained to me that of course, for LRA it was the most important thing to connect with their families and the people back home, because now they knew again from speaking to people during the peace talks that what the LRA was doing in the bush was the best for northern Uganda.[37]

Individual delegates expressed similar sentiments. They argued that bush fighters, exiled Ugandans and Ugandan civilians all shared the experience that the government was silencing them and was not providing peace and development. Kalyvas calls this a conflict's 'deep structure' that informs the most basic and persistence analysis of why a resolution is so difficult to achieve.[38] The LRA/M's 'deep structure' was their understanding that Museveni had robbed people of their political capacity to speak up against the very marginalisation that was, in turn, robbing them of their voice. It has been one of the remarkable characteristics of the conflict in northern Uganda that the LRA's mission to resist the government had in the most virulent years of the conflict lacked consistently vocal nonviolent competition, despite widely shared grievances. As a result, the LRA/M was guided in many of its actions by its understanding of itself as a social movement – or as the last man standing in an oppressive system.

This view of themselves is not surprising, as it increases the broader relevance of the fight and boundaries between violent civil wars and

---

[35] Author interview with Vincent Otti. Ri-Kwangba: 13 July 2007.
[36] Author interview with Vincent Otti. Ri-Kwangba: 22 September 2006.
[37] Author interview with Vincent Otti. Ri-Kwangba: 22 September 2006.
[38] Kalyvas (2006: 9).

social movements as expression of discontent.[39] The term 'social movement' is associated with, writes Charles Tilly, the participation of groups
claiming to represent larger groups with a limited political voice.[40] This
definition does not include demonstrative violent behaviour against the
very people the movement claims to represent. Yet describing the LRA as
a social movement is too benevolent regarding its methods and simplifies
the group's connection to its surroundings. Sidney Tarrow's definition of
a collective challenge to authorities might bring us closer to a suitable
description of what the LRA is.[41] Tilly and Tarrow establish that contentious politics can be expressed with both violence and nonviolence; the
mode of expression does not change the cause.[42] Such a perspective on
the LRA – as a group with a defined cause which has chosen violence to
pursue it – allows for a more nuanced and less judgemental perspective
on the LRA.

Such a perspective is important to understand how other actors utilise
the LRA/M and use their resistance as a catalyst to voice their own
grievances. When in the early days of the talks a range of actors, including
MPs from Uganda, claimed that the LRA's cause of resisting Museveni
was also their own, the LRA/M's view of themselves as representatives of
the broader political context was confirmed, even though they were a
little annoyed by the MPs' presence. A Ugandan journalist who was
covering the peace talks in Juba summed up why he felt the LRA/M's
view of themselves was justified:

Northern Uganda is definitely full of LRA supporters. Even people on [National
Resistance] Movement positions are very excited to see Kony. You cannot get
elected in northern Uganda unless you support the LRA. Even now people are
dying in the camps and an entire generation has been rendered useless. That is
why the LRA has become a political force to be reckoned with.[43]

Tilly talks about 'brokerage' to link actors in both violence and nonviolence.[44] The concept fits: One delegate described the LRA as the
channel through which others could voice their grievances. As an
example, he recounted that 'one LC 5 [Local Council representative]
in Soroti got up during consultations and said: "Kony might have messed

---

[39] Koopmans (2004).   [40] Tilly (2004).   [41] Tarrow (1994).
[42] Tilly and Tarrow (2006).
[43] Fieldnotes, Juba: 6 September 2006. Druckman's writing on ingroup-favouring bias
helps us to understand these shifts in attitudes and association. He makes the point
that 'the desire to form groups and to differentiate them from others is so strong that it is
easily activated under a variety of conditions' (Druckman 2006: 232).
[44] See Tilly (2003).

this war up by what he did. But it was not his war in the first place. If the government does not want to settle this issue, we might have to fight"'.[45]

Not everyone was enthusiastic about the 'brokering' that strengthened the LRA mandate through renewed ties. Colonel Bwone told me that he 'did not want to give more headache to my mum by seeing her and then going back to the bush again'.[46] Others were critical because families of LRA fighters were rounded up by RDC Ochora and MP Mao to come and visit, underscoring that there was a political currency in being seen to support the peace process with the LRA.[47] This feeling was strengthened in early December 2006 when Ochora brought Kony's ailing mother to the bush. In his angry swansong to the Juba Talks, written after the failed signing ceremony, former delegation spokesperson Olweny launched an all-out attack on the wider participation:

While it is recognized and appreciated that the cultural leaders, political leaders, administrators and elders in northern Uganda, particularly Acholi, would make a credible and substantive input into the talks as representatives and voices of the people, they instead sought to hijack the process and became themselves key movers and central figures in the process. It didn't help that some of them were sympathetic to the government. Many a time in the plenary hall, the LRA delegation were actually debating with this lot rather than the government delegation. It is commendable that some of the political leaders – MPs – have stood up firm against the government for the war in the region, but many other leaders lacked the spine to forthrightly tell the government off. Moreover, the victims of the war were never adequately and independently represented at the talks. The government side only used them to reinforce their arguments against the LRA.[48]

These were huge systemic issues to tackle – much bigger in the eyes of the delegates than, for example, negotiating a way to deal with the ICC warrants. Resignation set in swiftly, with delegates considering it almost impossible to take on the wider political context. The LRA/M delegates at times referred to the ill-fated Commission of Inquiry into Violations of Human Rights set up by Museveni to investigate government atrocities between 1962 and 1986. They agreed that not much had come of the Commission, despite what had been written about it on paper, and said that any negotiated agreement that looked good on paper might go the same way. Quinn, in her examination of the truth commission, comes to a similar assessment: she argues that the commission was left without funding and its ability to have an impact on the social fabric of Uganda

[45] LRA/M Peace Team (2009).
[46] Author interview with Col. Lubwoa Bwone and Lt. Col. Santo Alit (LRA). Ri-Kwangba: 22 September 2006.
[47] Fieldnotes, Juba: 19 November 2006.   [48] Olweny and Otukene (2008).

was deliberately undercut. The broader implication of this was that without a record of human rights abuses, victims of government atrocities were left without recourse and without a path towards social healing. If events are left unmentioned and unaddressed, victims lose their voice, whereas 'bringing these events out into the open, the power of the perpetrators over their victims is finally severed'.[49] This assessment echoes the LRA/M's often-repeated point that their voice to talk about the crimes against the Acholi had been silenced through violence and oppression.

They could have made a much stronger statement about the Commission's bias against the Acholi. For the LRA/M, this realisation translated into an implicit understanding that their own attempts to tell the truth and resolve the issues might also remain unheard. This would be the case even in an internationally sponsored peace process: 'Already our leaders feel that the international community, and indeed the ICC has already passed a verdict of guilty by the way the indictees are being called "killers," "murderers," "most wanted war criminals in Africa," etc', read one statement.[50] For the LRA/M, this was another indication that Museveni's power to control information and understanding was too far-reaching to be countered. As a further expression of the 'deep structure' of marginalisation and loss of voice, sceptics within the delegation argued that the talks had been set up by the GoU as a way to avoid touching on issues that would threaten Museveni's position. John Winslade has described such a phenomenon occurring in a conflict situation where actors develop narratives that 'see all events as taking place within, and being shaped by, larger stories. A whole mediation process itself might be seen as a plot development in the story of a particular relationship which endures through time'.[51]

This understanding of the negotiation process as being firmly embedded within an unchangeable hostile system also meant that any agreement would not only be a compromise, but a confirmation of the system. When bombs dropped on the LRA in December 2008, communication between Kony and others in the bush and their representatives outside broke down. For many critics of the Juba Talks, Kony's retreat into the bush served as proof that the representation had never worked in the first place. For some of the remaining delegates, however, it was proof that the hostile system had returned to its established tools. The LRA/M

---

[49] Quinn (2004: 406); see also Quinn (2010).
[50] Olweny (2006b). Calling someone a criminal before they have been found guilty of the crime by a court could be a libellous offence in some contexts.
[51] Winslade, Monk and Cotter (1998: 24).

argued after the talks that their mission to address Uganda's structural conflict had never stood a chance – it was, in their eyes, unfortunate but unavoidable that the LRA had also returned to its proven ways of operating as a highly mobile force committing atrocities against civilians.

8.3   System of Distrust

'Everybody lies and cheats in these talks, even on the delegation', one of the LRA/M delegates said to me.[52] Some delegates blamed the systemic political forces for the failure of the Juba Talks, but others were more critical of the role of the delegation. One delegate said that in the midst of the most comprehensive effort to address a national conflict, many of the delegates around the table had been pursuing personal agendas. They had indulged in their distrust of each other: 'If we all, in the delegation, had worked on one common goal, we would not have disintegrated to this level'. 'The Acholi in the early 1980s were very stupid', said one delegate, who was frank in describing the LRA's destructive role in the war. For him, the actions of previous generations, even though they had had it bad, had contributed to his terrible situation.[53]

They relied on their wealth and cattle and they failed to send their children to school. I myself missed out on seven years of school between 1983 and 1989. And because of that we now have a big problem in Acholiland, a general problem. We have become very disunited and stupid. People are only out for their own interest.[54]

Another delegate told me that in mid-2006, he had been living in the diaspora when he was contacted by others already working in the delegation. They had asked him to come to Juba, but he was shocked to hear who else had been appointed to the delegation. 'I could not believe it. [Name of one of the delegates]? Why him? He took amnesty. I could not believe it. You, [delegate's name]?' he explained his reaction. '[Another delegate] used to work for Ugandan intelligence. Why him?'[55] Another delegate recounted that the background of two of the original delegates was

not clear. People assumed [one of them] was close to Kony because he was somehow part of his security. [Another leading delegate] had worked for

---

[52] Fieldnotes, Juba: 19 November 2006.

[53] There is an element of 'competitive suffering' in LRA culture, a term Miller introduces. 'Competitive suffering' occurs when an essential part of one's personal identity is the ability to survive with that suffering identity intact. This captures one of the paradoxes of attempts to resolve this conflict (Miller 1996: 107).

[54] Fieldnotes, Juba: 18 December 2006.   [55] LRA/M Peace Team (2009).

internal affairs before joining the peace talks; [another delegate] was NRM and it was never clear how he came to be on the team. [Another delegate] was clearly Vincent's man and was working with the government. In addition, it was not clear why Justice Onega [from Uganda's Amnesty Commission] was the first to be contacted. Did Vincent want amnesty and a deal for himself? Kony seems to think so.[56]

I regularly encountered such assessments when asking people what they thought of their co-delegates. One delegate described a leading delegate as a 'well-known thug'.[57] Another delegate was known to double deal, working for both Kony and the GoU. One early delegate was so distrusted by the others that they wanted him arrested because he was accused of interference – but he had clearly been approved by the high command, since he was allowed to stay overnight in Ri-Kwangba. It was mentioned that some delegates had stolen money when Okello fell and were hoping that in exchange for bringing Kony to the table, their crimes would be forgotten.[58] One delegate explained 'members of the delegation are on file with the GoU. This information will be used to demoralise the delegation. They will walk on each and every single item that is brought up'.[59] For the delegate who was so shocked at who his colleagues were going to be, the make-up of the delegation was a sign that the GoU was firmly controlling the Juba Talks from the start. Nonetheless, he decided to join the delegation in Juba, precisely because he did not trust those at the centre of the peace effort.

Mistrust motivated many of the delegates. Other reasons for joining the delegation were kinship, a shared narrative of loss, or a shared antagonist identity. Some delegates were long-time associates of Kony, either inside Uganda, as organisers of LRA meetings in Nairobi, or as having travelled to LRA bases in Sudan to deliver goods for support. Others brought their own family relationships into the delegation.[60] Yet not all stories allowed the straightforward interpretation of a long-standing LRA connection. The story of how the delegation's legal advisor, Ayena, came to work in Juba shows the reach of the conflict across GoU and LRA affiliates, as well as how lack of trust created the delegation. Ayena said that he had been on the 2004–5 peace team as a member of the NRM 'until Betty Bigombe hijacked the process'. He claimed to have been instrumental in persuading Kolo to come out because our 'tactics back then was to weaken LRA by extracting key

---

[56] Fieldnotes, Nairobi: 11 November 2009.   [57] Fieldnotes: 24 November 2007.
[58] Author interview with local journalist. Juba: 31 January 2008.
[59] Author interview with member of the LRA/M delegation. Juba: 14 July 2006.
[60] Fieldnotes, Nabanga: 20 September 2006.

commanders to then speak strongly to LRA, but it did not work'. After withdrawing, he stopped following what happened between January 2005 and March 2006, but heard that the LRA 'was making quiet connections'.

In March 2006, two of the LRA's liaison people came to see him in Kampala and asked him to join their quest for peace talks. At the time, Ayena was recovering from a lost election campaign, having run on an NRM ticket so as to, as he said, 'work from within the system because I am a strong believer in national unity and national diversity'. At first, he did not believe that the LRA was starting a new peace process, but when his visitors showed photos of Onek, Assefa and Machar, he grew convinced that this was a genuine attempt. He flew to Nairobi on 31 May. At the time of his arrival in Juba in early June, he said, he did not know he was going to be on the delegation, but soon realised that he did not trust the delegates with the big job in hand: 'I am in the right place. I am the only one to draft all papers. I said yes when I saw the capacities of the delegation'.[61] Years later, Ayena would be Dominic Ongwen's controversial attorney at his trial at the ICC.

An internal letter by a former delegate demonstrates how this internal distrust also created opposition to everything the delegation negotiated:

Because of the weaknesses of the majority of the LRA delegates, [Two delegates], who are at least enlightened members of this delegation took advantage and hijacked the entire system and used it to articulate their personal interests and the national ones which do not auger well, not only for the Acholi community but also for the LRA at this time in question. In fact [two delegates] and [a Ugandan MP], are the ones to produce the position papers for the LRA and they do this at night in [a delegate's] hotel room. The following day they continued to the conference room to present the papers without discussing their contents with other members of delegation. Does this move surprise any Acholi when the interests of the LRA and those of Acholi community are not raised explicitly in such position papers? For instance the first agreement between the warring parties was Cessation of Hostilities. Here they agreed that the LRA soldiers who were still in Uganda should assemble at Owiny ki bul. Certainly this is UPDF control zone! The security of these soldiers was at stake. Secondly, the security of those in the IDPs camps were not also catered for in the agreement. Those in the camps have always been the victims of both UPDF and LRA, hence they required some protection from the observer team from this time until the comprehensive peace agreement is some and most of it, if not all, are implemented.[62]

---

[61] Fieldnotes, Juba: 11 October 2006.
[62] Name of writer withheld by author, 'Letter to Riek Machar re: Acholi Peace Conference in Juba', April 2007.

Another delegate accused some members of being government agents while calling others 'opportunists'. The sentiment that the GoU had planted agents within the delegation was shared by some of the Ugandan journalists who were covering the story. One reported that he had seen '[a delegate] with a Ugandan intelligence officer at midnight in Juba in a hidden place. He knows that I know what he was doing. I believe he is planted by the government to keep information flowing'.[63] President Museveni himself claimed in a meeting with US officials 'that the GOU had infiltrated the LRA and knew what its members were talking about'.[64] Some former LRA/M delegates were assumed in 2008 to be working closely with the GoU, since they were staying at the Fairway Hotel at government expense, presumably as informers.

Disillusionment amongst delegates about the delegation's and the LRA's behaviour was omnipresent; crucially, some delegates felt that improper and unprofessional behaviour made their already weak negotiation position even weaker. Delegates expressed despair that money given to the delegation leadership by IKV Pax Christi for the purchase of laptops went missing; other delegates remarked on a striking absence of receipts for supposed delegation purchases.[65] Delegation meetings centred on missing money as those seen as responsible were called to account.

8.4   Distrust and Approval

Being an LRA member, it transpired, meant permanently seeking validation. If one declares commitment to the cause, permanent scrutiny by other commanders followed. Approval could easily be withdrawn if Kony or the person's peers sensed a lack of commitment. However, it could also be reinstated, in a process of waxing and waning engagement or connect/disconnect that the LRA also used with outside actors. This process created a strong network of distrust and a permanent process of self-assessment and was mirrored in how the delegation acted in Juba. One delegate explained to me how the LRA/M associates control each other and keep watch on what each member is up to. Sometimes this was done in online discussions on Acolinet, sometimes it was obvious in the interactions. He said that nobody can ever be sure that they were trusted and dealing with trustworthy people.

He gave me an example: once one of the former LRA members had left the LRA, the former LRA member called the delegate several times from

[63] Personal email to author from Ugandan journalist (name withheld), 21 March 2007.
[64] US Embassy Kampala (2007f).   [65] Fieldnotes, Juba: 6 June 2006.

a satellite phone, pretending to be Bwone. The delegate thought this was an attempt to find out if he, the delegate, had been in touch with the high command, because the man who called him was planning to pretend to the high command that he himself was that very delegate in order to regain access to the inner circle.[66]

I encountered the idea that being an individual within the LRA meant undergoing a permanent approval process in various guises. Superficially, the coherence within the LRA seemed extremely tight. Even among lower ranks, connections established through the shared and often forced 'LRA identity' tended to continue even after individuals had left the bush. Former LRA fighters were likely to spend most of their time with comrades from the bush.[67] From the point of view of individual LRA members, however, individual identity as an LRA member was a lot less consistent than the group identity suggested. It seemed a rather fluid state to be an insider, and it was very easy for a previous insider to end up on the outside.

Two of the delegates, who were considered military representatives on the delegation, were soon regarded as outsiders by their comrades in the bush. Despite representing the LRA as public faces, those in the bush no longer saw them as belonging to the LRA. On the day the two came to visit the LRA in the bush, commanders in the bush said those two were not with the LRA anymore. In public meetings, one of them still acted as Kony's bodyguard, positioned behind Kony wearing a military vest and stony face behind sunglasses. However, he was no longer one of them, other commanders said.[68]

I asked the two military representatives on the delegation how they saw their own situation within the LRA; both gave a similar assessment. They were proud to have been part of the inner circle, trusted enough to be chosen as the outside ambassadors. Moreover, they were puzzled or uncertain why they had lost their former inner-circle status due to their elevated status as outside 'ambassadors'. They had expected to be elevated in the hierarchy, having proven their commitment. One of them explained that he and his colleagues on the delegation were now walking a tightrope:

I have to be honest with you, sometimes it is hard for us to be trusted. The guys [in the bush] think we have been in Juba, maybe we are a different person now. If I come, I have to empty my pockets and be searched. I am relying on the commander now to trust me. I cannot command.[69]

---

[66] Fieldnotes, Cologne: 24 September 2008.   [67] Allen and Schomerus (2006).
[68] Fieldnotes, Palotaka/Parajok: 3 October 2006.
[69] Fieldnotes, Juba/Magwi: 2 October 2006.

As soon as they were dismissed from the delegation in early 2008, other delegates pointed out that the two men, although they had always been greeted with great enthusiasm in the bush, had never truly been LRA members or trusted.

Abusing trust did not lead to being shunned. Instead, abuse of the system and an attempt to return to the inner circle could strengthen the bond. One of the early delegates [called O from here on] betrayed the LRA, but it did not lead to his exclusion. [O] had originally been part of the group sent out to make outside contacts in Uganda, Nairobi and Juba; he had introduced himself to me as a real nephew of Kony. He sat next to me when I first spoke to Otti on the phone. He was one of the men who established contact with IKV Pax Christi. After the first trip to see Otti, he was asked by IKV Pax Christi to take $10,000 to Kony. He did not go to see Kony; he did not deliver the money. Instead, he disappeared with the money and tipped off the UPDF about the route other LRA contact persons were about to travel. He told the army that they would be coming through Lira. The two denounced people narrowly escaped the UPDF.

When two of the initial delegates had to admit to IKV Pax Christi that [O] had stolen the money, they pleaded with IKV Pax Christi to not let Machar know. For IKV Pax Christi, this incident damaged confidence in the LRA/M delegation.[70] The LRA seemed to be less troubled by the incident. For a while, nobody knew where [O] was. Suddenly he reappeared in Juba in November 2006. I walked into the hotel yard to see the very delegate who had accused [O] of betraying him to the UPDF shake hands and greet him with enthusiasm. I asked him why he was happy to see [O] who had betrayed him. He answered: 'I will greet [O], but not talk to him'.

Delegates accused each other of having brought [O] back. One was very vocal: he said the issue of [O] was a big headache and that whoever brought [O] back should leave the delegation. He said if [O] went back to the bush, he would be killed. Nonetheless, [O] was given accommodation and hung around, usually by himself, outside his prefabricated room in Juba Bridge Hotel. When Dr Onek came for a meeting with the LRA to vent his anger at what the public perceived to be the LRA dragging their feet in the talks, he spotted [O]. He became very angry; after all, the money [O] had taken had been provided by an organisation. Onek publicly called [O] a 'thief' and the LRA/M 'idiots' for allowing him back. The delegation was very upset about the public humiliation, and

---

[70] Author interview with Sudanese advisor to peace talks. Juba: 8 December 2006.

now became very protective of [O].[71] Rather than being sent home, [O] was taken into the bush on the next journey. I saw him in Ri-Kwangba a couple of times after that. Clearly, no deadly revenge had been taken on him. Instead, he approached me and asked if I could give him $200. He later defected again from the bush with [another delegate] and was then jailed for trying to trick the GoU out of money.

Just after I had seen [O] back with the LRA in the bush, I spoke to one of the delegates and said how surprised I was about how [O] was treated. The delegate explained to me that watching each other strengthens the LRA, especially watching those you cannot trust. The delegation, he said, do not trust anybody because 'it keeps up attention' and 'you know better who your opponent is'. He elaborated that that was why the delegation could not really trust Machar, because they knew his history. However, because they knew his history, their distrust also meant that they trusted him to pay back his dues. It was a circle, he explained. Once you have done something wrong, the expectation that you will do it right next time is there. But mainly, said the delegate, his own distrust of Machar made it easier to understand what was being 'played', what the real intentions were. Distrust brought a sharper image of the truth.

An intriguing relationship between mistrust, distrust and the re-establishment of collaboration had long been part of the LRA. The frayed relationship with the Khartoum government provides another example. One LRA member explained to me that in the early days in Sudan, the LRA had no need to abduct fighters as they were 'well taken care of in Juba'. Nonetheless, the LRA did not trust Khartoum: 'Khartoum tried twice to arrest the chairman, in 2002 and 2004. In 2002, the chairman could only escape through a quick movement across the bridge'. Asking why Khartoum had turned against the LRA, the LRA commander said: 'Khartoum just thought we could be their slaves'.[72] Another story told amongst the LRA was that a confrontation between Machar, when he was still aligned with Khartoum, and Otti almost led to the killing of Otti. Otti was able to escape – reportedly without his clothes – but 'we thought we had lost him'. This experience of betrayal, however, as discussed earlier, was also a reason why the LRA trusted Machar with the Juba Talks.

Internally, distrust acted as a control mechanism. Externally, it contributed significantly to the LRA/M's failure to establish itself as a reliable negotiation partner. The struggle for recognition translated into having to pull together an unwieldy fabric of internal interests with often

---

[71] Fieldnotes, Juba: 6 November 2006.
[72] Fieldnotes, Ri Kwangba: 13 September 2006.

contradictory motivations. The most obvious manifestation of this was the steady growth of the LRA/M delegation in Juba – at one point, twenty-eight officially appointed members of the LRA/M delegation were seated at the negotiation table.[73] With more participation, turnover became rapid. Olweny lasted only a few months as spokesperson; Apire did not return to Juba in 2007. One South Sudanese member of the mediation team explained to me that it struck her as inward-looking of the LRA that

the LRA has not managed to form alliances with organisations here in Juba or with the media to advance their cause. Much of what is going on between Nabanga and here and getting more people on the team makes it rather unclear what is going on. All the LRA always say is the more the better; they seem to be quite open to have more people on the team.[74]

She thought rather than beefing up their numbers, the LRA/M would be better off focusing their demands regarding the safety of the assembly areas and working on a clear message to donor governments.

In wanting to include everyone, the delegation seemed increasingly dysfunctional. As LRA/M representation grew, so did the chief mediator's doubt that this approach would lead to a peace deal. Asked how he felt about the Nabanga meeting attended by more than a hundred family members, elders, community leaders and politicians in late July 2006 (at which I was not present), he said: 'You missed the show last week, but you did not miss much. I should have done something useful and gone to the funeral of my best friend'.[75]

Internal distrust and the belief that individuals were primarily pursuing personal agendas created speculation early on. As early as July 2006, the *East African* reported that 'parallel talks are likely to start in the next two weeks in the southern Sudan town of Maridi between the government, Kony, Acholi cultural leaders, elders and religious leaders' due to 'suspicion that some of the Lord's Resistance Army's negotiators are scheming to scuttle the ongoing Juba peace talks'[76] – although these never happened. From October 2006 onwards, it was however clear that a 'twin-track' had developed, with Gulu District Chairman Mao and RDC Ochora increasingly playing out their own rivalry.[77] The Mombasa meeting was another incarnation of such a parallel track. Museveni was said to be relying increasingly on direct feedback he was

---

[73] Fieldnotes, Juba: 12 September 2006.   [74] Fieldnotes, Juba: 12 September 2006.
[75] Fieldnotes, Maridi: 13 June 2006.
[76] 'LRA "externals" accused of killing talks' (2006).
[77] Fieldnotes, Juba: 11 October 2006.

getting from Ochora, rather than going through his own or Kony's delegation.[78] However, Museveni confirmed in a confidential meeting with US representatives, that he himself thought the parallel government track was 'foolery'.[79] The issue of representation had grown even more confused, and the level of distrust along with it.

The broader network of those wanting to attack the political system in Uganda also influenced progress and failure in Juba. The press release issued by Oloya on 10 April 2008, that said Kony would not sign the FPA and that the delegation had been infiltrated by the GoU, was the most obvious manifestation of distrust and infighting in the much broader network of LRA/M affiliates. Another example of internal distrust comes from late 2007, when LRA/M delegates travelled around northern Uganda to consult with the population on issues of accountability and reconciliation. While on the road, the LRA/M delegates received angry dispatches from members of the anti-Museveni diaspora. The delegates were accused of selling out to Museveni by even entering Uganda. One delegate told me, rather frustrated, that 'there was lots of trouble from the diaspora during consultations, people who complained that it could not be the real thing if they were not present'. I asked him why those who wanted to be present did not travel to join the consultations. 'Exactly', he answered. 'Why did they not come?'[80] His view was that they did not trust that they would be safe in Uganda, but that they also did not trust the delegates to make it safer for them in the future by negotiating a peace agreement. As a result, they believed so much in Museveni's power to spoil everything that in the end, they ended up wanting to spoil peace for everyone, he said.

Daniel Pécaut's work might help us in understanding what happens when the concrete geographical space of a rebellion is abandoned. His point is that by abandoning a particular location with which resistance is attributed, a new space is located in which damaging patterns can be projected: 'The non-place is the domain of generalized distrust'. The distrust within the vastly scattered Acholi diaspora is a good example of this phenomenon.[81]

In early 2008, after Otti's death had been confirmed, the delegation's leadership was handed to Matsanga. Matsanga – whose CV is a little unclear, including as to which university bestowed a PhD on him – had been meddling in Ugandan politics since the early 1980s, and had been on the fringe of the LRA/GoU conflict on and off since 1998. A brash presence, he was touted as the official LRA spokesperson in the late

---

[78] Fieldnotes, Juba: 6 December 2006.   [79] US Embassy Kampala (2007f).
[80] Fieldnotes, Juba: 28 January 2008.   [81] Pécaut (2000: 136).

1990s before publicly renouncing the LRA in 2000.[82] He became an image consultant for Zimbabwe's President Robert Mugabe through his UK PR company Africa World Media Ltd, also claiming that he was working as a Consultant Stringer for news outlets such as Sky News. His UK business address was given at the time of the Juba Talks as a hotel in London's neighbourhood Croydon – where nobody had heard of either Matsanga or his company.[83] In the early days of the Juba Talks, he had denounced the delegation's attempt as 'peace jokes' in polemical write-ups on his website in a typically audacious style.[84] After the Juba Talks ended, Matsanga has been active in criticising the ICC in its work on Kenya and DRC, and worked in Zimbabwean politics, documented under his Twitter handle @MatsangaDr.

When Matsanga first arrived in Juba, delegates showed a range of reactions towards him, from detachment to outright hostility. Publicly, they closed ranks. Internally, however, delegates were outraged. It did not help Matsanga's standing that he instantly sought one-on-one talks with Machar in which he reportedly denounced the delegation's work and offered his own services to bring the Juba Talks to a successful close. However, Matsanga seemed to have unlimited financial means to support the peace process, including money he spent on items for the LRA in the bush, so his membership of the delegation was not openly challenged.

After Kony had had Otti killed in October 2007 and his death had been confirmed, one of the leading delegates made clear that he was shocked about the turn of events. He called the loss terrible, both because he had had a personal relationship with Otti and because Otti had been indispensable to the peace talks. He also indicated that he felt the LRA/M delegation had been infiltrated by government agents – something he himself had been accused of being – and that it had been government agents who had convinced Kony that Otti had been making deals with the GoU behind his back, including taking money in exchange for guaranteeing a peace deal. Ojul explained that he had wanted to resign after the last visit to Nabanga in early 2008, but was persuaded by Ayoo to remain as chairman – only to then be publicly dismissed by Kony along with Ayoo.

Ojul, argued other delegates, had gambled his own credibility by pursuing parallel tracks with government representatives, first in Mombasa and then in Kampala. There was talk of money having been exchanged during Ojul's private late-night meeting with Museveni. An

---

[82] For example Kiwawulo (2009).   [83] Fieldnotes, London: 14 October 2007.
[84] For example Nyekorach-Matsanga (2007, 2006a, 2006b, 2006c).

international military advisor reiterated that the delegation had been outraged that two delegates had worked closely with Shortley while on consultations in Uganda and had responded to calls for individual meetings at State House without including the rest of the delegation.[85] One delegate argued that another delegate was a good example of how individuals had used the broader quest of the LRA/M for their personal advancement. He said that this delegate had always kept his government contacts open to assure his personal soft landing within the system. The dismissal/resignation had been part of a bigger plan: '[He] made his red carpet for this return by distancing himself from Kony'.[86]

Having dismissed Ojul, Kony nominated Matsanga as the delegation leader; Obita took Ayoo's position as the spokesperson. For some delegates, the change in leadership made little difference: both Ojul and Matsanga were equally suspected of being steered by the government. One delegate described Matsanga and Obita as opportunists, explaining that 'Obita's family is in Canada, and he did not get visa for Canada, so he came to Juba'.[87] Olweny wrote:

Internal schisms and rivalries, lack of cohesiveness, cliquism, greed and personal posturing began to unravel the delegation. It was already apparent that there were moles of the Uganda Government within the LRA delegation, lending credence to the claim that the Juba peace talks were actually between the two delegations of the Uganda Government![88]

Freshly dismissed, one of the now-former delegates expressed his distrust of the very organisation he had supported. He said that Kony's paranoia that everyone was out to get him was out of hand. He recounted that during his last meeting with Kony in the bush, Kony had complained that Chissano had received the inaugural Mo Ibrahim Prize for Achievement in African Leadership.[89] Kony had stated that Chissano had received the prize because of the work he had done with the LRA, arguing that he, Kony, was hence entitled to at least $250,000 of the $5 million prize money. According to one of his former spokespeople, this was yet again proof to Kony that nobody wanted to give the Acholi credit for their contributions and that the system was set up against them. 'These are the words of a lunatic', he said. 'Kony is now obsessed with

---

[85] Fieldnotes, Nabanga: 15 April 2008.   [86] Fieldnotes, Nabanga: 12 April 2008.
[87] Fieldnotes, Cologne: 24 September 2008.   [88] Olweny and Otukene (2008).
[89] The Mo Ibrahim Prize for Achievement in African Leadership was inaugurated in 2007. Due to the stringent conditions of the award, it is not awarded every year and had by 2019 only been awarded six times.

money. He wants to make a runner. He does not know that the planet has become too small for him'.[90]

With Ojul, Ayoo and Ongom leaving Juba, the delegation's numbers were quickly diminished; success in the final round of negotiations in early 2008 seemed unlikely. Yet under Matsanga's reign, outstanding agreements were signed in swift succession. In the eyes of the remaining delegates, such success came too quickly. They complained that Matsanga was not engaging Kony in the matter: he had failed to meet Kony in Ri-Kwangba on a number of occasions, citing personal security concerns as the reason for staying behind in Nabanga. Having concluded the final negotiations, Matsanga agreed to the ceremony to sign the FPA. When Kony failed to attend the 10 April 2008 ceremony, Matsanga resigned in a huff, citing Kony's lack of interest in ending the war as his reason – although it remained unclear whether he had actually ever communicated directly or met with Kony.

The lack of direct communication and Kony's failure to arrive in Ri-Kwangba confirmed what other delegates had suspected all along: 'Matsanga was a government agent hired to make it look as if Kony did not want to sign'.[91] Delegates had grown increasingly suspicious of Matsanga; the fact that he lived in a lavish suite at the Intercontinental Hotel in Nairobi when not in Juba and was freely spending money fuelled speculation.[92] In addition, Matsanga's information seemed to be different from anyone else's. From their own communication with Kony, delegates said Kony had asked for a detailed workshop on Agenda 3 after the protocol had been signed, but Matsanga had instead gone through with preparations for the signing ceremony.[93] Kony, delegates said, had understood the signing ceremony meetings in April, May and September 2008 as opportunities to read the negotiated agreements – but the lack of progress took its toll on delegates' belief in the Juba Talks. One delegate was so disillusioned with the failure to sign the FPA and the increased LRA violence that he said: 'If we treat the LRA as normal humans, we all lose. Kony is paranoid'.[94]

Such disillusionment from a formerly enthusiastic delegate confirmed that the LRA/M were also experiencing a contradictory group process. As the Juba Talks gained credibility, their position as members of the

---

[90] Fieldnotes, Juba: 28 January 2008.   [91] LRA/M Peace Team (2009).

[92] Matsanga countered the suspicions in a letter to Machar, written at the end of April 2008: 'I have used my hard earned money to buy clothes, shoes, and other humanitarian goods for the women and children in Garamba Park. I am Professional earning at least good money from my job that paid for my accommodation in Nairobi while in the peace process' (Nyekorach-Matsanga 2008).

[93] LRA/M Peace Team (2009).   [94] Fieldnotes, Cologne: 24 September 2008.

LRA/M became more credible. This also meant, however, that individuals within the group used that reputation for their own purposes. In the case of Ojul, delegates argued, he felt powerful enough to pursue his own interest, but in the process of doing so risked the accomplishments of the group. His dismissal was also an assertion of power and a reminder to the group that getting too close to the other side would be considered betrayal. A high-ranking SPLA intelligence officer who had been involved in the peace talks saw a similar mechanism leading up to Otti's death. When mistrust of Otti was growing, Kony had to re-establish control. Killing Otti was one part of that; minimising communication and giving the leadership of the delegation to someone who was not trusted was another way. '[Otti's death] reinforced the LRA's leadership in having more control and people became more scared', the officer explained.[95]

Matsanga, it seemed, spent most of April 2008 fuming over Kony's failure to sign the FPA. On the last day of the month, he sent a letter of almost 7,000 words to Machar, decrying the delegation's shortcomings and praising his own capacity to solve the conflict. He did not hold back when judging his fellow delegates – and specifically his spokesperson – and their criticism of his reign over the delegation: 'My debates during the negotiations can not be erased by any biological substance that looks like that of Dr James Obita whose genes are too short for my likings'.[96] To add another twist to the story of representation, Kony reinstated Matsanga as the leader of the delegation in the early summer of 2008, leaving question marks over whether he trusted Matsanga after all. Rather than speculating about this question, viewing Kony's reinstatement of Matsanga as another expression of distrust as a control mechanism might be more useful.

For the facilitators of the Juba Talks, Matsanga's larger-than-life presence caused confusion. Having been reinstated presumably to oversee the signing of the FPA, little tangible success seemed to be possible with Matsanga as the intermediary between Kony and the mediation team in Juba. Amongst facilitators, it was accepted knowledge that Matsanga was probably 'bought by Ugandan intelligence and that is why he had money to buy goodies'. An international advisor recounted that at one point the mediation team had decided that they needed to establish direct contact with Kony, as Matsanga's role as gatekeeper had stalled progress. The initiative fell flat: 'Kony called me and reiterated several times, shouting,

---

[95] Author interview with SPLA intelligence officer (name withheld by author). Juba: 1 March 2009.
[96] Nyekorach-Matsanga (2008).

that I should only talk to Matsanga and nobody else, that Matsanga was his only chairman. I think Kony was very cynical there. He liked the goodies, did not bother to meet Matsanga most of the time, and wanted us therefore to continue with him'.[97]

In September 2008, when delegates and leaders from Uganda met with Kony in Ri-Kwangba, Matsanga again failed to accompany them. He later explained that he had been harassed by Ugandan security in Nairobi and thus was unable to travel. Leading up to OLT in December 2008, the story of what happened and Matsanga's role in it gets ever murkier. Delegates explained to me that it had been communicated to Kony in late 2008 that the absolute final deadline for signing the FPA was 30 November 2008. On 18 November, Kony asked his delegation to come to discuss the document, but reportedly indicated to delegates that he was ready to sign. The delegation only managed to get to Nabanga by 28 November – too late to discuss and sign the final agreement. At that point, Matsanga had withdrawn entirely from discussing peace matters and did not join the delegation. Just over two weeks later, the UPDF dropped bombs on the LRA camp in Garamba Park. The following year, Matsanga physically assaulted two former delegates when they encountered each other in Nairobi in a radio station. The assault was so bad that the two former delegates reported Matsanga to the Kenyan police. Amongst some former delegates, OLT and the closed doors on the peace process served as proof that they had been betrayed again:

The LRA, however, is aware of certain forces at work behind the curtain, undermining and taking advantage of the great desire for peace in the region, by corrupting and attempting to divide the ranks of the LRA/M; to the extent that some of their operatives might have managed to infiltrate the ranks of the outgoing delegates[,]

read one communiqué.[98]

Why delegates had not withdrawn entirely from the process once they felt Matsanga and his suspected government connections undermined it, remained unclear to me. One delegate explained that everyone had benefited from Matsanga's lavish spending, despite being aware that he was possibly using government funds set aside specifically to keep LRA/M delegates quiet. Other delegates said they had accepted Matsanga on the team and later as a leader to avoid a replay of what had happened in previous peace negotiations when delegates had been killed. The most prominent case was the death of Kilama, as Dennis Pain writes, 'who had

[97] Personal email to author from international advisor to the Juba Talks, 7 August 2011.
[98] LRA/M (2008).

taken part in and surrendered following the 1988 Peace Agreement signed with the UPDA in Pece, Gulu, and had since been killed as well as other UPDA commanders'.[99] The question of what had happened to Kilama was of crucial importance to the LRA/M. It was one of the two main questions raised in the 1993–94 peace talks. With the question unanswered, having a government agent as delegation leader seemed to afford a certain protection to the rank and file of the delegation.[100]

Having listened to many complaints about Matsanga, I was surprised when in June 2008, a person who had played an important role for the LRA during the talks, decided to join the delegation under Matsanga. This new delegate had always been very critical of Matsanga. His move seemed to make no sense. When I had the chance to ask him about it, the new delegate explained that he had indeed always been deeply distrustful of Matsanga, but that he had also realised that Matsanga brought some skills that the delegation had been lacking, namely an ability to place items in the media. With Matsanga in charge, it had become easy to get an LRA message printed in the GoU-owned *New Vision*.[101] Before that, neither the Ugandan nor the international media had been willing to devote any reporting to the LRA/M message. Playing the hostile system by getting a voice through someone who was seen as a traitor, he argued, was better than not having a voice at all. From his point of view, by using distrust as an internal control mechanism he could at least partially counter the possible negatives of having a GoU agent on the delegation. Kony was also reportedly aware that Matsanga might be a government agent, which might have been the reason why he kept him on board, but only at arm's length. After all, a few times in conversations LRA/M delegates had quoted Sun Tzu's idea that it was best to keep one's friends close, but one's enemies closer.[102]

These developments created a strawman situation in the peace process, in which what was achieved on paper bore no resemblance to how indecisive and sluggish the LRA/M delegation had become. Crucially, the way distrust was handled also maintained the LRA/M's view of itself as caught in a system that would not allow the conflict to change. The LRA/M's only way to counter this was by also maintaining their status quo – or, in the words of the international advisor, by approaching the Juba Talks with great cynicism.

---

[99] Pain reports that in 1994 Kony stated, 'What happened to Kilama will not happen to me' (Pain 1997).
[100] Dolan (2005: 447).   [101] LRA/M Peace Team (2009).
[102] Paraphrased after Tzu (1971).

8.5   Maintaining the Status Quo

When the LRA/M entered the Juba Talks, they proclaimed grand aspirations that this would be the chance to comprehensively address the root
causes of the war. One root cause as identified by some delegates was the
GoU's lack of acceptance that the LRA/M had a legitimate political
agenda – a pattern that Christopher Dolan describes as the GoU's
tactical 'belittling of the LRA as having no political programme in the
1994 peace talks'.[103] From early on, however, the LRA/M thus found
itself in a bind: on the one hand, they were there to solve the conflict, on
the other, they found it hard to accept that solving the conflict might
involve dissolving the LRA/M. One delegate argued in July 2006 that

> the regime's mouthpiece, the New Vision Newspaper in an Editorial of July 21,
> says LRA is a defeated small rebel group whose demands must not be granted.
> The editorial advises the rebels to forget ever being part of a government of
> national unity. It says the best it can offer LRA is to integrate the rebel soldiers
> into the UPDF. To the NRM, one is only a criminal if he or she has picked arms
> against the regime, but one's crimes are washed away if one joins the regime.[104]

While the LRA/M said they had come to Juba for change, they also
wanted to maintain their own status rather than being dissolved into a
despised system. Negotiating their own organisation's dissolution –
which was clearly the aim of both the GoU and international facilitators –
turned out to be a frightening endeavour. Maintaining the status quo as
the marginalised group under permanent covert attack from the GoU
became an attractive option. At one point a Sudanese Acholi leader
commented on progress in the peace talks. He said it would be difficult
for the LRA to sign a peace deal because if they did 'they can then no
longer say that they are being mistreated'.[105]

Various participants and observers of the talks used different ways to
describe how they saw the LRA/M's behaviour in the talks. One delegate
described his colleagues' attempts to maintain the status quo: 'The
delegation is reluctant to accept outside advice. They feel threatened by
any kind of expertise'. Pointing out that the GoU delegation consisted of
state ministers with PhDs, he said: 'The power balance between delegations is indicative of the power balance between communities'.[106] Yet the
LRA/M was not using the support available to address this imbalance.
One day a delegate discussed with me the lack of research material
available to the LRA/M delegation. He said that research resources were

---

[103] Dolan (2005: 109).   [104] Ayoo, Godfrey. 2006b. 'Ethical debate', Cologne.
[105] Fieldnotes, Owiny-Kibul and Palotaka: 26 November 2006.
[106] Author interview with member of the LRA/M delegation. Juba: 14 July 2006.

a real problem and that this made it impossible for the LRA/M to genuinely participate in the Juba Talks. 'We have no statistics on the [IDP] camps', he explained to me, 'no people to do research. Instead we are told to get statistics off the Internet by Machar'. I did not find that unreasonable, considering that large amounts of data and analysis, particularly on conditions in the Ugandan IDP camps, were readily available online. The delegate was genuinely surprised – he had no idea that it would be easy for the LRA/M to back up their claims with published research.[107] In the end, no LRA/M statement or position paper showed evidence of having used the extensive resources available online. Instead, most arguments remained centred on the person of Museveni. One of the international advisors saw the LRA/M's maintenance of the status quo in their denial of current realities by aiming unrealistically high: 'The LRA/M need to be smarter in negotiating concessions, but they do not want to take advice because they still think they can negotiate Museveni out of power'.

In December 2006, a group of European ambassadors travelled to Juba to meet with participants of the Juba process, including the LRA/M delegates. Most of the delegates had gathered at the agreed meeting time with the ambassadors; delegation leader Ojul and legal advisor Ayena – arrived half an hour late. They explained their tardiness with their having forgotten a letter – a letter which they then proceeded to read to the ambassadors, rather than engaging in conversation. An observer explained that the letter was 'written in old communist UPC style about 1986 events', and the debate never moved much from there. Afterwards, however, members of the delegation were in a low mood, realising that their emphasis on the past paralysed them in their quest for a better future. 'We lost today', was how one delegate described the scenario.[108]

Pushing for change while maintaining the disempowered and marginalised status that gave the LRA carte blanche to use violence or remain reactive to GoU action proved an unsolvable dilemma. The LRA identity is caught in a perfect cycle of continued self-pollination, where the sheer existence of the LRA proves its need to exist. The ability to survive with the LRA identity intact is an essential element of this identity, setting up one of the paradoxes for resolving this conflict. Giving up this existence also would mean being reduced to meaninglessness. One of the international advisors described to me how he had experienced these internal dynamics of pushing for change and maintaining the status quo. He argued that

[107] Fieldnotes, Juba: 10 August 2006.   [108] Fieldnotes, Juba: 15 December 2006.

there is a small group of voluntary allies and a much larger group that in principle would like to get out. Juba was very instrumental in strengthening this group. So successful that Kony had to kill Otti to get the ghost back in the bottle. And that is why he was not able to say 'no' to the peace process categorically, that he had to be seen by his men to be seriously working on peace (indeed, to create the narrative that LRA is all for peace but that the outside world doesn't want it). And that explains a lot of the strange happenings especially in the last year.[109]

One former delegate would have disagreed with this assessment. He argued that the LRA/M were within their rights not to sign the FPA, because they had yet again become victims of the broader context in which government forces had infiltrated them and created rifts and internal distrust. He concluded that the best way forward was to rewind to the beginning and start again: 'Negotiations need to be reopened. So far, they can justifiably be considered worthless'.[110] With this statement, he maintained the status quo for his organisation, but also confirmed to many that negotiating with the LRA/M was a pointless endeavour.

8.6   Conclusion

The LRA/M's messy representation, and their way of justifying their own shortcomings as manifestations of their inhibition by a hostile system, created the impression that they were dysfunctional, and as such were not credible negotiation partners. This impression turned outside sentiment against them: donors withdrew and support waned when the label 'dysfunctional' became the dominant assessment. Yet the messy representation and reactive attitude fulfilled a function, allowing the LRA/M to blame outside interference for each shortcoming, including the often unclear position Kony was taking vis-à-vis the Juba Talks. Further, this chapter shows just how interdependent the interlocking structures between the LRA and the LRM, as well as between the LRA/M and the GoU, are. Most debates about the LRA and the LRM try to establish to what extent these are separate entities; a natural follow-on discussion is to what extent the GoU infiltrated the delegation. Such a fragmented interpretation of the three seemingly separate entities is misleading. Instead, part of the conflict dynamics stems precisely from the network of control, mistrust/distrust and infiltration – particularly because infiltration went both ways, with LRA/M sympathisers infiltrating the GoU, too.

---

[109] Personal email to author from international advisor to the Juba Talks, 7 August 2011.
[110] Fieldnotes, Cologne: 24 September 2008.

Unable to get a peace deal signed, the conflict system of LRA/M and GoU still emerged from the Juba Talks internally strengthened. Each actor in the 'system LRA' received confirmation that their behaviour continued to be necessary since nobody else could be trusted. This meant that the Juba Talks had served to confirm beliefs and the conviction that it was correct to act on them. Individual delegates maintained that the way Juba was conducted proved that conflict in Uganda was deeply rooted in a hostile system, confirming the need for resistance through an organisation such as the LRA/M. Fighters used the slow progress in the talks to maintain that the use of violence remained their only option.

Having been unable to find a way to navigate internal dynamics and use them constructively, Juba also confirmed the LRA/M's notion of their own position in the conflict, thus inadvertently strengthening the very conflict structures the talks were supposed to tackle, while in a parallel process initiating significant change beyond the LRA/M. Indeed, some of these insights come from lessons that could have been learned in earlier peace talks.

9   'We Are All Learning in This Peace Process'

Peacemaking and the Legacy of the Juba Peace Talks
with the Lord's Resistance Army

Today, northern Uganda *looks* like a peaceful place. Other parts of the region that might have benefitted from a peace deal between the LRA and the Ugandan government still face outright violence every day: South Sudan – including the areas in the Equatorian states that once were so affected by the LRA – is dealing with its own civil war, with government, opposition forces and numerous militias punctuating periods of brutal fighting with peace agreements. Eastern DRC is still a conflict zone, suffering attacks by often-unidentified groups. Eastern CAR continues to struggle due to its internal conflict and tensions and armed activity in neighbouring Darfur, Chad, South Sudan and DRC. It would be easy to conclude from this picture that, ultimately, it did not matter that the Juba Peace Talks turned out to be a broken process: civilians in the main conflict region got peace anyway; those in other affected parts continue to suffer because of their country's own conflict dynamics.

And yet, such a conclusion does not fully capture how northern Uganda's peace feels to its citizens. A broken process has created an incomplete peace with little political space or credible accountability mechanisms.[1] Speaking in northern Uganda's Palabek Kal in 2018, a man in his early thirties described how life in northern Uganda was for him:

I think by now we would have been fine if there was peace. There was this business of peace talks also and if it had finished, we would be good. The majority of people believe that the LRA can still return this side. Because based on the political system of Uganda, you hear that some other soldiers are still going somewhere. And people still think that the LRA might come back after working with those soldiers. So, people still think they might come back …

Somewhere is peace. To a small extent there is peace, but to another extent there is no peace. And the community is still struggling for land. Some

---

[1] An early assessment of the post-Juba Talk Ugandan situation comes from Atkinson (2010b).

are settling in the community, but others are already taking their land. So still there is no peace.[2]

The decade since Kony's missed signature was marked by subtle fall-out as described by this young man, a new brutal normal in political and military conflict in central Africa, and harsh humanitarian and political consequences. Immediately after the initial military strike of OLT against the LRA in December 2008, the situation became unsettled and unsettling. In early February 2009, Congolese IDP numbers stood at 160,674, with 20,000 having fled across the border; displacement was going to remain a long-term phenomenon in the region.[3] The World Food Program was at the time only able to access 54,511 of the IDPs – only those who had reached major towns or villages. Food delivery was slow on dry season roads. It took twelve days to take food from Beni to Dungu, a distance of 500 km; during wet season delivery was almost impossible. The area was at the time reportedly protected by 6,000 FARDC soldiers (who had little interest in fighting the LRA while battling their own problems in the Kivus), around 2,000 UPDF (although this number was never verified), and 400 MONUC troops.[4] Yet some IDP camps were too dangerous for humanitarian workers due to lack of protective army or police presence.[5] In early 2009, the LRA had killed 729 civilians since OLT; only 286 of 711 abductees had been rescued.[6] Throughout this military campaign, the UPDF insisted that the LRA was weakened, yet local civil society actors saw the LRA 'traverse the jungle with relative ease', most notably a new, young and strong generation of fighters.[7]

A conviction that an improved military response would end the conflict galvanized international actors into action. On 24 May 2010, US President Obama signed into law the LRA Disarmament and Northern Uganda Recovery Act, making ending LRA violence an obligation on which the government was accountable to Congress.[8]

In October 2010, representatives of LRA-affected countries and the AU met in Bangui, CAR, to establish an AU-backed Regional Task

---

[2] Author interview, Palabek Kal: 13 May 2018.   [3] IRIN (September 2013).
[4] Fieldnotes, Kampala: 15 February 2009.   [5] Fieldnotes, Kampala: 15 February 2009.
[6] Fieldnotes, Kampala: 15 February 2009.   [7] Fieldnotes, Kampala: 15 February 2009.
[8] 11th Congress of the United States of America (2010). There had been previous attempts to regulate Uganda's conflict through US law: U.S. House Congressional Resolution 309 had twelve years prior condemned 'Joseph Kony and the LRA's use of abductions and child soldiers' and called 'for the immediate release of all abducted children' and urged 'the US President and Secretary of State to support those groups attempting to end the abductions'. The resolution also called upon the UN to become more involved and for Sudan to stop supporting the LRA (US Congress 1998).

Force (AURTF) against the LRA threat – a threat that was somewhat repackaged to appeal to EU and US funding: 'For us, LRA elements are terrorists exactly like Al-Qaeda. The international community must not be stingy with the means to help Central Africa to get rid of the insecurity created by this rebellion', explained a Central African politician.[9] In October 2011, President Obama announced the deployment of a hundred special military advisors to help the regional armies in their hunt for Kony.[10] In March 2012, a video by the Californian advocacy group, Invisible Children, calling for Kony's arrest and continued US military support to the Ugandan army became the biggest social media sensation to date under the catch-phrase 'Kony2012'.

Violence against unprotected civilians particularly in DRC and CAR had become dramatic; LRA violence against civilians escalated or was more carefully recorded when international interest spiked, such as after the Kony2012 campaign.[11] With political representation of the LRA reduced to a few press releases, ending the conflict peacefully through political negotiations was off the table. In mid-2012, the AURTF against the LRA was strengthened with a further 2,000 UPDF soldiers and 500 SPLA.[12] Civil society leaders from Uganda and the region expressed their concern about the GoU's move to let the Amnesty Act for former fighters lapse, citing the Law's significant contribution to bringing stability to northern Uganda and the region, and calling on the GoU to reinstate it.[13] The US Senate passed Resolution 402, which condemns Kony and the LRA, commends AFRICOM for its work, and reiterates US military engagement and other commitments laid out in the LRA Act.[14] Meanwhile, the security situation in the affected areas remained bad, with numerous armed actors identified.

In 2013, South Sudan's government broke into factions; the end of that year saw the start of the young country's own civil war between the government and armed opposition. As a trusted long-term ally of the South Sudanese government, the UPDF dispatched two battalions to fight crucial battles for the government – a controversial move

---

[9] AFP (2010).   [10] Schomerus, Allen and Vlassenroot (2011).
[11] The LRA Crisis Tracker – run by Invisible Children and Resolve and in itself a controversial tool – shows that generally 'attacks and abductions by the LRA doubled in the first six months of 2012 relative to the latter half of 2011' and that in early 2012 'LRA violence in CAR spiked following Ugandan military operations' (AFP 2010).
[12] 'East Africa: Additional Ugandan and S. Sudanese Troops Join Anti-LRA Force' (2012).
[13] Traditional and Religious Leaders/Civil Society and other Organisations (2012).
[14] The Senate of the United States (2012).

that some saw as averting the worst, but that gave the government a crucial advantage.[15]

In early 2015, LRA commander Ongwen left the LRA and was handed over to US forces by Seneka rebels in CAR. The United States – who rejected the ICC – delivered the LRA commander to the Court in The Hague; his trial started in December 2016, with a verdict due in 2021. As part of a quickly broken peace deal signed by South Sudan's warring parties in 2015, Uganda withdrew from South Sudan. In 2017, all forces (including the United States) stopped military operations against the LRA, although it was widely acknowledged that for civilians in CAR and DRC, the situation was far from safe.[16] The multifaceted international system had not been able to find a way to address the violence that had radiated from the LRA conflict for decades.

Back in December 2006 in the LRA bush camp, Kony had addressed his delegation, UN staff and leaders from Uganda – amongst them Uganda's future deputy chief justice, Owiny Dollo – sat in a large circle. The visitors weighed Kony's every word, searching for an indication whether the LRA remained committed to the peace negotiations. The preceding months had been rocky, with attention primarily focussed on the challenges of safely assembling the LRA. Kony, speaking in Acholi, gave his assessment of the Juba Talks.[17] He explained that the LRA continued to be under threat from the UPDF and needed to protect itself. He criticised what he saw as the unjust approach of the ICC: 'I want to emphasise that in our view the fairest way to go about this matter: the ICC should avail themselves to come and talk to us so that at least they know our view about this matter'. In his analysis of how power and weakness played out in African and international politics he said:

The international justice system is insincere. If UN really wants the world at peace, UN should not turn to [provide/support] justice for [the] strong. If they see Kony as a weak man, they pursue him. If that is the rule of the game, the only option is to fight so that international community sees you are strong and let you walk free.

Museveni's hand was heavily involved in Rwanda and DRC, when Museveni went to support the late Kabila against Mobutu. After removal of Mobutu, there was disorder: Between Kabila and Kagame and Museveni on the other side. Museveni and Kagame supported the rebel group that [wanted to] remove the

[15] Alier (2014); Sudan Tribune (7 March 2014); Rolandsen, Heggli Sagmo and Nicolaisen (2015).
[16] Burke and Mwesigwa (1 May 2017).
[17] One of the LRA/M delegates translated Kony's words into English on the spot; it is his translation that is quoted here.

regime that was in power. Charles Taylor tried to help Sankoh who did not succeed. Taylor was taken to justice because he was now vulnerable.

If that is the rule of the game, it means that getting powerful is enough [to be safe]. If UN wants that to be the rule of the game, let it be clear.[18]

Kony argued that the reality of targeting the weak left the LRA in a bind: they had to continue to use violence to show strength or be powerless, but peaceful. Reiterating the LRA's commitment to resolving the problem, he concluded:

It would appear that we are hostage to our own pursuit. We seem to have built our own deathbed by committing to this peace process. We want government to be honest about it, no trickery about the peace talks. If its peace, let it be peace. If not, let's call it something else.[19]

In late 2006, this seemed a prematurely disillusioned assessment of the Juba Talks. Yet years later, the Juba Talks are generally considered a failure, maybe even an extravagant, naïve and doomed-to-fail undertaking. They are remembered as an insincere, messy and corrupt process, involving an unreliable LRA, an incompetent LRM, and a contradictory international framework that pitted international standards of justice against local needs, making a principled international approach impossible. With Ongwen on trial at the ICC, the international justice mechanism is now rebranded as the principled international stance. Measures of success, such as a signed FPA or a clear framework for dealing with the tension that arises from the intervention of the ICC, are absent.

Yet such cursory assessments overlook two crucial points: what the Juba Talks did achieve and the value of Juba's broader lessons about contemporary peacemaking. The insights are multilayered and possibly fleeting, as many of the lessons seem to be so context-specific. The Juba Talks were a unique process, yet the patterns and concerns – and the reasons why the personal experience of it broke the process – allow for broader lessons about peace processes in other contexts. Three critical inferences need to be considered: dynamics, entrenchment and understanding.

First, the focus on the primarily technical conduct and legal implications of the Juba Talks glossed over the developing dynamics of the process. In the end, it was the dynamics and events of the process, rather than technical or legal challenges, that reshaped the peace effort into the next stage of violent conflict. A significant change occurred, but almost as an unintended immediate consequence. Juba's most valuable

---

[18] Fieldnotes, Ri-Kwangba: 12 December 2006.
[19] Fieldnotes, Ri-Kwangba: 12 December 2006.

conceptual contribution might be an understanding that the experience of the process rather than finding solutions to technical problems or signing agreements holds the key to conflict transformation; and that measuring success through reached milestones can be misleading.

A second lesson is about entrenchment. Juba entrenched existing power dynamics between the GoU, the LRA/M and international actors. Because the achieved agreements were rather disconnected from how the process was experienced, the conflict system LRA – which includes actors from the LRA, the LRM and the GoU – retreated into their established ways of doing things. With an international community caught up in galvanic surges and unable to work with nuance over prolonged periods of time, the international peace machinery also reproduced itself without transformation.

Third, the Juba Talks also reveal the difficulties of 'understanding': they show how tricky it is to develop insights on a peace process. Recording, analysing and possibly utilising the dynamics of a peace process is a challenge – even more so if the aim of such analysis was to influence those dynamics in real time.

9.1   A Thumbnail Assessment of the Juba Talks

It is easy to look at the Juba Talks and the damaging military fallout and conclude that the talks were an overall failure. Yet many groundbreaking steps were taken along the way. Egeland summed up his assessment of the Juba Talks in 2009:

> To end up with a sustained cessation of hostilities and a situation where millions of people's lives are permanently improved, it seems that is not a bad result in the real world. Because the alternatives are not, as many believe, between perfect war and perfect peace. It is between perfect war and imperfect peace. Those are the two alternatives, I know so far in real life.[20]

Foremost, since the Juba Talks, northern Uganda has had reliable physical peace. The LRA activity in northern Uganda had been minimal just before the Talks started, possibly due to the changing environment since Sudan's CPA. Thus, direct attribution to the Juba Talks is impossible, but physical peace is an important achievement.

The Juba Talks led to a complete withdrawal of the LRA from northern Uganda. This achievement is now often falsely attributed to the UPDF having pushed the LRA out of Uganda or the ICC issuing

---

[20] Author's telephone interview with Jan Egeland, former UN-Undersecretary for Humanitarian Affairs: 27 August 2009.

warrants of arrest, with the implicit message being that in the end, it was the military or international justice that brought peace. In reality, the LRA left Uganda to fulfil the CoH agreement and the ICC's impact is too nebulous to allow such clear conclusions.

Civilians perceive a situation very differently if they know there is a largely inactive armed group nearby versus knowing that the group has left the area for good. A safe environment is more stable and allows other peaceful changes to be put in place, even though northern Ugandans still talk about how unstable their lives feel, sometimes adding that this is because insecurity or insurgency might return.[21]

Taking into account only the expense of two years of Juba Talks, physical peace in Uganda through LRA withdrawal cost US$ 15 million. Estimating the price of the military operations since 2008 is difficult, but it is easy to know that it was much, much higher: a fighter plane worth a few million dollars was lost in the first days of OLT; military operations went on for just under a decade. Creating more insecurity for civilians in DRC, South Sudan and CAR thus took considerably more time and money than bringing peace to northern Uganda through the Juba Talks.

The Juba Talks opened a discussion space. The often-tedious debates around the negotiation table helped spell out the intricacies of the conflict in a more public setting. These included current power relationships and underlying politics, the history of grievances and political voice in Uganda, divisions within the Acholi community, the complexities of peace and justice, as well as the operational challenges of what is euphemistically called a military 'solution'. Initiatives, such as the 'Beyond Juba Project' of the Refugee Law Project utilised this momentum and continue to do transformative peacebuilding work, including research, consultations and memorialisation, for example through the National Memory and Peace Documentation Centre in Kitgum. Programmes and research have shifted towards reconstruction and healing. None of this would have been possible without the changes brought on by the Juba Talks.[22]

Looking back, LRA/M delegates acknowledged that Juba had achieved something – although what exactly was hard to pin down. 'It is a step, but where to?' reminisced a former delegate in November 2008.[23] Former spokesperson Ayoo said that despite many outstanding issues, the

---

[21] Fieldnotes, Kitgum and Madi Opei: May 2018; Amanela et al. (2020).
[22] See for example Tuller (2018); Victor and Porter (2017); Osborne, Exelle and Verschoor (2017).
[23] Author interview with former member of LRA delegation and Cessation of Hostilities Monitoring Team. Nairobi: 10 November 2008.

LRA/M in the Juba Talks had 'achieved a lot. We got the government to admit that there is marginalisation'.[24] Indeed, the political debate had never been so public or garnered such intense regional and international interest. Uganda had previously neither been open to a broader UN role in ending the conflict, nor had accepted outside mediation. With Machar and Chissano in crucial roles, the process was to no small extent regionally owned. The Juba Talks were also the first time that the somewhat mysterious diaspora emerged in the bigger arena to address its own politics, even if that process remains inconclusive. Involving a broad range of affected people in consultations is in itself a remarkable achievement for a peace process.[25]

The Juba Talks challenged – at least temporarily – entrenched block thinking on military versus negotiated approaches. The peace versus justice debate became much more nuanced, nationally in Uganda, locally in affected areas, and internationally.[26] The debate on what kind of justice procedures would be possible drawing on the stipulations of Agenda 3 and previously unconsidered aspects and challenges of international justice became much more focused,[27] as did insights on how people in Acholiland articulate their justice needs.[28] The Agreement on Comprehensive Solutions included a commitment to facilitation of returns, as well as economic development of northern Uganda.[29] These agreements opened up a different kind of negotiation space in northern Uganda, where people – now disillusioned by the lack of visible impact of some of the reconstruction programmes put in place since the Juba Talks and by struggling to experience their own recovery[30] – continue to call on the government to fulfil its commitment to development in northern Uganda. These are important stepping stones to lasting conflict transformation.

In Uganda's broader political arena, the Juba Talks triggered unprecedented political engagement, perhaps the most promising transformative

---

[24] Fieldnotes, Juba: 28 January 2008.
[25] Hemmer argues that Juba's virtues became also its shortcomings: international influence became overpowering, the broadening of the process created 'a cacophony of voices' and blurred communication channels (Hemmer 2010).
[26] The delicate national judicial process on Agenda 3 was negotiated largely also as a political statement to allow some breathing space from the ICC.
[27] Clark has argued that the LRA case exposed a contradiction in the court system: since Uganda was not unwilling to prosecute, but unable to apprehend, international support was hardly needed for criminal prosecutions, but for apprehension, which is outside the ICC mandate (Clark 2008).
[28] For example Nouwen and Werner (2014).
[29] Government of the Republic of Uganda and Lord's Resistance Army/Movement (2007).
[30] Amanela et al. (2020).

aspect of the negotiations. People spoke up about the need for political debate, for example in an open letter to Museveni by one of his opponents, who argued that the President had treated 'every expression of opposition to your rule as a military, rather than a political matter'.[31] Dialogue between Museveni and opposition parties increased, with the President inviting leaders of the main political parties to State House to develop a framework for 'constructive dialogue with the opposition', as the Daily Monitor reported, calling the meeting 'a good start'.[32] Prior to the meeting, the opposition Uganda People's Congress submitted a list of neglected issues to discuss because

there is always a multiplicity of complimenting and competing ideas on any matter and especially on affairs of an entire nation like Uganda. It is this belief that has over the two decades of the NRM administration guided us in our constant demand for serious dialogue among the political stakeholders in Uganda. There has been no such dialogue.[33]

Mahmood Mamdani called those developments 'a good indication that the balance of power in Ugandan politics is shifting'.[34] It was one of the LRA/M's major shortcoming that they prioritised ownership of the Juba Talks over widening the political base for anti-government grievances.

Yet while Uganda's internal political debate and the discussion of peace and justice was at least temporarily boosted in its sophistication, the discourse on military intervention seemed to grow more monolithic, particularly in the United States and within US-headquartered advocacy organisations, who supported the notion of strengthening the Ugandan army in its pursuit of the LRA and broader anti-terror fight. In the end, the Juba talks ended with international support for what the LRA/M called a '"Rambo" type solution'.[35] A consequence of this was that also the political space that had for a while opened up was again closed down. With the Juba Talks receiving the label 'failure', some who had used the negotiations to push political dialogue were reluctant to continue to do so to avoid being affiliated with a failed endeavour and dodgy LRA/M participants. The slow and reluctant opposition to the abolishment of Uganda's Amnesty Act in 2012 might serve as an example for this backlash, as does the general rejection of the idea that the LRA conflict was solvable through negotiations, a sentiment that seems prevalent across most UN agencies and in US political circles.

The GoU reasserted control soon after the Juba Talks had opened up a space: in April 2011, UPDF soldiers and police killed nine people

---

[31] Oloka-Onyango (2006).   [32] Ssemogerere (2006).   [33] Obote (2006).
[34] Mamdani (2006).   [35] Lord's Resistance Army/Movement Peace Team (2010).

(in Kampala, Gulu and Masaka) who had been protesting against the government's management. Two demonstrators were shot in the back, two others were killed while inside a building. One of those killed in a building was a child. Several times, opposition leader Besigye was arrested and kept under house arrest in what was called 'preventive detention'.[36] While the events were noted internationally, pressure on the GoU was limited and US support to its military remained unchanged. The public outcry against the bill that removed age limits for the president – a bill that comfortably passed parliament – is another marker of an iron grip on power.[37]

In November 2009, one of the LRA/M delegates who remained active in voicing the need for a negotiated solution talked about the urgent necessity to shift from the military situation to something that yet again opened up space for change and negotiation. He made no excuses for LRA/M shortcomings in the talks and said that for him, the fact that there were now soldiers hunting young LRA men in DRC highlighted both the military's short fuse, but also the LRA/M's shortcomings: 'Military action exploits the weakness of the LRA, the weakness to communicate their grievances', he explained.[38] As a result, the LRA/M had also failed to settle on a shared understanding of what they wanted to achieve through negotiations and had not taken advantage of the momentum for change that had developed temporarily during the Juba Talks.

This list of success criteria of the Juba Talks seems to be in contradiction with my core argument that the process was more important in determining success and failure than the negotiated agreements. Yet the disconnect between the knock-on effects of the negotiated agreements and the continuing conflict injects meaning into the notion of holistic peace talks. Many actors from the LRA who directly experienced the dynamics of the process continued their armed struggle – in a different space, with different methods and, in later years, with much less public or international attention. Those for whose benefit the LRA/M purportedly negotiated during the process – the civilians of northern Uganda and the citizens who live under what the LRA/M describes as an oppressive regime – experience significant positive change in their situation, even if many challenges and political tensions remain.

This points to a broad contradiction in current peace talks setups: to be holistic, that is to encompass credible positive chance for all conflict actors and victims, process and agreements achieved ought to be aligned. Instead, the experience of the Juba Talks was not that of a peaceful path

---

[36] Human Rights Watch (October 2016).   [37] Library of Congress (2017).
[38] Fieldnotes, Nairobi: 1 November 2009.

to conflict resolution. Yet, in the more public arena of implementation of technical agreements, the situation was arguably changed for the better, with some changes in legislation and some corridors for political dialogue opened. That LRA violence continues, that northern actors feel disenfranchised and that under government pressure and land grabbing, people in the north have held up signs during demonstrations asking the LRA to help people resist government land grabs – and a murky process to end the outrage over such land grabs – highlights that a holistic process that sustainably changes dynamics is much more difficult to manage and implement.[39]

Implementation relies on technical agreements to act as road maps. Yet, ultimately implementation of these often fails, leaving behind a smattering of broken agreements with their own narratives and dynamics of failure attached. A holistic experience of a process that has changed dynamics for all actors possibly holds the key to supporting implementation when it flounders. Technical implementation without changed broader dynamics seems to most of the time run out of steam. Developments in Uganda since the Juba Talks – despite such initiatives as the Beyond Juba Project – are marked by an assertion of power, violent confrontation and lack of interest in changing the regime's grip on power. The heated debate around the removal of age limits for the President – signed into law by President Museveni in early 2018 against much protest – is an example of how the rules are changed to fit the interests of those who hold power.[40]

9.2   Dynamics

I have attempted to show how the LRA/M's everyday experience of the peace negotiations in the end posed a greater challenge to ending the conflict than having to figure out ways to navigate the ICC warrants. Henrietta Moore writes in her work on the importance of the individual experience of everyday lives that 'hopes, desires and satisfactions can never be fully captured by forms of regulation'.[41] Likewise, the end of a conflict such as this one cannot be achieved through expecting power dynamics to change. Such change needs to be noticeable during the negotiations. Transformation needs to be tangible in how the process is conducted and experienced. Mistakenly, the ICC caused actors in the Juba Talks to focus more on how to navigate the Rome Statute's regulations; one way of dealing with this technical aspect was seen as getting a

[39] Laing (15 April 2019); Serugo (15 June 2017).   [40] Daily Monitor (6 May 2018).
[41] Moore (2011: 22).

signature under an agreement which would, it was assumed, automatically open the door to the next steps. As such, the ICC warrants might have posed a technical challenge, but in garnering so much attention also reduced how success was measured in an unhelpful way.

The intense attention on technical challenges obscured the understanding of dynamics and events – game theory perspectives shaped the view on dynamics. Mark Duffield has criticised conflict resolution approaches as promising grand social engineering aimed at modifying behaviour, rather than tackling the context.[42] Applied to the Juba Talks, the aim was to modify the LRA's behaviour into signing a deal without attempting fundamental structural changes in Ugandan society. The dynamics of the talks, however, meant that the LRA/M did not go along with that as planned.

Machar, in a confidential meeting with US representatives before the failed signing ceremony, reportedly said that since the terms of the negotiated agreements were 'generous to the LRA, on the whole' and because the LRA had become so used to the comforts provided to them during the Juba Talks that 'even Kony was discovering that life is better with peace', a final signature was inevitable.[43] A former LRA/M delegate gave an assessment, a few months later, why this was a profound misjudgement. For the LRA/M, he argued, the Juba Talks had been conducted in an offhand manner, driven by the assumption that for the LRA/M any agreement would be a bonus and more than they could have hoped for. This created a sloppy process in which basic procedural oversights were compounded by the LRA/M's lack of capacity and professionalism. 'There was not even clear terms of reference set out for the exercise of the mandate for mediation. Imagine that! All this talk and somethings as simple as the terms of reference for the mediation are missing', the former delegate said.[44]

Eager to maintain that their fight had been legitimate and that the population of northern Uganda was facing physical threats and political repression by a corrupt government, the LRA/M upheld one major criticism about the Juba Talks: that they were never meant to be a political process. One delegate explained what he considered the peculiar logic of international support for the Juba Talks: if the international community had really believed that the conflict had legitimate root causes and that violence had been committed by the GoU, how could they square this with the expectation that military action against the rebels conducted by the GoU would bring peace? He argued that this

[42] Duffield (1997).   [43] US Embassy Khartoum (2008).
[44] LRA/M Peace Team (2009).

proved that in most people's minds the Juba Talks never moved beyond the notion of creating a 'soft landing'. In a 2006 statement, LRA/M spokesperson Ayoo wrote:

The NRM Kampala regime must know that the peace negotiations is [sic] an admission that the military option has failed, hence Juba becomes a political forum to arrive at some political end. Juba is not a moment to further war, but a venue and moment to get into a serious political search and discussion of the causes of the war and how to end it.[45]

'The conflict is still not accepted as a political conflict', said another former LRA/M delegate in November 2009. After three years of frustration with the GoU, the UN, his own delegation colleagues and the LRA leader, he seemed puzzled that the LRA/M had not managed to change this most basic perception about the war in northern Uganda. At that moment, he said, he did not even know what a future initiative for peace might look like or who could be a good mediator. From his perspective, everything that could have gone wrong in Juba went wrong. 'Of course, it's possible that Kony might get killed', he said. 'But it will not make a difference to the problem and the situation in the country'.[46]

From his point of view, the experience of the Juba Talks had turned out to be a monolithic choice between a state the LRA/M is comfortable with – war – and the rather vague idea of a peace agreement administered by the very structures of their adversary they had been fighting and that they were forced to sign through violence. The UNSC expressed a similar notion, albeit being supportive of it: 'There seems to be general agreement in the Council that only an effective military offensive can put enough pressure on the LRA to return to the negotiating table'.[47]

In 2006, one LRA member explained to me that because of the peace talks, his organisation was losing control over the analysis of the conflict and the portrayal of the conflict actors. For him, the Juba Talks were looking increasingly like an exercise in reducing the conflict to agreeable declarations and in making the LRA/M vulnerable. Another member of the LRA, who considered himself instrumental in bringing about the Juba Talks, explained how entering peace talks had exposed him to future trouble in an unchanged political landscape:

I was very committed to my work in the peace process. I now have a bad record in the government because I was also the one who brought on the peace process. And the government was trying to get out of the peace process. They were trying

---

[45] Ayoo, Godfrey. 2006a. 'The absence of Kony doesn't jeopardise the Juba Peace Negotiations', Draft paper from the LRA/M archive. RadioRhino: Cologne.
[46] Fieldnotes, Nairobi: 1 November 2009.   [47] UN Security Council (2009).

to give us money and said we might bring the women out of the bush who might be sick.[48]

In his December 2006 speech, Kony had emphasised what he saw as the most prominent obstacle to reaching a peace deal:

The thing I want to add for us is the reason why it is difficult to stop war in this situation – is the attitude of disrespect, disregard and abuse. Disregard is shown to us whereby ICC just ignores us, our sentiments, how this matter should have been handled. One morning we wake up and are told we are now wanted in The Hague. Undermining of people must stop and disregard and disrespect. If there is a level of understanding of this conflict, [it is] like at the crucifixion.

Because of this disregard and lies made it was the case between Barabbas and Jesus who should be released. Crucify Jesus, they said, he is the sinner and criminal. It is the same with ICC: emphasis is on those who have committed less crimes, not on those who have committed massive crimes that are just being pushed under.[49]

After the Juba Talks had turned into the gateway for the next military phase of this conflict, another delegate gave me his view on what had happened. For him, the threat of military action as the antidote to a negotiated peace agreement had been paralysing from the start. With OLT, his worst fears about how both the GoU and the international community were juxtaposing the signature with a military strike in an either/or option had come true. He explained why he felt that the either/or choice was so damaging:

In reality, solving conflict through the military and solving conflict through a peace process are as related as battling the banking crisis by giving the banks more power and allowing them to issue more shares, rather than limiting their power and making the bank's balance sheet a weaker incentive for bank's performances.[50]

In his opinion, the use of military leverage in a peace process had not only ended the Juba Talks but had also discredited the integrity of the process itself as a way to resolve the long-standing conflict. It was, to him, proof that the Juba Talks had missed the point.

Another separate set of dynamics also warrants attention: the dynamics of what I have called the galvanic surge of international opinion. External actors for months and years perpetuated the notion of their own capacity to solve the situation, convincing themselves that a properly imple-mented solution was just around the corner. After the issuing of the

[48] Fieldnotes, Juba: 18 December 2006.
[49] Fieldnotes, Ri-Kwangba: 12 December 2006.
[50] Fieldnotes, Nairobi: 1 November 2009.

ICC warrants in 2005, the Washington Post wrote 'there are growing indications ... that the days of this bizarre and brutal rebel force might be numbered'. The article quoted Kofi Annan saying that the warrants 'had sent a "very powerful message" that "would-be warlords" must be held accountable for their actions'.[51] At an August 2009 conference in South Africa, a representative of a European government dismissed my point that a solution to the LRA problem was not to be found through the threat of prosecution or a military strike. He argued that international contacts at an informal level were already being forged and that it was just a matter of weeks until an international LRA strategy would be made public: 'LRA festive days are over'.[52] To whom these days were supposed to have been festive was not clear to me.

In January 2011, I was told by one of the main funders for a US advocacy group that they were certain that within the following twelve to eighteen months, the LRA would be defeated militarily.[53] This was at odds with the opinions held by those closely engaged on the ground: Three and a half years after OLT started, six months after the deployment of US military advisers and two months after waves of enthusiasm for a quick military solution brought on by the Kony2012 campaign, a resident of Yambio was told by the commanding UPDF officer in his area that the UPDF was convinced that they would have to stay in the area for 'ten years' to end the LRA insurgency.[54] In the end, they did stay that long, but without defeating the LRA entirely.

South Sudan's own civil war brought first an end to UPDF presence in South Sudan in 2015 and then as a force hunting the LRA in 2017 – yet remnants of the LRA still roam and constitute a threat to civilian lives primarily, it seems, in DRC, CAR and the Darfur region. Yet the dynamics of the galvanic surge regularly drowned out these realities because being engaged in offering a solution is great currency – for acknowledgement, for fundraising, for Hollywood film scripts, for potential Nobel Peace Prize nominations, for graphic novels, for scholarship, for viral social media campaigns and for doctoral dissertations.

9.3   Entrenchment

When the FPA remained unsigned, analysts, observers and those affected by the conflict gave a whole list of reasons. Conspicuously absent was the explanation that with a signed agreement, the LRA/M would

[51] Wax (2005).
[52] Fieldnotes, ISS/Egmont conference on DRC, Kloofzicht, South Africa: 25 August 2009.
[53] Fieldnotes, Juba: 6 January 2011.   [54] Fieldnotes, London: 18 May 2012.

have entered into a partnership with the same enemy that they had experienced as unchanged and unchanging during the negotiations. The basic contradiction of ending violent resistance in an untransformed political environment remained largely unaddressed.

Change was difficult for all actors. The LRA/M to a great extent maintained its own reputation as an unreliable and violent negotiation partner torn apart by infighting. The GoU was seen as making few genuine political concessions and instead relying on the military; the international actors failed to establish themselves as principled with clear guidelines and in some cases maintained the often-criticised complicity with the GoU. These dynamics had been present in the conflict and continued during the Juba Talks and beyond, confirming the LRA/M's perception of being trapped in a hostile and unchangeable system. Being themselves caught up in their narrative that the GoU was solely adversarial, entering into a peace agreement would have also come with the concession that the GoU was capable of change – and would have required the LRA/M to change, too.

The scholarship on peace negotiations mostly falls short of empirically capturing these finer dynamics of peace processes, although the argument that peace talks can entrench conflict dynamics rather than change them is well established. Matthew Sinn uses the concept of 'viable peace' introduced by Michael Dziedzic and Leonard Hawley, which, amongst other things, stipulates that for peace talks to work 'violence-prone power structures must be dislodged'.[55] If that does not happen, peace talks victimise: Adek – a long-term ally of Kony and the most senior member of the delegation – at one point commented that the disrespect the LRA/M experienced in Juba was similar to what was happening at home. It was all too familiar, he said, because 'I have been a victim of peacetalks before'.[56]

Ann Lesch writes about the Sudanese peace talks that 'the negotiations illustrated the pitfalls of negotiating in a polarised political context in which talks heightened mistrust rather than bridged differences'.[57] Karl DeRouen and David Sobek make the point that in a civil war, 'defeat could mean the loss of existence. The high stakes generally make compromise difficult'.[58] Politically, argues Mamdani, the Juba Talks were

---

[55] Sinn (2010); Dziedzic and Hawley (2005: 14).
[56] Fieldnotes, Ri-Kwangba: 11 June 2006. Adek had also been imprisoned on charges of collaborating with the rebels and had been on probation with the need to regularly report to the police.
[57] Lesch (1999).   [58] DeRouen and Sobek (2004).

likely to constitute the most serious political challenge for both Kony and Museveni. As more political options open up for the northern political class, Kony will run the risk of being eclipsed by another, more explicitly political movement, whether armed or not.[59]

However, 'dislodging' the existing structures poses an existential problem to those who exist to oppose them. William Zartman outlines the contradiction inherent in negotiations between the state and rebels:

Rebels need the recognition that negotiation brings, but they also need iron-clad assurances of continued existence and recognition once combat is terminated. Formulas that dissolve the rebels into the current political and military structures deny the basic needs of the rebels and are non-starters.[60]

Kony had put the same argument into his own words (muddling the mandates of the ICC and the International Court of Justice):

The solution for the peace talks is war. In the past, many great things have happened. In Rwanda, people died in thousands. The cause is Museveni. And what happened in Congo? It is Museveni. Museveni was accused in International Court of Justice. He was not arrested. Why? Because he is in power. That means we should also capture power.[61]

To settle on peace within those power structures would for the LRA have meant to solidify them without access to recourse through the waging of war. If, however, continuation of having access to this recourse, no matter the cost to civilians, is the motivation behind the war, the LRA has been tremendously successful – as has the GoU in maintaining its enemy and all the benefits that brings.

The notion of conflict resolution as a reduced and regulated process that can be captured in models or conducted along legal guidelines reduces the range of internationally acceptable options to end conflicts, entrenching the limited and often unsuccessful toolkit that is available. To understand the broader implications of this, it is useful to take a look at the context that unfolded around the Juba Talks.

Critics have long argued that criminalisation of violent conflict or the notion of legal frameworks as conflict resolution tools are problematic. From the LRA/M's point of view, legislating peace and disarmament rang hollow. Having called for equal justice for all perpetrators – although to what extent the LRA leadership was prepared to go to court is hard to say – they argued that notions of justice in this conflict suffered a considerable setback when on 12 February 2008, a UPDF colonel

---

[59] Mamdani (2006).   [60] Zartman (2006: 260).
[61] Fieldnotes, Ri-Kwangba: 12 December 2006.

accused of having committed human rights abuses in northern Uganda, was promoted to a prominent position within the UPDF, while the United States signalled its preparedness to support the UPDF in its strike against the LRA.[62] Even after the botched and disastrous operation, the UPDF seemed certain of their friendship with the Americans since they had in 2009, as François Grignon writes, given 'a new shopping list of requests from the Ugandan government to help them hunt down' the LRA.[63]

From the point of view of the opposition parties in Uganda, this was a strengthening of the existing structures of militarised politics, which the UPC had criticised in a memorandum to Museveni: 'The NRM legacy on politics is one of fostering militarism as a pillar of politics .... As a nation, we must discuss practical means to de-militarise our politics once and for all'.[64] That support for a military operation contributed to militarisation seemingly came as a surprise to international observers, including the US sponsors of Ugandan military activity against the LRA. Most international observers were reportedly nonplussed by the number of Ugandan troops in DRC following the implementation of 'Plan B' against the LRA. The GoU had always emphasised the Congolese ownership of the military operation, hiding the rather large number of its own troops. A US report in June 2009 noted 'the Ugandan Government has deliberately (and successfully) kept quiet its troop strength and regular engagements with the LRA in order to keep a Congolese face on the operation'.[65] Not long after, Kinshasa asked the UPDF to leave and withdrew its support to the AU force put in charge of hunting the LRA.

Besides entrenching uneven justice and military structures, the crucial structure that was confirmed in the Juba Talks was the depoliticisation of the LRA/M's grievance. Noam Chomsky, in his evaluation of NATO's engagement in Kosovo, states that open dissent was systematically suppressed with a very easy blow: whoever criticised NATO's bombs was labelled a supporter of Milosevic.[66] David Keen has written about the repeating pattern in conflict situations of stymying discourse.[67] Chaim Kaufmann describes a similar process of monopolising discourse in the lead-up and during the Iraq war. Sold as an honourable intervention to liberate oppressed Iraqis, the systematic streamlining of coverage, including the embedding of journalists, made Kaufmann describe the situation as a 'failure of the democratic marketplace of ideas'.[68] For many of those arguing against military strikes against the LRA and for political

---

[62] See also Schomerus (2012)   [63] Grignon (2009).   [64] Obote (2006).
[65] US Embassy Kampala (2009b).   [66] Chomsky (1999).   [67] Keen (2008).
[68] Kaufmann (2004: 30).

dialogue – including myself – being labelled an LRA apologist is a familiar experience.

Along with passing the LRA Bill, the United States took further steps to entrench its viewpoint that peace, especially with unsavoury groups, was not to be gained through political processes. In June 2010, the US Supreme Court ruled that 'knowingly providing any service, training, expert advice or assistance to any foreign organization designated by the US State Department as terrorist' even without any proof that the aid was 'intended to further any act of terrorism or violence by the foreign group' could lead to a prison sentence of up to fifteen years.[69] The law, first adopted in 1996 and strengthened by the Patriot Act, had been questioned by the Obama administration after a ruling of the US Appeals court had declared 'parts of the law unconstitutionally vague'.[70] In the definition of the US Supreme Court, assistance now includes giving advice on how to find a peaceful solution.

As the LRA was still a terrorist organisation in US definition, the ruling strengthened the point that finding a solution through talking – and giving advice on international criminal procedures – would be almost impossible for a US organisation. Andy Carl wrote in an op-ed piece for the BBC that the US government was on the one hand 'calling for inclusive and political solutions to the world's most intractable conflicts' and that this naturally 'sometimes means talking to "terrorists"'.[71] He pointed out that 'the quiet diplomacy with [the Irish Republican Army] and loyalist paramilitaries which helped bring about the Good Friday agreement – meetings, training seminars and facilitated dialogues – would now be deemed a terrorist offence' including for US citizens working abroad for organisations that do not fall under US jurisdiction or receive US funding.[72] Similar, although somewhat vague, legal provisions exist in the UK under the Terrorism Act 2000. As this makes organisations vulnerable to prosecution, pursuing peace by peaceful means falls back onto governments or the UN – which also has strict guidelines on not engaging with groups deemed terrorist.[73]

As laws, conflict resolution, peacemaking, military intervention and humanitarianism continue to blur, concerns that are seemingly specific to each of these areas lose clarity, allowing for entrenchment of ideologies that support particular actions. Fiona Terry's discussion of how refugee camps in Congo were used strategically by Hutu genocidaires to find cover and regroup has fueled concerns that feeding the LRA would legitimise them politically and facilitate their return to violence.[74] To

---

[69] Vinci (2010).   [70] Vinci (2010).   [71] Carl (2010).   [72] Carl (2010).
[73] Carl (2010); see also Haspeslagh (2014).   [74] Terry (2002).

avoid such politicisation of the LRA, the negotiations suffered from depoliticisation. Achille Mbembé draws a clear line of distinction between politics and war. To shift war into politics, 'a project of autonomy' needs to be developed and 'agreement among a collectivity through communication and recognition' needs to be achieved.[75] Neither is possible in a situation in which one partner needed for the agreement has both depoliticised itself and is systematically depoliticised by its negotiation partners. Thus, the crucial element of politics needed for a more 'holistic' peace process remained elusive.[76]

9.4   Understanding

Vincent Otti, in a conversation, admitted that while everyone involved in the talks wanted to maintain the notion of being in control and knowledgeable about what was going, the opposite was more the case: 'See, for the UN this peace process is difficult. For the LRA, this peace process is difficult. For the VP, this peace process is difficult. We are all learning in this peace process'.[77]

I, too, learned in this peace process. Trying to understand why the LRA did not make peace presented by a range of methodological and analytical challenges which are just as important to consider as the more practical or political lessons learned by other actors. Yet the focus on predicting behaviour contributed to a game-theoretical view of the process with a focus on two crucial elements of political game theory as identified by Nolan McCarthy and Adam Meirowitz: who is to get which concession and whether the outcome is achieved in an efficient manner.[78] The model replaced a deeper engagement needed to understand how the LRA/M experienced the talks and what the ways were to find out. An untangling of the complex dynamics could not happen using measurable indicators without deeper understanding that needs to be achieved in ways other than through modelling.

Scholarship on modern peacemaking tends to look for the spoilers – readily identifiable actors that pursue a counterproductive interest that can be tackled to bring a conflict to a resolution. This sits in stark contrast to the idea of a holistic peace process – one that encompasses many aspects of life with violence and many perspectives of a conflict situation. What the Juba Talks in their complexity, fluidity and their vast range of individual and group actors have shown is that no single spoiler

---

[75] Mbembé (2003: 13).   [76] Nan (2009).
[77] Author interview with Vincent Otti, Ri-Kwangba: 13 July 2007.
[78] McCarthy and Meirowitz (2007: 275).

exists, nor does the notion hold water that once actors have made concessions and investments in the process, there is a point of no return. A more holistic perspective – and one that clearly identified holistic to mean moving away from notions of linearity and singular interests – might have made the shortcomings of that perspective clearer sooner.

Instead, the realisation that peace talks are a multi-layered part of a conflict trajectory also means that individual experiences matter, possibly more so than the technical matters discussed at the table. Yet what to do with this realisation that throws open more questions than it answers? My answer was to hone in on the individual experience, guided by James Fearon who writes that 'a creeping lack of confidence among social scientists as to whether they can really provide universally applicable explanations makes it all the more important not to ignore people's own understanding of why they act'.[79]

Adequately capturing that individual understanding is a daunting task. It is a challenge to understand the rich human tapestry as it requires thorough and time-consuming investigation of a nonlinear coalescence of ever-changing events, experiences and context through detailed multi-disciplinary observation. This would need to include engagement with all actors. Ideally, this would allow a process after which the researcher would emerge as an omniscient narrator able to produce a sequential analysis of unsystematic human experiences. Ordering would have to come with an appreciation that success and failure need new measurements if the whole process and all the dynamics it sets into motion were to be taken into account. The impossibility of this ideal scenario highlights that investigating complex peace processes with a holistic perspective presents a scholarly challenge.

A scholarly approach that provides reliable information on years of multifaceted and ever-changing motivations in a developing process – with ever-changing access – and then draws constructive conclusions that help make the peace talks a success is realistically outside the remit of individual researchers. Scholarship has yet to learn how to investigate complex processes with incomplete and manipulated information and draw nuanced, yet operationally informative conclusions – while at the same time being mindful with what authority a researcher is delving into these most personal of experiences. I did and often do wonder: does my access give me the overall picture as well as the detail that I need? Or more importantly, is this really my story to tell, with my words and my interpretations and my snippets of information?

---

[79] Fearon (2004: 420).

9.5   Implications for Contemporary Peacemaking

The three main insights from the Juba Talks on dynamics, entrenchment, and understanding serve as a reminder that transformation of
conflict also requires a self-reflective process. For this to happen, facilitators and conflict actors need to find a way to record and contemplate
ongoing non-linear experiences in a confusing environment. External
actors need to examine the occurrences of galvanic surges and cognitive
dissonance to be able to recognise them. This means scrutinising
whether decisions taken are supported by realistic insights or by ideological beliefs that a particular approach simply ought to work. It sounds
obvious and easy, but it is neither. When the Juba Talks came to be called
a failure, broader achievements were dismissed, such as the improved
situation in northern Uganda, the starting point for dealing with war
crimes in Uganda as stipulated in Agenda 3, or the at least temporarily
improved political dialogue in Uganda. Crucially, the peace process was
entirely abandoned as a lost cause, replaced by an uncertain military
approach and a dishonest discourse that stipulated that broader political
issues could only be tackled once the military problem was solved.

To allow a reflective transformative process to happen without fur-
thering entrenchment as seen in Juba, it is necessary to radically rethink
what a peace process is and is supposed to achieve. Most peace processes
are still run as if they can be project managed, with a clearly defined start
and endpoint. Notably, signed agreements are considered the most
important aspect of a peace process. This is at odds with how actors
experience change – through realisation, experience, relationships, narratives, a transformed perspective and a lived reality of such transformed
perspective, rather than through signatures.

'We are aware of our limitations, but we cannot quit now', said a
former LRA/M delegate in November 2009. He and a few of the others
had maintained a voice as the 'LRA/M Peace Team', primarily to issue
press releases to comment on military and political developments. It was
not clear to me what they thought they might be able to do, particularly
considering that the press releases generally were not much more than
rebuttals. 'We will try to change the thinking on this issue', he said, and

I want to find funding for a permanent peace secretariat that looks at
peacebuilding without a signature, to look at all the issues that need to be
resolved to make Uganda a peaceful country without judging success of making
peace on signing an agreement or hunting down Kony.[80]

---

[80] Fieldnotes, Nairobi: 1 November 2009.

Considering that the LRA/M failed to establish itself as a credible peace-maker during the Juba Talks and the Talks generally developed a tainted reputation, it is not surprising that funding dried up and no organisation ever worked credibly with LRA/M representatives again. Yet for peace-making to work, it is likely that it is this kind of long-term engagement with conflict actors that can become transformative.

The Juba Talks illustrate, however, that both information and analysis pose challenges: information is difficult to get, impartial analysis that acknowledges the extent to which evolving dynamics influence how information is viewed poses an intellectual and operational challenge. In the Juba Talks, an ongoing record of what happened and how the actors viewed the events was not kept, but an analysis of such information could have served as an additional track to maintain focus on the present, rather than on root causes or a future military threat. It is difficult to know how exactly such records could have been helpful and establishing a theoretical counterfactual devalues my point that the key to conflict transformation lies in unpredictable dynamics. In the end, the broader lesson from the Juba Talks does not come as a concrete recommenda-tion, but as a list of omissions. Since the Juba Talks and other similar peace processes tend to bring limited success, close attention to these omissions might be the key to understanding how conflicts are transformed.

I discussed the gap between theory and practice in contemporary peacemaking, using this book to show the practice of peacemaking and the constraints experienced by all actors: the LRA/M's internal limita-tions and external pressures, as well as the contradictory and often template-driven approaches of an international community that found itself in unchartered waters between international justice and regional peace. Yet how precisely does the experience of the Juba Talks allow for broader theoretical insights?

The answer to this question lies in how the LRA/M conceptualised the peace process for which they were hoping, the moments of failure when the negotiation space tightened from transformative to technical and the lack of a broader political vision. This follows scholarship that introduced the notion of conflict transformation – such as Louise Diamond's dis-tinction between conflict resolution – which seeks 'to discover, identify and resolve the underlying root causes of the conflict' – and the trans-formative process which endeavours 'to change the conditions that give rise to the underlying root causes of the conflict',[81] or Johan Galtung's

---

[81] Diamond (1994: 3) cited in Botes (2003).

rejection of the idea of conflict resolution in favour of viewing conflict as part of political life that needs to be managed to remain constructive.[82] Only with a holistic approach to managing the ebbs and flows of political conflict can interaction and systems in entrenched situations be changed over the long term.

Transformation scholars such as Raimo Väyrynen have identified the various ways in which transformation occurs: through internal change in actors, through a changed understanding of the issues at the heart of a conflict, through changed or new rules that regulate how actors behave with each other, and through structural transformation that makes up the broadest change to the system in which the conflict occurs.[83] Eileen Babbit, Diana Chigas and Robert Wilkinson speak about the type of change that is needed to mitigate or even manage conflict: change in attitudes, change in behaviours, and change in institutions.[84] Each of these theoretical themes prominent in conflict resolution resonates directly with the analysis of the Juba Talks presented here and why they failed to transform the dynamics of the conflict.

9.6   In Place of a Conclusion: How It Continues

In November 2012, I attended 'Move: DC'. It was the in-person follow-up to the Invisible Children Kony2012 campaign, with supporters of the campaign gathering in Washington, DC for a day of events and a march to the White House. When I arrived, I was told to 'stop by the legacy table to pick up your wristband and get a high five'. People, kitted out in the ubiquitous Kony2012 T-Shirt, were taking snapshots in the photo booth before a black background with letters spelling out MOVE. A stage of multiple screens, donning flags – among them, the United States, Uganda, DRC, CAR, South Sudan, ICC and UN – served as a popular backdrop for selfies with hands held up in peace signs. The dim light in the room made the White House projected onto the screen look like a beacon. Most attendants watching the thirty-minutes-to-start countdown on a big clock were teenagers, maybe some in their early twenties. A mother sitting behind me reminded her young daughter to remember to eat lunch amongst all the excitement.

When the event kicked off, the audience first got to see a film clip about Martin Luther King recruiting children to walk for civil rights – and how he was criticized for using children for his cause but persisted despite the criticism. The voice-over urged to keep the Kony 2012

---

[82] Galtung (1995).   [83] Väyrynen (1991: 163).
[84] Babbit, Chigas and Wilkinson (2013).

movement going despite the difficulties it and its supporters had faced.[85] Jason Russel – one of the founders of Invisible Children – arrived on stage to big cheers. He told everyone to 'Take a deep breath and look around … you made it'. Made it to what he then described as an 'incredibly important meeting', even *the* most important summit on LRA in the history of the world. What this summit wants, he explained, was to get Kony arrested and watch his trial before the ICC. But, Russel asked, what should come after that has been achieved? His answer was to tell the audience that they were beautiful and powerful and that they had impressed the world with what they had been doing and that this was a soundtrack they ought to repeat in their minds.

One after the other, important Invisible Children actors came on stage. Those introduced as survivors of the conflict got a big cheer. Political representatives of the governments of Uganda, South Sudan, CAR and the United States appeared, along with a representative of the AU. The US assistant secretary of state for African Affairs Johnnie Carson's speech was followed in French by the Deputy Defense Minister of CAR; however, notwithstanding translation, there was a notable movement towards the concession stands during the latter's speech. And yet … despite the world's most infamous wanted African warlord, the most infamous social media campaign Kony2012, the presence of high-level politicians, the mobilisation of thousands of American teenagers and a new benchmark set for advocacy campaigns of the future, the situation that created all this activity remains unresolved. It does because, at the core, all these attempts misunderstood that a shift was needed.

The LRA still exists – as an armed entity somewhat miraculously in what Day calls 'survival mode', as well as in people's minds.[86] And much like there were many familiar faces among those who gathered for the opening of the Juba Talks in July 2006, many of the faces of the Juba Talks continue to be important actors: Riek Machar as the controversial leader of the armed opposition in South Sudan which he somehow commanded while under house arrest in South Africa. Ayena, former LRA/M delegate, as the defence attorney for Ongwen in The Hague who, critics say, failed to do enough research for the defence. Dominic Ongwen himself, defendant in the ICC case *The Prosecutor v. Dominic Ongwen*, who had expected to be returned to Uganda based on arrangements agreed during the Juba Talks, rather than finding himself in the

---

[85] See Timms and Heimans (2018) for an analysis of the challenges Invisible Children faced with Kony2012.

[86] Day (2017).

dock in Europe. One of the chief justices in Uganda's Constitutional Court ruling over the constitutionality of removing age limits on Uganda's president is now Alfonse Owiny Dollo – once said to have dressed up as a woman to act as a messenger to bring the LRA to the negotiation table and visitor to the LRA in the bush to advice during the Juba Talks.

Whether Kony is alive or dead, whether he is in CAR, DRC or Darfur is unclear and depends on whose intelligence one believes. There has been no credible sustained communication with the LRA leadership since the Juba Talks broke down. Many – maybe most – people consider the LRA defeated, although people continue also to live in fear or point towards the LRA's ability to survive and regroup.[87] And even those who are convinced that the LRA is no longer a fighting force acknowledge its continuing influence as the symbol of war and the symbol of issues unaddressed: during a recent land conflict, reported an interviewee, 'people say "please LRA come and save us … the government is taking our land, Joseph Kony come and help us"'.[88]

As the next generations live with the continuing aftermath of the violence previous generations endured, experienced and perpetrated, going 'to the bush' to fight a political cause has become something like a national laughing stock: In his 2018 Labour Day speech, President Museveni joked that he had been so frustrated with medical doctors striking for better working conditions that he had himself considered to go 'back to the bush' over the matter.[89] The suggestion did receive a few good chuckles. Uganda's doctors did not get better working conditions; instead, the Ugandan government planned to follow Kenya's lead and hire Cuban doctors to bypass the dispute. Political contestation, so was the message, was not to be taken seriously – and only one serious bush fighter remained anyway and that was the president.

In 2005, Vincent Otti had written me a letter. He had asked who I was, whether I was trustworthy and whether I could buy

two good mobile phones with enough airtime in the line of Celtel because with M.T.N or U.T.L. (mango), it is easy for it to be trapped or monitored. The mobile phone the chairman had, one of the high ranking commanders surrendered with it so currently there is nothing.

Nobody could speak to the LRA, his representatives in Gulu told me, because there was no way to communicate. Also, nobody trusted the

---

[87] For example Faber (2017).
[88] Author interview at National Memory and Peace Documentation Centre: 9 May 2018; see also Serugo (15 June 2017).
[89] Muwulya (1 May 2018).

LRA. 'Nothing more to say', Otti had concluded in his letter. 'But more will come its way' if I managed to get the phones and stay in touch with him while I was in Europe. 'I understand you are soon going back'.[90]

When I had first spoken to Otti, he wanted to know more about the ICC. He thought he would be publicly executed if the ICC got him. The last time I saw him, some weeks before he was killed on order of this boss, I asked him if he now knew what to expect from the ICC. 'Hm hm', Otti replied, somewhat vaguely. 'It is very hard to understand how you get to peace'. He changed the subject, asking me if I at least had now come to fully understand the LRA. I was not sure, I replied, it was all very complicated. 'It is very difficult to understand LRA, to understand Uganda', he replied.

We have a big problem in Uganda and it needs to be solved. I want peace, but the problem needs to be solved. It is good you understand because we need a lot of support. Some who understand, after a while they go back home to their country. We are still here.[91]

---

[90] Vincent Otti personal letter to author: 25 August 2005.
[91] Author interview with Vincent Otti, Ri-Kwangba: 13 July 2007.

References

11th Congress of the United States of America. 2010. 'Lord's Resistance Army Disarmament and Northern Uganda Recovery Act of 2009', Public Law 111–172.

Accorsi, Sandro, Massimo Fabiani, Barbara Nattabi, Bruno Corrado, Robert Iriso, EmingtoneO. Ayella, Bongomin Pido, Paul A. Onek, Martin Ogwang, and Silvia Declich2005. 'The disease profile of poverty: Morbidity and mortality in northern Uganda in the context of war, population displacement and HIV/AIDS', *Transactions of the Royal Society of Tropical Medicine and Hygiene*, 99: 226–33.

van Acker, Frank. 2004. 'Uganda and the Lord's Resistance Army: The new order no one ordered', *African Affairs*, 103.

Acker, Joan, Kate Barry and Joke Essveld. 1991. 'Objectivity and truth: Problems in doing feminist research', in Mary Margaret Fonow and Judith A. Cook (eds.), *Beyond Methodology: Feminist Scholarship as Lived Research* (Indiana University Press: Bloomington).

Afako, Barney. 2002a. *Promoting Reconciliation: A Brief Review of the Amnesty Process in Uganda* (CSOPNU: Kampala).

—— 2002b. 'Reconciliation and justice: "Mato oput" and the Amnesty Act', in Okella Lucima (ed.), *Protracted Conflict, Elusive Peace: Initiative to End the Violence in Northern Uganda* (Conciliation Resources/Accord: London).

—— October 2006. 'Traditional drink unites Ugandans', *BBC Focus on Africa Magazine*, http://news.bbc.co.uk/1/hi/world/africa/5382816.stm.

—— 2010. 'Negotiating in the shadow of justice', in Elizabeth Drew (ed.), *Initiatives to End the Violence in Northern Uganda* (Conciliation Resources: London).

AFP. 25 September 2006. 'Ugandan army vows immediate attacks on LRA if peace talks fail'.

—— 14 October 2010. 'Central Africa says "fight LRA like Al-Qaeda"'.

Agamben, Giorgio. 1993. *The Coming Community* (University of Minnesota Press: Minneapolis).

—— 2002. *Remnants of Auschwitz: The Witness and the Archive* (Zone Books: Princeton).

Agbonifo, John. 2004. 'Beyond greed and grievance: Negotiating political settlement and peace in Africa', *Peace, Conflict and Development*, April, Issue 4: 1–14.

Ahere, John, and Grace Maina. 2013. 'The never-ending pursuit of the Lord's Resistance Army: An analysis of the Regional Cooperative Initiative for the Elimination of the LRA', *Policy & Practice Brief*, Issue 24. ACCORD.

Ahimbisibwe, Fortunate. 3 October 2006. 'LRA war resumes', *The New Vision*.

Akec, John A. 2006. 'Can South Africa help dismantle Ugandan apartheid?', *JohnAkecSouthSudan Blog*.

Alava, Henni. 2019. 'The everyday and spectacle of subdued citizenship in northern Uganda', in Katariina Holma and Tiina Kontinen (eds.), *Practices of Citizenship in East Africa: Perspectives from Philosophical Pragmatism* (Routledge: London).

Alier, Panther. 2014. 'Tragedy averted: On Uganda's involvement in S Sudan', *Al Jazeera*.

Allen, Tim. 1991. 'Understanding Alice: Uganda's holy spirit movement in context', *Africa*, 61: 370–99.

1994. 'Ethnicity and tribalism on the Sudan-Uganda border', In Katsuyoshi, Fukui , and Markakis, John (eds.), *Ethnicity and Conflict in the Horn of Africa*, London: James Currey: 112–139.

2006. *Trial justice: The International Criminal Court and the Lord's Resistance Army* (London: Zed Books).

2007. 'The International Criminal Court and the invention of traditional justice in Northern Uganda', *Politique Africaine*, 107: 147–66.

Allen, Tim, and Mareike Schomerus. 2006. 'A hard homecoming: Lessons learned from the reception center process in northern Uganda', *USAID/UNICEF*, 1–119.

Allen, Tim, and Jean Seaton. 1999. 'Introduction', in Tim Allen and Jean Seaton (eds.), *The Media of Conflict: War Reporting and Representation of Ethnic Violence* (Zed Books: London).

Allio, Emmy. 28 September 2006. 'Museveni gives $1m for Juba peace talks', *The New Vision*.

13 October 2006. 'LRA return to Garamba', *The New Vision*.

Amanela, Suleiman , Tracy Flora Ayee, Stephanie Buell, Alice Escande, Tony Quinlan, Anouk S. Rigterink, Mareike Schomerus, Sam Sharp, and Sarah Swanson. 2020. *Part 1: The Mmental Llandscape of Ppost-Cconflict Llife in Nnorthern Uganda*, Parts 1–7. (Secure Livelihoods Research Consortium (SLRC), (ODI: London).

Amnesty International. 1999. 'Uganda Country Report' (Amnesty International: London).

2010. 'Uganda: Human rights violations in Karamoja region guarantees impunity' (Amnesty International: Kampala).

Amony, Evelyn. 2015. *I Am Evelyn Amony: Reclaiming My Life from the Lord's Resistance Army* (edited with an Introduction by Erin Baines) (University of Wisconsin Press: Madison).

Amoru, Paul, and Andrew Mugyema. 4 June 2008. 'Uganda: Government resumes war on LRA rebels', *The Monitor*.

Annan, Jeannie, Christopher Blattman, Dyan Mazurana and Khristopher Carlson. 2009. 'Women and girls at war: "Wives", mothers, and fighters in the Lord's Resistance Army', HiCN Working Papers 63 (Households in Conflict Network).

Annan, Kofi. F. 'Letter dated 30 November 2006 from the Secretary-General to the President of the Security Council (S/2006/930)' (United Nations: New York), https://digitallibrary.un.org/record/587727?ln=en.

Associatated Press. 28 August 2006. 'Ugandan rebels say war is over after 19 years', *AP*.

Apuuli, Kasaija Phillip. 2005. 'Amnesty and international law: The case of the Lord's Resistance Army insurgents in northern Uganda', *African Journal on Conflict Resolution*, 5: 57.

Assefa, Hizekias. 1992. 'The challenge of mediation in internal wars: Reflections on the INN experience in the Ethiopian/Eritrean conflict', *Security Dialogue*, 23: 101–6.

Atkinson, Ronald R. 2009a. 'Revisiting "Operation Lightning Thunder"', *The Independent* (Kampala).

2009b. 'From Uganda to the Congo and beyond: Pursuing the Lord's Resistance Army'. New York: International Peace Institute.

2010a. '"The realists in Juba"? An analysis of the Juba Peace Talks', in Tim Allen and Koen Vlassenroot (eds.), *The Lord's Resistance Army: Myth and Reality* (Zed Books: London/New York).

2010b. *The Roots of Ethnicity: The Origins of the Acholi in Uganda* (Fountain Press: Kampala).

Atkinson, Ronald R., Phil Lancaster, Ledio Cakaj and Guilaume Lacaille. 2012. 'Do no harm: Assessing a military approach to the Lord's Resistance Army', *Journal of Eastern African Studies*, 6: 371–82.

Baaré, Anton. 2008. 'Opinion Paper Juba Process: Security arrangements and DDR', Draft document.

Babbit, Eileen., Diana Chigas and Robert Wilkinson. 2013. *Theories and Indicators of Change Briefing Paper: Concepts and Primers for Conflict Management and Mitigation* (USAID: Washington, DC).

Baines, Erin. 2009. 'Complex political perpetrators: Reflections on Dominic Ongwen', *Journal of Modern African Studies*, 47: 163–91.

Baines, Erin, and Lara Rosenoff Gauvin. 2014. 'Motherhood and social repair after war and displacement in northern Uganda', *Journal of Refugee Studies*, 27: 282–300.

Barnes, Catherine, and Lucima Okello. 2002. 'Introduction', in Lucima Okello (ed.), *Accord: Protracted Conflict, Elusive Peace: Initiatives to End the Violence in Northern Uganda* (Conciliation Resources: London).

Baruch Bush, Robert A. Baruch and Joseph P. Folger. 1994. *The Promise of Mediation* (Jossey-Bass Publishers: San Francisco).

Bates, Robert, Avner Greif and Margaret Levi. 2000. 'Analytic narratives revisited', *Social Science History*, 24: 685–96.

BBC News. 2 June 2006. 'Interpol push for Uganda arrests', *BBC News*.

6 November 2006. 'Uganda rebel chief wants UN talks', BBC News.com.

21 October 2006. 'Museveni meets Ugandan LRA rebels', *BBC News*.

2007. 'Rebels snub Ugandan peace talks', Nairobi/Kampala.

2008. 'Congo "to attack Ugandan rebels"', *BBC News Online*.

Beattie, John H. M. 1959. 'Understanding and explanation in social anthropology', *British Journal of Sociology*, 10: 45–59.

Behrend, Heike. 1993. *Alice und die Geister: Krieg im Norden Ugandas* (Trickster: Munich).

1999a. *Alice Lakwena and the Holy Spirits* (James Currey: Oxford).

1999b. 'Power to heal, power to kill. Spirit possession and war in northern Uganda (1986–1994)', in Heike Behrend and Ute Luig (eds.), *Spirit Possession, Modernity and Power in Africa* (James Currey: Oxford).

Berg-Schlosser, Dirk, and Rainer Siegler. 1990. *Political Stability and Development: A Comparative Analysis of Kenya, Tanzania and Uganda* (Lynne Rienner Publishers: Boulder).

Bergner, Jeffrey T. (Assistant Secretary, Legislative Affairs, United States Department of State). 2007. 'Letter to Senator Feingold of Wisconsin', Washington, DC.

Bigombe, Betty, and John Prendergast. 2006. 'Stop the crisis in northern Uganda', *The Philadelphia Inquirer*, 21 February.

Bogdan, Robert. C., and Sari Knopp Biklen. 1982. *Qualitative Research for Education: An Introduction to Theory and Methods* (Allyn & Bacon, Inc.: Boston).

Botes, Johannes. 2003. 'Conflict Transformation: A debate over semantics or a crucial shift in theory and practice of peace and conflict studies?', *The International Journal of Peace Studies*, 8: 1–44.

Boulding, Kenneth. 1962. *Conflict and Defense* (Harper & Row: New York).

Bourdieu, Pierre. 1990 (1980). *The Logic of Practice* (Stanford University Press: Stanford).

Branch, Adam. 2005. 'Political violence and the peasantry in northern Uganda, 1986–1998', *African Studies Quarterly*, 8: 1–31.

2007. 'Uganda's civil war and the politics of ICC intervention', *Ethics & International Affairs*, 21: 179–98.

2008a. 'Against humanitarian impunity: Rethinking responsibility for displacement and disaster in northern Uganda', *Journal of Intervention and Statebuilding*, 2: 151–73.

2008b. 'Gulu town in war ... and peace? Displacement, humanitarianism and post-war crisis', Crisis States Working Paper, 1–26.

2011. *Displacing Human Rights: War and Intervention in Northern Uganda* (Oxford University Press: New York).

2017. 'Dominic Ongwen on trial: The ICC's African Dilemmas', *International Journal of Transitional Justice*, 11: 30–49.

Bukuluki, Paul. 2011. *Negotiating Retributive and Restorative Justice in Conflict Transformation Efforts: The Case of Northern Uganda* (LIT Verlag: Zurich).

Burgess, Heidi, and Guy Burgess (eds.). 1997. *Encyclopedia of Conflict Resolution* (ABC-CLIO Inc.: Santa Barbara, CA).

Burke, Jason, and Alon Mwesigwa. 2017 (May 1). 'Central Africa fears return of LRA after hunt for Joseph Kony ends', *The Guardian*.

Burton, John. 1996. *Conflict Resolution: Its Language and Processes* (The Scarecrow Press, Inc.: Lanham, MD).

Buruma, Ian, and Avishai Margalit. 2005. *Occidentalism: A Short History of Anti-Westernism* (Penguin: New York).

Bussmann, Jane. 2010. *The Worst Date Ever: War Crimes, Hollywood Heart-Throbs and Other Abominations or How It Took a Comedy Writer to Expose Africa's Secret War* (Pan Macmillan: New York).

Buteera, Richard. 2003. 'The reach of terrorist financing and combating it – The links between terrorism and ordinary crime', in IAP Annual Conference, Washington, DC.

Cakaj, Ledio. 2016. *When the Walking Defeats You: One Man's Journey as Joseph Kony's Bodyguard* (Zed Press: London).

Carl, Andy. 2010. 'Viewpoint: Ending wars peacefully just got harder', *BBC News*, 29 June.

Cerasini, Marc. 2002. *The Complete Idiot's Guide to US Special Operations Forces* (Penguin: New York).

Chirot, Daniel, and Clark McCauley. 2006. *Why Not Kill Them All? The Logic and Prevention of Political Mass Murder* (Princeton University Press: Princeton/Oxford).

Chiwengo, Ngwarsungu. 2008. 'When wounds and corpses fail to speak: Narratives of violence and rape in Congo (DRC)', *Comparative Studies of South Asia, Africa and the Middle East*, 28: 78–92.

Chomsky, Noam. 1999. *The New Military Humanism: Lessons from Kosovo* (Common Courage Press: Monroe).

Clancy, Tom. 2001. *Special Forces: A Guided Tour of US Army Special Forces* (Berkeley Publishing Corporation: Berkeley, CA).

Clandinin, D. Jean, and F. Michael Connelly. 2000. *Narrative Inquiry: Experience and Story in Qualitative Research* (Jossey Bass: San Francisco).

Clark, Janine Natalya. 2010a. 'The ICC, Uganda and the LRA: Re-framing the debate', *African Studies*, 69: 141–60.

Clark, Phil. 2008. 'Law, politics and pragmatism: The ICC and case selection in Uganda and the Democratic Republic of Congo', in Nicholas Waddel and Phil Clarke (eds.), *Courting Conflict? Justice, Peace and the ICC in Africa* (Royal African Society: London).

2010b. *The Gacaca Courts, Post-Genocide Justice and Reconciliation in Rwanda* (Cambridge University Press: Cambridge).

2011. 'Chasing cases: The ICC and the politics of state referral in the Democratic Republic of Congo and Uganda', in Carsten Stahn and Mohamed M. El Zeidy (eds.), *The International Criminal Court and Complementarity: From Theory to Practice*, vol. II (Cambridge University Press: Cambridge).

von Clausewitz, Carl. 1973 (originally published 1873). *Vom Kriege* (rororo: Hamburg).

Cockett, Richard. 2010. *Sudan: Darfur and the Failure of an African State* (Yale University Press: New Haven, CT, and London).

Cocks, Tim. 20 October 2006. 'Commander denies LRA rebels killed civilians in Sudan', *Reuters*.

27 September 2006. 'Ugandan rebel commander overrules own peace team', *Reuters*.

Cole, Alison. 2011. 'Gaddafi might have been arrested by now if the ICC's warrant had been sealed', *The Guardian Legal Network*, 31 August.

Coleman, James S. 1956. *Community Conflict* (Free Press: New York).

Collins, Alan, Caroline Cox and Nick Pamment. 2017. 'Culture, conservation and crime: Regulating ivory markets for antiques and crafts', *Ecological Economics*, 135: 186–94.

Comerford, Michael Gerard. 2003. *The public sphere and the construction of peace narratives in Angola: From the bicesse accords to the death of Savimbi*, PhD thesis, University of Leeds.

Cook, Kathy. 2007. *Stolen Angels: The Kidnapped Girls of Uganda* (Penguin: Toronto).

Crook, John R. 2012. 'United States sends military forces to Central Africa to aid in combating the Lord's Resistance Army', *American Journal of International Law*, 106: 168–69.

Cunningham, David E., and Douglas Lemke. 2013. 'Combining civil and interstate wars', *International Organization*, 67: 609–27.

The Daily Monitor. 23 September 2006. 'LRA's Otti accuses Sudan of favouring Ugandan govt', *The Daily Monitor*.

24 January 2007. 'South Sudan's Kiir warns Ugandan LRA of military action'. *The Daily Monitor*.

2018 (6 May). 'Age limit ruling a litmus test for Uganda courts'.

Day, Christopher R. 2017. '"Survival Mode": Rebel resilience and the Lord's Resistance Army', *Terrorism and Political Violence*, 31(5). 966–86.

Demmers, Jolle, and Lauren Gould. 2018. 'An assemblage approach to liquid warfare: AFRICOM and the "hunt" for Joseph Kony', *Security Dialogue*, 49(5): 364–81.

DeRouen, Karl, and David Sobek. 2004. 'The dynamics of civil war duration and outcome', *Journal of Peace Research*, 41: 303–20.

Diamond, Louise. 1994. 'On developing a common vocabulary: The conflict continuum', *Peace Builder*, 1(4): 3.

Dolan, Chris. 2009. *Social Torture: The Case of Northern Uganda, 1986–2006* (Berghahn Books: Oxford/New York).

Dolan, Chris, and Lucy Hovil. 2006. 'Humanitarian protection in Uganda: A Trojan Horse?' (ODI: London).

Dolan, Christopher Gerald. 2005. 'Understanding war and its continuation: The case of northern Uganda', PhD thesis (London School of Economics and Political Science: London).

Doom, Ruddy, and Koen Vlassenroot. 1999. 'Kony's message: A new Koine? The Lord's Resistance Army in Uganda', *African Affairs*, 98: 5–36.

Dowden, Richard. 2006. 'Inspiration behind the "terror gang"', *The Observer*, 2 April.

2008. *Africa: Altered States, Ordinary Miracles* (Portobello Books: London).

Drew, Elizabeth (ed.). 2010. *Initiatives to End the Violence in Northern Uganda* (Conciliation Resources: London).

Drexler, Elizabeth F. 2007. 'The social life of conflict narratives: Violent antagonists, imagined histories, and foreclosed futures in Aceh, Indonesia', *Anthropological Quarterly*, 80: 961–95.

Druckman, Daniel. 2006. 'Group attachments in negotiation and collective action', *International Negotiation*, 11: 229–52.

Duffield, Mark. 1997. *Evaluating Conflict Resolution: Contexts, Models and Methodology* (Chr Michelsen Institute: Bergemn).

Dutta, Prajit K. 1999. *Strategies and Games: Theory and Practice* (MIT: Boston, MA).

Dziedzic, Michael J., and Len Hawley. 2005. 'Introduction', in Jock Covey, Michael J. Dziedzic and Len Hawley (eds.), *The Quest for Viable Peace:*

International Intervention and Strategies for Conflict Transformation (USIP: Washington, DC).

'East Africa: Additional Ugandan and S. Sudanese Troops Join Anti-LRA Force'. 2012. *Sudan Tribune*, 18 September.

Eaton, Dave. 2008. 'The business of peace: Raiding and peace along the Kenya–Uganda border (part II)', *African Affairs*, 107: 243–59.

'Editorial: Uganda's image at stake in CAR'. 2012. *The Observer*, 2 March.

Egadu, Samuel, Emmanuel Gyezaho, Grace Matsiko and Charles Akena. 5 September 2006. 'Top Kony rebel contacts UPDF', *The Daily Monitor*.

Egadu, Samuel O., and Charles Akena. 2007. 'Museveni issues directive over Lakwena burial', *The Daily Monitor*, 26 January.

Egeland, Jan. 2008. *A Billion Lives: An Eyewitness Report from the Frontlines of Humanity* (Simon & Schuster: New York).

Eichstaedt, Peter H. 2009. *First Kill Your Family: Child Soldiers of Uganda and the Lord's Resistance Army* (Lawrence Hill Books: Chicago).

von Engelhardt, Johannes, and Jeroen Jansz. 2014. 'Challenging humanitarian communication: An empirical exploration of Kony 2012', *International Communication Gazette*, 76: 464–84.

Epstein, Helen. 2017. *Another Fine Mess: America, Uganda, and the War on Terror* (Columbia Global Reports: New York).

Eriku, James. 9 November 2006. 'Gulu orders night centres to close', *The Daily Monitor*.

Etukuri, Charles. 20 December 2005. 'LRA accepts southern Sudan peace mediation', *The New Vision*.

Evera, Stephen Van. 2002. 'Why states believe foolish ideas: Non-self evaluation by states and societies', in A. K. Hanami (ed.), *Perspectives on Structural Realism* (Palgrave Macmillan: New York).

Faber, Pamela. 2017. *Sources of Resilience in the Lord's Resistance Army* (CNA: Arlington, VA).

FARDC, UPDF, SPLA. 2008. 'Press statement on the joint operation against the LRA', UPDF: Brig James Mugira (Chief of Military Intelligence), SPLA: Brig Matual Majok (Chief of Military Intelligence), FARDC: Brig Deodenne Kitenge (Chief of Military Intelligence) (eds.). Office of the President, Uganda Media Centre: Kampala.

Fearon, James D. 2004. 'Why do some civil wars last so much longer than others', *Journal of Peace Research*, 41: 275–301.

Fearon, James D., and David Laitin. 2005. 'Civil war narratives', Estudios/Working Papers, Instituto Juan March de Estudios e Investigaciones.

Feldman, Major Robert. 2007. 'A deal with the devil: Issues in offering Joseph Kony amnesty to resolve the conflict in Uganda', *Small Wars and Insurgencies*, 18: 134–43.

Finnstroem, Sverker. 2003. *Living with Bad Surroundings: War and Existential Uncertainty in Acholiland, Northern Uganda* (Uppsala Studies in Cultural Anthropology: Uppsala).

2008a. 'An African hell of colonial imagination? The Lord's Resistance Army/Movement in Uganda, another story', *Politique Africaine*, 112: 1–21.

2008b. *Living with Bad Surroundings: War, History, and Everyday Moments in Northern Uganda (The Cultures and Practices of Violence)* (Duke University Press: Durham, NC).

2009. 'Gendered war and rumours of Saddam Hussein in Uganda', *Anthropology and Humanism*, 34: 61–70.

Fisher, Jonathan. 2014. 'Framing Kony: Uganda's war, Obama's advisers and the nature of "influence" in Western foreign policy making', *Third World Quarterly*, 35: 686–704.

Frazer, Jendayi E. 2009. 'Four ways to help Africa: The U.S. African Command should move from Germany to Liberia', *The Wall Street Journal*, 25 August.

Freeman, Mark. 2002. 'The presence of what is missing: Memory, poetry, and the ride home', in R. J. Pellegrini and T. R. Sarbin (eds.), *Between Fathers and Sons: Critical Incident Narratives in the Development of Men's Lives* (Haworth Clinical Practice Press: New York).

Galtung, Johan. 1995. 'Conflict transformation', in Kumar Rupesinghe (ed.), *Conflict Transformation* (St. Martin's Press: New York).

Gardner, Graham. 2001. 'Unreliable memories and other contingencies: Problems with biographical knowledge', *Qualitative Research*, 1: 185–204.

Gegout, Catherine. 2013. 'The International Criminal Court: Limits, potential and conditions for the promotion of justice and peace', *Third World Quarterly*, 34: 800–18.

Gersony, Robert. 1997. *The Anguish of Northern Uganda: Results of a Field-Based Assessment of the Civil Conflicts in Northern Uganda* (USAID Mission, US Embassy: Kampala).

Giddens, Anthony. 1984. *The Constituiton of Society: Outline of the Theory of Structuration* (Polity Press: Cambridge).

Girling, Frank Knowles. 1960. *The Acholi of Uganda* (HMSO: London).

Giro, Mario. 1998. 'The community of Saint Egidio and its peace-making activities', *The International Spectator*, XXXIII.

Gissel, Line Engbo. 2017. 'Legitimising the Juba peace agreement on accountability and reconciliation: The International Criminal Court as a third-party actor?', *Journal of Eastern African Studies*, 11: 367–87.

Government of the Republic of Uganda and Lord's Resistance Army/Movement. 26 August 2006. 'Agreement on cessation of hostilities', Government of the Republic of Uganda/Lord's Resistance Army/Movement.

2007. 'Agreement on Comprehensive Solutions' Juba.

29 June 2007. 'Agreement on accountability and reconciliation between the Government of the Republic of Uganda and the Lord's Resistance Army/ Movement' Juba.

Government of Southern Sudan, Office of the Vice-President(Riek Machar Teny-Dhurgon). 2008. 'Statement of the Chief Mediator concerning the status of the peace process between the Government of Uganda and the Lord's Resistance Army', Juba.

The Governments of Sudan and Uganda. 1999. 'Nairobi Agreement', Nairobi.

Government of Uganda/Lord's Resistance Army/Movement. 14 April 2007. 'Ri-Kwangba Communique'.

2007. 'Cessation of hostilities agreement between the Government of the Republic of Uganda and the Lord's Resistance Army/Movement: Addendum 3', Released by Government of Southern Sudan (GoSS).

29 February 2008a. 'Agreement on disarmament, demobilisation and reintegration', Juba.

29 February 2008b. "Agreement on implementation and monitoring mechanisms', Juba.

Grabher, Gernot, and David Stark. 1997. 'Organizing diversity: Evolutionary theory, network analysis and postsocialism', *Regional Studies*, 31: 533–44.

Graham, Suzanne. 2008. 'Mother and slaughter: A comparative analysis of the female terrorist in the LRA and FARC', in Joelien Pretorius (ed.), *African Politics: Beyond the Third Wave of Democratisation* (Juta and Co: Cape Town).

Grainger, Sarah. 16 October 2006. 'Uganda "attack" threatens talks', *BBC News*.

27 September 2006. 'Uganda's LRA rebels "on the move"', Gulu: BBC News Online/Focus on Africa.

Greater North Women's Voices for Peace Network/Ugandan Women's Coalition for Peace/Women's Initiatives for Gender Justice. August 2007. 'Position paper: View of women from North and North Eastern Uganda on the Peace Talks, mechanisms for accountability and reconciliation'.

Green, Matthew. 2008. *The Wizard of the Nile: The Hunt for Africa's Most Wanted* (Portobello Books: London).

Grignon, François. 2009. *African Peace-Building Agenda: 'Elements of a New Strategy to Disarm the LRA'* (International Crisis Group: Brussels).

Grono, Nick, and Adam O'Brien. 2007. 'Justice in conflict: The International Criminal Court and peace processes in Africa', *Royal African Society*, 1–8.

Gyezaho, Emmanuel, Paul Harera and Grace Matsiko. 27 September 2006. 'Otti endorses Rugunda, tells of LRA Juba team', *The Daily Monitor*.

Gyezaho, Emmanuel and Frank Nyakairu. 11 October 2006. 'Govt still wants ICC to rest Kony, Otti', *The Daily Monitor*.

Harrington, C., and S. Engle Merry. 1988. 'Ideological production: The making of community mediation', *Law and Society Review*, 22: 708–35.

Haspeslagh, Sophie. 2014. 'Listing terrorists: The impact of proscription on third-party efforts to engage armed groups in peace processes – A practitioner's perspective', in Ioannis Tellidis and Harmonie Toros (eds.), *Terrorism: Bridging the Gap with Peace and Conflict Studies* (Routledge: London).

Hassen, M. K. A., and M. H. A. Keating. 2004. 'The responsibility to protect: A plan of action for northern Uganda'. Liu Institute for Global Issues: Vancouver.

Hazan, Pierre. 2017. 'Uganda's amnesty law and the peace/justice dilemma'. Blog: http://pierrehazan.com/en/2017/07/ugandas-amnesty-law-and-the-peacejustice-dilemma/.

Hemmer, Bruce, Paula Garb, Marlett Phillips and John L. Graham. 2005. 'Putting the "Up" in bottom-up peacebuilding: Broadening the concept of international negotiations', *International Negotiation*, 11: 129–62.

Hemmer, Jort. 2010. 'The Lord's Resistance Army: In search for a new approach', *Clingendael Institute*, 1–10.

Herwig, Holger H. 1987. 'Clio deceived: Patrotic self-censorship in Germany after the Great War', *International Security*, 12: 5–44.

Hoffman, Danny. 2005. 'West-African warscapes: Violent events as narrative blocs: The disarmament at Bo, Sierra Leone', *Anthropological Quarterly*, 79: 328–53.

Holmes, Richard. 1970. *Acts of War: The Behaviour of Men in Battle* (Free Press: London).

Hovil, Lucy, and Zachary Lomo. 2005. Whose Justice? Perceptions of Uganda's Amnesty Act 2000: The Potential for Conflict Resolution and Long-Term Reconciliation. Kampala.

Human Rights Focus. 2002. '"Between two fires." The plight of IDPs in northern Uganda: The human rights situation in the "protected camps" in Gulu District, northern Uganda'. Kampala.

Human Rights Watch. 1994. *Civilian Devastation: Abuses by All Parties in the War in Southern Sudan* (HRW: New York).

    2006. 'Uganda: No amnesty for atrocities – Turning a blind eye to justice undermines durable Peace' (HRW: New York).

    2009. 'The Christmas Massacres: LRA attacks on Civilian in Northern Congo' (HRW: New York).

    2012. *Justice for Serious Crimes before National Courts Uganda's International Crimes Division* (HRW: New York).

    2015. *Uganda: War Crimes Trials Face Challenges, Local Effort May Offer Insights for Other Countries* (HRW: New York).

    2016 (October). *Universal Periodic Review Submission Uganda: Addendum to UPR Submission* (HRW: New York/Kampala).

IKV Pax Christi. 2007. 'Mombasa consultations between the government of Uganda and the Lord's Resistance army may unblock Juba negotiations'.

International Court of Justice. 2005. 'Case concerning armed activities on the territory of the Congo (Democratic Republic of the Congo v. Uganda) (ICJ: The Hague)

International Criminal Court. 2005. 'Warrant of arrest unsealed against five LRA commanders'. (ICJ: The Hague.)

International Crisis Group. 2008. 'Northern Uganda: The road to peace, with or without Kony', Africa Report, Nairobi/Brussels.

    2010. 'LRA: A regional strategy beyond killing Kony' Africa Report 157, Brussels.

IRIN. 13 January 2006. 'Uganda – Year in brief 2005 – A chronology of key events', *IRIN*.

    18 October 2006. 'Gov't says LRA killed army officer, demands action', *IRIN*.

    26 October 2006. 'Dispute over truce terms holds up peace talks', *IRIN*.

    30 August 2006. 'Uganda: Key events in the northern conflict since May', *IRIN*.

    2005. 'Uganda: Year in review 2005 – Rebel activity and political upheaval', *IRIN*.

    2006. 'Uganda: Chronology of key events in 2006', *IRIN*.

    2013 (September). 'Making the best of displacement in DRC', *IRIN*.

Iya, Ronald. 2010. 'Encountering Kony: A Madi perspective', in Tim Allen and Koen Vlassenroot (eds.), *The Lord's Resistance Army: Myth and Reality* (Zed Books: London/New York).

Izama, Angelo. 5 November 2006. 'New "LRA" group emerges in Sudan', *Sunday Monitor*.

Izama, Angelo, and Emmanuel Gyezaho. 2006. 'More hurdles in Juba talks', *The Monitor*, 19 July.

Jackson, Paul. 2009. '"Negotiating with ghosts": Religion, conflict and peace in northern Uganda', *The Round Table*, 98: 319–31.

Jada, Hillary, and David Toure Pouch. 15 June 2006. 'LRA deny attack on Juba outskirts', *Juba Post*.

Jo, Hyeran, and Beth A. Simmons. 2016. 'Can the International Criminal Court deter atrocity?', *International Organization*, 70: 443–75.

Johnson, Douglas H. 2003. *The Root Causes of Sudan's Civil Wars: Peace or Truce* (Bloomington: Oxford).

Juba Post. 6 November 2006. 'Man gunned down in town, Juba residents run scared', *Juba Post*.

Kabonero, Richard Tumusime. 2006. 'No genocide in Uganda', *Uganda Net*.

Kalyvas, Stathis N. 2006. *The Logic of Violence in Civil War* (Cambridge University Press: Cambridge).

Kamara, Joseph K., Sheila Cyril and Andre M. N. Renzaho. 2017. 'The social and political dimensions of internal displacement in Uganda: Challenges and opportunities – A systematic review', *African Studies*, 76: 444–73.

Kaplan, Jeffrey. 2007. 'The fifth wave: The new tribalism?', *Terrorism and Political Violence*, 19: 545–70.

Kaufmann, Chaim. 2004. 'Threat inflation and the failure of the marketplace of ideas: The selling of the Iraq war', *International Security*, 29: 5–48.

Keen, David. 2008. *Complex Emergencies* (Polity: London).

Keller, Linda M. 2017. 'The continuing peace with justice debate: Recent events in Uganda and the International Criminal Court', *The University of the Pacific Law Review*, 48: 265.

Kenyi, Bullen. 17 August 2006. 'LRA delegation prossess on with peace process', *Juba Post*.

22 June 2006. 'Onek denies being head of the LRA delegation', *Juba Post*.

Kersten, Mark. 2012. 'Peace from Juba: Peace talks between the LRA and the Government of Uganda (2006–2008)', in Amanda Taub (ed.), *Beyond Kony 2012* (Leanpub (e-book)).

2016. *Justice in Conflict: The Effects of the International Criminal Court's Interventions on Ending Wars and Building Peace* (Oxford University Press: New York).

Kiwawulo, Chris. 2009. 'Who is David Nyekorach Matsanga?', *Daily Vision*, 15 August.

Kleinman, Arthur, Veena Das and Margaret M. Lock. 1997 *Social Suffering* (University of California Press: Berkeley).

Koopmans, Ruud. 2004. 'Protest in time and space: The evolution of waves of contention', in David A. Snow, Sarah A. Soule and Hanspeter Kriesi (eds.), *The Blackwell Companion to Social Movements* (Blackwell: Oxford).

Körppen, Daniela, Norbert Ropers and Hans J. Gießmann (eds.). 2011. *The Non-Linearity of Peace Processes – Theory and Practice of Systemic Conflict Transformation* (Barbara Budrich Verlag: Opladen/Farmington Hills).

Kriesberg, Louis. 1989. 'Conclusion', in Louis Kriesberg, Terrel A. Northrup and Stuart Thorson (eds.), *Intractable Conflicts and Their Transformation* (Syracuse University Press: Syracuse).

2015. *Realizing Peace: A Constructive Conflict Approach* (Oxford University Press: Oxford/New York).

Kriesberg, Louis, Terrel A. Northrup and Stuart J. Thorson (eds.). 1989. *Intractable Conflicts and Their Transformation* (Syracuse University Press: Syracuse).

Kulubya, Sheila C. 2003. 'Torture victim to get Shs 60m', *The Daily Monitor*, 26 February.

Kwera, Francis. 22 September 2006. 'Uganda's Museveni says wants to steer LRA talks'. *Reuters*.

Labeja, Justin. 2009. 'Open letter: LRA/M private bag, RE: L.R.A. DOCUMENT ON JUBA PEACE TALKS'. Nairobi.

Laing, Tessa. 2019 (15 April). Contesting compensation in Uganda's Apaa land conflict. Blog Africa at LSE. https://blogs.lse.ac.uk/africaatlse/2019/04/15/uganda-apaa-land-conflict/

Laitin, David. n.d. 'Random narratives'. www.stanford.edu/group/ethnic/Random Narratives/random narratives.htm.

Lamwaka, Caroline. 2002. 'The peace process in northern Uganda 1986–1990', *Conciliation Resources/Accord*, Protracred conflict, elusive peace: Initiative to end the violence in northern Uganda.

2011. *The Raging Storm: Civil War and Failed Peace Processes in Northern Uganda, 1986–2005* (Fountain: Kampala).

Lederach, John Paul. 1995. 'Transforming violent intercommunal conflict', in Kumar Rupesinghe (ed.), *Conflict Transformation* (St. Martin's Press: New York).

Leonardi, Cherry. 2007a. '"Liberation" or capture: Youth in between "hakuma", and "home" during civil war and its aftermath in southern Sudan', *African Affairs*, 106: 391–412.

2007b. 'The poison in the ink bottle: Poison cases and the moral economy of knowledge in 1930s Equatoria, Sudan', *Journal of Eastern African Studies*, 1: 34–56.

Leopold, Mark. 2005. *Inside West Nile: Violence, History and Representation on an African Frontier* (James Currey, School of American Research Press, and Fountain Publishers: Oxford, Santa Fe, and Kampala).

Lepore, Jill. 1998. *The Name of War: King Philip's War and the Origins of American Identity* (Vintage Books/Random House: New York).

Lesch, Ann. 1999. *The Sudan-Contested National Identities* (Indiana University Press: Bloomington).

Library of Congress. 2017. Uganda: Bill Eliminating Presidential Age Limit and Extending Parliamentary Term Passed. *Global Legal Monitor*

Lloyd, Genevieve. 1993. *Being in Time: Selves and Narrators in Philosphy and Literature* (Routledge: London).

Lomo, Zachary, and Lucy Hovil. 2004. 'Negotiating peace: Resolution of conflicts in Uganda's west Nile region', Refugee Law Project Working Paper (Faculty of Law, Makerere University: Kampala).

Lord's Resistance Army/Movement Peace Team. 2010. 'Press statement on the Bangui meeting on the Lord's Resistance Army', edited by Justin Labeja. Nairobi.

LRA Crisis Tracker. 'www.lracrisistracker.com/'.

'LRA "externals" accused of killing talks'. 2006. *The East African*, 24 July.

LRA/M. 2006. 'Press release 26 September 2006', edited by Martin Ojul. LRA/M: Juba.

    2008. 'LRA condemn Gunboat tactics being used by Uganda', edited by Alex Oloya. LRA/M: London.

LRA/M (attributed to Joseph Kony). 2008. 'Press release Lord's Resistance Army/Movement: Peace talks between LRA and Uganda Government is suspended', edited by Alex Oloya. LRA/M: Juba.

LRA/M delegation in Juba. 2006. 'Agenda for peace and all-inclusive political tolerance in Uganda'. LRA/M: Juba.

    (23 September 2006). 'LRA/M press release'. LRA/M: Juba.

LRA/M Peace Team. 2009. 'Juba Peace talks: The record of sabotage by the Government of Uganda; the reasons General Joseph Kony wants the peace agreement revisited; and, the way forward', by Justin Labeja and Michael Anywar. LRA/M Peace Team: Nairobi.

    2012. 'Behind the "Kony2012" facade: The fear of the political triumph of native and indegenous African people and other hidden and real reasons for the United States' led "Rambo" type military campaign in central Africa'. LRA/M Peace Team.

Lucima, Okello (ed.). 2002. *Protracted Conflict, Elusive Peace: Initiatives to End the Violence in Northern Uganda (Accord Issue 11)* (Conciliation Resources: London).

Luttwak, Edward N. 1999. 'Give war a chance', *Foreign Affairs*, July/August.

Mac Ginty, Roger and Alpaslan Özerdem. 2019. 'Introduction: why compare peace processes?, in Roger Mac Ginty and Alpaslan Özerdem (eds.), *Comparing Peace Processes* (Routledge: Abingdon).

Macdonald, Anna. 2017. '"In the interests of justice?" The International Criminal Court, peace talks and the failed quest for war crimes accountability in northern Uganda', *Journal of Eastern African Studies*, 11: 628–48.

Macdonald, Anna, and Holly Porter. 2016. 'The trial of Thomas Kwoyelo: Opportunity or spectre? Reflections from the ground on the first LRA prosecution', *Africa*, 86: 698–722.

Mamdani, Mahmood. 2006. 'Kony not the real issue in peace talks', *The New Vision*, 10 July.

Mao, Norbert. 8 November 2006. '"It is good ..."', *The New Vision*.

Marchal, Roland. 2007. 'Warlordism and terrorism: How to obscure an already confusing crisis? The case of Somalia', *International Affairs*, 83: 1091–106.

Matia, Apollonia. 5 October 2006. 'LRA soldiers missing, peace talks continue', *Juba Post*.

    26 October 2006. 'Attacks continue around Juba', *Juba Post*.

Matsiko, Grace. 8 November 2006. 'Govt rejects LRA demand for ministry', *The Daily Monitor*.

    9 September 2006. 'Canadian nude photos mess up Juba talks', *The Daily Monitor*.

Matsiko, Grace, Frank Nyakairu and Emmanuel Gyezaho. 28 September 2006. 'Kony orders rebels to quit assembly points/LRA threaten to leave talks in 7 days', *The Daily Monitor*.

Mawson, Andrew. 1999. 'Breaking the circle: Protecting human rights in the northern war zone'. Amnesty International: London.

Mayer, Bernard. 2003. *The Dynamics of Conflict Resolution: A Practitioner's Guide* (Jossey-Bass Publishers: San Francisco).

Mayom, Manyang, and Apiok Kur. 2007. 'Ismail Kony joins SPLM and pludges [sic] and end to raids', *The Juba Post*, 20 April.

Mbembé, Achille. 2003. 'Necropolitics', *Public Culture*, 15: 11–40.

Mbembé, Achille, and Steven Rendall. 2002. 'African modes of self-writing', *Public Culture*, 14: 239–73.

McCarthy, Nolan, and Adam Meirowitz. 2007. *Political Game Theory: An Introduction* (Cambridge University Press: New York).

Menkhaus, Ken. 2009. 'False start in AFRICOM', *Security Policy*, 30: 53–57.

Mergelsberg, Ben. 2010. 'Between two worlds: Former LRA soldiers in northern Uganda', in Tim Allen and K. Vlassenroot (eds.), *The Lord's Resistance Army: Myth and Reality* (Zed Books: London).

Miller, Nancy K. 1996. *Bequest and Betrayal: Memoirs of a Parent's Death* (Indiana University Press: Bloomington/Indianapolis).

Minh, Ho-Chi. 18 February 1946. Letter from Ho Chi Minh to President Harry Truman; 1/18/1946; 800 Indochina 1946; General Records, 1946 - 1948; Records of the Foreign Service Posts of the Department of State, Record Group 84; National Archives at College Park, College Park, MD. [Online Version, https://www.docsteach.org/documents/document/ho-chi-minh-truman, November 21, 2020]

Mkandawire, Thandika. 2002. 'The terrible toll of post-colonial "rebel movements" in Africa: Towards and explanation of the violence against the peasantry', *The Journal of Modern African Studies*, 40: 181–215.

Moffett, Luke. 2015. 'Accountability for forced displacement in Democratic Republic of Congo and Uganda before the International Criminal Court', *African Journal of International Criminal Justice*, 2: 129–52.

2016. 'Complementarity's monopoly on justice in Uganda: The International Criminal Court, victims and Thomas Kwoyelo', *International Criminal Law Review*, 16: 503–24.

Moore, Henrietta L. 2011. *Still Life: Hopes, Desires and Satisfactions* (Polity Press: Cambridge).

Moro, Justin, and Chris Ocowun. 26 September 2006. 'M7 talk angers Acholi leaders', *The New Vision*.

Mpagi, Charles Mwanguhya 2007. 'Uganda: Changing faces of Santa Okot', *The Daily Monitor*, 2 May.

Muhumuza, Rodney. 30 October 2006. 'Kabila okays plan to capture Kony', *The Daily Monitor*.

2006. 'Museveni asks U.S. to back plan B against LRA', *The Daily Monitor*, 3 October.

Muhumuza, Rodney, and Emmanuel Gyezaho. 7 September 2006. 'No deal on arrest warrants, ICC tells Kony', *The Daily Monitor*.

Muhumuza, Rodney, Frank Nyakairu and Simon Kasyate. 10 October 2006. 'Kony rebels refuse to sign peace deal', *The Daily Monitor*.

Mukasa, Henry. 5 November 2006. 'LRA tactics irk govt', *The New Vision*.

27 October 2006. 'Five people killed in Juba gunfire', *The New Vision*.

2006. 'Uganda: Monitors set to visit scene of LRA clashes', *New Vision*, 4 December.

Mukasa, Henry, and Felix Osike. 22 October 2006. 'Museveni to meet LRA', *The New Vision*.

Mukasa, Henry, and Alfred Wasike. 1 October 2006. 'Uganda: Govt snubs LRA demand', *The New Vision*.

Mukwana, Ruth, and Katinka Ridderbos. 2009. 'Uganda's response to displacement: Contrasting policy and practice', *Forced Migration Review*, Special Issue: Ten Years of the Guiding Principles. 10: 21 – 22.

Musamali, Geresome. 27 October 2006. 'Stop LRA food supply, government tells Machar', *The New Vision*.

Museveni, Yoweri Kaguta. 30 October 2006. 'Statement about prospects for durable peace in Uganda'. *The Monitor*.

1997a. 'Letter to James Obita (secretary for foreign affairs LRA/M).

1997b. *Sowing the Mustard Seed: The Struggle for Freedom and Democracy in Uganda* (Macmillan Education: New York).

Mutumba, Richard, Grace Natabaalo and Rodney Muhumuza. 8 September 2006. 'Otti gives LRA rebels Sept.19 deadline', *The Daily Monitor*.

Muwulya, Moses. 2018 (May 1). 'I wanted to return to the bush over doctors' strike, says Museveni', *Daily Monitor*.

Mwaniki, David and Manasseh Wepundi. 2007 "The Juba Peace Talks: The chequered road to peace for Northern Uganda". Global Crisis Solutions.

Nan, Susan Allen. 2009. 'Shifting from coherent towards holistic peace processes', in Dennis Sandole, Sean Byrne and Ingrid Sandole-Staroste (eds.), *Handbook of Conflict Analysis and Resolution* (Routledge: London/New York).

The New Vision. 26 September 2006. 'LRA warrants to stay, says ICC', *The New Vision*.

Nganda, Ssemujju Ibrahim, and Benon Herbert Oluka. 2006. 'Behind scenes: Mecca in DRC jungle', *The Weekly Observer*, 10 August.

Nnyago, Omar Kalinge 2007. 'Lakwena's death opens new wounds in the north', *Daily Monitor*, January 30.

Nouwen, Sarah M. H. 2013. *Complementarity in the Line of Fire: The Catalysing Effect of the International Criminal Court in Uganda and Sudan* (Cambridge University Press: Cambridge and New York).

Nouwen, Sarah M. H., and Wouter Werner. 2014. 'Monopolizing global justice: International Criminal Law as challenge to human diversity', *SSRN Electronic Journal*.

Nyakairu, Frank. 22 October 2006. 'Museveni meets LRA face to face', *The Sunday Monitor*.

Nyakairu, Frank, Emmanuel Gyezaho and Paul Harera. 17 October 2006. 'Museveni heads to Juba', *The Daily Monitor*.

Nyakairu, Frank, Paul Harera and Grace Matsiko. 26 October 2006. 'SPLA orders UPDF out of Owiny ki-Bul', *The Daily Monitor*.

Nyakairu, Frank, and Egadu Okiror. 10 August 2006. 'Govt rejects ceasefire', *The Daily Monitor*.

Nyekorach-Matsanga, David. 2006a. 'UGANDA: The dishonesty of the peace process in Juba'. *Africa News Flash* (Khartoum).

2006b. 'UGANDA: The dark clouds on the Uganda/LRA peace talks. Frankly speaking column. The last lap of marathon in Juba talks peace'. *Africa News Flash* (London).

2006c. '"UGANDA" What a tragedy for LRA/Uganda talks?' *Africa News Flash* (London).

2007. 'UGANDA EXCLUSIVE: I have quit casino politics of Uganda'. *Africa News Flash* (London.)

2008. 'Letter to Riek Machar re: Continued support for the peace process and clarification'.

O'Kadameri, Billie. 2002. 'LRA/Government negotiations 1993–94', in Okello Lucima (ed.), *Protracted Conflict, Elusive Peace: Initiatives to End the Violence in Northern Uganda (Accord Issue 11)* (Conciliation Resources: London).

Obita, James. 2002. 'First international peace efforts 1996–98', in Okello Lucima (ed.), *Protracted Conflict, Elusive Peace: Initiatives to End the Violence in Northern Uganda (Accord Issue 11)* (Conciliation Resources: London).

Obita, James (LRA/M Secretary for Foreign Affairs). 1997. 'Letter to his excellency Yoweri Kaguta Museveni, president of the Republic of Uganda, State House, Kampala, Uganda'.

Obote, A. Milton. 1990. 'Notes on concealment of genocide in Uganda'. Lusaka, Zambia.

Obote, Uganda Peoples Congress signed by Mama Miria Kalule. 2006. 'Memorandum submitted to H.E. The President of Uganda Yoweri Kaguta Museveni by The Uganda Peoples Congress at State House, Nakasero, Kampala'. Kampala.

Ocowun, Chris. 14 September 2006. 'ICC blocking peace talks, says LRA's Otti', *The New Vision*.

29 August 2006. 'Army to halt military escorts', *The New Vision*.

30 August 2006. 'UPDF withdraws', *The New Vision*.

Ocowun, Chris, and Caroline Ayugi. 26 October 2006. 'Two Sudanese killed by LRA rebels', *The New Vision*.

Ocowun, Chris, and Charles Mukiibi. 4 September 2006. 'Top LRA meets UPDF', *The New Vision*.

Oguru Otto, Patrick. 2002. *Kacoke Madit: The Quest for Peace in Northern Uganda* (Kacoke Madit Secretariat: London).

Ojwee, Dennis, and Cornes Lubangakene. 28 August 2006. 'Stop killing, Otti orders', *The New Vision*.

Okidi-Olal, Jongomoi. 2006. 'Proposal by Lwo Development Incorporated Chairman'. Lwo Development Inc.: Washington, DC.

Okot, Arthur. 31 August 2006. 'North celebrates LRA truce', *The New Vision*.

Oloka-Onyango, J. 2006. 'Open letter to President Museveni and the Movement Caucus', *Uganda Net*.

Olweny, Obonyo. 2006a. 'First position paper of the LRA Peace Delegation during negotiations'. Juba.

2006b. 'LRA/M opening speech at first Juba Peace Talks opening ceremony'. Juba.

Olweny, Obonyo, and Joshua Otukene. 2008. 'Re: Juba Peace Talks: Who should be blamed for the refusal of Joseph Kony to sign the peace agreement?" Nairobi.

Omach, Paul. 2002. 'Civil war and internal displacement in Northern Uganda: 1986–1998', Network of Ugandan Researchers and Research Users ((NURRU).

Onyango-Obbo, Charles 2007. 'Kony is crazy, so why does Riek love him?', *The Monitor*, 27 June.

Oosterom, Marjoke A. 2016. 'Internal displacement, the camp and the construction of citizenship: Perspectives from northern Uganda', *Journal of Refugee Studies*, 29: 363–87.

Osborne, Matthew, Ben Exelle and Arjan Verschoor. 2017. 'Truly reconciled? A dyadic analysis of post-conflict social reintegration in northern Uganda', *Journal of Peace Research*, 55: 107–21.

Otti, Vincent. 13 September 2006. 'The hot seat show panel'. KFM.

Otunnu, Olara. 2005. 'Saving our children from the scourge of war: The Sydney Peace Prize 2005 acceptance speech'. University of Sydney: Sydney, www .sydney.edu.au/news/84.html?newscategoryid=4&newsstoryid=764.

2006. 'The secret genocide', *Foreign Policy*, July/August, 45–46.

p'Bitek, Okot. 1964 (1997). 'Acholi love', in, *The Anniversary Issue: Selections from Transition, 1961–1976* (Indiana University Press: Bloomington).

Pain, Dennis. 1997. '*The Bending of Spears': Producing Consensus for Peace & Development in Northern Uganda* (International Alert/Kacoke Madit: London).

Parrott, Louise. 2006. 'The role of the International Criminal Court in Uganda: Ensuring that the pursuit of justice does not come at the price of peace', *Australian Journal of Peace Studies*, 1.

Pax Christi Netherlands. 2006 (29 August). 'Pax Christi International und Sant´ Egidio halfen mit beim Friedensabkommen in Uganda'.

Pécaut, Daniel. 2000. 'Configurations of space, time, and subjectivity in a context of terror: The Colombian example', *International Journal of Politics, Culture, and Society*, 14: 129–50.

Pham, Phuong, Patrick Vinck, Eric Stover, A. Moss, M. Wierda, and R. Bailey. 2007. 'When the war ends: A populations-based survey on attitudes about peace, justice, and social reconstruction in northern Uganda'. : Human Rights Center (University of California, Berkely), Payson Center for International Development (Tulane University), International Center for Transitional Justice: Berkeley/New York.

Ploch, Lauren. 2011. 'Africa command: U.S. strategic interests and the role of the U.S. military in Africa'. Congressional Research Service: Washington, DC.

Pollner, Melvin, and Robert M. Emerson. 2001. 'Ethnomethodology and Ethnography', in Paul Atkinson, Amanda Coffey, Sara Delamont, John Lofland and Lyn H. Lofland (eds.), *Handbook of Ethnography* (Sage: London).

Porter, Holly. 2016. *After Rape: Violence, Justice, and Social Harmony in Uganda* (Cambridge University Press: Cambridge).

Porter, Holly E. 2012. 'Justice and rape on the periphery: The supremacy of social harmony in the space between local solutions and formal judicial systems in northern Uganda', *Journal of Eastern African Studies*, 6: 81–97.

Prorok, Alyssa K. 2017. 'The (In)compatibility of peace and justice? The International Criminal Court and Civil Conflict Termination', *International Organization*, 71: 213–43.

Pruitt, Dean G. 1981. *Negotiation Behavior* (Academic Press: New York).

Prunier, Gerard. 2004. 'Rebel movements and proxy warfare: Uganda, Sudan and the Congo (1986–99)', *African Affairs*, 103: 359–83.

Quaranto, Peter. J. 2006. 'Ending the real nightmares of northern Uganda', *Peace Review*, 18: 137–44.

Quinn, Joanna R. 2004. 'Constraints: The un-doing of the Ugandan Truth Commission', *Human Rights Quarterly*, 26: 401–27.

2009. 'Getting to peace? Negotiating with the LRA in northern Uganda', *Human Rights Review*, 55: 55–71.

2010. *The Politics of Acknowledgement: Truth Commissions in Uganda and Haiti* (UBC Press: Vancouver).

Radner, Roy, and Robert Rosenthal. 1982. 'Private information and pure strategy equilibrium', *Mathematics of Operations Research*, 7: 401–9.

Raffaele, Paul. 2008. *Among the Cannibals: Adventures on the Trail of Man's Darkest Ritual* (Smithsonian Books: Collins: New York).

Ramsbotham, Oliver, Tom Woodhouse and Hugh Miall. 2005. *Contemporary Conflict Resolution* (Second Edition) (Polity: Cambridge).

Rauxloh, Regina. 2017. 'Kony is so "last month": Lessons from social media stunt "Kony 2012"', in Anthony Amatrudo and Regina Rauxloh (eds.), *Law in Popular Belief: Myth and Reality* (Manchester University Press: Manchester).

Reid, Richard. 2017. *A History of Modern Uganda* (Cambridge University Press: Cambridge).

Resolve Uganda. 2007. 'Give peace a real chance: Rethinking U.S. policy toward northern Uganda'. Washington, DC.

Reuters. 4 October 2006. 'Ugandan army resumes offensive against LRA rebels', *Reuters*.

13 October 2006. 'Ugandan LRA rebels violate truce – Monitors', *Reuters*.

16 October 2006. 'Ugandan rebels accuse army of launching attack', *Reuters*.

20 September 2006. 'Uganda dismisses LRA appeal over arrest warrants', *Reuters*.

27 September 2006. 'Top LRA leader violates ceasefire – Ugandan army', *Reuters*.

Richards, Paul. 2005. 'New war: An ethnographic approach', in Paul Richards (ed.), *No Peace No War: An Anthropology of Contemporary Armed Conflicts* (Ohio University Press/James Currey: Athens/Oxford).

Ricoeur, Paul. 1992. *Oneself as Another* (Chicago University Press: Chicago).

Rigterink, Anouk S., and Mareike Schomerus. 2017. 'The fear factor is a main thing: How radio influences anxiety and political attitudes', *Journal of Development Studies*, 53: 1123–46.

Roberts, Bayard, Kaducu Felix Ocaka, John Browne, Thomas Oyok and Egbert Sondorp. 2011. 'Alcohol disorder amongst forcibly displaced persons in northern Uganda', *Addictive Behaviors*, 36: 870–73.

Rodman, Kenneth A. 2009. 'Is peace in the Interests of Justice? The case for broad prosecutorial discretion at the International Criminal Court', *Leiden Journal of International Law*, 22: 99–126.

Rodriguez, Fr. Carlos. 2004. 'The northern Uganda war: The "small conflict" that became the world's worst humanitarian crisis', *Health Policy and Development Journal/Health Policy and Development Department of Health Sciences of Uganda Martyrs University*, 2: 81–84.

Rodríguez Soto, Carlos. 2009. *Tall Grass: Stories of Suffering and Peace in Northern Uganda* (Fountain Publishers: Kampala).

Rolandsen, Øystein H., Tove Heggli Sagmo and Fanny Nicolaisen. 2015. 'South Sudan – Uganda relations: The cost of peace', *Conflict Trends*, 4: 33–40.

Rubinstein, Ariel. 1991. 'Comments on the interpretation of game theory', *Econometrica*, 59: 909–24.

Russell Lee, Matthew. 2007. 'UN's Louise Arbour calls Lord's Resistance Army a "criminal enterprise" with no political agenda'. New York: Inner City Press.

Sarrica, Mauro, and Alberta Contarello. 2004. 'Peace, war and conflict: Social representations shared by peace activists and non-activists', *Journal of Peace Research*, 41: 549–68.

Schomerus, Mareike. 2007. *The Lord's Resistance Army in Sudan: A History and Overview* (The Small Arms Survey: Geneva).

    2010a. 'Chasing the Kony Story', in Tim Allen and Koen Vlassenroot (eds.), *The Lord's Resistance Army: Myth and Reality* (Zed Books: London).

    2010b. '"A terrorist it not a person like me": An interview with Joseph Kony', in Tim Allen and Koen Vlassenroot (eds.), *The Lord's Resistance Army: Myth and Reality* (Zed Books: London).

    2012. 'They forget what they came for: Uganda's army in Sudan', *Journal of Eastern African Studies*, 6: 124–53.

    2015a. 'International Criminal Law in peace processes: The case of the ICC and the Lord's Resistance Army', in Morten Bergsmo, Wui Ling Cheah, Tianying Song and Ping Yi (eds.), *Historical Origins of International Criminal Law*, vol. 4 (Torkel Opsahl Academic EPublisher: Brussels).

    2015b. '"Make Him Famous": The single conflict narrative of Kony and Kony2012', in Alex de Waal (ed.), *Reclaiming Activism: Western Advocacy in Contention* (Zed Books: London).

Schomerus, Mareike, Tim Allen and Koen Vlassenroot. 2011. 'Obama takes on the LRA: Why Washington sent troops to Central Africa', *Foreign Affairs*, 15 November.

Schomerus, Mareike, and Kennedy Tumutegyereize. 2009. 'After operation lightning thunder: Protecting communities and building peace'. London: Conciliation Resources.

The Senate of the United States. 2006. 'Resolution 573 SRS ATS'. 109th Congress 2nd session. US Senate: Washington, DC.

    2012. 'S.Res. 402: Condemning Joseph Kony and the Lord's Resistance Army for commiting crimes against humanity and mass atrocities, and supporting ongoing efforts by the United States Government and governments and regional organizations in central Africa to remove Joseph Kony and Lord's Resistance Army commanders from the battlefield'. US Senate: Washington, DC.

Seguya, Neema. 2010. *Challenges in Conflict Resolution: Case of the Juba Talks in Uganda: Challenges Faces at the Juba Peace Talks in Uganda (2006–2010)* (Lambert Academic Publishing: Saarbruecken).

Serugo, Geoffrey. 15 June 2017. 'Museveni to meet Northern Uganda leaders over Apaa land dispute', *Eagle Online*, 15 June.

Simonse, Simon, Willemijn Verkoren and Gerd Junne. 2010. 'NGO involvement in the Juba peace talks: The role and dilemmas of IKV PAx Christi', in Tim Allen and Koen Vlassenroot (eds.), *The Lord's Resistance Army: Myth and Reality* (Zed Books: London/New York).

Sinn, Matthew. 2010. 'Sudan: In search of a model', in Alex de Waal (ed.), *SSRC: Making Sense of Sudan.*(SSRC: New York).

Sørbø, Gunnar, Joanna Macrae and Lennart Wohlgemuth. 1997. 'NGOs in conflict – An evaluation of international alert', CMI Series.Chr. Michelsen Institute: Bergen.

Spector, Bertram I. 2006. 'Negotiation in an insecure world', *International Negotiation*, 11: 225–28.

Spiegel, Julia, and John Prendergast. 2008. 'A new peace strategy for northern Uganda and the LRA', *ENOUGH strategy paper* ENOUGH – The project to end genocide and crimes against humanity. Washington, DC.

Ssemogerere, Karoli. 2006. 'Will Juba turn out to be a historical mistake?', *The Monitor*, 26 July.

Stark, Lindsay, Les Roberts, Wendy Wheaton, Anne Acham, Neil Boothby, and Alastair Ager. 2009. 'Measuring violence against women amidst war and displacement in northern Uganda using the "neighborhood method"', *Journal of Epidemiology & Community Health*,64(12): 1056–61.

Sudan Tribune. 2014 (7 March). 'Preferential treatment of UPDF sparked Juba violence: Rebels'.

Sudan Tribune and Daily Monitor. 21 August 2006. 'Sudan's Kiir says LRA must disclose troops positions for ceasefire', *Sudan Tribune*.

The Sunday Times. 2017 (October 8). 'Angelina Jolie "volunteered" to snare warlord Joseph Kony in dinner honeytrap'. London.

Tarrow, Sidney. 1994. *Power in Movement: Collective Action, Social Movements and Politics* (Cambridge University Press: Cambridge).

  2007. 'Inside insurgencies: Politics and violence in an age of civil war', *Perspectives on Politics*, 5: 587–600.

Taub, Amanda (ed.). 2012. *Beyond Kony 2012: Atrocity, Awareness and Activism in the Internet Age* (Leanpub (e-book)).

Tella, Oluwaseun. 2016. 'AFRICOM: Hard or soft power initiative?', *African Security Review*, 25: 393–406.

Terry, Fiona. 2002. *Condemned to Repeat? The Paradox of Humanitarian Action* (Cornell University Press: Ithaca, NY).

Tilly, Charles. 2003. *The Politics of Collective Violence* (Cambridge University Press: New York).

  2004. *Social Movements, 1768–2004* (Paradigm Publishers: Boulder).

Tilly, Charles, and Sidney Tarrow. 2006. *Contentious Politics* (Paradigm Press: Boulder).

Timms, Henry, and Jeremy Heimans. 2018. *#newpower: Why Outsiders Are Winning, Institutions Are Failing, and How the Rest of Us Can Keep up in th Age of Mass Participation* (Picador: London).

Titeca, Kristof. 2010. 'The spiritual order of the LRA', in Tim Allen and Koen Vlassenroot (eds.), *The Lord's Resistance Army: Myth and Reality* (Zed Books: London).

  2013. 'Conference presentation: An LRA for everyone. How different actors construct different images of the LRA, and instrumentalise the conflict'. ECAS conference paper, Lisbon.

  2018. 'Illegal ivory trade as transnational organized crime? An empirical study into ivory traders in Uganda', *The British Journal of Criminology*, 59(1): 24–44.

Titeca, Kristof, and Theophile Costeur. 2015. 'An LRA for everyone: How different actors frame the Lord's Resistance Army', *African Affairs*, 114: 92–114.

Toft, Monica Duffy. 2010. *Securing the Peace: The Durable Settlement of Civil Wars* (Princeton University Press: Princeton).

Traditional and Religious Leaders/Civil Society and other Organisations. 2012. '"Fairway communique of traditional and religious leaders, civil society and other organisations concerning the decision of the Minister of Internal Affairs of Uganda to declare, on 23rd May, 2012, the lapse of the amnesty provisions of the Amnesty Act of Uganda (The Amnesty Act (Declaration of Lapse of the Operation of Part II) Instrument'.

Trujillo, Mary Adams, S. Y. Bowland, Linda James Myers, Phillip M. Richards and Beth Roy. 2008. 'Introduction: Conflict, culture and knowledge', in Mary Adams Trujillo, S. Y. Bowland, Linda James Myers, Phillip M. Richards and Beth Roy (eds.), *Re-Centering Culture and Knowledge in Conflict Resolution Practice* (Syracuse University Press: Syracuse).

Tuller, Hugh. 2018. 'Translating forensic science in northern Uganda', *Practicing Anthropology*, 40: 6–10.

Tzu, Sun. 1971. *The Art of War* (Oxford University Press: Oxford).

UNICEF Sudan. 2006. 'List of requirements for the non-combatant population – Women and children – In LRA camps'. Juba.

U.N. Mission of the USA. 2006. '06USUNNEWYORK1404 (For official use only): Gambari, Kalomoh, Guehenno, Egeland attend core group meeting on Northern Uganda'.Wikileaks: New York.

UN News Service. 2005. 'Annan hails International Criminal Courts' arrest warrants for five Ugandan rebels'.

UN Security Council. 2006. 'Statement by the President of the Security Council (S/PRST/2006/45)'. United Nations Security Council: New York.

  2008 (December). 'Security council report: Northern Uganda and LRA-affected areas'.

  2009. 'Update report: Northern Uganda and LRA-affected areas'. New York.

UN System Southern Sudan. 2006. 'Southern Sudan care and protection and women and children associated with the Lord's Resistance Army status report'.UNOCHA/ UNICEF: Juba.

UNHCR. 9 March 2006. 'UNHCR Sudan operations: Sudan/Chad situation update 50'. UNHCR: Juba.

United Nations. 2006. 'United Nations launches Juba Initiative Fund to aid peace in northern Uganda (AFR/1439; IHA/1239)'. UN.

UNOCHA–IRIN. 2005. 'Sudan-Uganda: SPLM/A leader pledges to help Ugandan peace effort', 31 January.

'UPDF Denies LRA Claims'. 2006. *The New Vision*, 3 December.

UPDF Spokesperson. 7 November 2006. 'LRA has committed gross violations of truce', *The New Vision*.

US Congress. 1998. 'Congressional Resolution 309', Washington, DC.

US Embassy Kampala. 2007. '07KAMPALA1853 (classified): Northern Uganda notes (November 3–30)'. US Embassy: Kampala.

2007a. '03 KAMPALA 001426 (Confidential): Senator Feingold raises regional and domestic issues with Ugandan President'.Wikileaks: Kampala.

2007b. '07KAMPALA1172: Uganda: Roundup on Staffdel Smith and Kuiken visit UGANDA: ROUNDUP ON STAFFDEL SMITH AND'.Wikileaks: Kampala.

2007c. '07KAMPALA1351 (for official use only): Northern Uganda notes: (Aug 11–Aug 24, 2007)'.: Wikileaks: Kampala.

2007d. '07KAMPALA1360: Africa bureau senior advisor on conflict resolution travels to northern Uganda'. Kampala.

2007e. '07KAMPALA1419: Senator Feingold discusses northern Ugandan issues'. Wikileaks: Kampala.

2007f. '07KAMPALA1449 (Classified Secret): Uganda: A/S Frazier discusses LRA, Congo, and Somalia with President Museveni'. Wikileaks: Kampala.

2007g. '07KAMPALA1894 (Confidential): LRA Peace process update'. Wikileaks: Kampala.

2007h. '08KAMPALA197 (confidential): Northern Uganda: U.N. Envoy on resumption of talks'. Wikileaks: Kampala.

2008a. "08KAMPALA203 (confidential): Northern Uganda: Juba Peace Talks Resume, Lra Sorts Out Internal Issues." In.

2008b. '08KAMPALA410 (classified Secret): Ugandan officials not surprised by Kony's movement into CAR' Wikileaks: Kampala.

2008c. '08KAMPALA1579 (confidential): Uganda: Kony living in a fool's paradise'. Wikileaks: Kampala.

2008d. 'KAMPALA 000284 (Confidential): Northern Uganda: Government views on progress at Juba, reported LRA attacks'. Wikileaks: Kampala:.

2009a. '09KAMPALA207 (confidential): Uganda/DRC: Museveni and Kabila summit set for March 1'. Kampala.

2009b. '09KAMPALA551: Uganda/DRC: Operation Rudia II Update'. Wikileaks: Kampala.

2009c. '09KAMPALA587 (confidential) Uganda: Games the Acholi Diaspora continue to play'. Wikileaks: Kampala.

2009d. '09KAMPALA1397 (confidential): Uganda: Intelligence Sharing Agreement'. Wikileaks: Kampala.

US Embassy Khartoum. 2006. '06KHARTOUM2564 (Confidential): GoSS Vice President tells Special Envoy that "distrust" pervades LRA peace talks'. Wikileaks: Khartoum.

2007. '07KHARTOUM351: UN Envoy meets with LRA chief Kony; peace talks may resume'. Khartoum.

2008a. '08KHARTOUM429: LRA Peace Talks to resume in Juba'. Khartoum.

2008b. '08KHARTOUM324: LRA Peace Talks conclude, await signing of final agreement'. Khartoum.

US Embassy Kinshasa. 2007. '07KINSHASA1361 (Classified Confidential): President Kabila's December 11 meeting with ambassador and AF senior advisor shortley'. Wikileaks: Kinshasa.

US State Department. 2008. 'Resumption of the Peace Talks in Juba (2008/ 068)'. Washington, DC.

USAID. 2006. 'Analysis of lessons learned from past efforts to end the conflict in northern Uganda'. Washington, DC.

Uvin, Peter. 2001. 'Reading the Rwandan genocide', *International Studies Review*, 3: 75–99.

Väyrynen, Raimo. 1991. 'To settle or to transform? Perspectives on the resolution of national and international conflicts', in R. Väyrynen (ed.), *New Directions in Conflict Theory: Conflict Resolution and Conflict Transformation* (Sage: London).

Vertin, Zach. 2018. *A Poisoned Well: Lessons in Mediation from South Sudan's Troubled Peace Process* (International Peace Institute: New York).

Victor, Letha, and Holly Porter. 2017. 'Dirty things: Spiritual pollution and life after the Lord's Resistance Army', *Journal of Eastern African Studies*, 11: 590–608.

Vinci, Anthony. 2005. 'The strategic use of fear by the Lord's Resistance Army', *Small Wars and Insurgencies*, 16: 360–81.

2006. 'Beyond terror and insurgency: The LRA's dirty war in northern Uganda', in George Kassimeris (ed.), *Warrior's Dishonour: Barbarity, Morality and Torture in Modern Warfare* (Ashgate Publishing Limited: Hampshire).

2007. 'Existential motivations in the Lord's Resistance Army continuing conflict', *Studies in Conflict and Terrorism*, 30: 337–52.

Vinci, James. 2010. 'Supreme Court upholds terrorism support law'.Reuters: Washington, DC.

Waddel, Nicholas, and Phil Clarke (eds.). 2008. *Courting Conflict? Justice, Peace and the ICC in Africa* (Royal African Society: London).

Wallensteen, Peter. 2007. *Understanding Conflict Resolution* (Sage Publications: London).

Wallensteen, Peter, and Mikael Eriksson. 2009. *Negotiating Peace: Lessons from Three Comprehensive Peace Agreements* (Uppsala University/Mediation Support Unit UN: Uppsala/New York).

Wasike, Alfred. 15 October 2006. 'LRA must assemble', *The New Vision*.

27 September 2006. 'LRA vanish from Kibul', *The New Vision*.

29 August 2006. 'UPDF/LRA truce starts', *The New Vision*.

Wassermann, Stanley, and Katherine Faust. 1994. *Social Network Analysis: Methods and Applications* (Cambridge University Press: Cambridge).

Watson, Cate. 2006. 'Unreliable narrators? "Inconsistency" and some inconstancy) in interviews', *Qualitative Research*, 6: 367–84.

Watson, J. 2002. *Strategy: An Introduction to Game Theory* (Norton: New York).

Wax, Emily. 2005. 'Net tightens around northern Uganda's brutal rebel militia', *Washington Post*, 8 October.

Weeks, Willet. 2002. 'Pushing the envelope: Moving beyond "protected villages" in Northern Uganda', *UNOCHA*, 1–53.

Weinstein, Jeremy M. 2007. *Inside Rebellion: The Politics of Insurgent Violence* (Cambridge University Press: Cambridge).

Westbrook, B. David. 2000. 'The torment of Northern Uganda: A legacy of missed opportunities', *Online Journal for Peace and Conflict Resolution*, June.

White, Natasha 2014. 'The political economy of ivory as a "Conflict Resource"', *Peace and Conflict Studies*, 21, Article 6.

Whitmore, Todd David. 2010. 'Genocide or just another "casualty of war"? The implications of the memo attributed to President Yoweri K. Museveni of Uganda', *Practical Matters*, 3: 1–49.

'Why do Ugandan exiles support LRA?'. 2006. *The New Vision*, 16 September.

Wierda, Marieke, and Michael Otim. 2011. 'Courts, conflict and complementarity in Uganda', in Carsten Stahn and Mohamed M. El Zeidy (eds.), *The International Criminal Court and Complementarity: From Theory to Practice*, vol. II (Cambridge University Press: Cambridge).

Wijeyaratne, Surendrini. 2008. 'Promoting an inclusive peace: A call to strengthen Canada's peace-making capacity: Country Study Peace and Justice in Northern Uganda'.CCIC: Ottawa.

Winslade, John, Gerald Monk and Alison Cotter. 1998. 'In theory: A narrative approach to the practice of mediation', *Negotiation Journal*, 14: 21–41.

Worden, Scott. 2009. 'The justice dilemma in Uganda'. USIP: Washington, DC.

World Health Organization/Ministry of Health. 2005. *Health and Mortality Survey among Internally Displaced Persons in Gulu, Kitgum and Pader Districts, Northern Uganda* (The Republic of Uganda, Ministry of Health: Kampala).

Yawanarajah, Nita, and Julian Ouellet. 2003. 'Peace Agreements', University of Colorado. www.beyondintractability.org/essay/structuring_peace_agree.

Zartman, William. 2006. 'Negotiating internal, ethnic and identity conflicts in a globalized world', *International Negotiation*, 11: 253–72.

Index

Acholi, 33
  accusations against in Sudan, 179
  diaspora, 5, 25, 33, 44, 58, 70, 187, 211, 231, 250, 268
  elders, 35, 42, 117, 167, 208, 219, 234
  leaders, 46, 48, 81, 104, 106, 140, 147, 219
  religious leaders, 47, 58, 214
Advocacy, 186, *See* Invisible Children
African Union (AU)
  on ceasefire monitoring team, 74
  as observers, 77, 91, 140, 181, 202
  Regional Task Force, 263
Africanisation
  African solution for African problems, 182
  as a way to deal with the ICC, 181
  of the conflict, 168
  of the negotiations, 172
AFRICOM *See* USA
Agenda 2, 97, 143–44, 174, 197
Agenda 3, 145, 197, 202, 253, 268
Agenda 5, 203
Al Jazeera. *See* Media
Amnesty, 44
  Act, 45, 164, 263, 269
  Commission, 45, 50
  as incentive, 46
  rejected by LRA, 56
Apology *See* Kony, Joseph
Assembly
  challenges, 78, 82, 100, 139, 142, 174
  confusion over, 81
  disturbance through press trip, 84, 89
  Nabanga as location, 74
  Owiny-Kibul as location, 76, 78, 88
  as part of Cessation of Hostilities, 75–81, 83–85, 88, 90, 94, 99–101, 105, 109, 143, 216
  Ri-Kwangba as location, 80
  in safe zones, 46
  UPDF assessment of, 93, 99

UPDF deployment, 83–84, 88–89, 91–94, 102–4, 109, 139, 174, 197, 214, 217
  assessment of Operation Lightning Thunder, 224
Atrocities. *See* UPDF atrocities, *See* Government of Uganda: atrocities, *See* LRA atrocities, *See* NRA atrocities
Attacks
  during talks, 94, 96, 200. *See also* LRA; UPDF
Attempts at peace talks. *See* Peace attempts
AU. *See* African Union
Ayena, Krispus Odongo, 82, 141, 175, 204, 234, 243, 258, 285

Bandwagoning. *See* galvanic surge
BBC *See* media
Besigye, Kizza, 38
Bigombe, Betty, 41, 47, 161, 243

CAR. *See* Central African Republic
Ceasefire, 73
Central African Republic (CAR), 1, 6–7, 151, 187, 199, 223, 261, 263–64, 267
  LRA presence in, 187
  UPDF presence in, 224
Ceremonies of the Juba Talks. *See* LRA/M opening ceremony, 2
Cessation of Hostilities (CoH), 70
  conditions, 75
  Monitoring Team (CHMT), 74, 77, 87, 139
  negotiations over, 74
  start of, 77
  UPDF orders on, 77
  violations of, 88, 91, 93
Chissano, Joaquim, 72, 105, 140, 143, 146, 155, 181, 191, 198, 202, 210, 212, 216, 218, 222, 252, 268
CHMT. *See* Cessation of Hostilities
Civil society. *See* Acholi leaders
CoH. *See* Cessation of Hostilities (CoH)